The London Medieval and Renaissance Series

General Editor A. V. C. Schmidt

Sir Thomas Malory

LE MORTE DARTHUR
The Seventh and Eighth Tales

Edited by P. J. C. Field, B.Litt., M.A.

Lecturer in English, University College of North Wales, Bangor

HODDER AND STOUGHTON
LONDON SYDNEY AUCKLAND TORONTO

To Susan and Mike

ISBN 0 340 09899 6 Paper

First published in this edition 1978
Second impression 1982

Printed and bound in Hong Kong for
Hodder and Stoughton Educational,
a division of Hodder and Stoughton Ltd,
Mill Road, Dunton Green, Sevenoaks, Kent,
by Colorcraft Ltd.

Contents

Preface

There are two surviving texts of *Le Morte Darthur*: an edition published by Caxton in 1485, of which two copies remain, and a manuscript discovered in 1934. The manuscript is undated, but may have been written at about the time when Caxton published his edition; like the edition, it is at least two stages of copying removed from the manuscript that Malory himself wrote. All previous editions have shown a strong preference for one of these texts over the other. This edition, although based on the manuscript, assumes the two to be of more nearly equal authority.

The lexical footnotes below the text are meant to explain it rather than translate it, and so have been kept short and literal. Where two meanings are given, the first is the more literal, the second a translation.

This edition has profited from suggestions made by Sister Alban of the Sisters of Charity of St Paul, Newbold Revel, and Mother Stanislaus of the same house and order, by Mr J. M. G. Blakiston, sometime Fellows' Librarian at Winchester College, Professor J. A. W. Bennett, Miss Janet Cowen, Professor Norman Davis, Miss Nadine Eynon, Mrs Rachel Hands, Miss Ruth Anne Henderson, Revd Dr D. A. Jackson, the late Revd Professor Dom David Knowles, o.s.b., Miss Margaret Locherbie-Cameron, Dr Terence McCarthy, Dr Caterina Maddalena, Dr Pauline Matarasso, Mrs Margaret Malpas, Mr B. D. H. Miller, Mr A. D. Mills, Revd Fr. Joseph Mizzi, archivist of the Sovereign Military Order of Malta, Professor Shunichi Noguchi, Miss Carole Rawcliffe, Mrs Vivien Thomas, Mrs Gweneth Whitteridge, Mr P. Yeats-Edwards, present Librarian at Winchester College, and by the General Editor; and from the accurate typing of Mrs Joyce Williams. It has been sustained by the patience of the General Editor and that of my family. Surviving mistakes, omissions and inadequacies are my own.

P. J. C. Field
University College
Bangor

1977

2491–8. Here for the last time Malory attributes to his sources what they ought to have said instead of what they did say. According to the French book, Lancelot's kinsmen spent the rest of their lives 'in the service of Our Lord'. The author of the English poem correctly inferred that this meant in the regular monastic life; but Malory, who had several kinsmen in the greatest of the military religious orders, preferred and substituted the service to which they were devoted: fighting against the *myscreantes*. (*Myscreantes* means primarily 'mis-believers', 'people with a false religion': the actions expected of mis-believers added the subordinate sense 'vile wretches', which is now the only meaning.)

Since 1300 a new, ferocious and apparently irresistible Moslem people, the Ottoman Turks, had become a steadily increasing danger to Christendom. They captured Constantinople in 1453, and plainly did not intend to stop there. They were to be at the gates of Vienna less than a century later, and were not to be decisively beaten back for over two hundred years. To thinking men, a crusade seemed an urgent necessity of self-defence as well as a visionary religious ideal, and it seemed no less necessary because the states of north-west Europe preferred squabbling among themselves to taking part in it (cf. l. 2109n). For these reasons, even an Elizabethan Englishman could think of crusading as a good way to die. Shakespeare in *Richard II* describes with obvious admiration Mowbray's death:

> Streaming the ensign of the Christian cross
> Against black pagans, Turks, and Saracens.
>
> IV. i. 94

(Cf. also *K Jn*, II. i. 4; *Ric II*, II. i. 53–6, IV. i. 92–100; 1 *H IV*, I i. 18–102; 2 *H IV*, III, i. 108, IV, iv, 3–4, IV, v, 210–241; *H V* V. ii. 203–207.)

The great lord's responsibility for his lands and people is emphasised for the last time in l. 2494: before he leaves them, even for a crusade, he must see that their government is in good hands. T. S. Eliot echoes these words, after an allusion to the Grail, at the end of *The Waste Land* (l. 425).

2498. The ultimate inspiration of this is the alliterative *Morte Arthure* (ll. 3430–31).

2508. The ninth year of King Edward IV: 4 March 1469 to 3 March 1470 inclusive.

283

Suggestions for Further Reading

Further information on Arthur and his age can be found in Leslie
Alcock, *Arthur's Britain* (Harmondsworth: Penguin Books, 1973); on
chivalry in Richard Barber, *The Knight and Chivalry* (London: Longman,
1970), and Arthur Ferguson, *The Indian Summer of English Chivalry*
(Durham, N.C.: Duke University Press, 1960); on courtly love in
C. S. Lewis, *The Allegory of Love* (Oxford: Clarendon Press, 1936); on
romance in John Stevens, *Medieval Romance* (London: Hutchinson,
1972); and on the medieval English language in Tauno Mustanoja,
A Middle English Syntax (Helsinki: Société Néophilologique, 1960). There
is a sound text of *La Queste del Saint Graal*, edited by Albert Pauphilet
(Paris: Champion, 1923), and a good translation by Pauline Matarasso
(Harmondsworth: Penguin Books, 1969). The standard edition of *La
Mort Artu* is by Jean Frappier (Paris: Champion, 1956), translated by
James Cable (Harmondsworth: Penguin Books, 1971). The stanzaic
Le Morte Arthur is available in the edition of James Bruce (Oxford:
Early English Text Society, 1903) and the alliterative *Morte Arthure* in
that of Edmund Brock (Oxford: Early English Text Society, 1871).
The most authoritative edition of Caxton's text is *Le Morte Darthur*, ed.
Heinrich Sommer (London: Nutt, 1889–91), and of the manuscript's,
The Works of Sir Thomas Malory, ed. Eugène Vinaver (Oxford: Claren-
don Press, 1973). Noteworthy literary assessments of the *Morte Darthur*
will be found in Eugène Vinaver, *Malory* (Oxford: Clarendon Press,
1929), Muriel Bradbrook, *Sir Thomas Malory* (London: Longmans,
1958), *Essays on Malory*, ed. J. A. W. Bennett (Oxford: Clarendon
Press, 1963) and *Malory's Originality*, ed. Robert Lumiansky (Baltimore,
Md.: Johns Hopkins Press, 1964). My own *Romance and Chronicle*
(London: Barrie and Jenkins, 1971) focuses on Malory's style. William
Matthews' *The Ill-Framed Knight* (Berkeley, Cal.: University of Cali-
fornia Press, 1966) gives a witty and controversial account of all the
suggested authors of *Le Morte Darthur*. Most of these books contain
bibliographies, but there is a particularly useful one in Vinaver's
edition, and one in some ways still more comprehensive in *A Manual of
Writings in Middle English 1050–1500*, ed. J. B. Severs and Albert
Hartung (New Haven, Conn.: Connecticut Academy of Arts and
Sciences, 1967–   ), *III*, 757–70 and 909–24.

Introduction

King Arthur is the most famous of all the inhabitants of medieval Britain. Stories about him survive in thousands of manuscripts in a dozen languages: in medieval English alone there are thirty of these stories, varying from short anecdotes to vast romances longer than most modern novels. He is the central character of Spenser's *Faerie Queene*; Milton at one time thought of writing his epic on Arthur rather than on Paradise Lost; and Dryden and Purcell wrote an opera about him. Tennyson's most ambitious poem is about Arthur, and Mark Twain satirised him in a historical novel. In our own time there has been an unbroken stream of novels, poems, films and plays about him; Arthurian societies flourish at Tintagel and other places associated with him; and his name has helped to attract publicity to investigations at South Cadbury, Castle Dore, and other sites that would otherwise have been of interest only to students of archaeology. His name is one of the very few from the period of nearly a thousand years of British history between Julius Caesar and Alfred the Great that are familiar to everyone today. Nevertheless, the first question that must be asked about Arthur is whether or not he really existed. The answer to this question helps to explain the kinds of stories that were told about him later, by Sir Thomas Malory and by others.

Arthur

In 400 AD, the Roman Empire, of which Britain had been a province for nearly four centuries, comprised Europe south-west of the Rhine and Danube, and much of North Africa and the Middle East. The Romans had ruled these areas for hundreds of years, but in the next decade barbarian invasions overran the western half of the Empire, and province after province fell permanently outside Roman authority. In about 410, the last Roman legions were withdrawn from Britain, and it ceased to be part of the Empire. At the end of the next century, communications with the continent were restored by missionaries sent by Pope Gregory to convert the pagan Anglo-Saxon invaders who now ruled nearly all England. The period between 410 and 597 is the most obscure in British history, and it can only be pieced together from a few documents (many of which are of much later date and not written as historical records) and from archaeological remains.

Nearly all we know of Arthur come from four such documents. In about 540, Gildas wrote *On the Fall of Britain* to denounce the vices of his day. In it he says that there had been forty-four years of comparative peace since the Saxons had been finally defeated at the siege of

1

Mount Badon. He does not say where Mount Badon is (most guesses put it near Bath), nor mention Arthur's name. A Welsh poem called *Y Gododdin*, written in about 600, describes a certain warrior as having 'glutted black ravens upon the ramparts, although he was not Arthur' (that is, his prowess in killing the enemy was second only to Arthur's). These words would be early enough to establish the existence of Arthur, if we could be certain they were not one of the later additions to the poem. The fullest apparently historical account of Arthur comes much later, in Nennius' *History of the Britons*, written in about 800. This tells us that after a barbarian settlement in Kent (which the *Anglo-Saxon Chronicle* dates in 488), 'Arthur fought against them with the kings of the Britons, and he was the Commander-in-Chief' (*dux bellorum*). Nennius then gives a list of twelve victories won by Arthur. The sites of some are unidentifiable; the most probable locations for the others are in southern Scotland, Lincolnshire, Chester, and wherever Mount Badon is. He adds a few details about two of the battles that suggest that Arthur had a reputation for piety and great personal courage. Finally, there are two relevant entries in the tenth-century *Annals of Wales*. The first, for 518, speaks of 'the battle of Badon, in which Arthur bore the cross of Our Lord Jesus Christ three days and three nights on his shoulders, and the Britons were victorious'. The second, for 539, reads: 'The battle of Camlann, in which Arthur and Medraut fell'. *Medraut* must be Malory's *Mordred*, but one cannot tell from this brief passage whether Medraut was Arthur's enemy or his ally, let alone if he was his nephew and betrayer, as in later stories. Where Camlann was is unknown.

This evidence has been much argued over. Nennius' words have been construed by some to mean that Arthur was a king, and by others to mean that he was not. It has been argued that *dux bellorum* meant a mere tribal war-leader chosen for particular campaigns, and alternatively a late-Roman military rank like that of the *dux Britanniae*, one of the senior generals under the Empire. Some historians have said that the battle-sites are so far apart because Nennius supplied the place of forgotten names with half-remembered ones, like that of the battle of Chester in 616, in which the Britons were defeated. Others have explained it by saying that the British kings appointed Arthur to defend the whole country, and gave him a highly mobile cavalry force to do it. Such a force would be not unlikely in the fifth century: after the battle of Adrianople in 387, in which Gothic horsemen killed the Emperor and wiped out his mainly infantry army, the Romans had discovered by desperate experiment a combination of lancers and horse-archers that could defeat the invaders. The use of this kind of army would also account for the victories since, well-handled, it always beat infantry —and the Saxons fought on foot. But there is no direct evidence.

Not even Arthur's existence is beyond question, but there are some probabilities. There was probably a supreme British military commander of genius in the late fifth century, who had the Roman-derived name of Arthur (though we cannot infer much about his background from his name), who fought against the Saxons in campaigns that culminated in a great victory in Wessex about 500 AD, and may have been killed about twenty years later in one of the civil wars mentioned by Gildas. His deeds were told in traditional oral literature, which Nennius summarised in Latin.

The Legends

It was in oral literature that the historical general evolved into the marvellous 'Emperor' of later Arthurian legend. Myth and folk-tale and the stories of historical figures of other periods came to be attached to the soldier who had staved off the downfall of Britain for half a century. Perhaps no marvel seemed improbable when attributed to the man who had achieved that. Consequently, by the time the stories came to be written down, it was impossible to separate the fiction from the truth. Many of the characters in Malory clearly had nothing to do with the historical Arthur. Merlin, who appears as Arthur's magician in the later stories, seems to have been an invented figure round whom gathered tales of various prophets and wizards and the legendary Wild Man of the Woods. Of the Knights of the Round Table, Lancelot has an even more unexpected origin: his name first appears in a long list of Arthur's companions, as one of a trio of folk-heroes who had originally been Celtic pagan gods. The names of Tristram, Ywain, and probably Gawain belonged to historical princes of different periods from Arthur and one another, who all became famous fighting in north Britain. Kay and Bedivere appear in one of the earliest narratives about Arthur, a Welsh poem (number XXXI in the *Black Book of Carmarthen*) of the tenth or eleventh centuries; and no trace of history shows in either— Bedivere is remarkable mainly for his four-pronged spear, and Kay for being a destroyer of lions and witches and for having fought a demonic cat called Cath Palug. In another poem, *Culhwch and Olwen*, Arthur's companions include Calchas the soothsayer from the siege of Troy, Gildas, and Clust the son of Clustfeinad, who, though buried seven fathoms underground, could hear an ant fifty miles away stirring from its nest in the morning. Among the adventures attributed to Arthur

3

himself are a boar-hunt across Ireland, the Irish Sea and Wales, and a journey to the other world to obtain a magic cauldron. By 1100, a flourishing body of legends, oral and written, told of an age of heroism and wonders beyond common experience, in which Arthur was the central figure. One of the most widespread legends was the prophecy that Arthur would one day return to Britain.

The Social and Intellectual Background

It was at this time that the Arthurian story took on the form in which it has traditionally been known. That form reflects the realities and ideals of life in France, the cultural heartland of Europe. The experience of the previous five hundred years had taught men throughout the continent to take a condition of war as normal and one of peace as the exception. This attitude was reflected both in life and in thought. Politically and socially, eleventh-century France was controlled by a fierce and independent knightly class defined by its military power. The invention of the stirrup and the horseshoe, and the use of the lance underarm in the charge—instead of its being thrown overarm—had made heavy cavalry even more irresistible than it had been in Arthur's day. Only the knight could afford the war-horse, the helmet and mail-coat, the lance and shield and sword, and the time needed to learn to use them efficiently together. The name 'chivalry' comes from the most important and difficult of these skills, horse-mastery (French *cheval* = 'horse'). But the knights, even those higher members of the class distinguished by titles and extensive lands, lived in a plain style. Like the rest of Europe, France was recovering from half a millennium of devastation and anarchy, and simply did not produce enough wealth for luxury.

Society was feudal: that is, it was organised as a hierarchy of reciprocal personal obligations based on the holding of land. The peasants held land of and were protected by the lord of their manor (the *fief* or *fee*, words closely related to *feudal*), and in return provided him with his woollen clothes, coarse food and wooden house. The knight held his fief of and was protected by his overlord, and in return owed him advice and military service. The overlord in turn held his fief of a superior, and so on up to the king. Peasant and duke alike acquired land by doing homage to its lord, becoming his vassal. Land-holdings soon became hereditary, though this was not logically necessary. In theory, no man was to do homage to more than one lord; and the relationship created was to be lifelong, unless one party failed to fulfil his obligations, in which case the other could repudiate it. At each level, these obligations were interpreted by the feudal court: the vassals under the presidency of their lord. The customary obligations, above the level of the peasants, were light: principally advice on marriage alliances and war; and, in war, forty days military service a year. But the feudal system worked more successfully in repelling foreign invasions than in preventing civil war. A lord had little power to punish even a breach of feudal obligation among his knightly vassals, especially if the vassal's house were built on a palisaded mound that could withstand forty days' siege. Often the military service for a fief, however large, was only one knight for forty days—so a baron who was the overlord of twenty knights might be able to field a force as large as that of an earl who was the overlord of twenty barons. If there was little control over how a knight behaved towards his lord or his fellow-vassals, there was none at all over how he behaved towards others. For the knightly class of the eleventh century, private war was a pleasure, a duty and a means of livelihood. Private wars were fought incessantly, for castles, land, cattle and ransoms. Consequently, the toughest fighters were much competed for by fathers of unmarried daughters and princes with fiefs to dispose of. The winner, like William the Conqueror, might gain a kingdom: the loser disappeared into a monastery or the grave.

The feudal system never encompassed every man and every acre, even in France, where it flourished most; but it was dominant in Europe and lands conquered by Europeans. A knight from Scotland would recognise a knight from Syria, friend or enemy, as a being akin to himself. It was dominant most of all in men's imaginations. Idealists interpreted their profoundest loves, human and divine, in terms of homage and personal service: in contrast, on a far from idealistic level, one Surrey manor is said to have been held of the King of England by service of being Marshal of the Court Prostitutes. The system was finally undermined less by its failings—mostly arising from inheritance or divided allegiance—than by its successes. It helped to produce an age that was, in contrast with the previous five hundred years, one of increasing peace and prosperity, money and trade. This was the point of economic 'take-off', after which prosperity generates more prosperity, that economists now eagerly look for in developing countries. Fiefs could be held safely by knights unnatural enough not to enjoy fighting, or descend by inheritance to women and children without their being speedily and forcibly dispossessed; and such people could afford to give the king money to hire soldiers to serve in their places. Kings were glad to do this, because many country knights were both

5

less efficient and more independent-minded—particularly about going abroad to fight—than professional soldiers. The increasing prosperity of the thirteenth and fourteenth centuries continued this process. Most of the money went to the knightly class: the higher the more. The titled nobility ate imported spices, sugar and oranges, wore silks and exotic furs, and built fine stone castles. In order to do this, many of them commuted the customary services to which they were entitled into money rents, or even sold them for cash. But at the very time when this increasingly expensive style of life was expected of the knightly class, the money they used to pay for it was being devalued by successive periods of inflation. Only kings and a few very great nobles kept up and even improved their positions. In the eleventh century, these princes had had to use their vassals—lesser nobles and knights—to make war, because there was no other way to do it. As their income increased, from taxes paid by non-fighters and from other sources, they became able to hire poor knights, younger sons of nobles, even townsmen, as administrators and judges to supervise their laws, and as soldiers to enforce them. In 1192, the King of France was unable to invade Normandy in defiance of a prohibition from the Pope, because his barons refused to follow him. A hundred years later, his successor could pay an army to do it, whatever his barons thought. By that time, the gigantic gamble of private war was no longer possible for the ordinary knight or lesser baron, though a variety of setbacks prevented the establishment of royal authority over the greatest nobles until the end of the fifteenth century.

The stresses of both peace and war generated divisions among members of the knightly class. Knighthood was not only an ideal: it was a social fact; and from the thirteenth century on, knighthood and fighting and governing and landholding and the status of being a gentleman began slowly to diverge. In England, the law imposed on knights an increasing number of expensive and time-consuming duties in local government, so that the gentry began to avoid taking up knighthood, and remained all their lives mere 'esquires' or 'gentlemen'. Local government had to be done by such formally unqualified men as could be persuaded to do it: some from the class that would earlier have been knighted, others who would not. One of the latter is Chaucer's Franklin, who is not quite a gentleman—apart from any formal qualifications, he talks too much and too anxiously about *gentilesse*, instead of simply living it. Most of the gentry, knights or not, no longer followed their lords to the king's army in war: they paid taxes instead to support a minority of professional soldiers. And even good professional soldiers often avoided knighthood, a high rank that might make it difficult for them to stay out of the cavalry. The cavalry had prestige, but it had grown more expensive as crossbow and long-bow made it necessary to have armour more elaborate than the mail-coat, and less effective as fourteenth-century military experiment found ways to contain and eventually defeat its charge. These pro-fessionals, though squires themselves, fought and captained men, manoeuvring the lighter cavalry, yeomen archers and (at the end of the Middle Ages) cannon. Men who did take on knighthood tended to have stationary incomes and rising costs, which compelled them to depart yet further from the knightly ideal: in peace to full-time estate farming, to career administration for a king or a great lord, or even into trade; in war, to mercenary ruthlessness, and on returning from it, to selling their skills on contract to competing armed factions with less of the old personal, permanent and exclusive loyalty to one lord.

From the early twelfth century, some of the increasing amount of money available had gone to townsmen, enabling them too to live luxuriously, buy land, and even occasionally be ennobled, if they gained the king's favour. But the king's favour was the last privilege of the knightly class, who did their best to monopolise it. By 1500, even the great nobles had lost most of their freedom and political and military power, but they were still the preferred leisure companions of kings. And there they spent a good deal of time in secular Orders of Chivalry intended to recall and revive the legendary knightliness of Arthur and Charlemagne. The first and most famous of them all, the English Order of the Garter, was originally to have been called 'The Order of the Round Table'. Whatever their statutes said, however, these Orders did little beyond holding impressive and expensive cere-monies focused on the person of the sovereign, thus unwittingly magni-fying the importance of kingly power and money, the two things most subversive of the ideals and reality of knighthood.

Feudal Chivalry

Which virtues a society admires most will depend largely on its tradi-tions and needs. The knight's place in feudal society brought it about that the three essential chivalric virtues should be prowess, loyalty and generosity. *Prowess*—the ability to win in battle—was vital because the knight's occupation was war; *loyalty*, particularly to his lord and to his word of honour, because, there being no means of compulsion, the alternative was an anarchy that prowess would only aggravate; and *generosity*, because gifts were a sign of love and evoked loyalty in re-

7

turn. In practice, the French and Anglo-Norman nobility seem, as far as can now be judged, to have fought well and been loyal to their obligations as they understood them: in particular, violation of one's freely given solemn word was very rare. Generosity was usually remarkable by modern standards, and was often taken to the point of ruinous extravagance. In a warrior society of horsemen, where a man must frequently be ready to gamble his life cheerfully and without hesitation on his fighting skill, anxiety over possessions irrelevant to war is likely to seem contemptibly petty. Any kind of judicious calculation will probably be despised, but that over material possessions most of all. Generosity was practised, that is, in a spirit characteristic of such a society: a spirit of proud, impulsive and reckless gallantry.

This was the spirit that won medieval knights nearly all the battles of the Middle Ages, and needlessly lost them some disastrous exceptions. It explains why two more ambivalent virtues, courtesy and the desire for glory, were as much admired as prowess, loyalty, and generosity. *Courtesy* in this context is a misleading name for a virtue that belongs to the battlefield, not the court. Respect for a formidable enemy can develop into generous treatment of him: a code of fair play between knights. It came to be felt that one knight should not attack another when he was unarmed or unawares, or take part in an attack two or more to one, that he should spare the lives of vanquished knights, demand ransoms that were less than ruinous, and release prisoners on parole. Those knights who went on crusade to the Holy Land learnt more of this virtue from the sophisticated society of their Moslem enemies. Both sides were often ruthless, but when Saladin heard that his enemy Richard the Lionheart was ill, he sent him a gift of fruit. No Christian would wish to be less magnanimous than that. The *desire for glory* was linked to this, since the reputation men prized was one for both prowess and courtesy. As, during the thirteenth and fourteenth centuries, wars came to be fought on an ever-larger scale between armies made up more and more of mercenary soldiers, it became increasingly difficult for a knight to maintain that he was defending his fief or serving his lord, and neither king nor country yet evoked great devotion. So knights fought for profit and enjoyment and glory. Profit and enjoyment were considered disreputable, and so it was glory that was increasingly professed—and sought, often enough at the cost of military effectiveness. The individual's desire for glory all too often subverted disciplined coordination; and extravagantly honourable behaviour led knights to throw away both victory and profit. St Louis' brother lost an entire war by leading a charge despite orders to hold back, and Sir Philip Sidney in the sixteenth century lost his life because he threw away his thigh-armour rather than ride into battle better protected than his friend.

But in the fifteenth century, both the desire for glory and the practice of courtesy were on the wane. The wars were more bitterly fought and probably more nationalistic; there were fewer knights in the armies, and those few were hard pressed for money. They returned to the twelfth-century custom of talking about glory and acting for profit, in (for instance) holding noblewomen to ransom and leading mercenary bands in plundering the countryside, things almost unheard of in the two preceding centuries.

Some knights found glory in war itself, others in the mimic war of *tournaments*. Tournaments were devised in France just before the Norman Conquest, and were imported into England by King Stephen, although the Pope had forbidden them because they occasioned the shedding of Christian blood. They changed a good deal as armour grew heavier and more expensive, but always remained a combat between two sides, using all sorts of weapons. Some of the early tournaments were so large that infantry was used in them as well as cavalry. A tournament might begin with the most devastating weapons of all, lances used in a massed charge, but neither side would willingly allow the other time to retire, form up, and charge again. The tournament would therefore break up into fighting between individuals or small groups. Any knight who had or could get an unbroken lance and a clear run at one of the opposite party would use that, otherwise he would use his other weapons, including his mailed fist, at close quarters. If unhorsed, he was allowed to continue to fight on foot if he could, hoping to get or be found another horse before he was defeated and made to admit it by someone on the other side. The fighting might continue from morning until night, and it could go on all over the neighbouring countryside, which explains why ambushes are possible in the tournaments of the *Morte Darthur*. In the later Middle Ages, tournaments were normally fought with blunted weapons and under certain other restrictions, but serious injury and death were still not uncommon. Chaucer's *Knight's Tale* gives a vivid and detailed picture of this kind of tournament: the restrictions include having the entire affair take place in an enclosed arena. Tournaments gave ordinary knights an exciting combination of dangerous sport, spectacular entertainment, useful military training, a chance to mix with the very great, and—though it is not seen in the *Morte Darthur*—gambling, since a knight won the valuable warhorse of any rider he could unseat, and an even more valuable ransom from any man he could capture and compel to admit defeat. The vanquished could lose everything, and the consistently

9

successful could become rich and famous: at the end of the twelfth century William Marshal, the landless fourth son of an unimportant baron, who had to borrow a horse to take part in his first tournament, rose by means of them to become Earl of Pembroke and Regent of England. Pure sportsmanship was not always the rule. It was possible (though frowned on) to set on a man half-a-dozen at a time, to unseat an opponent by deliberately killing his horse, or to wait until most of the contestants were exhausted, and then go in and score spectacular successes. But these risks were themselves an attraction, and kings as well as poor knights-errant found tournaments addictive. Malory's sources gave him a picture of them more or less as they were in their heyday: he must have felt that the changes visible in his own age showed a definite decline.

During the later Middle Ages, as the expense of the equipment made it increasingly difficult to gather a party large enough for realistic miniature battles, the tournament was replaced by the *joust*, a combat with lances between two mounted men. A series of jousts could be run, either consecutively or concurrently, before or instead of a tournament, to practise skills with the lance. Having each pair of knights fighting separately much improved safety, and the Pope reallowed the sport in 1316. Other changes soon made it safer still. A long barrier (the 'tilt') was put down the centre of the lists, and the jousters rode down opposite sides of it, aiming their lances at one another across it. Armour grew impenetrable, and saddles were fastened on even more firmly. It became almost impossible to unhorse an opponent, even by accident, and winners were assessed on a complicated points system. Tilting became the standard martial show in Malory's time, and was usually accompanied by a number of comparably artificial exercises, such as exchanging a fixed number of sword-strokes with a mounted opponent, and fighting with various weapons against an opponent on foot on the other side of a barrier. Prizes and penalties were brought within bounds. The new exercises were almost as spectacular as the tournament proper, and safer (if only relatively—a sixteenth-century king of France was killed while tilting). As armoured mounted lancers gradually ceased to be irresistible in war, it came to matter less that tilting was not the effective training for war that tournaments had been. Out of a kind of military nostalgia, the shield and the great helm were still used in tilting, although the development of plate armour had made them obsolete on the battlefield. Around tilting, ceremonial, heraldry and costume were elaborated in splendid and highly symbolic pageantry that sometimes required the fighting itself to be 'fixed'. Like the secular Orders of Chivalry, these magnificent shows focused not a living chivalry but national pride and devotion to the person of the sovereign. This symbolism and the attractions it inherited from the tournament proper kept tilting in use in England until 1622 as spectacular entertainment for great occasions.

Church and Court

Feudal chivalry did a great deal to civilise the proud and aggressive behaviour of knights towards one another, whether as friends or enemies, as equals or as lord and vassal. But it did nothing to restrain a knight's behaviour towards anyone who could not stand up and fight him: the old, the poor, women, priests, cripples, peasants, merchants, children and Jews. Feudal chivalry was an exclusive code, and they were all excluded. The very pride of a society of mounted warriors might occasionally make a knight gratify a generous impulse towards such people, but more often it would stifle any sympathy for those who seemed to be of another and inferior species. Common sense might make a knight treat his inferiors on his fief as well as he did his cattle (if not as well as he did his war-horse), but it would not make him anything but a predator towards strangers. Chaucer saw a real affinity when in *The Parliament of Fowls* he presented his three knights as hawks, the hunting birds with which knights loved to ride marshy riverbanks: fierce, strong, beautiful, their deadly high-strung reflexes keeping them on the brink of madness. If the ideal, let alone the reality, of medieval knighthood were ever to include compassion for those who were not knights, some external factor would have to modify the killing machines that feudal chivalry would otherwise produce. The two principal external factors that did so were *Christianity* and *the Court*.

Even after the barbarian invasions, the Christian message was preached to the whole of what had been the Empire in the West. That message was primarily a statement about the relationship between God and Man. Individual moral behaviour, and still more the moral behaviour of men in society, came second; but it came a close second, directly and by no remote inference. No other available set of ideas about man and his condition could rival Christian theology and morality in comprehensiveness, sophistication, or profundity. And this message was as relevant to the knight as to the priest or the peasant. The most successful of fighting men would take no pride in his finite strength, skill and virtues, if he began to set them against the infinite perfections of God, saw them as gifts only kept in being by God's providence, or reflected that pride was the deadliest of sins, a ridiculous assertion of self-sufficiency that invited disaster in this world and damnation in the next. He would not mistreat the weak if he thought that their ultimate worth came, like his, from God's love and an eternal destiny, two infinites in which they might exceed him, in which his success might depend on how he treated them, and which dwarfed all the differences between them. This theory could not be refuted: it could only be ignored. The violence, robbery and lust of the sixth to eleventh centuries show how often and how much it was ignored; but in time, part of the practical implication of this teaching became incorporated in the specifically knightly code of ideals. The knight was obliged to treat all his fellow-men, not as his social or political equals —that would have seemed ludicrous—but as beings of infinite worth in the eyes of God. He could make an exception only (if at all) of himself. The ideal has left its marks even on the language in use centuries later: the *gentleman* was obliged to *gentleness* and *generosity* to all. To fail in this was not only un-Christian; it was also unknightly. The superficial familiarity of this ideal conceals from modern Europeans and those educated in the same ethos how odd a growth it was in a society that was masculine, aggressive and based on war. Yet it pervades the most famous description in English of a knight, the one in the General Prologue to Chaucer's *Canterbury Tales*. It is not at all surprising that the Knight should love the five feudal chivalric virtues:

> Chivalrye,
> Trouthe and honour, fredom and curteisye
>
> *Cant. Tales*, A 45

(*Chivalrye* is approximately prowess, *trouthe* is loyalty, and *fredom* is generosity of spirit.) But when Chaucer explains the Knight's courtesy, he begins, with fine poetic instinct, with a simile that stands out sharply against the catalogue of masculine soldierly achievement that preceded it:

> And of his port as meke *as is a mayde*.
> He never yet no vyleinye ne sayde
> In al his lyf unto no maner wight. . . .
>
> *Cant. Tales*, A 70

The quadruple explicit negative is extremely forceful, but the most forceful item of all is the implicit negative *vyleinye*, 'something-not-proper-to-a-gentleman', behaviour that might be expected of a villein or peasant. Under the gravitational pull of the Christian virtue of being *meke*, the social virtue of good breeding has extended itself beyond a man's equals in battle, beyond the women and priests of their families, to *all maner wight*. This was exemplified historically, for instance, when Sir Philip Sidney, dying as the result of his own chivalrous folly, gave away his drinking water, not to a fellow-knight, not to one of his own men, but to a wounded common soldier—because he was there.

But the Church did more to change the character of knighthood than merely impose on knights a general obligation to behave as Christians. It had faced the brutalities of royal power in the Dark Ages by evolving a theory of kingship that would Christianise (and civilise) the Merovingian kings, and it attempted to bring this theory home to the kings by teaching, both verbal and symbolic. One symbol, which survives to the present day, was that of an anointing as part of the coronation, as though the king were a kind of bishop. This reminded the king that his power was ultimately held from and dependent upon God. Similarly, the Church evolved a *theory of knighthood*, which was again expressed in both verbal and symbolic terms. As early as 950, the secular ceremony of dubbing a knight could include a religious element. As a token that he would serve God, the new-made knight had his sword blessed before he girded it on, or offered it on the altar of a church. With time, this ceremony was elaborated more and more, as was the theory implied in it, though it remained common practice, especially before a battle, for knighthood to be conferred in a very short simple form like that used today.

Knighthood, according to the theory, was not a mere social condition of certain adult males in society trained and equipped for war; it was an *Order* in society comparable to the priestly order and bringing its members both privileges and responsibilities. The state—that is, society insofar as it is organised—was thought of almost exclusively in terms of its most basic function: protection. The knight's duty was to provide this protection. He should bring about by force what the priest urged in words: peace, justice, and Christian orthodoxy. It was essential for a knight to be able to fight: no lord, it was said, should knight a man who was too maimed (or too fat) to be able to do so. But the prospective knight should not be chosen merely for his ability in war, or even for his excellence in all the chivalric virtues taken together. The Church's theory took account of two difficulties that the feudal code alone did not: the knight as a danger to others and the knight as a danger to himself. He should have a wide range of virtues besides the feudal chivalric ones—notably humility, temperance, pity, chastity and wisdom. He should also have the noble descent that would make it likely that these virtues would be firmly rooted, and his training should strengthen these moral qualities, as well as his warlike skills. Then he would be able to master not only the enemy but also, in himself, rage, avarice, lust, quarrelsomeness, and most of all the pride and naked aggression that were so nearly uncontrolled in feudal chivalry, and which would needlessly and unjustly make enemies of his lord, his fellows, and his vassals.

The fundamental assumption of feudal chivalry was that the preservation of the state and the welfare of society depended directly on the virtues of the governing class. The Church's theory was a more radical and comprehensive version of this, and tended to reinforce that assumption. And so the Church always said that the principal danger to knighthood was not any force external to it but the knight who failed to acquire the Christian virtues. Some failings are picked out for particular condemnation: killing one's lord, sleeping with one's lord's wife, betraying a castle he had committed to one's trust, and robbery —whether of property by theft or of honour by defamation. All the theorists are ferocious in condemning these failings, and unanimous in declaring that it is the duty of the true knight to deal with the delinquent one (though the ways suggested range from varieties of social ostracism such as banning him from tournaments through public degradation to challenging him to mortal combat). If the knights as a body were virtuous, the rest, it was thought, would follow easily: invaders could be fought off and rebels put down, the law enforced and the Church protected, and widows, orphans, and the poor provided for. And it was the knight's duty to protect society that made it both right and necessary that he should have the privileges he possessed: horses and weapons, and power, and the wealth and leisure to live in an impressive style. These ideas are accepted as much by the radical—as can be seen, for instance, in Langland's *Piers Plowman* (B text, Passus VI) — as by the conservative.

The third and most demanding level at which Christianity could affect knighthood was that at which the knight put himself entirely at the service of the Church: by going on a crusade against the pagans in Prussia or the Moslems in Spain (Chaucer has his Knight do both), or the Moslems in the Holy Land; or by joining a military-religious order like the Hospitallers of St John of Jerusalem, which might also take him to the crusades, where the military orders were always in the forefront. Neither mode of life was ever thought essential for every knight, but the gallantry and idealism of the crusaders and the military orders in victory and defeat made a deep impression on the imagination of all Christendom.

The notion of the knight as a sort of policeman enforcing a Christian

peace became immensely popular, and is standardised in the innumerable formulae that divide society into those who fight, those who pray,
and those who labour. The courtesy expected of a knight became a
much broader virtue, including much of what the clerical theorists
prescribed; and was more broadly applied, although there were always
some who felt it was only obligatory on members of the knightly class
in their dealings with one another. And the sentiment that the moral
virtue of the governing class is the basis of peace and justice is stated or
assumed by many secular manuals of behaviour, and explains the importance they give to manners. But the Church's own more practical
prescriptions were often disregarded. Although the moralists forbade
jousting, and the stricter ones hunting as well, some churchmen argued
that a knight *ought* to joust and hunt, to keep him in training for war,
while the Church's prohibition of private war, tournaments, and the
taking of ransoms and other loot in war, along with its embarrassing
insistence on restitution before forgiveness could be granted, were very
widely evaded or ignored—something many clerics must have con-
nived at. Most knights seem to have felt that if they were *preux* (had
prowess), loyal, generous and courteous, God would turn a blind eye
to a certain carelessness about homicide and the rights of the clergy and
other non-combatants.

The second great civilising influence on the knight was that of *the
court*. The knight was not just a cavalry soldier: he was also a magnate
whose military service provided him with land; and, at each level in
the feudal hierarchy, land meant courts. Courts in the Middle Ages
had functions that even then were beginning to separate from one another, and have now done so entirely. At the top of the hierarchy, the
royal court, the king would on formal occasions gather the great men to
make great decisions, particularly men versed in the law when a legal
principle had to be clarified, particularly the politically powerful when
the matter was one of state, such as a declaration of war. These now
separate bodies are respectively the Law Courts and what in Britain is
still occasionally called the High Court of Parliament. But the king's
court also managed the ceaseless round of detailed administration and
legal minutiae, of petitions and patronage and running the royal
estates; and its other functions made it the focus of honour and the
centre of high society. Some members of the court, of all ranks, were
almost permanently in attendance, but a much larger number paid
visits of varying lengths at intervals. This in turn made the court the
natural centre for influences of many other kinds, in art, fighting,
finance, religion, sport, intellectual matters and dress. The number of

people at court, like the number of things controlled (as opposed to influenced) was small, and so the court was naturally a very personal institution. Socially, as economically, comparisons with developing countries are more illuminating than those with modern constitutional monarchies. The most important person by far was the king: his character affected everything done or not done at court, he took many decisions himself, and he always knew that a wrong decision on an important issue might cost him his life. But the king himself was much influenced in issues great and small, official and private, by members of his court—and not only by the high-ranking ones. Almost anyone at court might have some sort of access to the king, and those who did not could work on those who did. For the courtiers were not only the employees and customers of the business of government, they were also the king's family and circle of friends and his sounding-board for public opinion. (As late as the nineteenth century, British ministers could judge the popularity of their policies by the glaziers' bills for mending broken windows.)

At each level in society, the pattern of the king's court was reproduced on a smaller scale. The ordinary knight would attend the court of his lord at least on great occasions, and he would preside in his own manor court, dispensing justice to his vassals, settling disputes among them, and administering the manor with a wary eye for encroachments on his own rights. On occasions when he had great decisions to make, he would gather together a small 'parliament'—his relatives, friends, neighbours, and senior vassals—to advise him on a decision that would affect all of them; or perhaps so as to persuade them of the wisdom of a decision he had already made. Even in Chaucer's time, when the king's authority could override lower feudal authority, when the knights administered the local government for the king as much as or more than for their immediate feudal superiors, the pattern of the feudal court seemed perfectly natural. Chaucer's *Merchant's Tale* shows an ordinary knight who wants to marry calling his own personal court together—and ignoring all the sensible advice he gets, because he has already made up his mind what he wants.

Having to run his manor and at least help administer his lord's fief tended to impress on the knight the importance of one other virtue outside the feudal ones: wisdom—not a virtue that grows naturally among cavalrymen. Seeing the natural tension between prudence and the impetuous heroism of chivalry, Chaucer firmly asserts both of his Knight, saying 'Tho that he were worthy' (that is, had a deserved reputation for honour) 'he was wys'. This is the only virtue besides the feudal–chivalric five that Chaucer explicitly attributes to his Knight.

When a country was poor, and the struggle for lands fierce, the primacy of the feudal virtues could hardly be challenged. But with even a limited increase in prosperity and security, the intimate involvement of a country's power structure and surplus wealth with the lords' social and domestic life would make other personal qualities besides wisdom useful to a vassal—some of them less unequivocally admirable. To be charming and agreeable could be as quick a way to riches as was fighting ability; and it might be a great deal safer. The counterpart in medieval political satire of the modern heartless bureaucrat is the smooth-tongued flatterer who, because he knows how to make himself agreeable, can monopolise the royal patronage, cut the king off from the natural advisers who would tell him what needs doing, and lead him into folly, evil and disaster. But this was only the reverse side, the corruption of a virtue so essential to court life that it took its name from the court: *courtesy*. Courtesy was the kind of unselfishness and consideration for others that was essential to smoothing the rubs of living in a small crowded community with little privacy, short tempers, long memories, and an arsenal of weapons. So essential was courtesy that it was developed into an elaborate code that specified each person's precedence and rights in many situations. When a deer was killed, every participant from the Master of the Hunt to the hounds had his appointed part of the carcase—there was even one piece to be thrown to the crows. Religion might provide the ultimate justification and war the most spectacular examples of courtesy, but it was the court that provided the opportunity and incentive to practise it most frequently. That was why it was *the* court virtue, at once a personal quality 'natural' to men of knightly descent, and an art to be learned as the basis of social life.

Courtesy became still more important as peace and prosperity brought leisure, and, with leisure, boredom. The principal pastimes were arts that could hardly be distinguished from courtesy itself, in a broad sense. The young squire learned not only how to carve and serve at table, to arm a knight, and to understand a little of the international languages of French and Latin, but the proper way to welcome a stranger, dance, hunt, sing, and above all to talk, the medieval art *par excellence*. The *Canterbury Tales* celebrate the importance of this art at all levels in society.

But the supreme 'art' that leisure and courtesy developed was the Art of Love. Passionate love between man and woman was hardly new in the Middle Ages, but reverence for it was. The medieval notion that love was the centre of the noble life and the source of all the virtues was more than just new: it was revolutionary. Before the twelfth century, a medieval woman was always subject to some man: father, husband, or guardian, she was a minor in his charge. She could be publicly beaten without redress, and her marriage was an alliance between two families about which she was not consulted. Nevertheless, she was an important, if junior, partner in the family, not a brood mare or a harem toy. She was mistress of the household, and, in her husband's absence, of the castle and fief; and she could speak her mind freely to him if she were prepared to risk the consequences. Marriages such as these might produce affection or friendship, but rarely passion. So it it not surprising that when passionate love appeared, it was either hostile or indifferent to marriage.

The ideas of what significantly came to be called 'courtly love'—or even *courtoisie*, as if it were or implied the whole of the courteous life— first appeared in the lyric poetry composed and sung by troubadours at the small, rich, and peaceful courts of early twelfth-century southern France. The theory behind them, whether stated or implied, is bizarre but confident with a certainty derived from novel, exciting and intense experience. It made women, or rather one woman, not the poet's equal but infinitely his superior. Love was defined as the emotion caused by unrestrained admiration for a lady. This admiration was caused by her virtues; her lover's awareness of it dominated his life and generated virtues in him. The virtues expected of him naturally resembled those of the other kinds of chivalry: the exclusive, passionate, and lifelong service given by a vassal to a good lord or by a religious man to God. The most extreme exponents of love said that one could not be a good knight or a good anything else without it. They also maintained that this love was its own justification and reward. The real lover, they said, did not care whether he was rewarded with kisses, or more, or nothing; or even if the lady was pleased at being worshipped. Love was a debt of justice, which she deserved and he could not help paying: it was not an act of ingratiation.

The notion that he should try to please and that she should respond with passion is found later in the century in the north of France. It was the product of further experience, though sometimes attributed to the influence of Ovid (a classical author gave some respectability to even the oddest ideas). But though Ovid's poetry did not produce the new kind of love, it helped the lovers understand their own feelings, because, while the love he described might not be either virtuous or fully serious, it was both intense and sexual. And sex is essential to love as described by the chief twelfth-century authority: the *Art of Love* Andreas Capellanus wrote for Marie, Countess of Champagne. Andreas explored all kinds of contradictory ideas, and it is hard to know when he is being serious. He and Marie's court were both subtle enough to know that a 'joke' may be the only way to explore a para-doxical or forbidden subject; and that the best and most effective joke may be something outrageous said with a straight face, to enrage the strait-laced or entice the eccentric into further oddities. Writing about love in the form of a textbook, an *Art of* ——, was itself a joke, and Andreas' definition of love sounds uneasily like a parody: a passion produced by thinking excessively about the body of someone of the opposite sex, and producing in turn an overwhelming desire for inter-course. But he plainly thought that love was a sexual matter, and that it was mutual: the lover must therefore learn to be pleasing. And like previous writers, he maintained that it was aristocratic and extra-marital. Although, he conceded, love is produced by and produces virtue and is therefore possible for those of low birth, the requisite qualities are so unlikely in the low-born that a knight irresistibly attracted by a peasant woman should rape her rather than waste his courtesy trying to evoke love. And love is quite incompatible with marriage, because sex must be voluntarily given by lovers (whereas married people cannot refuse one another) and because lovers must be jealous (which for married people would be a sin).

These ideas were popularised by the courtly romances that domi-nated northern French literature, the most famous of which were those written by Chrétien de Troyes. So many of them are about the new emotion and contain long discussions of it in its special language that they presuppose the existence of an audience eager to find out what this new emotion was, and what they ought to feel. And the image of love remained remarkably stable in medieval literature from this time on. A knight must love a lady: some said platonically, some said in marriage, but many—especially in France—expected his love to be both physical and extramarital. He must be brave and loyal, but also *cavaliere servente*: handsome, richly and elegantly dressed, with clean teeth and fingernails, able to sing and play an instrument and perhaps compose his own songs, and a courteous and witty conversationist adept in the ambiguous language of love. His first concern must be his lady's honour, which he must increase by his deeds of prowess; but he must also preserve her reputation by keeping his love secret. (These apparent incompatibles could be reconciled by discretion about physical favours.) Some expected him to prove his worth by long ser-vice before he was so much as granted permission to serve her; others spoke as though the only virtue a lady produced was fighting ability, and this deserved a speedy physical reward. All agreed that for his lady's sake the lover should honour and protect all ladies. Chaucer's description of the Squire in the General Prologue to the *Canterbury Tales* gives a comprehensive portrait of an ideal lover.

Life was very different from literature. Although wives were not usually chosen for love and certainly not for love alone, adultery was unanimously condemned. Geoffrey de la Tour Landry put on record in his book of manners his regret that transgressors were no longer buried alive. But many gradually came to accept the less radical precepts of courtly love: that love was an honourable and efficient spur to prowess, and that a knight should treat ladies with courtesy and make himself agreeable to them. Some said that these elaborate attentions to women promoted immorality; and certainly, if there was any widespread acceptance of the recommendation that platonic and honourable lovers should sleep together naked, the pessimists were probably right. Shakespeare's Iago torments Othello with a nightmare vision of his wife extending this courtesy to her 'friend' (a basic ambiguity in the language of love: French *ami* = 'friend' and 'lover'). But the very elaboration prescribed may actually have reduced the incidence of adultery: we can never know. The spectacular examples of courtesy to ladies that the chronicles record and the fragmentary evidence of ordinary life both suggest that men were beginning to be much more gentle and considerate to ladies, even to their wives. The final lesson experience taught contradicted both the clerics and the court poets: as Chaucer's *Franklin's Tale* contends, loving one's own wife or husband could be much more satisfying than loving someone else's. Between them, love and court life seem to have taught the knight to be an agreeable companion both in his own home and away from it.

The End of an Ideal

At the very time of chivalry's greatest diffusion, a number of tensions affected the way men thought of it. Some of these tensions were internal: feudal, religious and courtly chivalry were, in their most extreme forms, irreconcilable with one another; so the proponents of each criticised the others. The Church admired the virtues that were the basis of feudal chivalry, but criticised the circumstances in which those virtues were practised. The Church's definition of a just war was too strict for most of the wars actually fought: it is notable that although England and France were at war for the whole of Chaucer's lifetime, in the career of his ideal Knight he names only campaigns against Moslems and pagans. But, however uneasy idealists were at the thought of Christians shedding one another's blood, some justification could usually be given for each case in context. So idealistic uneasiness was more often directed at three concomitants of war than at war itself or particular wars. The Church condemned *homicide*, particularly in tournaments; it condemned the feudal ideal of *glory* as vainglory— boasting and pursuing groundless human admiration instead of the glory of God; and it condemned *robbery*, including the taking of ransoms and war booty, except on certain (nearly impossible) conditions. Courtesy in manners had the Church's high approval as a form of applied charity, but *courtoisie* in the sense of courtly love was condemned without reserve. When it was mentioned at all, the virtues it proclaimed were categorised as vices. Sexual intercourse outside marriage had of course always been forbidden; and passionate obsession with one person was condemned as offensive alike to reason and to grace. Neither aspect of love was often dignified with the elaborate consideration given to war. Occasional handbooks for confessors include questions about lascivious conversation, 'petting', and writing love-songs; occasional moralists complain that modern manners—unlike those of a tougher and wiser past—are frivolous and self-indulgent; but the only systematic refutation on religious principles of the claims of courtly love comes, oddly enough, in the last book of Andreas's *Art of Love*.

Andreas's self-refutation shows the overwhelming intellectual superiority of the *logic* of the theologians over the immediate *experience* of feudal chivalry and courtly love. Partisans of both avoided arguments they would have been bound to lose; those of feudal chivalry expounded the agreed fundamentals and ignored the differences of application; those of courtly love stated their own ideas and left criticism of the Church's teaching on sexual morals tacit or ironic or buried in obscure corners. But these internal tensions left it open to different authors to think of chivalry in different ways, according to the weight given to each of its competing ideals. These weightings were usually implicit rather than overtly didactic, and few authors tried to exclude any of the three elements entirely, but every possible degree of seriousness and combination of elements is found, in histories and chronicles as well as in romances and love poems.

Almost from the beginning, however, as society changed, the conditions that sustained chivalry were being undermined from outside. Something has already been said of this above (pp. 4–7). Yet as, in the fourteenth and fifteenth centuries, modern war and the modern state began to take shape, the confusions and uncertainties of the process made most men hold yet more firmly to the old ideals. This applied not only to those who took up knighthood and to the squires from the same background who avoided it, but also to the rich townsmen for whom feudal reality and chivalric theory provided no place in the social structure. Ambitious burgesses like Chaucer's five guildsmen, who held no land by feudal tenure and rendered no military service, began to call themselves 'gentlemen' and adopt as much as they could adapt of chivalry. There was no coherent alternative, and the very abstractness of the ideal in England saved it from much of the criticism it suffered in France, where it is for the first time systematically criticised as militarily ineffective: amateurish, undisciplined, and leading to neglect of army organisation. But in England, though the feudal structure no longer sustained government and war, the quasi-religious atmosphere, the aesthetic values, the ideals of personal conduct, the snob-appeal of heraldry, and the associated but separable element of courtly love remained popular and credible with all the lay rulers of medieval society. The chroniclers treat chivalry as a living ideal from which they hope for a remedy for the times, and a standard by which they condemn the evils they record. In war, a kind of international law was administered by heralds' courts, which enforced the payment of ransoms and punished dishonourable behaviour such as breaches of allegiance: conviction could mean death, or social, professional and financial ruin. Chivalry still formalised the best side of aristocratic pride, and instilled courage and mercy into men anxious to keep their own self-respect.

But the virtues of chivalry—feudal, religious, or courtly—were *private* virtues. And even though they were capable of being broadened to include what the twentieth century regards as public issues, there were limits to the extent to which chivalry could survive this. The fifteenth century saw an increasing awareness of a separate public sphere of action. A new ideal took shape, elevating virtues that the old chivalry hardly recognised: patriotism, eloquence, and a wisdom that needed knowledge far beyond common sense—knowledge particularly of law and of the classics of Greece and Rome. The medieval knight was too international in outlook for patriotism, and typically despised learning in members of his own class, though respecting it in 'clerks'. In contrast, at the end of the sixteenth century, Shakespeare's Ophelia admires Hamlet as a courtier, soldier and *scholar*. It is these new virtues, finding their outlet in *public* service rather than in the personal service of a lord, that mark out the new man of the Renaissance. In the new world, soldiering is merely one profession among many, jousting is (as Francis Bacon saw it in his *Essays* in 1625) a mere appendix to the subject of masques and triumphs, and war is part of a continuous struggle of states to which chivalry is irrelevant. But to the private lives and manners of the public men, in which the new practicality and classical ideas might have produced mere ruthless schemers, the ideals of chivalry made a humanising and permanent contribution.

The Romances

The Arthurian stories circulated in the Celtic world of Wales, Cornwall and Brittany, and were popularised in the courts and baronial halls of France by minstrels, probably Bretons. Some Bretons were descended from the thousands of insular Celts who had fled to Brittany during the Anglo-Saxon invasion, and the Bretons as a people were passionately devoted to the memory of Arthur. One twelfth-century commentator said that anyone who denied in Brittany that Arthur was still alive would be lucky to avoid being stoned to death. The minstrels, bilingual in Breton and French, found a ready audience for their tales of wonders wherever French was understood. Their stories, brought up to date in taste and costume and manners, were able to fascinate kings and counts who had no racial affinity with the British hero, and who lived well beyond the Norman–French sphere of influence. The earliest recorded appearance of Arthur and his knights in pictorial art is in Modena, in a carving made about 1100 in the cathedral. It shows Arthur, Kay, and Gawain rescuing Guenivere from a fortress held by Arthur's enemy Caradoc. And from all over Europe came stories of the king surviving, either in a golden island of perpetual summer, or asleep with his knights in a cave under a mountain.

It was probably the Breton minstrels who made the stories about Arthur popular, and who brought them back across the Channel to England after the Norman Conquest; but it was Geoffrey of Monmouth who made them coherent and respectable. Geoffrey was an ambitious cleric who wrote a Latin *History of the Kings of Britain* about 1135 in a bid for royal favour. His popular and fraudulent work claimed to be based on 'a very old British book', and provided a complete history of Britain from the earliest times to the Saxon conquest: William of Newburgh, one of the few contemporary sceptics, said scathingly that Geoffrey had 'disguised under the honourable name of history, thanks to his ability to write in Latin, the legends about Arthur which he took from the ancient fictions of the Britons and increased out of his own head'. This sums Geoffrey up as a historian, but as a story-teller he occupies a high rank. He stole from many authors to make his story, and did so with a sure eye for verisimilitude. Vivid, down-to-earth and sophisticated, his mixture of borrowed facts and invented details convinced nearly all his contemporaries, because Geoffrey's characters behaved just as they themselves would have done.

It was Geoffrey who first told the tale of Arthur's mysterious conception: how Merlin helped Uther Pendragon by enchantment to sleep with Igrayne, Duchess of Cornwall, so that Arthur was begotten, and how Uther married Igrayne after the death of the duke and died shortly after Arthur was born. Geoffrey transformed the fantastic heroes of Celtic legend into nobles and barons from many parts of Europe, giving some of them real names picked at random from old genealogies, and so made Arthur's court a more splendid version of the courts he knew. Although he was a cleric, the qualities which Geoffrey presented as admirable in his kings were ruthless efficiency, generosity and foreign conquest. He made Arthur's career one of continuous battles, some taken from Nennius and elaborated, others manufactured out of whole cloth. The subjection of England is followed by that of Scotland, Ireland, Norway, Denmark and finally of the Rome of 'the Emperor Lucius'. As far as we know, the overseas conquests are Geoffrey's invention. A hero so great could fall only by treachery: so, if Mordred's rôle was not traditionally that of a traitor, Geoffrey made it so. In the last battle, the traitor is killed, but Arthur is 'mortally wounded' and is carried to the Isle of Avalon 'for his wounds to be healed'. Geoffrey leaves his readers to resolve the conflict of phrases for themselves: whether the 'healing' was a mere intention that a 'mortal' wound would make impossible, or whether—necessarily by magic or miracle—the wound was healed. He himself says nothing of Arthur's death or burial. Nor does he explain that 'the Isle of Avalon' was a name sometimes used for Glastonbury Tor—not an island proper but a high mound between rivers in a marshy lowland.

The life of Arthur has been taken as the high point of Geoffrey's *History* by readers of all periods, as he obviously intended; but he established many other stories, including that of King Lear, as historical. His book was immensely popular, was translated into at least five other languages, and was used as a historical authority up to the time of Henry VII, who called his eldest son Arthur.

The best of the translations of the *History* is the Norman–French one completed by Wace in 1155. Although his material was rather different, his treatment of it is similar to Malory's. A medieval historian, however intelligent, sceptical and hard-working, lived before the invention of printing had made possible a wide diffusion of cheap and accurately printed sources. If he wanted to tell a story, he would be faced with a few manuscripts and a number of oral accounts of it or parts of it, which would vary a great deal in fullness and accuracy. There were no great libraries of printed and indexed records in which he could cross-check the facts and opinions of other historians about the prejudice, propaganda, credulity, or wholesale fraud of his sources. He could only rely on his native sense of what was likely, the reputations of his authors if they were famous, and the probability that most of them were telling the truth most of the time; but he knew, from the discrepancies between their stories, that all of them were probably wrong in small ways. So he might conflate or omit at will, add a description, a speech, or even a whole scene, without feeling that that took him further from the unattainable whole truth than any of his sources were. It must also be remembered that history, in the Middle Ages and long afterwards, was not dominated by economics and sociology as it is today. Historians, more like modern journalists, took as their subjects the stories of kings and bishops and saints, the love-affairs of the great, battles and natural calamities, great ceremonies and strikingly unusual happenings. Since this was also the subject-matter of romance, which often grew up around historical figures like Arthur, it is not surprising that most medieval people made no distinction between the two.

Wace turned upon Geoffrey's pseudo-history a critical and enquiring historian's mind, and one fully aware of what might bore or shock. He cut some of the miracles, the account of the evangelisation of Britain, the tortures that Arthur inflicted on the Picts, and some passages of exaggerated sentiment. He used the Bible, Nennius, and contemporary chronicles to develop the story, and his familiarity with the geography of southern England to make the action more probable. He also carefully collected oral traditions: indeed, he blames himself for not having heard more. Oral tradition presumably gave him the three novelties that he adds to the story of Arthur: the forest of Broceliande in which marvels occurred; the Round Table which Arthur had made to stop quarrels over precedence among his nobles; and explicit mention of Arthur's survival. Of the last he says cautiously that, although the Bretons still expect Arthur's return, he himself will say no more than Merlin, who had said that Arthur's death would be mysterious; and for his own part he thinks people will never know whether Arthur is alive or dead.

His story did not please everybody. Henry II tried to dispose of the uncertainty and at the same time of a possible, albeit unlikely, rival by inducing the monks of Glastonbury in 1191 to discover Arthur's and Guenivere's 'remains' in their graveyard. The discovery increased Geoffrey's reputation for accuracy but failed to kill off the legend of Arthur.

Wace's translation was itself translated into vigorous English verse about 1200 by an obscure English priest called Layamon. Layamon's *Brut* is the first Arthurian story in English, and it makes a number of additions to Wace, probably from French or Breton poets. Two of these lasted: Arthur's dream obscurely foretelling his betrayal by Mordred, and his final departure in a small boat to Avalon to be healed of his wounds by the queen of the fays.

But well before this, about 1170, some much more celebrated Arthurian poems had been written in France. The literature of northern France had changed in accordance with the changing tastes of the nobility who were its patrons. The most conspicuous effect on literature was the rise of courtly love, but writers also show an increased consciousness of their art, which is visible in the various poems about the love of Tristan and Isolt (some of which followed fashion and attached the story to King Arthur's court). They all share the same basic plot and all glorify love; but the love varies from earthy passion to elevated erotic idealism. The poet's art lay in presenting the story so as to embody in it what he thought was the truth about love.

The most influential Arthurian poet of this generation was Chrétien de Troyes. He was fascinated by the novelty, beauty and literary potential of the Arthurian story, and he took five self-contained Arthurian adventures from Wace and minstrels' tales and turned them into long, elegant, well-constructed and often amusing poems, combining marvels in the action with clear and perceptive psychology. The first four are about love, and three of them present the true-love marriage as the ideal union. Chrétien had clearly been repelled by the way the Tristan story exalted love adulterous, uncontrolled, and heedless of honour. Though he never denied the doctrines of the Church, he was more concerned with this world than the next; and he condemned adulterous passion less on religious grounds than as mere futile excess. Ironically, it is not his three stories about love in marriage that had the greatest influence on the developing Arthurian legend, but the other two.

The first of these was his *Lancelot, or the Knight of the Cart*, about which he says that he has been given both the story and the implied message by Marie of Champagne (the countess who was Andreas Capellanus's patron). Previously, Lancelot seems to have been a mere name among Arthur's knights. Chrétien adapted to Arthur's court an ancient Celtic myth in which a mysterious stranger claims a married woman, and either by force or by obtaining a rash promise from her husband, carries her away to his supernatural realm. The husband pursues, triumphs over all obstacles, enters the strange land, and wins back his wife. The Modena sculpture shows that Guenivere was already the heroine of a similar story before Chrétien's time, but now it is the newly-developed knight, Lancelot, who rescues her from the consequences of Arthur's folly. It is Lancelot who suffers danger and disgrace for Guenivere, and who is eventually welcomed to her bed. Kay, who first tries to rescue the queen from the stranger, Mellyagaunte, is wounded and captured. Gawain, Arthur's premier knight, and Lancelot set out in pursuit, but are separated. Lancelot's horse is killed, and his only method of transport is a cart like those used to carry prisoners to execution. Lancelot hesitates for only two steps before mounting the vehicle of shame. Overcoming numerous adversaries on his journey, he eventually crosses the sword-bridge to Mellyagaunte's castle. Though badly wounded, he defeats Mellyagaunte, only to find that the queen treats him with cold disdain, because he had hesitated before mounting the cart. But later a false report of his death changes her mind, and she summons him to her window at night. He tears out the window-bars (cutting his hands badly), kneels before her as if she were a saint, and spends the night with her. In the morning, Mellyagaunte finds bloodstains on the bed, and accuses the queen of adultery with Kay. Lancelot, of course, offers to fight for her. On the way back to Arthur's court, he takes part in a tournament in which, at the queen's command, he first plays the coward and later carries off the prize. Captured afterwards, he escapes just in time to defend the queen in the judicial combat, and kills Mellyagaunte.

This sketch reveals something of Chrétien's problem. At Marie's command, he had to make credible and if possible admirable a hero who, though supreme in physical prowess, was also ecstatically submissive to a tyrannical woman. It was a challenge to him as an artist, as more congenial stories were not. His success is revealed in the sharp, individual characters of Lancelot and Guenivere. Lancelot's chivalrous courtesy finds its natural outlet in love-ecstasy, and his swoons are carefully modelled on those of a religious mystic. But between his trances we see a practical man of action, who takes prudent advice and keeps cool in grave danger. Guenivere too is profoundly understood. Beneath her cruel pleasure in imposing humiliating trials on a brave knight, Chrétien shows us a despairing woman who knows herself guilty of grievous wrong to her lover. The truth to life of this story established the triangle Arthur–Guenivere–Lancelot for future generations, as the most important characteristic of Arthur's court.

The influence of Chrétien's unfinished last romance, *Perceval, or the Story of the Grail*, was second only to that of his *Lancelot*. Once again (although this is much disputed) Chrétien seems to have received a

Celtic story from his patron, and adapted it to an Arthurian knight, Perceval, who beforehand had been little more than a name. Once again he was challenged by a story which he might not have chosen for himself. But this time his patron was no longer Marie, the champion of adulterous love, but the Crusader, Philip of Alsace, and the story was about religion. As in the *Lancelot*, there seems to be a deliberate contrast between Gawain and the hero. Though the elegant, courteous, honourable Gawain is far above the boastfulness and cruelty of Kay, he is still worldly, fundamentally frivolous, and given to casual amours. He is distracted from his part in the Grail-quest by what seems to be sheer thoughtlessness. At first, Perceval, who has been brought up far from courts and knights, contrasts laughably with Arthur's elegant nephew; and his deeper faults prevent him from finding out the nature of the Grail or healing the wounded king who guards it. But he learns the worldly graces and virtues by advice and example until he can respond to courtesy with equal courtesy, and he and Gawain are on the same level. Perceval, however, rises higher, taking up again in remorse and humility the quest in which he has failed, learning from a hermit his faults and their remedy through submission to God's will, and reaching a third plane of which Gawain never dreams. Presumably, if Chrétien had lived to complete the poem, Perceval would have returned to the Grail-castle, made wise by experience, and healed the king. Here we have the quest which was to be the climax of the Round Table story. Though the characters shift in the later versions, we have the seeds of the final form: the conflict of worldly and spiritual values working themselves out in King Arthur's court.

In the early thirteenth century, Arthurian romance, while still profiting from Chrétien's example, took on a new interest, of which Malory's work is the fullest expression. More and more stories were gathered into the circle of Arthurian influence, and various authors tried to extract from them a coherent and authoritative complete story of Arthur and his knights. Chrétien's work had established no order of events for Arthur's reign, and many of the most popular tales, like those of Tristan and Isolt, were only loosely related to it. The most widely-read attempt to produce order was an enormously long compilation that was later called the Vulgate Cycle. The Vulgate Cycle explained mysterious events in its sources and gave unfulfilled prophecies an outcome. It was made up of five prose romances by various authors: *The History of the Holy Grail*, the prose *Merlin*, the prose *Lancelot*, *The Quest of the Holy Grail* and *The Death of Arthur*.

The first two romances were probably written last. The *History* was written, with more piety than literary skill, to explain how the Grail came to Britain. It is a long and often confused story, telling how Joseph of Arimathea collected the blood of the crucified Christ in a dish used at the Last Supper, and after experiencing voyages, tempests, disappearances, searches, dreams, temptations, and the assaults of violent men and demons, converted Britain and entrusted the holy dish to his nephew, the first of the kings who were to guard it in the castle of Corbenic and wait for the destined Grail-knight. Its plot is aimless, its characters crudely drawn, and its religion a wild flurry of miracles, but it shows the strength of the thirteenth-century impulse to unify the story of Arthur's kingdom.

The *Merlin* is an even more striking illustration of this impulse, for there were several hands involved in it. The writer of the first part gives an account of the early life of Merlin, the son of a fiend who took sexual possession of a virtuous woman in her sleep. She devotes herself to piety, and her son, though born with a hairy body and supernatural powers, inherits nothing of his father's will to evil except a mischievous sense of humour. Merlin's enchantment and knowledge of the future play a large part in the Britons' war against the Saxons, the decision to make the Round Table, and the conception of Arthur. It is Merlin who arranges for Arthur's safe upbringing until he can try the sword in the stone, which only the rightful king can draw. Arthur passes the test and is finally crowned, though his barons remain unconvinced. The whole story is set within the cosmic struggle of God and the Devil for men's souls, and focuses on the establishment by Arthur of the Round Table, seen as a symbol of the highest ideal of chivalry: it is a replica of the table of the Last Supper.

Two successive continuations fill the gap between Arthur's coronation and his established greatness. They make up a long chronicle of victorious war, in which Gawain and many other knights achieve the youthful exploits that explain their full stature in the prose *Lancelot*. The presence of Merlin gives continuity to the whole: when he is finally buried alive by an enchantress and the king is victorious, the Arthurian cycle is complete.

But the story continues with the prose *Lancelot*, the first half of which gives the life of its hero from his birth to the preparation for the Grail-quest, the second half the immediate preparation for the quest. The underlying theme of the story of quests, magic and fighting is to be found in Lancelot's relationships with the king, who knights him, and the queen, who rectifies Arthur's extraordinary omission at the ceremony and gives Lancelot a sword, and with whom he falls in love at first sight. He becomes established as Arthur's greatest knight, wins the castle of Joyous Garde as his own, and overcomes Arthur's most dangerous enemy, Galahault, who becomes Lancelot's close friend. It is Galahault, who, according to the familiar medieval pattern, arranges the crucial interview with his beloved, after which they become lovers. But Galahault becomes jealous of Guenivere's power over his friend, and dies in withdrawn and melancholy pride. The second part of the romance resembles the first in its profusion of jousting, enchantments, and strange encounters, but here the underlying theme is the begetting of Galahad at Corbenic, when Lancelot is tricked into sleeping with the king's daughter, after drinking a potion which makes him think she is Guenivere. Portents, such as the adventures that Gawain and Lancelot's cousin Bors find at the Grail-castle, foreshadow the fates of the characters in and after the Grail-quest. Lancelot ignores these and attributes his increasing misfortunes to chance. But the queen recognises what is happening and her passion becomes so mixed with guilt and jealousy of the Grail-king's daughter that it drives Lancelot insane. In his wanderings, he comes to Corbenic and is healed by the Grail. The structure of the prose *Lancelot* is majestic, and the prose masterly, but the book as a whole is divided in spirit. At first all the sympathy is with the lovers and their friend, and love seems the source of all good: adultery, lying, and disloyalty are accepted as necessary (though not glorified, as they are in Chrétien's *Lancelot*). The second part is more ambiguous, but clearly asserts at times that adulterous love is a sin and brings on disaster.

In contrast, *The Quest of the Holy Grail* is uncompromisingly ascetic. It opens with Galahad, the long awaited Grail-knight, arriving at Arthur's court. When the knights are assembled in the great hall, there is a clap of thunder and an intense light, and the Grail appears. It circulates round the table apparently unsupported and serves each knight with the food he desires. It then vanishes, the knights swear to go in quest of it, and each finds adventures that reveal his moral worth. Most, including Gawain and Lancelot's brother Ector, meet only obstacles and humiliations, and return to court. Galahad, Perceval and Bors, searchingly tested by their adventures, achieve the vision of the Grail, and Galahad and Perceval die. Lancelot stands between the two levels. He develops through a series of crises: the shock of discovering that in the world of the Grail he is no longer invincible, the loss of joy, the inward struggle leading up to repentance and a life of penance. As a result he is able to reach the Grail-castle and achieve a limited vision of the Grail before, like Bors, he returns to the world of ordinary life.

The last romance, *The Death of Arthur*, or *Mort Artu*, tells of the ruin of the Round Table. Lancelot returns to Arthur's court and relapses into his adultery with Guenivere. Their affair is the theme of the first part of the romance. Wounded in a tournament, Lancelot takes refuge at the house of the Fair Maid of Astolat, who nurses him and falls desperately in love with him. Rumours reach the court that Lancelot loves her, and Guenivere is racked by jealousy, until one day a boat floats down the river bearing the body of the Maid of Astolat and a letter saying that Lancelot's rejection of her love had killed her. But Arthur's suspicions are aroused by a visit to his sister Morgan, who shows him pictures that Lancelot had painted while imprisoned, telling the story of his affair with Guenivere. The queen is falsely charged with poisoning a knight, and is saved only by Lancelot's victory in a judicial combat. The lovers are finally trapped together by their enemy Aggravayne, and when Lancelot rescues Guenivere he unwittingly kills Gareth, Gawain's beloved brother.

Gawain's bitter enmity is the theme of this second part of the romance. He and Arthur besiege the lovers in Joyous Garde, and when the Pope makes peace—Arthur taking Guenivere back and Lancelot retiring to his kingdom of Benwick in France—Gawain makes Arthur pursue him. Only when Gawain is severely wounded does Arthur withdraw. He then learns that the Romans have invaded his continental lands. He defeats them and kills the Emperor, but immediately hears news that Mordred, whom he left as regent in England, has rebelled. In the last part of the romance, Arthur sails back to England to punish the traitor. Gawain is killed in the landing at Dover, but Arthur kills Mordred in a battle on Salisbury Plain. He is himself mortally wounded, and is carried away by his sister Morgan in a small boat: later his tomb is found near by. Guenivere enters a convent. Lancelot and his kinsmen return to Britain, kill the sons of Mordred in battle, and spend the rest of their lives as hermits. When Lancelot dies, his soul is carried heavenwards by angels and his body buried with Galahault's in Joyous Garde.

The material for the *Mort Artu*, like that for the other Vulgate Cycle romances, comes from a great many sources. But this romance has a tighter chain of cause and effect than the others. Once the adultery is suspected, everything else follows. The author also shows considerable insight into character: Gawain's vindictiveness, Guenivere's jealousy, and the pathetic suspicions that torment Arthur. Complex emotions interact when the queen discusses with Lancelot and his kinsmen Arthur's offer to take her back with honour: political calculation and weariness mix with unselfish love and the spirit of sacrifice. This sacrifice brings the reckless Lancelot of the early scenes a spiritual regeneration that makes him able to love even his mortal enemy Gawain, and gives conviction to the end of the story. It completes a long, uneven, but immensely popular collection of romances, which presented chivalry in different ways as a noble ideal to a society that was often far from noble.

At about the same time, the story of Tristan was made into what was virtually a companion volume to the Vulgate Cycle. Style and subject matter are very similar. Tristan becomes a knight-errant of the same kind as Lancelot, and the climax of his adventures is his being made a member of the Round Table. In the poems, Mark was Tristan's lord, and Tristan's allegiance to Mark and his love for Mark's wife were in tragic conflict. In the prose *Tristan*, Mark is a villainous enemy of knighthood, and it is Tristan's duty, not his misfortune, to be his rival and, with the wholehearted support of Arthur's knights, to keep him in check. Chivalric adventures take up most of the story, which ends with the death of Tristan, whom Mark murders as he sits singing to the harp for Isolt. Two new major characters are introduced: Palomides the Saracen, who, despite his unrequited love for Isolt, is generous and faithful to his successful rival; and Tristan's worldly, mocking friend, Dinadan. Dinadan thinks that passionate love is not worth the misery it produces, nor knight-errantry worth wounds and death. Though his mockery is entertaining, it is a symptom of the disunity of the *Tristan* when compared with the *Lancelot*. It is a mere succession of incidents with no coherent ethic, however peculiar. Some of these incidents have no connection with chivalry, and some, like the incidental life of Alexander the Orphan, none with the main story.

Arthurian romance was as popular in England as in continental Europe, and nearly a quarter of the surviving English medieval romances are Arthurian. Malory's is the most important of them, but two others must be mentioned: poems with confusingly similar titles, which were both among his sources. The first of these, the *Morte Arthure*, was written (most probably between 1360 and 1375), in the native alliterative metre inherited from the Anglo-Saxons. Its principal source is a version of Wace very like the one Layamon used, and it owes nothing to any of the French romances considered above. Some of the French romances make Arthur's court only a place for the hero to start and finish his adventure, but the emphasis of the alliterative poem is on the king's part throughout. The poem is a narrative masterpiece. It recounts the rise of a brave and noble king, and his fall, occasioned by his leaving his kingdom under the regency of the traitor Mordred while he himself fights a war abroad. After a list of Arthur's conquests, the *Morte Arthure* tells how messengers from Lucius, Emperor of Rome, summon Arthur to do homage. Arthur's barons promise to support him, and after an elaborately described banquet, the messengers are sent back carrying Arthur's defiance. Arthur sails for France, and after a voyage during which he has a dream prophetic of the outcome of the war, lands in Brittany, where he kills the giant of Mont St Michel. In the battle against Lucius, the British knights fulfil their promises and Arthur himself kills the Emperor. Arthur advances triumphantly into Italy, receives the submission of the Romans at Viterbo, and prepares to go to Rome, to be crowned as Emperor. But an ominous second dream tells him that for him Fortune's wheel has reached its highest point, and he should repent the excesses pride has led him into, before the wheel whirls him down to disaster. News arrives that Mordred has betrayed Arthur, and the king returns hastily to Britain. There he defeats Mordred's navy and forces a landing, in which Gawain is killed. He gives battle, wins, and kills Mordred, but is himself fatally wounded. He does not pass to Avalon, but is carried to Glastonbury, where he dies and is buried with great solemnity. The characterisation of the poem is full of strong, if not subtle, contrasts, and the rich descriptions are more vivid than any in the French romances.

The second poem, called *Le Morte Arthur*, was written in about 1400 in eight-line stanzas, and is based on the *Mort Artu*. The poet tells his story with economy and suspense, and reduces description, psychological analysis and commentary to a minimum, though there are occasional hints of compassion for those who have not lived up to the ideals of chivalry. When he laid down his pen, the list of the books that Malory is known to have used was complete.

Sir Thomas Malory

Although Sir Thomas Malory lived a thousand years later than the events that gave his story its origin, not much more is known with certainty about him than about the historical Arthur. All that is certain is found in his book, mostly in the *explicits* (the closing words) of the eight tales that make up the *Morte Darthur*. In the *explicit* to the last tale, he tells us his name, that he was a knight and a prisoner, that he wanted his readers to pray for him, and that he finished his book between 3 March 1469 and 4 March 1470. The earlier *explicits* confirm all but the last of these statements, and the first *explicit* makes it clear that when Malory wrote it he did not expect to write anything else afterwards. The book as a whole shows that he had access to some very expensive manuscripts, that he knew French and was proud of it, and that he loved hunting, tournaments and chivalry. He once speaks, with feeling but without mentioning himself, of how an illness in prison made Sir Tristram suicidally depressed, which is probably a reminiscence of a serious prison-illness of his own. Medieval prisons being extremely unhealthy, a serious illness would not be in the least surprising, and it is characteristic of Malory that he should say nothing directly about himself: his attention is all on the story he is telling. His language suggests that he was not a southerner, but where in the Midlands or North he came from is disputed: the best opinion suggests (with reservations) Lincolnshire. His politics may have been Lancastrian. Writing under a Yorkist king who had seized the crown from a Lancastrian, he reproached Englishmen with their ingratitude to good kings (see p. 213); and one or two incidents in the narrative seem to point in the same direction, as when the traitor Mordred raises troops against Arthur in a Yorkist part of the country (see p. 217). The very guardedness of Malory's words strengthens this suggestion. But certainty is impossible: the guardedness may be common caution; there are reasons of narrative convenience that could explain the incidents in the story; and a Yorkist, or any Englishman who knew what civil war meant, might equally fear his countrymen's fickleness in politics. When Malory reproached them, the English were about to expel the Yorkists and restore the Lancastrians, and the signs may have been evident even to a prisoner.

Everything else about the author of *Le Morte Darthur* is even less certain. The book can hardly have taken less than two years to write, but we cannot guess when it was begun, since the writing may very well not have been continuous. Illness, freedom, loss of interest, legal processes and lack of sources may all have affected the author, and the *explicit* of the first tale sounds as if written when Malory was expecting some such interruption. Neither can it be assumed that the eight tales were written in their present order. They are in this order now to make up what Malory called the 'whole book of King Arthur', with his birth at the beginning, his death at the end, and other things in place between. Readers have generally agreed that the later tales are better than the earlier ones; but this proves nothing, since authors do not always improve with age. Moreover, the improvement is not simple: parts of the earlier tales, especially of the third and fourth ones, are among the best in the book. Malory must have read other things besides the romances that were his immediate sources, but almost the only book that can be even tentatively suggested as in this class is John Hardyng's *Chronicle*, a Lancastrian history completed in 1457 and reissued in the following five years in a revised 'Yorkist' version.

The book, then, does not reveal much about its author. But there are equally great difficulties in trying to use the author's life to explain the book. The greatest difficulty is in identifying him. Fifteenth-century records are sketchy: most men died leaving no written trace of their lives, and where there are records, what seems at first to be the career of one man may turn out to be the careers of two, and vice versa. A century of literary detective work has identified five Thomas Malorys alive at about the right time, but no external evidence has been found to connect any of them with the *Morte Darthur*. There may be others undiscovered, since Malory was not a very uncommon name. But fortunately the internal evidence of the book shows that its author did not come from the social class of which fewest records survive. This internal evidence also excludes two of the five known Thomas Malorys: a Northamptonshire priest, and an agricultural labourer from Tachbrook Mallory in Warwickshire. Neither of them could have been a knight; and it is probable that the labourer could not read English and almost certain that he could not read French, even if he had been interested in and able to gain access to the Arthurian manuscripts. But the other three are not so disqualified. The Cambridgeshire, Yorkshire, and Warwickshire branches of the Malory family each had a Thomas alive in 1469–70, though none of them is known to have led either a bookish or a knightly life. As far as the known records go, the dominant feature of their lives seems rather to have been bad luck, as the name Malory suggests (Fr. *malheur* = 'misfortune').

The first of the three was the son of a Sir William Malory, who is said to have been MP for Cambridgeshire in 1433. His main estates were at Papworth St Agnes in Cambridgeshire and at Shawbury in Shropshire, but he also held two Lincolnshire manors until 1442–3. He died in 1445. Thomas, his son and heir, was born in Shropshire and was twenty when his father died. It seems that, as was usual in the Middle Ages, the first man to get the ear of the court was made his guardian, and took control of Thomas's lands for what he could make out of them. Thomas was unable to get full possession of them until 1451, when he was twenty-five. Despite this handicap, he held a number of minor offices in local government, made connections in the London cloth trade, married and begot ten children, and performed one or two less praiseworthy exploits. Sir William, when one of his kinsmen died, had stolen an estate in Northamptonshire from the widow, whose family only managed to regain it after Sir William's death. As soon as he could, Thomas seized it back from his relatives, who only recovered it again after he died. On another occasion, he armed himself with a variety of fearsome weapons, kidnapped his parish priest, and carried the unfortunate man round the countryside threatening his life until he agreed to resign his church to Malory or forfeit £100. Despite these things, there is no record that he was ever in prison, and throughout his life and even after his death he is always referred to as an esquire, never as a knight. In deciding the authorship of the *Morte Darthur*, those things must offset his father's Lincolnshire manors. He made his will in September 1469 and was dead by 27 October 1469.

Of the second Thomas Malory, even less is known. His father was William Malory, an esquire of Hutton Conyers in Yorkshire, who was born in 1417 and died in 1475. Thomas was one of fourteen children, and was probably illegitimate. He is only mentioned (as far as is known) in two documents during his lifetime: a record of fines in 1444, and the Ripon Cathedral records in 1471, the latter as having cited one of his neighbours, a well-known troublemaker, before the Cathedral Chapter. Two of his brothers were probably killed fighting for the Lancastrians. If Thomas joined in, it would have increased his chances of imprisonment or knighthood or both, but there are no other grounds for suggesting that he was ever a knight or a prisoner.

The third Thomas Malory was certainly imprisoned—though perhaps at the wrong time—and knighted, and in the present state of knowledge this must make him the favourite for authorship. He was the son of John Malory, an esquire whose not very extensive lands centred on Newbold Revel in Warwickshire, and who was Member of Parliament for that county five times from 1413 to 1427. The first record of Thomas connects him with the war that was being waged between England and France from 1337 to 1453. In 1414, Thomas enlisted with Richard Beauchamp, Earl of Warwick, to serve with one lance and two archers in his retinue for the siege of Calais. Beauchamp, who was famous throughout Christendom as a pattern of chivalry, spent much of the next twenty-five years in Normandy fighting a war of skirmishes and sieges against the French. Where Malory spent these years is not known. He must have inherited the family when his father died in 1433-4, and in 1439 he reappears as a respectable country landowner with a growing interest in politics. He took a mortgage on some of his brother-in-law's lands, was knighted, acted as a parliamentary elector, and witnessed documents in a neighbouring family's land settlement. A discordant note was sounded in 1443: he was charged with wounding and imprisoning Thomas Smythe and stealing his goods, but the charge apparently fell through. In 1445 he became Member of Parliament for Warwickshire, and in this and the following year served on a parliamentary commission to assess tax-exemptions for the impoverished towns of the county. He may have married about this time, because his son Robert was born in 1447–8. In 1449 he acquired outright the lands that had been mortgaged to him, and in September of that year the Duke of Buckingham, who had been on the earlier commission with him and who controlled the constituency of Bedwin in Wiltshire, had Malory elected to parliament for that borough. To a background of serious unrest in the country, which was eventually to turn into civil war, parliament met in November and December, and dispersed for Christmas on 17 December.

With the new decade, Malory's life, for no known reason, underwent a sudden and startling change. On 4 January 1450, he and 26 other armed men laid an ambush to murder his patron Buckingham, at Coombe near Newbold Revel. This was followed by many other crimes, or at least many very well-supported allegations of crimes. He seems to have behaved himself while parliament was in session again in London, but it was adjourned to Leicester in April, and the later charges accused him of committing rape and theft and extortion around Newbold Revel from May to August.

Despite this, when a new parliament met in September 1450, Malory was returned to it as the Member for Wareham in Dorset, which was controlled by the Duke of York. York needed experienced parliamentary help against the government, and Malory needed a protector. Although a warrant was issued halfway through this parliament for his arrest 'for divers felonies', he may have attended parliament until it was dissolved in May. A few weeks later, he and his accomplices were stealing cattle in Warwickshire. While Buckingham was trying to catch up with him, Malory raided Buckingham's hunting-lodge, carried off his deer, and did an enormous amount of damage. He was arrested and imprisoned at Coleshill, but two days later swam the moat and escaped. He then twice raided a nearby abbey with a large band of men, breaking down the doors, insulting the monks, and stealing a great deal of money. He was charged with nearly all these crimes at a court at Nuneaton, over which, disregarding his own involvement, Buckingham presided. Malory may still have been free, but by January 1452 he was in prison, in London, where he spent most of the next eight years, waiting for a trial that never came.

Patient waiting was not in Malory's character. During 1453, when the first battle of the civil war took place, and the country was polarising into the York and Lancaster factions, he seems to have escaped again—this time perhaps by bribery—and been recaptured in the Midlands. When the Duke of Norfolk's men bailed him out for six months in 1454, he joined an old crony on a horse-stealing expedition across East Anglia that ended in Colchester jail. From here he escaped again, 'using swords, daggers, and halberds', but was again recaptured and sent back to prison in London. After this he was shifted frequently from prison to prison, and the penalties put on his jailers for his secure keeping reached a record for medieval England. During Henry VI's insanity, Malory was given a royal pardon by the Lord Protector, the Duke of York. But this was the lowest point in his fortunes: the courts refused to accept his pardon, he was twice sued for small debts he could not repay, and he did not even get beyond the walls in the attempted mass-escape from Newgate prison in 1456. Soon after it, he was moved to another prison. However, late in 1457 the Earl of Warwick's men bailed him out for two months, and he seems to have been free again briefly in 1459. He was moved to a more secure prison when the Yorkists invaded in 1460, but after they had expelled the Lancastrians he was freed and pardoned. He seems never to have been tried on any of the charges brought against him.

The new decade looked more promising for Malory. He repaid the attentions the Yorkist lords had given him when he was in prison by following them north in 1462 to the siege of the castles of Alnwick, Bamborough, and Dunstanborough, which the Lancastrians had seized. He was over age, but he may have known more about sieges than any younger man. The castles were taken, and Malory settled down to a more peaceful life. In 1464 he witnessed another land-settlement, and in 1466 his grandson Nicholas was born. But by July 1468, when King Edward was beginning to be at odds with his chief supporters, Warwick's family, the Warwickshire knight appears to have changed sides again. Between June 1468 and March 1470, his name appears six times in lists of Lancastrians who were excluded from royal pardons for any crimes they might have committed. It is possible that he, like most of those excluded, was not in prison; but it seems more reasonable to assume that the Sir Thomas Malory whom the government wanted under lock and key was the Sir Thomas Malory who was in prison at this time completing the *Morte Darthur*.

Outside the prison, the balance of power shifted uncertainly. In October 1470 a sudden invasion brought the Lancastrians back, and among their first acts in London was to free those of their party who were in prison. Six months later, on 14 March 1471, Thomas Malory of Newbold Revel died, and was buried in Greyfriars, Newgate, which, despite its proximity to one of the gaols in which he had been imprisoned, was the most fashionable church in London. On the day of Malory's death, King Edward landed in Yorkshire, and two months after that the Yorkists were back in power. When the administration held an inquiry into Malory's estate, the jurors testified that he had died owning nothing. In a prudent moment, the rash Sir Thomas had made all his lands over to his wife. She was left in possession of them, and he was left to rest in peace until 1547, when Henry VIII had all the tombstones in Greyfriars sold for whatever they would fetch.

'The Whole Book of King Arthur'

Why Malory wrote his book no one knows. (The commonest motive writers professed at the time was the Avoidance of Idleness, and a prisoner would have had plenty of time on his hands.) But once he had taken his decision, he faced problems very different from those of a modern novelist. Just as medieval history is unexpectedly like romance, so medieval romance is unexpectedly like history. The greatest stories, such as those of Arthur, Charlemagne and Troy, were partly independent of their tellers: many of the 'facts' were so widely known as to be unalterable. The audience not only, in the classic phrase, suspended its disbelief: it believed. History itself was less certain than it is nowadays; and even the sceptical would believe that these famous stories contained some truth. The less sceptical would accept them, without debating the issue much, as being very largely true—as true as history. Moreover, even an extreme sceptic would still know, for instance, that certain components *were* the story of Tristram and Isolt, and accept them as that. Tampering with the accepted components, of which the plot was usually the most firmly established, was likely to destroy all three kinds of belief, and with them the audience's interest. Like a modern historical novelist, the author had to respect at least the well-known facts, and use his skill with pace, proportion, perspective, characterisation and detail to tell the story more interestingly than before. Like the historical novelist, he could omit repellent or boring parts of his story, and fill gaps from his imagination or from new sources he had found, or pretended to find.

He told a story set, like a historical novel, in the distant past. Nevertheless, it was not a historical novel, recreating a world distanced from the author's own by innumerable tiny differences, yet coherent in itself. These differences, which make up the pastness of the past, were something few people before the nineteenth century were aware of, and fewer interested in. For most people, the whole of the past was a play in modern dress. The romance writer most commonly stressed what past and present had in common and assimilated unavoidable differences, such as the paganism of Greek and Roman heroes, with the minimum of fuss, perhaps hardly noticing what he was doing. His purposes were different, to tell the story well and bring out whatever message he felt was implicit in it. This message might not be the one his predecessors had seen there. He could not end the story of Tristram and Isolt with a happy marriage, but he could present it as anything between high tragedy and pornographic farce.

If Malory had been pressed on the point, he would no doubt have said that the Arthurian stories he used contained much more truth than fiction. His remark on the ingratitude of the English to good kings implied that their ingratitude to Arthur was real; and he requested prayers for Sir Tristram's soul just as he did for his own release from prison. But even had he thought otherwise, the quasi-objective status of the story would have imposed much the same restrictions on him. He had to find the story of Arthur in 'authorised books' (to use his own words), and then retell it to the best of his ability. His almost-history allowed, as has been said, a good deal of latitude in style and presentation. Even the action could be altered to some extent if a particular incident were distasteful or incredible. For instance, in the French prose *Tristan*, Lancelot fights Tristram and gets rather the worst of it. Malory evened things up, to fit his idea of Lancelot's supreme prowess. A good many of the things that he changed he concealed by ascribing them to his French sources (for the section edited here, the Commentary says which of his ascriptions are genuine). But the overall structure of the story he could not alter: in particular, although he admired both Sir Lancelot and the Round Table, he must show the Round Table destroyed by Lancelot's misdeeds.

But there were advantages as well as problems for a medieval author ambitious enough to attempt one of the famous stories of his age. An author's talents could be drawn out supremely by the difficulties themselves: by the conflict, for instance, between the inexorable situation and the sympathy he felt for a character whom he might not like or approve of in any ordinary sense, but whom his own imagination, half discovering, half creating, had made him first understand and then sympathise with. Chrétien's Lancelot, Chaucer's Criseyde and Shakespeare's Falstaff are greater than the roles they were originally intended to fill, greater even than the books they appear in. Malory likewise presents his Lancelot with a grasp of character and tragic situation that he never achieves in the less challenging story of his second knight-hero Sir Tristram. More directly, the author could be sure of his audience's interest, since the fame of the subject guaranteed quality, authenticity and a kind of truth; their knowledge of the action allowed economy of explanation and counterpoint of mood, a setting of the present against the final outcome; and the resolution of a particularly

difficult puzzle of situation or character would make the more know-
ledgeable among them share with him a special pleasure in discovering
'the way it must have been'. And, although a pre-existing story might
contain elements that its would-be teller could neither omit nor successfully integrate into the action as he understood it—and there are
several such elements in the *Morte Darthur*—it might also have poten-
tialities the author could respond to and develop, but which he himself would never have been able to devise. Malory's sources give, with
many discrepancies, a picture of the rise, prosperity and fall of a great
kingdom. There is no sign in his book that he could have thought of
this idea without prompting; but he appreciated it and developed it
further than any of his sources had, and it became the master-symbol
of his story of Arthur.

He began his book with incisive independence. The Vulgate Cycle
was his principal source, but he cut away the whole of *The History of the
Holy Grail* and a substantial part of the prose *Merlin*, and began with
Arthur's conception. Merlin's magic makes this possible, and ensures
that Arthur is brought up secretly as the foster-son of one of his father's
vassals, to keep him safe during the anarchy after his father's death.
When Arthur comes of age, he proves himself the rightful king by
drawing the miraculous sword from the stone. Most of his barons refuse to accept him; and, with Merlin's advice, he fights a tough and
skilful campaign against them. During a truce, he and his half-sister,
not knowing their kinship, have an affair in which he begets Mordred.
Merlin warns him that this incest will eventually be his destruction,
but again assists him by helping him obtain the sword Excalibur from
the Lady of the Lake. When the war is won, Arthur falls in love with
and marries Guenivere. The Round Table is her dowry, and Arthur
reorganises it as an Order of Chivalry to fight for peace and justice.
The king and his knights face oppression, new rebellions, hostile magic
and treachery within his family and the Order; and they lose Merlin's
help when he is outwitted and buried alive by a sorceress. But, although some knights come shabbily or shamefully out of their adventures, by the end of the tale Arthur is undisputed king of all
Britain.

The second tale, an adaptation of the Roman war in the alliterative
Morte Arthure, takes this kingship for granted. The Emperor's messengers demand tribute of Arthur; but he, with his barons' enthusiastic
agreement, defies them and invades France (himself killing, *en passant*,
the predatory giant of Mont St Michel), and outfights the Romans.
The newly knighted Lancelot particularly distinguishes himself, but all
the barons fulfil their vows of support, and Arthur himself kills the

Emperor in the climactic battle. He is crowned Emperor in Rome, establishes sound government there, and returns triumphantly with his knights to Britain. To harmonise the source with the rest of the book, Malory changed its tragic end, saved from death several knights who have parts to play later, and increased Lancelot's part from six passing mentions to that of a principal character, the rising star of chivalry.

The third tale sets several incidents, nearly all from the French prose *Lancelot*, in a frame of Malory's own making. It is the end of the Roman war, and Lancelot is in love with Guenivere. But the tale shows the growth not of their love but of his reputation. In the adventure-filled forest, force, trickery and the supernatural break without warning upon the solitary questing knight. Lancelot discovers himself sufficient to handle every kind of danger, to protect the weak, defeat the king's enemies and send a steady stream of the latter to submit themselves to Guenivere—an incomparable present. Lancelot's discovery of his own capacity to achieve difficult ideals gives the story its tone: an exultant and youthful gallantry. There is as yet nothing to set his ideals at odds: in particular, no sign that his love is more than platonic. His achievements gain him many friends—some of them past enemies—and the reputation of the greatest knight in the world.

The source of the fourth tale is almost certainly a lost English poem about Sir Gawain's younger brother, adapted by transferring much of Gawain's rôle to Lancelot. Arthur is now said to be at the height of his power, and Lancelot is his friend and most famous knight. A young man comes to ask Arthur for three boons. His first request is for a year's sustenance, which he has to work for in the kitchens. Then a girl comes to ask Arthur for help for her sister, Lady Liones, whose castle is besieged. The young man asks for knighthood at Lancelot's hands and this quest, and is granted them. The girl at first jeers at him as a kitchen-boy, but he overcomes opponent after opponent and finally Liones's enemy, all of whom do him homage. In the tale's second half, which has many inconsistencies, the hero is revealed to be Gawain's brother Gareth; his new vassals make their peace with Arthur; and he wins Liones's hand in a tournament and marries her. He avoids Gawain because of his vindictiveness, and becomes one of Lancelot's closest friends.

The fifth tale is based on the French prose *Tristan*, first summarising its hero's birth and upbringing. He is knighted by his uncle, King Mark of Cornwall, and fights a duel to decide an Irish claim for tribute. He kills his opponent, but receives a poisoned wound that can only be cured in Ireland. He goes there incognito, and Isolt, who is being wooed by Palomides the Saracen, cures him. They fall in love, but

Tristram is recognised and banished. Mark comes to hate his nephew, and, hoping that he will be killed, sends him to Ireland to ask that Isolt should marry Mark. Tristram loyally does so, but on the return voyage he and Isolt accidentally drink a magic potion that makes them lovers for life. Most of the tale presents adventures in a profusion like life itself; but some themes stand out and there are elusive hints of others. The whole Arthurian world is involved, but Tristram is the main character. Despite Mark's treachery, Palomides' rivalry and Dinadan's teasing, he becomes a knight of the Round Table and Lancelot's friend. When he and Isolt have to flee from Cornwall, Lancelot gives them his own castle, Joyous Garde. Within the Round Table, ominous factions slowly crystallise round Lancelot, Gawain and Lamorak. Gawain and the other sons of King Lot of Orkney (except Gareth) murder Lamorak, and Lancelot's devoted supporters become a potential danger as more and more people suspect him of adultery with the queen. Several incidents foreshadow the Grail-quest. In one, interpolated into the *Tristan* from the prose *Lancelot*, Lancelot is tricked into sleeping with Elaine of Corbenic, believing she is Guenivere. So Galahad is conceived by the very act that tells us that the rumours of adultery are true. Tristram's consistent generosity of mind throughout the second half of the tale makes Palomides into his friend and a Christian, and Palomides' baptism ends the tale. Malory left out the last section of his source, a Grail-quest that would have been incompatible with his next tale.

The source of Malory's sixth tale is the Vulgate Cycle *Quest of the Holy Grail*. He follows it more closely than any other source, and the account already given of its plot (p. 30) exactly describes his tale.

The seventh tale opens with Lancelot returning from the Grail-quest, and relapsing into his adultery. The tale divides into five chapters, the first two of which have a double source, the French *Mort Artu* and the English stanzaic *Le Morte Arthur*. The stories in the first part of the *Mort Artu* are interwoven with one another in short sections. The corresponding portion of the stanzaic *Morte Arthur* separates out the most important, the stories of the poisoning and of the Fair Maid of Astolat, into four alternating blocks *a b a b*, and omits everything else. Malory's two separate chapters complete this process, though his narrative itself generally remains closer to his French than to his English source. His third chapter, an account of a tournament, he may have invented himself. His fourth chapter, the story of the Knight of the Cart, is a free adaptation of Chrétien's *Lancelot* or perhaps of the version of Chrétien's story that was incorporated into the prose *Lancelot*. His last chapter, about the healing of Sir Urry, he probably elaborated from another incident in the prose *Lancelot*. The five incidents are presented as happening one after another during about a year, each in turn endangering the secrecy of Lancelot's affair with the queen.

The eighth tale is set an unspecified time later, and begins with a sixth incident, in which the secret is discovered. This sets in motion the sequence of events that destroys both Arthur and his Order of Chivalry. The sources are again the *Mort Artu* and *Le Morte Arthur*. The French romance's narrative is less complicated here, but the English poem again simplifies by omission, notably of the Roman war and the war against the sons of Mordred. Malory not only follows it in this—the story of the Roman war he had told already—but quite often echoes its wording. In both these last tales, he handles the narrative with a masterly freedom that reveals that he understands and is in control of both what he changes and what he keeps unaltered.

The different stories of Malory's sources have become one coherent narrative, and so consistently so that it must be his deliberate creation. The first four tales form one chronological sequence, and the last four another later one. The beginning of the fifth must overlap to some degree with some of its predecessors, but Malory was inconsistent about the extent of the overlap. This and a few other contradictions within and between tales are no doubt due to the difficult conditions under which he was working. The progress of his story is revealed partly by the explicit time-references at the beginning and end of many of the tales, partly by the many references to what has happened in previous tales or will happen in future ones, and partly by reference to events that are not described at all: Arthur's wars with Claudas, Lancelot's first appearance at court and his capture of Joyous Garde. They exist in the fictional but objective world formed by the consensus of all existing Arthurian romances; and events dated by reference to them have an apparently historical solidity. The progress of the story is also revealed by the development of the action itself: the characters' changes of situation, personality and relationship, and the effect these have on the king and the Round Table. The dozen or so leading characters are followed through the story, and, where sources disagree, personality as well as action is harmonised. Lancelot's attractive and chivalrous nature draws people to him in nearly every tale; King Arthur is consistently shown as generous and honourable, despite sources that attempted to palliate the adultery by making him suspicious and violent. Hence their conflict is tragic. And the tragedy is shared by hundreds of minor characters who move in and out of the story. Many of these Malory created, by giving names to the mysterious anonymous characters the French romances abound in: names from the Vulgate Cycle or his English sources in incidents from the *Tristan*, and vice versa; and sometimes names from obscure romances that he may never have read, only heard of. The cumulative effect of this is the creation of a complete society, growing, flowering and decaying. The pattern of rise, supremacy and fall is universal in human experience: Malory saw it and brought it to life in the story of King Arthur.

The Morte Darthur *and the World of Knighthood*

Part of the unity of the *Morte Darthur* comes from its genre, chivalric romance. As a romance, it is a story of events that are strange and heroic, and therefore interesting. The tone is varied by strategic verisimilitude in parts of the first tale and Homeric heroic warfare in the second, by folk-tale patterns of action in the fourth and the workings of a mysterious spiritual cause-and-effect in the sixth; but it remains romance.

A good deal of it is at least based on history. Throughout, the main occupation of the characters is knight-errantry. It is not quite historical knight-errantry, but history tempers the romance. In the heyday of knighthood it had been possible, if never easy, for a young and landless knight to rise to real political power by success in tournaments, or to travel to a distant country and win a principality by his sword. Most of Malory's sources were written at or shortly after this time, and the endless quests they contain reflect these possibilities, and sometimes show flashes of real political insight. In this respect, the knightly class of Malory's day was justified, at least as far as its own members were concerned, in sharing the widespread medieval belief that the past was much like the present, but better. Success in tournaments might still bring popularity and influence at court, but poor knights could not afford to take part. A very successful soldier might still win a title, power and lands; but with greater difficulty, and from beginning to end he would be more in the power of the king than his predecessor had been in the power of his liege-lord. Nevertheless, Malory's romance shows a part of early medieval life that had survived in attenuated form into his own time, and to this he added much from his own age, making—no doubt unconsciously—a mixture that is of no one period. For instance, he sees the Round Table as a *late* medieval institution, an Order of Chivalry. It has the distinctive attributes: devotion to the sovereign, a fixed number of knight-companions as members, regular meetings and statutes that the companions were sworn to observe. Arthur promulgates these when he reorganises the Round Table, and those then mentioned are largely concerned with practical justice and keeping the peace. They strongly resemble fifteenth-century Ordinances of War (standing orders for armies on campaign), such as those issued by Henry V for his wars in France. We learn in passing that the companions have to swear not to fight one another—a common feature of fifteenth-century brotherhood-in-arms.

The *Morte Darthur* has occasional even closer correspondence with particular historical events—but it is not a political allegory. Nor is it a set of examples showing how a country should be run—such a book would have been unthinkable at the time without, for instance, an extensive treatment of flatterers. It is a *romance*, made up mainly of elements from, but not intended to be a picture of, everyday medieval life. Romance naturally contains much that is at or even beyond the limits of common experience. Surprising things happen, some of them magical or miraculous. But there *are* limits to what can happen. The powers that produce supernatural effects are themselves apparently subject to rules, although the powers and the rules, and their relationship to fate and providence, all remain mysterious. Lancelot's cure of Sir Urry may be magic, the automatic consequence of his prowess; or it may be a miracle, the result of divine intervention in nature. Some of the characters understand something of these forces, and use them, both for and against Arthur's knights. But the knights (like the reader) know these forces only by particular commands, visions and prophecies, and they cannot use them at all: their achievements are the product of their chivalry alone. The actions the rules dictate may often be odd and unkind, but enormous unknown consequences depend upon them. Before Arthur is taken to Avalon, his sword Excalibur must be thrown back into the lake from which it first came, even at the risk of the king's life. Why this is necessary is not explained, and the king himself may not know. Arthur is conveyed to Avalon by queens powerful in the supernatural sphere who were previously enemies, and this hints—but no more—that some ultimate reconciliation is taking place between the deepest and most conflicting forces of Malory's world.

Like the events, the characters of Malory's world also tend to extremes. Strong sudden passions often make his knights outstandingly heroic or wicked, and sometimes both by turns. Pellinore defeats Arthur in a fight, and then tries to kill him in case Arthur should hold the defeat against him; but Merlin, who speaks with authority, shortly afterwards calls Pellinore the worthiest of all the Knights of the Round Table. The knights' lives are simplified by the omission of administrative responsibilities and (usually) of pressing need for money; and by the absence of peasants, lawyers and merchants. The Knight is reduced to his essence, the fighting-man able and perhaps willing to fight for land or reputation or justice; and, within the Order of Knighthood itself, the Knights of the Round Table are sustained by their companions in an active Order of Chivalry that comes closer than any historical one did to the professed aims of such Orders.

Paradoxically, the literary effectiveness of this world comes largely from its exaggerations and limitations, from its conspicuous avoidance of 'naturalism'—the literary reproduction of common experience and nothing else. It is because the knight's activities in chivalric romance are limited in variety and slightly unreal that they are a ready symbol of any man's activities. Romance is selective even within the range of activities of the historical knight-errant. Its knight is a man on horseback, dominating nature yet part of it. He follows his quests alone, with such courage, perseverance and loyalty as he can muster against unpredictable obstacles. He may have a particular objective, or he may simply be looking for what chance will bring; but at any time events may force him to show by his actions what he really is, with no guarantee of victory or life or honour. His fighting capacity makes him the potential helper or oppressor of everyone he meets, but even his fighting is partly stylised: little is seen of campaigning conditions, or loot, or experiment with different kinds of weapons, and the mess and pain of fighting are normally played down. The quest, like the voyage and the pilgrimage, is an apt symbol of any one man's way through life, and this simplification emphasises its symbolic effect, which is particularly conspicuous in the long central fifth tale, whose length and lack of any real plot make the fact of questing its dominant feature. In a similar way, since social relationships vary more than most things with time and place, the kings and lords and knights of the *Morte Darthur* are made by the almost complete elimination of other social classes into a distanced and universalised society. The rise and fall of a kingdom is as natural a symbol for collective human enterprise as the quest is for individual ones, and the avoidance of naturalism brings out the symbolic function of the kingdom in the *Morte Darthur* as a whole.

Chivalric romances embody many different kinds of chivalry, and Malory rarely pauses to expound his. This brevity suggests that he did not want to explain his ideals in abstract terms, and his sometimes confused words suggest that he could not have done so clearly if he had wished. He usually narrated actions both good and bad without comment, and his admirable characters are independent enough to behave badly at times and to voice views with which he did not agree. He was willing to praise good even when mixed with bad, and he did not always assimilate his sources perfectly. Nevertheless, throughout the *Morte Darthur*, judgments made in passing, the implications of words and the way the sources are altered reveal a coherent set of preferences and aversions; and paradoxically, whereas the action of his story is idealised, its ideals form a code by which men of his time could and did try to live.

The essence of chivalry, for Malory, was its unity. It is not merely that he had little taste or talent for making intellectual distinctions: he saw, almost certainly more intuitively than consciously, the various virtues as generating and sustaining one another in war, love and religion, from the most elevated nobility of mind to competence in action. He recognises individual variations—that one knight may have more stamina and another more strength, that a third may be brave but cruel—but his whole book stresses the tendency of the virtues to generate one another and to produce action in the world.

He sees chivalry in the state as naturally practical, maintaining peace and justice, and defending the state and Christendom as a whole. The importance of this brings the feudal–chivalric virtues to the fore, *prowess* and *loyalty* most of all. When Gawain is trying to find the most compressed insult he can hurl at Lancelot, he repeatedly calls him a disloyal coward. Malory rarely indicates prowess by describing particular blows, or the skills by which one knight outfights another. A knight is praised for qualities of mind, or of mind and body together, as tough, brave, agile, or energetic, and we are left to infer from this how he would fight. But the fighting these qualities produce is so important that several characters who are behaving discreditably are incongruously called 'noble knights' for their prowess alone. Loyalty is just as important: it is from one point of view the subject of the whole *Morte Darthur*, and the lack of this virtue in his own day provokes Malory to a unique outburst, his only comment on fifteenth-century politics (lines p. 213). As in the case of prowess, he spends more time on the virtue itself than on its manifestation in effective ambushes and battle-formations; implying that if the virtue is sound, the rest follows. A lord with the feudal–chivalric virtues will attract knights to his service, and men will come to be knighted by him, which will create a special bond between them. Family unity is another bond of loyalty, so strong that a whole family may feel tainted by the disgrace of one member. These factors together create powerful fellowships that can maintain the peace. Yet their very success can be dangerous: loyalty to the lord of the fellowship may be stronger than loyalty to the king. Moreover, the lords and the king himself will be to a great extent in the power of their united followers. Arthur and Lancelot are at different times compelled by their followers to continue fighting one another. To ensure this, Gawain even threatens Arthur with a *diffidatio*, a formal renunciation of allegiance.

Among the interdependences of the virtues, the effect of generous courtesy on loyalty and prowess is particularly clear. A reputation for not being generous nearly costs Guenivere her life. Nevertheless, Malory rather takes it for granted that the good knight will normally be generous with land and other possessions, and only picks out for special mention spectacular examples of this, as when Lancelot gives away an entire kingdom. Similarly with courtesy. He rarely describes any court ceremonial: important as the idea of the Order of Knighthood was to him, he never describes the knighting ceremony, even in its simple form; and in his seventh tale he leaves out much of the procedure of the trial by combat. What he does describe and even comment on is spontaneous but difficult acts of generosity and courtesy: giving someone else one's horse in battle, refusing to suspect a friend, taming violent passions into gentleness. When Lancelot takes Guenivere back to her husband, this, their greatest act of self-sacrifice, is highlighted by the most detailed description of ceremonial in the *Morte Darthur*. The four virtues that dominate Lancelot's eulogy on his friend Gareth (p. 111) are prowess, loyalty, generosity and courtesy—generosity extending to straightforward sincere behaviour, and courtesy to humility, to being 'meke and milde', a phrase recalling Chaucer's Knight. This is the nearest Malory ever comes to a definition of the ideal knight; and it is noticeable that the eulogy, like the book as a whole, neglects some gifts and virtues highly valued in later times: among them knowledge, intelligence, wit, good looks and the careless grace many Renaissance thinkers felt to be essential to the good life.

The fifth of the feudal–chivalric virtues, the desire for glory, is also omitted from Lancelot's eulogy, but throughout the book something like it underlies all the others. For Malory, nobility of mind—having the whole range of chivalric virtues—generates every kind of chivalric achievement, just as particular traits of mind produce particular kinds of fighting; and the key to nobility of mind is the desire for *worship*. But *worship* is an ambiguous idea, meaning 'honour' in two senses: *noble idealism* of mind and *high reputation*. Malory leaves the ambiguity to be resolved by the action. Sometimes the *Morte Darthur* presents discrepancies between reputation and merit; but more often they correspond, as no doubt would normally happen in a small family-like court whose members knew one another well. Kay is a boaster, but he deceives no one. For Malory, the chivalric virtues include the desire for worship in both senses together, for *deserved* reputation. Nobility of mind, that is, includes the desire to increase in worth; and therefore —since Malory sees all virtues as outgoing—to act in the most worthwhile way; and, in consequence, to be known to be honourable. The most worthwhile action is seeking out and rectifying injustice, for which the *quest* is both opportunity and symbol. A knight successful in quests will increase in worship (in the chivalric virtues and the reputation for them), and he may enjoy himself enormously and win lands. But his most important achievement will be establishing justice, without which the rest would be selfishness, more or less high-minded. The need for justice means that a knight *ought* to undertake quests; and the higher his rank, the greater his obligation.

Malory's view of *love*, except for what is in a single incoherent passage of explanation (see pp. 129–30 and Commentary), has to be discovered in the same way as his view of chivalry. Like the classic exponents of courtly love, he portrays sexual passion as a powerful arbitrary force, difficult to resist but impossible to conjure into existence if it will not come of itself. But after that, his view and courtly love diverge. Love takes many forms, some neither beneficent nor admirable. It can inspire great feats of chivalry, but it can also destroy virtue, sanity, happiness and life itself. It drives Morgan le Fay to the attempted murder of her husband and brother, keeps Tristram at home during the Roman War, and leaves Merlin 'besotted'. Like a knight's chivalry, a lover's feelings and actions are produced by and reveal his innermost being; but the noble character may find love most destructive, just as a brave knight may be killed while a coward escapes. But widespread, various and powerful though it is, love is not universal. Some good knights are never said to be in love, and those that are seem more often to undertake adventures for the sake of justice or adventure itself than for their ladies. Despite this, love is as natural to a knight as war. Nobility of mind, Malory says, predisposes one to love, and when a noble man loves a noble woman, his character and achievements will draw her irresistibly to love him. Knights, however, sometimes find their ladies regrettably able to resist: Gareth complains to Liones that he has earned her love with the best blood in his body, and Tristram reproaches Isolt with the lands he gave up for her.

For Malory, true love is very like feudal chivalry. It has the same virtues, and resourceful courage (the equivalent of prowess) and loyalty are foremost among them. Arthur falls in love with Guenivere for her courage and beauty, and his love makes him in turn braver. Loyalty is given a special importance: in love, too, contemporary disloyalty provokes Malory to a unique outburst about his own time (the passage in which he tries to explain the nature of love). Lovers too should be courteous and generous, and the emphasis is again on spontaneous virtue in difficult circumstances. Chaucer's Squire's many social accomplishments, and the delight in 'love-talking' and the special vocabulary that Malory's age had inherited from courtly love, are all virtually ignored; and even beauty is mentioned surprisingly infrequently. *Jantyl servyse*, as Malory calls generosity and courtesy together, is real service, but one in which both lovers, not merely the man, seek to please and to obey. The lover should desire *worship*, but for his beloved not for himself: Isolt insists on Tristram's going to tournaments instead of staying with her, and Lancelot tries to protect Guenivere's reputation by avoiding her company. 'True love' will have these virtues, whereas 'modern love' is fickle, promiscuous and selfish, and deserves to be despised.

But *true* love is incomplete without another quality. If it is to become *virtuous* love, it must 'reserve the honour unto God': it must be chaste. The literature of courtly love often showed marriage as an impediment to love, or an irrelevance. Chaucer's *Book of the Duchess* describes at length a lover mourning for his dead mistress, and never mentions that they had been married for ten years. But in the *Morte Darthur*, the true end of love is marriage. Lancelot says that even an affair between unmarried lovers is shameful, a sin, and will bring the lover bad luck; and the course of the story bears him out. An adulterous affair is worse, and the only honourable course for a man who falls in love with another's wife is platonic love. The sin is graver, and Tristram's refusal to fight his mistress's husband because he has wronged him too much already shows how the shame inevitably involves the husband too. If the wronged husband is one's lord, the sin and shame are compounded. Malory disliked showing Lancelot behaving dishonourably, and presumably for that reason he used the prose *Tristan* instead of the prose *Lancelot* as the centre of his book, and told only selected incidents from the *Lancelot* that left Lancelot's adultery in doubt for as long as possible. This unavoidably brought Tristram's adultery into prominence instead, but that at least had Mark's viciousness to palliate it. But despite this and the fact that Tristram's was 'true' love, the idea that it had been adulterously consummated was so shameful that Perceval refused to believe it of so honourable a knight. Lancelot and Guenivere's affair is necessary to the last two tales; but even then, Malory only relates the act of adultery itself where the plot requires it, as in the Knight of the Cart episode: where it does not, as when Aggravayne traps the lovers together, he casts doubt on its having taken place. As narrator he seems to feel (and as author he may really have felt) embarrassed at the diminution of Lancelot's excellence, but he could not alter the story.

In the *Morte Darthur*, true love that is not virtuous is wrong, and the very strength its good qualities give it may make it immensely destructive. But the real good in it makes it respectable enough for the world to turn a blind eye to it: when Tristram brings Isolt to Arthur's court, everyone speaks and acts as though Tristram were merely chivalrously acting as her escort. Such love may also be strong enough to be an education for the love of God: Malory seems to agree with Elaine of Astolat that all good love comes from God (whatever the lover may make of it later), and he says as narrator that Guenivere's true love earns her her good end. It is part of the paradox that, their true love having destroyed everything else they value, all that either she or Lancelot then has left is the honour they had previously failed to reserve to God.

Religion in the *Morte Darthur* is Catholic and entirely orthodox, though Malory shows no more inclination towards theological exposition than towards expounding the theory of chivalry. He accepts the theology of his sources, sometimes abbreviating their explanations; and almost the only idea he adds is his hint that even sinful true love may become part of the lover's way to God. The world he portrays is sustained by God, whose presence and mysterious purposes are occasionally revealed by miracles, visions, and prophecies. Men move towards God by grace or away from Him by sin. He may punish by death a serious sin like incest, and lovers who commit suicide know they are damned. Many medieval religious institutions appear in Malory's book, though there are no pardoners offering old pillowcases as Our Lady's veil and no parish priests excommunicating for their tithes, and though Malory's hermits (like Shakespeare's friars) can, when the plot demands, behave with a freedom that would turn an ecclesiastical superior's hair white. But the book includes popes and bishops, monasteries and chantries, the seven sacraments, the liturgy, and the Church calendar. Religion has harmonised the virtues of chivalry and love with itself. Though most of this harmony came to Malory in his sources from the experience and theological thought of earlier centuries, he extended the process, and not only in the case of chastity in love. He stressed humility in love and in chivalry; and sometimes, like Chaucer, supplemented the feudal virtues with wisdom, which he apparently understood as a practical temperateness (*mesure*) and prudence, which would shut Aggravayne's dangerous 'open mouth' and show lovers' fickleness to be stupid as well as shameful. Most of the practical disputes between feudal and religious chivalry do not arise:

Arthur's wars are just, his knights do not need ransom-money, and the good knights usually manage to avoid killing anyone in tournaments, however serious the injuries they inflict. So religious and feudal–chivalric virtues reinforce one another naturally, as when a knight guilty of robbery and rape is blamed because he is breaking his knightly oath. Religion gives knighthood itself its dignity: Malory as narrator calls it again and again the High *Order* of Knighthood.

The *Morte Darthur* contains no heretics or atheists, and none of its characters thinks the virtues of war and love form a system independent of God. But for all their religious surroundings, the characters can forget God. 'Forgetting' does not mean total oblivion, but letting things slip to the back of one's mind: so lovers in winter 'forget' past kindnesses, but springtime brings them to mind again (pp. 128–9). Malory's characters are prone to forgetting: Tristram 'almost forgets' Isolt on one long absence, and Lancelot 'forgets' his promise of reform soon after the Grail-quest. Those who forget God think of their faults only in terms of *shame*, never of *sin*; they do not refer their actions to God, but try to gain reputation with the world at large, or love from one person, or their own self-respect. Lancelot does all three. They may have many real virtues—Lancelot is immeasurably better than King Mark—but they have no safeguard to prevent their virtues being distorted into vices. So Gawain falls into pride, and Lancelot and Guenivere into illicit love. God in His courtesy sends the Grail-quest, the quest for Himself, as a remedy; all the Round Table know it to be the highest of all quests, and pursue it, but few persevere. Gawain makes excuses early on, and Lancelot, who wants to want God, is unable to change himself enough to do so. He is condemned as lacking loyalty (*stabilité*) towards God, the virtue Malory prized above all.

A vivid awareness of God makes progress in loving him and so in the other virtues possible. Awareness of God may come from 'great goodness', as in Galahad or the hermit in the Knight of the Cart episode, or from repenting sins by seeing their consequences. Gawain is brought out of his pride and Lancelot and Guenivere out of their adultery by the disaster their sins cause, which brings out in each an objectivity and selflessness far beyond what would (if only it could have been shown earlier) have averted the disaster itself. The awareness of God puts one into a service as personal as that of a human lord, and demands the same virtues, but in different form. Lancelot's prowess is shown again in the wholeheartedness of his life of penance, and generous courtesy in the hermit who gives away all his great possessions for God; but the *'worship'* sought is entirely supernatural, and of its nature shuns fame. God's service is most perfect in the monastic life, but is also possible in war. Both, though they may demand the willing acceptance of suffering as penance for sin, are active: the one in performing the liturgy and giving hospitality to travellers; the other in crusading to the Holy Land. To those whose love becomes perfect, God responds with His own generous courtesy, as can be seen in the angelic escort that receives Lancelot's soul.

Style

The narrative style of the *Morte Darthur* is based on speech, a business-like 'paratactic' prose predominantly of straightforward declarative sentences and clauses, joined by conjunctions such as *and*, *but*, and *then*, with little antithesis, parallelism, or subordination of one element to another, and usually in simple past tenses. Parataxis is common in medieval English prose: most literature was then read aloud, and a more complicated style would have been difficult for listeners to understand fully. Because parataxis can recount competently a series of events happening or things seen one after another, it was much used in English chronicles of the time. Like those of the spoken language, Malory's sentences sometimes repeat words to remind the hearer of the subject when it is not logically necessary, and omit words that logical completeness would demand but that the hearer can supply without confusion. Like that of speech, Malory's grammar is occasionally careless in small ways, in, for instance, sequence of tenses, number and gender. Very occasionally this becomes ambiguous or even misleading, most often when two clauses appear in an order different from that of the events they describe. Malory's diction is as straightforward as his syntax, making powerful use of ordinary words and phrases (often phrases in the same kind of common use as proverbs), and sparing in the use of adjectives.

Malory never uses the elaborate figures of speech, heavy alliteration, or polysyllabic French or Latin-derived words that medieval formal rhetoric recommended for an impressive style. He does use a number of French words, many of them short, but, except for a very few copied without thought from his sources, they were a natural part of the English spoken by the knightly class he belonged to. His style, however, has a kind of instinctive rhetoric: a tendency towards forceful brevity of expression and towards emphasising important points by unobtrusive alliteration and patterns of repetition, particularly the use of pairs of synonyms such as 'prayers and orisons', and the thematic repetition of a word or phrase throughout a whole passage. Some words and phrases, such as 'out of measure' and 'noble knights' accumulate special associations and acquire significance by repetition throughout the whole book.

In storytelling, narration and description are opposite poles: the more a writer describes, the more slowly his story will proceed. Physical causality is relatively unimportant in Malory's story, and he gives very little physical description. He regularly omits circumstantial detail and occasionally even leaves the reader to assume part of a sequence of actions. Most of his story is told in direct narration. The adjectives, descriptive phrases, and formal similes are few and taken from ordinary common speech. The story highlights chivalry and characterisation, and characters will be described as noble, and actions and speeches reported to show what their nobility consists of; but the reader must nearly always imagine their appearance for himself. A few physical details are mentioned because they are strikingly odd, or because they change the course of events, like the scar by which the hermit recognises Lancelot. It is only at climactic moments—and not all of those— that the physical scene is visualised, whether in some striking symbolic aspect or in a full description. This is another side of the practical speech-derived style of fifteenth-century chronicles.

Because the description is limited, the story moves fast. But Malory controls its speed with a sense of pace worthy of a skilful film-director. Repetitions, description and dialogue in different ways slow the action and provide touches of emphasis, and a break-and-link technique adds suspense at the ends of incidents, notably on page 160 and page 211. Allusions to events not recounted in the narrative give the story an extra dimension, a context and a past, as is particularly evident in the Healing of Sir Urry. These allusions can also hold and stress a desirable image for a moment, as in the link passage between the seventh and eighth tales. This catches Lancelot characteristically on quest, at the zenith of his and King Arthur's fame, in the moment before the peace and order of the kingdom breaks down, and so strengthens the contrast between what precedes and what follows.

In the dialogue of the *Morte Darthur*, syntax and diction are very much like those in the narration, except that in dialogue the syntax is sometimes a little more complicated and the diction a little more colloquial, so that the characters seem more vivid than the narrator. Expression again shows no sign of formal rhetoric; and, as in real-life speech, is forceful rather than precise. But again pace and emphasis are skilfully controlled, partly as in narration and partly by means special to dialogue, such as interjections, oaths, and vocatives. These means can slow down the pace of a speech and make it deliberate and dignified. And across the whole book, key phrases build up a cumulative effect: Lancelot's reputation as 'the best knight of the world' is established largely by the repetition of that phrase by the other characters. In many speeches, the repetition of words reveals strong feelings, but, especially in emotional speeches of explanation, the logical structure is often less complete than the patterns of words. General judgments about life are restricted almost entirely to proverbs, usually spoken by the characters rather than the narrator, and often helping to instil courage or an unembittered endurance of suffering. Proverbs are the product of collective rather than individual experience, and they act as a reminder that Malory's characters are facing the same difficulties and defeats as those who used the proverbs before them. (Particular instances of these traits of style are noticed in the Commentary.)

Malory's dialogue is not much differentiated by the rank or temperament or place or origin of speakers. Different moods are finely distinguished, but different men in the same mood speak in the same way, even in the same words; and the different social classes have the same linguistic usages—even with the class-distinguishing pronouns *ye* and *thou*. *Ye* was once merely the plural pronoun and *thou* the singular; but it came to be thought courteous to use *ye* and *you* to one's superiors, and then later to one's equals. By Malory's time, *thou* and *thee* were used to God in prayer, to a close member of one's family (especially at emotional moments), and to a social inferior. A king could call a knight *thou* —though Arthur normally uses *ye* to his own knights—but for one knight to use it to another was to insult him by demoting him. So knights who were fighting or about to fight call one another *thou*— Lancelot's unique use of *ye* to Gawain during their two fights at Benwick (pp. 205–11) is a measure of his courtesy, his love and respect for Gawain, and his unwillingness in conscience to fight. Mellyagaunte's carter adds insult to injury by refusing Lancelot a lift and then calling him *thou*. The usages can be mixed: when Guenivere calls Lancelot *thou*, she is both insulting him and reminding him of her higher rank. Arthur apparently calls Urry *thou* partly because he is a stranger and partly because his injury brings out in a healthy man a sympathetic superiority such as he might feel to a likeable but not-yet-grown-up cousin: when Urry recovers, the king calls him *ye*. But Arthur's use of *thou* to the dying Gawain and Ector's over Lancelot's body are the simple product of intense family grief.

Very occasionally a particular phrase will be so much the product of one temperament as to be unattributable to any but one speaker, or a phrase from war or hunting, religion, or law, will suggest a character's occupation, as when the Bishop of Rochester distinguishes smoothly between the Pope's 'worship' and his own mere 'poor honesty'. But this is rare: Malory's knights do not continually discuss the details of war in military jargon. Their speech is often knightly, but for another reason. Malory says as narrator that speeches showing courage and presence of mind are knightly, and those qualities are often shown in his knights' speech by direct and forceful brevity. Knights often respond to startling news with laconic stereotyped phrases such as 'That is truth', and 'I will well', where other writers, such as those of Malory's French sources, would prefer long eloquent speeches. Knights usually avoid exaggeration and emotionalism, whatever their situation, and prefer understatement, even irony. They rarely attempt long explanations, and those explanations they do give usually show some degree of incoherence. The knights' very lack of fluency suggests an uncomplaining courage in enduring what they do not fully comprehend; and, by contrast, the few long and well-organised explanations, such as Lancelot's great defence of Guenivere, seem to be given their form by the sheer pressure of intolerable emotion. This kind of speech is appropriate to knighthood, and it is knights who speak it most often and most memorably, though other characters—Guenivere, for instance— at times speak with a terse courage worthy of any knight. Because this knightly speech embodies the essence of chivalry without the technicalities of war, it reinforces the universal symbolism of quest and kingdom: Malory's knights seem to stand for Everyman.

Every story gives its readers some impression of the kind of person who is telling it, who chose these words and this way of narration rather than that. A narrator must exist, although his character may be, by accident or design, very different from that of the real author. The pilgrims who narrate their separate tales on the road to Canterbury are very different from one another, and from the historical Geoffrey Chaucer who created them all. The narrator may break into his story to comment on it or to address his audience directly: the Canterbury pilgrims do both. But Malory as narrator rarely does either, so the main impression his readers get of him comes from the narrative itself. The simplicity of narration and description makes him seem honest and unobtrusive. If, very occasionally, a word needs now to be explained in more than one sense, its senses do not make up a pun but are meanings that were felt as one in Malory's time and that have diverged since. The simplicity of narration gives the story verisimilitude, immediacy, dignity and pathos; and it makes the story objective, standing free of the narrator and distanced by the past tenses of its verbs. Its unalterable historical separateness is reinforced by the short formulas like 'Now turn we to so-and-so', and 'The French book says such-and-such', which comprise the majority of the narrator's remarks; by the handful of longer and more individual comments on the differences between King Arthur's days and his own; and by the link passage between the last two tales, where he confesses that part of the story has escaped him.

The narrator's knowledge of his world is incomplete in other ways. The most pervasive kind of knowledge of all comes from irony in narration. Irony embodies a knowledge that the narrator shares with at least the more discerning among his audience, but which is hidden from others. Chaucer is a master of this, as is shown in his agreement that his Monk should not stay within the cloister to labour, or

> How shal the world be served?
>
> *Cant. Tales*, A 187

The reader shares the narrator's superior knowledge of divine realities and of the way of the world; the Monk's ignorance of how the world should really be served puts him below them. Malory's characters can be ironic towards one another, but he as narrator is never ironic towards them. His few explicit observations on the world at large are simple and usually proverbial. Behind his story lie the mysterious workings of fate or providence; but such explanation as is given of them comes mostly from the characters, both privileged ones like Merlin and ordinary knights like Dinadan. Many of them seem to know more than the narrator, whose longest appearance in person is to complain (like so many of his predecessors) that he has not been able to discover Arthur's ultimate fate (p. 226). His explanations seem even more liable to confusion than do those of his characters, though this lack of eloquence has its own impressiveness: it is incoherence that gives the 'love and summer' passage (pp. 128–9) its passionate urgency. Furthermore, he does not exploit a creator's omniscience about the characters' thoughts and feelings, rarely saying more than common observation could deduce; and though as author he manages his characters' behaviour with profound understanding, as narrator his generalisations about it are remarkably naïve. He appears to be not a showman, superior to his characters, but a companion on their level or a little below it, and the story's seeming independence of him gives the heroism of the characters and the tragedy of their situation an extraordinary authenticity.

What little information the narrator discloses about himself is almost all in the *explicits* of the various tales, where a totally different style, interlarded with scraps of English verse and French and Latin, marks a genre as different from romance as a curtain-call is from a play. In the text, except for a comment apiece on the politics and morals of his day, he actually avoids speaking about himself and his ideas, directly or by ironic implication. The nearest he ever comes to irony is his sad observation that 'men say'—as if his contemporaries did not know it by experience—that modern Englishmen are still fickle in their loyalty to good rulers. In the progress of simple narration and laconic dialogue, with their built-in chivalric value-judgements and relative neglect of physical causality, the events are seen *through* the clear medium of his style: style and narrator alike are almost invisible. Yet, on his few appearances, his very limitations reinforce the verisimilitude that the story derives from its directness and its independence of him. He seems a naïve man trying to tell a plain blunt tale, who could not deceive if he wanted to; not controlling the action, but observing, suffering, and trying to understand.

Tragedy, Mystery and Triumph

Given the narrator's limitations, what Malory's characters are is necessarily shown mainly by their own words and actions; and what the characters are is to destroy them and the Round Table. The seventh tale opens with Arthur and his knights too firmly in power to be endangered by external threat; but Lancelot and Guenivere's adultery begins again. It is the major theme of the tale: the repeated risk it brings of discovery and disaster for Arthur's world, and the contradictory effects it has on the lovers, their natures tending to ennoble it, its nature driving them to act in ways unworthy of each other. At the beginning of the first episode, careless and malicious gossip is already spreading and Lancelot is torn by conflicting impulses: the selfless part of his love makes him avoid Guenivere, and his memories of the Grail make him still want to do God's will. He undertakes quests on behalf of defenceless women from this last motive, and also (we may infer) to try to compound with God for his adultery by extraordinary virtue in other respects. In consequence, Guenivere feels insecure and provokes a quarrel, which displays these and other motives. Close reading, as in many of Malory's dialogues, shows more than narrator or participants seem conscious of. Guilt and resentment drive the lovers to try to hurt each other, and their long-enduring love gives them weapons. Lancelot's are the more powerful: he has sacrificed his *worship* for her in the past, and may have to rescue her from the consequences of her own folly in the future. (Prescience like this, by which a character foresees or guesses much of a future disaster without being able to avert

it, adds a sense of fatality to the story here and at several later points.)
Unwittingly, Lancelot's arguments expose another flaw: he may have
begun his present quests for God alone, but he now also thinks of them
as camouflage for his adultery. But Guenivere, on even shakier ground
morally, does not reply directly to his arguments. She responds instead
to the wish to hurt that underlies them, and takes it as proof that he
does not love her at all. Determined to hit back at whatever cost, she
accuses him of every fault she can think of and banishes him from the
court.

This disedifying but revealing exchange provokes Guenivere into
giving the ill-fated dinner at which she is accused of poisoning one of
her guests. Arthur is very shaken by the charge and by her inability to
find a champion to defend her in the consequent trial by battle. As
king, he is the only husband in the country who cannot fight for a wife
he believes innocent. He must preside over such trials, and, if the
prisoner cannot find another champion, he must see her burnt. In an
excruciating situation, he acts with justice, dignity and speed: arrang-
ing the trial as the law demands, but being merciful where he can; and
then trying to find a champion for her. Of Lancelot's kinsmen, Bors is
nearest to him in prowess, and Guenivere asks him to fight for her. At
first he refuses, because in the heat of the moment, full of resentment at
her banishing Lancelot, he believes her guilty. Calmer thought and
persuasion by Arthur change his mind, and he agrees to fight, though
he continues to dislike her. By taking Bors's place in the battle and
winning it, Lancelot is reconciled with the queen, and soon afterwards
other events confirm her innocence beyond doubt.

The second episode in this tale is also sparked off by a disagreement
between the lovers, though one more muted and more ambiguously
motivated. Lancelot goes to the tournament at Winchester as Guenivere wants him to, but in a thoroughly resentful frame of mind. When
Elayne, daughter of his host at Astolat, presses him to wear a favour of
hers in the tournament, he breaks a life-long custom and accepts, telling
himself that it is only a disguise. His thoughtless acceptance encourages
Elayne in a passion that eventually kills her, and his disguise is so
successful that his kinsmen nearly kill him. Elayne helps to nurse him
back to health, and, Lancelot being what he is, her love continues to
grow, although he does nothing else to encourage it. In courage and
generosity and all the chivalric virtues she is his equal, and both Bors
and Gawain wish that he would return her love. That would solve
every problem but Guenivere's—and Guenivere's problem is something both knights want to know as little about as possible. Lancelot
does not fall in love with Elayne, but Guenivere hears an account,

magnified by accident and gossip, of what is happening, and is as furious as any disgruntled lover's subconscious could wish. Malory shows in little ways the suffering that Elayne feels and refuses to flinch from, but she is as stoical in pain and as unshaken by the prospect of her own death as any knight, and at first the others do not realise the damage her love is doing her. Finally, she asks Lancelot to marry her, or at least to take her as his mistress. His clumsy refusal, in which with unintentional cruelty he says every single thing he should not, precipitates her breakdown and death. Her deathbed speech is pure grief —intense but free from distortion, resentment, or self-pity. She acknowledges her love to have been 'out of measure', and her ability to place herself and love objectively in the divine order despite her pain displays once more her heroic quality of mind. When Guenivere hears the true story and sees the dead body of her rival, her natural generosity reasserts itself, and with splendid inconsistency she suggests to Lancelot that he should have been kinder to Elayne to save her life. Lancelot less generously gives an ambiguous reply: his explanation of why he could not is also a covert rebuke to the queen. Guenivere perseveres and apologises to him for her anger, he grudgingly accepts, and they are once again reconciled. The queen's generosity, however, has limits: in his next tournament she throws discretion to the winds and evens the score with Elayne by making him wear a favour of her own.

In the Knight of the Cart episode, Mellyagaunte kidnaps Guenivere: he has been infatuated with her and has been shown as detesting Lancelot as early as the fifth tale of the *Morte Darthur*. The lovers appear to better advantage coping with the practical urgencies of rescue, particularly in contrast with the mercurial Mellyagaunte, who is quick to seize an opportunity, but sly, irresolute and incompetent. Even in his moment of triumph (p. 132), his feelings are mixed: as much resigned to danger as exulting in success. Guenivere coolly and skilfully exploits every advantage in her circumstances and her captor's character until Lancelot arrives, and then her instant sympathy for him and joy in his prowess banish thought for herself. Yet she retains her presence of mind, calmly accepting Mellyagaunte's panic-stricken surrender at one moment, and teasing her furious lover out of fighting madness at the next. Her agreement to forget the whole affair is both far-sighted and magnanimous: Mellyagaunte has made a formal unconditional surrender, and the laws of war entitle the victors to kill him out of hand if they choose. In all this, Guenivere is credibly the woman Lancelot could not stop himself loving.

But from the next morning, the narrative is shot through with ironies. Mellyagaunte finds Lancelot's blood on Guenivere's bedclothes, and concludes that it came from one of her escort, all of whom were wounded. With the same impulsive unscrupulousness that made him kidnap the queen, he now seizes the chance to hide his previous crimes by out-accusing his potential accusers, although they had not harmed him and Guenivere was his queen, his guest, and (so he had said) his love. Febrile excitement in scheming, absolute certainty that he is right, and his still-evolving plans overcome his normal cowardice, and he warns Lancelot, Guenivere's champion, that 'God will have a stroke in every battle', a proverb one would only expect in such desperate straits from a better man than he—from Lancelot, for instance. Yet it is the traitor who is in the right: both halves of his challenge as he first delivers it are word-for-word true; and, in taking it up, only by verbal trickery can the best knight in the world get any shadow of justice on his side. Strictly speaking, Mellyagaunte should challenge Guenivere, and Lancelot accept the challenge as her champion. By accusing Mellyagaunte of lying, Lancelot is able to manoeuvre him into wording the accusation so that Guenivere, though guilty in fact, is innocent as charged. Mellyagaunte then manoeuvres Lancelot on to a trapdoor that drops him into a prison cell, which is Mellyagaunte's idea of the way God intervenes in battles. Characteristically, however, he fails to exploit his advantage fully, and Lancelot escapes in time for the queen's trial. The shameful story of Mellyagaunte's actions embarrasses the whole court, and provokes Arthur into a single tiny lapse from his painful impartiality in the conduct of the trial. In the battle, Mellyagaunte is inevitably soon grovelling for mercy. By human standards he deserves to die: by the criminal law as the loser in trial by battle; and by natural justice because, after Guenivere forgave him a capital crime, he tried to have her burnt alive under the form of law. But Lancelot has often, as Christianity and the statutes of the Round Table alike demanded, given mercy to those who asked for it, even though they did not deserve it; and by the criminal law Guenivere, though technically innocent, deserves the death she has just escaped. Nevertheless, she signals to Lancelot to kill, and he accepts her decision. Malory gives no hint of her motives: whether Mellyagaunte has exhausted her generosity, or whether she fears what he might say later —even on his way to execution, if the king refuses to ratify Lancelot's pardon. Now Lancelot in turn uses the process of law for deliberate homicide. The law entitles him to kill the loser on the spot; but instead he relies on his supreme prowess and offers Mellyagaunte further combat at apparently ridiculously favourable odds: in fact, certain death. Consistent to the end in bad judgment and eagerness to seize any advantage, particularly an unfair one, Mellyagaunte accepts, and the lovers are once more safe.

In the last episode of this tale, Sir Urry is brought to Arthur's court suffering from wounds that only the best knight in the world can cure. Lancelot has performed several such feats in earlier tales, each time behaving as if he were prepared, for the good of the sufferer, to act on an assumption that his humility made him want to deny. In these cures, as in other ways, Galahad superseded him during the Grail-quest; but Galahad is dead. All the knights at court attempt to cure Urry, providing incidentally a recapitulation of the major themes of the *Morte Darthur*: Arthur's love for his knights, their past achievements, the fellowships linking and dividing them, the Grail, Lancelot's pre-eminence and weaknesses, and the enemies who lie in wait for him and Guenivere. All the other knights fail—even Bors, the only survivor of the three who achieved the Grail—and Lancelot succeeds; but the outcome shakes him as it never had before, and he weeps as if relieved of a great tension. It seems as if his hesitation about presumption was only part of his unwillingness to try to cure Urry: he was also afraid that his renewed adultery had made him no longer the best knight in the world, that this would prevent the cure everyone expected of him, and that that would be taken as proving the gossip about his adultery true. So he prays most urgently for a miracle to supplement the possible deficiencies of magic; and, whether by magic or in answer to his prayer, ends the tale supernaturally confirmed as still the best knight in the world.

As the seventh tale' had opened with Lancelot and Guenivere's secret love, so the eighth opens with Aggravayne and Mordred's secret hate, incongruous in May, the season of new love. Their hate sparks off the tragedy; but although the narrator seems not to look beyond it, in fact almost everyone who suffers in the tragedy contributes in some degree to it; and before they die Gawain, Guenivere and Lancelot each acknowledge part of the responsibility. Hatred disguised as duty impels Aggravayne and Mordred to tell the king about the adultery, despite their brothers' counter-arguments of prudence and gratitude. Significantly, no one even mentions the possibility of Guenivere's innocence. For a third time a charge is made, and for a third time Arthur, whose generous mind had previously suppressed its own suspicions, has to act impartially, allowing Aggravayne and his kinsmen to set a trap that catches Lancelot in the queen's chamber at night. At this point, the narrator himself seems (like Arthur) to be trying, without complete success, to convince himself that the lovers might have been doing nothing more culpable than playing chess. Unlike their enemies, the lovers are commendably terse, brave, decisive and selfless: expecting to die, each still thinks first of the other. But there are stains on the shining fabric: he speaks casually of having fought for her 'in right and in wrong'; even if they have not just committed the crime the king's knights are trying to arrest them for, they are habitually guilty of it; and when, against all odds, Lancelot escapes and gathers his friends for the now inevitable fight, Bors says that whether Lancelot had done right or wrong *before*, it is his duty to defend the queen *now*. Bors, the closest to Lancelot of all his kinsmen, does not know or want to know the truth about Lancelot's nocturnal visits to the queen.

To the news that one knight without armour has killed thirteen fully-armed ones, even Arthur first responds with admiration; but admiration is rapidly succeeded by grief, resolve and anger at what he has been forced into and those who have forced him into it. Although Gawain argues that the queen might be innocent, she is summarily condemned to death. Lancelot and his friends rescue her, but in the mêlée they kill dozens of Arthur's knights, and Lancelot himself kills his friend Gareth.

The rescue affects Arthur and Gawain very differently, yet in both the heart of the tragedy is revealed: the pain that people who love one another inflict on one another. The king speaks with the simple honesty of desolation. At the beginning of his reign he loved the Round Table second only to Guenivere, and he loved Guenivere enough to marry her although Merlin warned him of the consequences. Malory shows, as usual without explanation, the result of the years when she loved Lancelot and Arthur did not allow himself to suspect them. His Order of Chivalry had become his first love; but he still loved her. Now he has lost them both: he has had to sentence her to death, and more than twenty of his Order have deserted him and nearly forty have been killed. To make it worse, he can foresee that Gawain will put irresistible moral and political pressure on him to make war on Lancelot. From this point on, he is a broken man. In Gawain, Malory shows a violent and passionate nature shocked out of precarious emotional equilibrium. During the short while before the full impact takes effect on him, Gawain can argue with apparent cogency that what has happened cannot have happened. This is followed by physical collapse when the mental strain becomes intolerable, then by exploration of the disaster even through simple affirmation of obvious facts ('which were two noble knights'), seeking for some kind of bearings in chaos. Then comes a solemn resolve when a new purpose, revenge, is discovered. Like falling in love or religious conversion, it seems to be imposed upon him by a force from outside himself. It seems to him to be his duty to Lancelot to kill him: hence his macabre promise not to 'fail' Lancelot until one or other of them is dead.

But Lancelot takes Guenivere and his uneasy conscience off to Joyous Garde, and will not fight. After months of siege, he and Gawain are drawn into an argument across the battlements. In the heat of it, truth is mixed on one side with equivocation, exaggeration, and raking up the past, and on the other with distortion, obsession, and deliberately provocative insult. Gawain's provocation is successful indirectly: Lancelot's knights force him to fight; but Lancelot, feeling continually that what he is doing is wrong, cannot bring himself to slaughter his way to the victory that is within his grasp. After this, the Pope makes peace, and Lancelot hands Guenivere back to the king, making in her defence one last superb blasphemous speech in which he cites his victory over the thirteen knights as God's testimony to her innocence. But Gawain cannot now be moved by this, or by reminders of debts of gratitude, or by generous offers of reparation and public penance for the death of Gareth. With Arthur's acquiescence, he banishes Lancelot from England and promises to follow him wherever he may go. Lancelot returns to his lands in France, divides them among his knights, leaving nothing for himself, and prepares for the attack.

The French invasion is the nadir for Arthur and Gawain. The king allows Gawain to refuse generous peace terms, and to begin the war with a campaign of devastation against civilians. In Gawain himself, the constraints put by Christianity and courtesy upon martial extremism have tragically collapsed, and the chivalrous knight regresses into a fierce warrior of the pre-feudal age, the age in which the primary social duty was revenge for slaughtered kinsmen. Lancelot's proud knights are eager to fight back; but he will not, until in the end he is compelled twice to fight Gawain himself. Both before and after these fights, Gawain's obsessive energy contrasts sharply with Lancelot's unhappy conscience and weary courtesy; but it is Lancelot who wins.

Mordred's usurpation and his attempt to marry Guenivere partly restore Arthur to his old self. He has something urgent, practical and right to do, instead of having to watch the two men he most loves attempting to destroy each other, while he wonders which of them is the more in the wrong. He ships his army home, and himself, fierce and irresistible, leads the landing. In the fighting, Gawain receives a mortal blow on the old wound that Lancelot had given him in France. This jolts him out of his vengeful pride, and makes him confess his own guilt and fallibility. Before he dies, he writes a letter to Lancelot seeking reconciliation, and assuring him that his death was his own fault, not Lancelot's, even though the old wound was part-cause of it. He had got the wound by his obstinacy in pursuing Lancelot: Lancelot had not wished it, and did not deserve the misfortune of being even accidentally among the causes of his death. If Gawain had been equally objective about Gareth's death, the tragedy would have gone no further.

Amid portents and omens, the king pursues Mordred to the final battle at Salisbury, where all but two of his remaining Knights of the Round Table are killed, and he ends the war by killing his son. That sharply visualised moment symbolises both the self-destructiveness of evil, and the dissolution of the natural ties that held the Round Table together: the closest of all those bonds are broken when a father kills his son, and the son (so it seems) his father. The annihilation of the Round Table as an instrument for preserving peace and justice is vividly brought home when, after the battle, Arthur's last two knights have to look on while their dead and dying fellows are murdered and robbed by pillagers. At the same time, the mystery around the king himself deepens further, in the unexplained necessities of returning the sword Excalibur to the lake, and in the ambiguity of his passing to Avalon. Even among omens that seem supernaturally inspired, some point firmly to his death, others no less firmly to his survival and return; and between them, the narrator has to confess himself at a loss.

When Lancelot receives Gawain's letter and brings an army to England, the Round Table is already destroyed, and Guenivere has disappeared, having secretly entered a convent, where she has been made abbess. Lancelot finds her, but greatly changed. Her sins had sparked off the preceding catastrophe; that had shocked her into seeing their seriousness; and she has set about making reparation for them by a life of penance, in which there can be no place for an ex-lover. She steels herself by speaking before her ladies and using *thou* to force him to a suitable inferiority; and, invoking both their old love and her new authority as abbess, banishes him from her presence for the last time and forever. His duty now is to rule his lands; and, she adds with ruthless logic, to marry (to ensure descendants and an orderly succession). But Lancelot has already provided for the government of his lands, and chooses instead to enter the religious life himself. Love and honour obliged him to remain in the secular life as long as she did, to protect her. But the hunger the Grail-quest had aroused in him for perfection and the love of God has not died; and, like her, he has sins to do penance for. The first step is the hardest, because their old love is still dangerously hot under the ashes: when he took her back to Arthur under suspicion of adultery, honour and etiquette allowed him a farewell kiss in front of the whole court; but now, the total commitment of their new vocations must forbid it. The seeming callousness of Guenivere's last words to Lancelot are an index of how difficult this is.

Lancelot enters the first religious house he comes to, the hermitage of a fugitive bishop, where Arthur is buried and the last Knight of the Round Table serves as a lay-brother. Lancelot's kinsmen send the army home and set out to look for him; and within six months his old magnetism has drawn eight of them into the monastic life. The completeness of the change is symbolised by their turning loose their horses, the knight's most essential possession. Two of Lancelot's closest kinsmen are missing: Lionel, killed in a casual skirmish; and Ector, whose search is still going on: they were the two of the family who failed conspicuously in the Grail-quest. After six years, Lancelot is ordained priest; and a year later, Guenivere dies. He and his companions are warned by a vision to fetch her body and bury her beside Arthur. When Lancelot sees their bodies lying together, his heart is wrung by the memory of their beauty and nobility, which have perished as all earthly things must; by the visual reminder of the marriage he had violated; and so by a renewed awareness of how his sinfulness had helped to set the two people he most owed love and loyalty to against one another, destroyed their marriage, and killed them. He intensifies his life of penance as previously he would have summoned up his last reserve of energy in a fight; and physically broken, but spiritually perfected, gains in death the victory he seeks. Of this victory his companions are given supernatural confirmation.

They bury Lancelot not with Arthur and Guenivere, but the length of England away, in his own castle of Joyous Garde. Ector finds him there at last and too late, and delivers over his body the most famous and moving of all chivalric laments. It sets the tragedy of what has been lost in human terms against the confidently evoked triumph of Lancelot's death, creating a complete perspective. After what the closest of Lancelot's kinsmen have endured, there can be no return to ordinary life, whether ruling their own lands or assisting Arthur's capable successor Constantine in governing England. The Grail-quest is beyond recall, but they put their own lands in order and go as crusaders to the Holy Land, to fight and die for Jerusalem.

Lancelot and Guenivere

I

So aftir the quest of the Sankgreall[1] was fulfylled and all knyghtes
that were leffte on lyve[2] were com home agayne unto the Table
Rownde—as *The Booke of the Sankgreall* makith mencion—than
was there grete joy in the courte, and en especiall[4] Kynge Arthure
and Quene Gwenyvere made grete joy of the remenaunte that   5
were com home. And passyng[6] gladde was the kynge and the
quene of Sir Launcelot and of Sir Bors, for they had bene passynge
longe away in the queste of the Sankgreall.

Than, as the booke seyth,[9] Sir Launcelot began to resorte unto
Quene Gwenivere agayne, and forgate[10] the promyse and the   10
perfeccion that he made[11] in the queste; for, as the booke seyth, had
nat Sir Launcelot bene in his prevy[12] thoughtes and in hys myndis
so sette[13] inwardly to the quene as he was in semynge outewarde to
God, there had no knyght passed[14] hym in the queste of the
Sankgreall. But ever his thoughtis prevyly were on the quene, and   15
so they loved togydirs[16] more hotter than they dud toforehonde, and
had many such prevy draughtis[17] togydir that many in the courte
spake of hit, and in especiall Sir Aggravayne, Sir Gawaynes
brothir, for he was ever opynne-mowthed.[19]

So hit befelle that Sir Launcelot had many resortis[20] of ladyes   20
and damesels which dayly resorted unto hym, that besoughte hym
to be their champion. In all such maters of ryght Sir Launcelot
applyed hym dayly for to do for the plesure of oure Lorde Jesu
Cryst, and ever as much as he myght he withdrew hym fro the
company and felaweship of Quene Gwenyvere for to eschew the   25

---

[1] *Sankgreall*, Holy Grail (French *Saint Graal*)
[2] *on lyve*, alive
[4] *en especiall*, especially
[6] *passyng*, very   *was*, were
[9] *seyth*, says;   and see Commentary. (In subsequent notes, *Commentary* will be abbre-
viated to C and *note* and *notes* to n and nn respectively.)
[10] *forgate*, forgot
[11] *made*, achieved
[12] *prevy*, secret   *myndis*, intentions
[13] *sette*, devoted   *semynge*, appearance   *outewarde*, outwardly
[14] *there had no knyght passed*, no knight would have surpassed
[16] *togydirs*, together   *dud toforehonde*, did beforehand
[17] *prevy draughtis* (C)
[19] *opynne-mowthed*, a blabber-mouth
[20] *resortis of*, appeals for help from
[22–3] Translate: 'In all such questions of justice, Sir Lancelot tried continually to
act so as to please ...'

sclawndir and noyse. Wherefore the quene waxed wrothe with Sir Launcelot.

So on a day she called hym to hir chambir and seyd thus: 'Sir Launcelot, I se and fele dayly that youre love begynnyth to slake, for ye have no joy to be in my presence, but ever ye ar oute of thys courte, and quarels and maters ye have nowadayes for ladyes, madyns, and jantillwomen, more than ever ye were wonte to have beforehande.'   30

'A, madame,' seyde Sir Launcelot, 'in thys ye must holde me excused for dyvers causis: one ys, I was but late in the quest of the Sankgreall, and I thanke God of Hys grete mercy, and never of my deservynge, that I saw in that my queste as much as ever saw ony synfull man lyvynge, and so was hit tolde me. And if that I had nat had my prevy thoughtis to returne to youre love agayne as I do, I had sene as grete mysteryes as ever saw my sonne Sir Galahad, Percivale, other Sir Bors. And therefore, madam, I was but late in that queste, and wyte you well, madam, hit may nat be yet lyghtly forgotyn, the hyghe servyse in whom I dud my dyligente laboure.   35

                                                                            40

'Also, madame, wyte you well that there be many men spekith of oure love in thys courte and have you and me gretely in awayte, as thes Sir Aggravayne and Sir Mordred. And, madam, wyte you well I drede them more for youre sake than for ony feare I have of them myselffe, for I may happyn to ascape and ryde myselff in a grete nede where, madame, ye muste abyde all that woll be seyde unto you. And than, if that ye falle in ony distresse thorow wyllfull foly, than ys there none other remedy other helpe but by me and my bloode.   45

                                                                            50

'And wyte you well, madam, the boldnesse of you and me woll

watch

26 *noyse*, gossip
28 *on a day*, one day
29 *slake*, slacken
35 *dyvers*, various   *but late*, only recently
36-7 Understand: 'I thank God that, because of his mercy (and not at all because of my deserving), I saw ...'
38 *hit*, it
39 *my prevy thoughtis* (C)
41 *other*, or   *therefore*, so
43 *lyghtly*, quickly   *whom*, which
46-7 *have you and me gretely in awayte*, are eagerly trying to trap us
47 *thes*, these
50 *in a grete nede*, in a desperate situation
52 *foly*, folly   *none*, no
53 *bloode*, family, kin

brynge us to shame and sclaundir, and that were me lothe to se 55
you dishonoured. And that is the cause I take uppon me more for
to do for damesels and maydyns than ever y ded toforne, that
men sholde undirstonde my joy and my delite ys my plesure to
have ado for damesels and maydyns.'

All thys whyle the quene stoode stylle and lete Sir Launcelot 60
sey what he wolde; and whan he had all seyde she braste oute
on wepynge, and so she sobbed and awepte a grete whyle. And
whan she myght speke she seyde,

'Sir Launcelot, now I well understonde that thou arte a false,
recrayed knyght and a comon lechourere, and lovyste and 65
holdiste othir ladyes, and of me thou haste dysdayne and scorne.
For wyte thou well, now I undirstonde thy falsehede I shall
never love the more, and loke thou be never so hardy to com in
my syght. And ryght here I dyscharge the thys courte that thou
never com within hit, and I forfende the my felyship, and uppon 70
payne of thy hede that thou se me nevermore!'

Ryght so Sir Launcelot departed with grete hevynes, that
unneth he myght susteyne hymselff for grete dole-makynge.
Than he called Sir Bors, Sir Ector de Maris, and Sir Lyonell,
and tolde hem how the quene had forfended hym the courte, 75
and so he was in wyll to departe into hys owne contrey.

'Fayre sir,' seyde Sir Bors de Ganys, 'ye shall not departe oute
of thys londe by myne advyce, for ye muste remembir you what
ye ar, and renomed the moste nobelyst knyght of the worlde,
and many grete maters ye have in honde. And women in their 80
hastynesse woll do oftyntymes that aftir hem sore repentith. And
therefore, be myne advyce, ye shall take youre horse and ryde to

---

55 *that were me lothe*, that would be hateful to me (C)
57 *y*, I   *toforne*, before
58-9 *my plesure to have ado for*, understand: 'the pleasure I take in fighting (lit.
'acting') for'
61 *all seyde*, said everything [he had to say]   *braste*, burst
62 *on*, in   *awept*, wept
63 *myghte*, could
65 *recrayed*, craven
66 *holdiste*, possess sexually
67 *falsehede*, falsehood
68 *the*, thee, you   *hardy*, bold (Fr. *hardi*)
70 *forfende*, forbid
71 *that thou see me* (C)
73 *unneth*, scarcely   *dole*, sorrow (cf. *doleful*)
76 *was in wyll*, wanted
79 *renomed*, renowned as   *moste nobelyst* (C)
81 *that aftir hem sore repentith*, what they afterwards bitterly regret

the good ermyte here besyde Wyndesore, that somtyme was a
good knyght, hys name ys Sir Brascias. And there shall ye abyde
tyll that I sende you worde of bettir tydynges.'   85

'Brother,' seyde Sir Launcelot, 'wyte you well I am full loth
to departe oute of thys reallme, but the quene hath defended me
so hyghly that mesemyth she woll never be my good lady as she
hath bene.'

'Sey ye never so,' seyde Sir Bors, 'for many tymys or this she   90
hath bene wroth with you, and aftir that she was the first that
repented hit.'

'Ye sey well,' seyde Sir Launcelot, 'for now woll I do by your
counceyle, and take myne horse and myne harneyse and ryde to
the ermyte Sir Brastias, and there woll I repose me tille I hyre   95
som maner of tydynges frome you. But, fayre brother, in that
ye can, gete me the love of my lady Quene Gwenyvere.'

'Sir,' seyde Sir Bors, 'ye nede nat to meve me of such maters,
for well ye wote, I woll do what I may to please you.'

And than the noble knyght Sir Launcelot departed with ryght   100
hevy chere suddeynly, that no erthely creature wyst of hym nor
where he was becom but Sir Bors. So whan Sir Launcelot was
departed the quene outewarde made no maner of sorow in
shewyng to none of his bloode nor to none other, but wyte ye well,
inwardely, as the booke seythe, she toke grete thought; but she   105
bare hit oute with a proude countenaunce, as thoughe she felte
no thynge nor thought no daungere.

So the quene lete make a pryvy dynere in London unto the
knyghtes of the Rownde Table, and all was for to shew out-
warde that she had as grete joy in all other knyghtes of the   110

---

83 *ermyte*, hermit
86 *Brother* (C)   *wyte you*, know
87–8 *defended . . . hyghly*, forbidden . . . strictly
90 *or*, ere
95 *hyre*, hear
98 *meve*, persuade   *of*, in
99 *wote*, know
100–1 *with ryght hevy chere*, in a most downcast way
101 *wyst*, knew
102 *becom*, gone
103–4 *in shewyng*, in appearance
104 See C.
105 *toke grete thought*, fell into deep dejection
107 *daungere*, danger
108 *lete make*, arranged (lit. 'had made')

Rounde Table as she had in Sir Launcelot. So there was all only
at that dyner Sir Gawayne and his brethern, that ys for to sey,
Sir Aggravayne, Sir Gaherys, Sir Gareth, and Sir Mordred.
Also there was Sir Bors de Ganis, Sir Blamour de Ganys, Sir
Bleobris de Ganys, Sir Galihud, Sir Galyhodyn, Sir Ector de   115
Maris, Sir Lyonell, Sir Palamydes, Sir Safyr his brothir, Sir
La Cote Male Tayle, Sir Persaunte, Sir Ironsyde, Sir Braundeles, Sir Kay le Senysciall, Sir Madore de la Porte, Sir Patrise
a knyght of Irelonde, Sir Alyduke, Sir Ascamoure, and Sir
Pynell le Saveayge, whych was cosyne to Sir Lameroke de Galis,   120
the good knyght that Sir Gawayne and hys brethirn slew by
treson. And so thes four-and-twenty knyghtes sholde dyne with
the quene in a prevy place by themselff, and there was made a
grete feste of all maner of deyntees.

But Sir Gawayne had a custom that he used dayly at mete and   125
at supper: that he loved well all maner of fruyte, and in especiall
appyls and pearys. And therefore whosomever dyned other
fested Sir Gawayne wolde comonly purvey for good fruyte for
hym; and so ded the quene: for to please Sir Gawayne she lette
purvey for hym all maner of fruyte. For Sir Gawayne was a   130
passyng hote knyght of nature, and thys Sir Pyonell hated Sir
Gawayne bycause of hys kynnesman Sir Lamorakes dethe; and
therefore, for pure envy and hate, Sir Pyonell enpoysonde sertayn
appylls for to enpoysen Sir Gawayne.

So thys was well yet unto the ende of mete, and so hit befylle   135
by myssefortune a good knyght, Sir Patryse, which was cosyn
unto Sir Mador de la Porte, toke an appyll, for he was enchaffed with hete of wyne. And hit myssehapped hym to take a
poysonde apple. And whan he had etyn hit he swall sore tylle he
braste, and there Sir Patryse felle downe suddeynly dede amonge   140

---

[111] *all only*, these and only these (lit. 'alonely')
[112–20] See C.
[122] *sholde*, were to
[123] *prevy*, private
[124] *deyntees*, delicacies
[125] *used*, observed, kept to   *mete*, dinner
[127] *other*, or
[129–30] *lette purvey*, had had provided
[131] *hote*, hot-tempered
[133] *pure*, sheer
[135] *thys was*, understand 'things were'
[137–8] *enchaffed*, heated (cf. l. 1048n below)
[139] *etyn*, eaten   *swall*, swelled

hem. Than every knyght lepe frome the bourde ashamed and
araged for wratthe oute of hir wittis, for they wyst nat what to sey;
considerynge Queen Gwenyvere made the feste and dyner they
had all suspeccion unto hir.

'My lady the quene!' seyde Sir Gawayne. 'Madam, wyte you   145
that thys dyner was made for me and my felowis, for all folkes
that knowith my condicion undirstonde that I love well fruyte.
And now I se well I had nere be slayne. Therefore, madam, I
drede me leste ye woll be shamed.'

Than the quene stood stylle and was so sore abaysshed that   150
she wyst nat what to sey.

'Thys shall nat so be ended,' seyde Sir Mador de la Porte, 'for
here have I loste a full noble knyght of my bloode, and therefore
upon thys shame and dispite I woll be revenged to the utteraunce!'

accused And there opynly Sir Mador appeled the quene of the deth   155
of hys cousyn Sir Patryse. Than stood they all stylle, that none
wolde speke a worde ayenste hym, for they all had grete suspeccion unto the quene bycause she lete make that dyner. And
the quene was so abaysshed that she cowde none otherwayes do
but wepte so hartely that she felle on a swowghe. So with thys   160
noyse and crye cam to them Kynge Arthure, and whan he wyste
of the trowble he was a passyng hevy man. And ever Sir Madore
stood stylle before the kynge and appeled the quene of treson.
(For the custom was such at that tyme that all maner of shamefull deth was called treson.)   165

'Fayre lordys,' seyd Kynge Arthure, 'me repentith of thys
trouble, but the case ys so I may nat have ado in thys mater, for
I muste be a ryghtfull juge. And that repentith me that I may
nat do batayle for my wyff, for, as I deme, thys dede com never

---

[141] *lepe*, leapt
[142] *araged for wratthe out of hir wittis*, driven (lit. 'enraged') out of their minds by
anger (C)   *for*, and
[143-4] *they had all*, they had all
[146] *for*, and (C)
[149] *shamed*, disgracefully exposed
[154] *dispite*, insult   *to the utterance*, to the death (lit. 'to the uttermost'; Fr. *à l' outrance*)
[155] *opynly*, openly   *appeled*, accused (C)
[160] *hartely*, passionately   *felle on a swowghe*, fainted
[161] *crye*, uproar
[166-7] *me repentith of thys trouble*, this trouble grieves me   See C and cf. ll. 516 and
773.
[167] *have ado*, act (i.e. fight)
[169] *deme*, believe   *com*, came

by her. And therefor I suppose she shall nat be all distayned, but 170
that somme good knyght shall put hys body in jouperté for my
quene rather than she sholde be brente in a wronge quarell. And
therefore, Sir Madore, be nat so hasty; for, perdé, hit may
happyn she shall nat be all frendeles. And therefore desyre thou
thy day of batayle, and she shall purvey hir of som good knyght 175
that shall answere you, other ellis hit were to me grete shame,
and to all my courte.'

'My gracious lorde,' seyde Sir Madore, 'ye muste holde me
excused, for thoughe ye be oure kynge, in that degré ye ar but a
knyght as we are, and ye ar sworne unto knyghthode als welle 180
as we be. And therefore I beseche you that ye be nat displeased,
for there ys none of all thes four-and-twenty knyghtes that were
bodyn to thys dyner but all they have grete suspeccion unto the
quene. What sey ye all, my lordys?' seyde Sir Madore.

Than they answerde by and by and seyde they coude nat 185
excuse the quene for why she made the dyner, and other hit
muste com by her other by her servauntis.

'Alas,' seyde the quene, 'I made thys dyner for a good entente
and never for none evyll, so Allmyghty Jesu helpe me in my
ryght, as I was never purposed to do such evyll dedes, and that I 190
reporte me unto God.'

'My lorde the kynge,' seyde Sir Madore, 'I requyre you, as ye
beth a ryghteuous kynge, gyffe me my day that I may have
justyse.'

'Well,' seyde the kynge, 'I gyve the the day thys day fiftene 195
dayes, that thou be redy armed on horsebak in the medow besydes Wynchestir. And if hit so falle that there be ony knyght to
encountir ayenste you, there may you do youre beste, and God

---

170 *distayned*, dishonoured (lit. 'stained')
171 *jouperté*, jeopardy (Fr. *jeu parti*)
172 *wronge quarell*, unjust trial
173 *perdé*, by God (Fr. *par Dieu*)
175 *purvey hir of*, provide herself with, obtain
178–9 See C. *in that degré*, in this respect (i.e., as the husband of the accused)
180 *als*, as
183 *bodyn*, bidden
185 *by and by*, at once
186 *for why*, because
186–7 *other . . . other*, either . . . or
189–90 *my right*, my [cause, which has] justice [on its side] (C)
191 *report me unto God*, call God to witness
193 *beth*, are   *gyffe*, appoint
195 *the the*, you (lit. 'thee') the

spede the ryght. And if so befalle that there be no knyght redy at that day, than muste my quene be brente, and there she shall be redy to have hir jugemente.' 200

'I am answerde,' seyde Sir Mador.

And every knyght yode where hym lyked. So whan the kyng and the quene were togidirs the kynge asked the quene how this case befelle. Than the quene seyde, 'Sir, as Jesu be my helpe!' 205 She wyst nat how, nother in what manere.

'Where ys Sir Launcelot?' seyde kynge Arthure. 'And he were here he wolde nat grucche to do batayle for you.'

'Sir,' seyde the quene, 'I wote nat where he ys, but hys brother and hys kynnesmen deme that he be nat within thys 210 realme.'

'That me repentith,' seyde Kyng Arthure, 'for and he were here, he wolde sone stynte thys stryffe. Well, than I woll counceyle you,' seyde the kyng, 'that ye go unto Sir Bors and pray hym for to do batayle for you for Sir Launcelottis sake, and 215 uppon my lyff he woll nat refuse you. For well I se', seyde the kynge, 'that none of the four-and-twenty knyghtes that were at your dyner where Sir Patryse was slayne woll do batayle for you, nother none of hem woll sey well of you, and that shall be grete sclaundir to you in thys courte.' 220

'Allas,' seyde the quene, 'and I may not do withalle, but now I mysse Sir Launcelot, for and he were here he wolde sone putte me in my hartis ease.'

'What aylith you,' seyde the kynge, 'that ye can nat kepe Sir Launcelot uppon youre syde? For wyte you well,' seyde the 225 kynge, 'who that hath Sir Launcelot uppon his party hath the moste man of worship in thys worlde uppon hys syde. Now go youre way,' seyde the kynge unto the quene, 'and requyre Sir Bors to do batayle for you for Sir Launcelottis sake.'

---

199 *spede*, prosper
201 *jugement*, execution of sentence
203 *yode*, went
206 *nother*, nor
207 *and*, if
208 *grucche to do*, make difficulties about doing
213 *sone*, soon   *stynte*, stop
214 *pray*, ask
217 *none* (C)
221 *and I may not do withalle*, that I can't do anything about that
224–5 See C.

So the quene departed frome the kynge and sente for Sir Bors 230
into her chambir. And whan he cam she besought hym of succour.

'Madam,' seyde he, 'what wolde ye that I ded? For I may nat
with my worship have ado in thys mater, because I was at the
same dyner, for drede that ony of tho knyghtes wolde have me in 235
suspeccion.

'Also, madam,' seyde Sir Bors, 'now mysse ye Sir Launcelot,
for he wolde nat a fayled you in youre ryght nother in youre
wronge, as ye have wel preved, for whan ye have bene in ryght
grete daungers he hath succoured you; and now ye have drevyn 240
hym oute of thys contrey by whom ye and all we were dayly
worshipped by; therefore, madame, I mervayle how ye dare for
shame to requyre me to do onythynge for you, insomuche ye have
enchaced hym oute of your courte by whom we were up borne
and honoured.' 245

'Alas, fayre knyght,' seyde the quene, 'I put me holé in youre
grace, and all that ys done amysse I woll amende as ye woll
counceyle me.' And therewith she kneled downe upon both hir
kneys and besought Sir Bors to have mercy uppon her, 'other
ellis I shall have a shamefull dethe, and thereto I never offended.' 250

Ryght so cam Kynge Arthure and founde the quene knelynge
afore Sir Bors. And than Sir Bors toke hir up and seyde, 'Madam,
ye do me grete dishonoure.'

'A, jantill knyght,' seyde the kynge, 'have mercy uppon my
quene, curteyse knyght, for I am now in sertayne she ys untruly 255
defamed. And therefore, curteyse knyght,' the kynge seyde,
'promyse her to do batayle for her, I requyre you, for the love
ye owghe unto Sir Launcelot.'

'My lord,' seyde Sir Bors, 'ye requyre me the grettist thynge
that ony man may requyre me. And wyte you well, if I graunte 260

230–1 *sente for . . . into*, sent for . . . [to come] into
233–45 See C.
234 *worship*, honour
238 *a*, have
238–9 *in youre ryght nother in youre wronge*, whether you were in the right or in the
wrong, cf. ll. 189–90
239 *preved*, discovered by experience   *for*, and
241–2 *by whom ye . . . were . . . worshipped by*, from whom you . . . gained honour; the
second *by* is redundant.
244 *enchaced*, driven
246 *holé*, wholly
250 *thereto*, either 'moreover' or 'so as to deserve that'
255 *am in sertayne*, am sure

to do batayle for the quene I shall wretth many of my felyship of
the Table Rounde. But as for that,' seyde Sir Bors, 'I woll
graunte my lorde that for my lorde Sir Launcelottis sake, and
for youre sake : I woll at that day be the quenys champyon, onles
there com by adventures a better knyght than I am to do batayle   265
for her.'

'Woll ye promyse me this,' seyde the kynge, 'by youre fayth?'

'Yee, sir,' seyd Sir Bors, 'of that I shall nat fayle you nother her,
but if there com a bettir knyght than I am : than shall he have
the batayle.'   270

Than was the kynge and the quene passynge gladde, and so
departed and thanked hym hertely.

Than Sir Bors departed secretly upon a day and rode unto
Sir Launcelot thereas he was with the heremyte Sir Brastias, and
tolde hym of all thys adventure.   275

'A, Jesu,' Sir Launcelot seyde, 'thys ys com happely as I wolde
have hit. And therefore I pray you make you redy to do batayle,
but loke that ye tarry tylle ye se me com as longe as ye may. For
I am sure Sir Madore ys an hote knyght whan he ys inchaffed,
for the more ye suffyr hym the hastyer woll he be to batayle.'   280

'Sir,' seyde Sir Bors, 'latte me deale with hym. Doute ye nat ye
shall have all youre wylle.'

So departed Sir Bors frome hym and cam to the courte agayne.
Than was hit noysed in all the courte that Sir Bors sholde do
batayle for the quene, wherefore many knyghtes were displeased   285
with hym that he wolde take uppon hym to do batayle in the
quenys quarell; for there were but fewe knyghtes in all the
courte but they demed the quene was in the wronge and that she
had done that treson. So Sir Bors answered thus to hys felowys of
the Table Rounde: 290

'Wete you well, my fayre lordis, hit were shame to us all and
we suffird to se the moste noble quene of the worlde to be shamed

261 *wretth*, anger
265 *by adventures*, by [any] chance
268 *Yee*, Yes (lit. 'Yea')
269 *but if*, unless
271 *was*, were
271–2 See C.
273 *uppon a day*, on a certain day
274 *thereas*, where
276 *happely*, by a lucky chance
284 *noysed*, rumoured
291 *and*, if
292 *we suffird*, we allowed ourselves   *of*, in

opynly, consyderyng her lorde and oure lorde ys the man of
moste worship of the worlde and moste crystynde, and he hath
ever worshipped us all in all placis.'   295

Many answerd hym agayne: 'As for oure moste noble Kynge
Arthure, we love hym and honoure hym as well as ye do; but as
for Quene Gwenyvere, we love hir nat, because she ys a destroyer of good knyghts.'

'Fayre lordis,' seyde Sir Bors, 'mesemyth ye sey nat as ye   300
sholde sey, for never yet in my dayes knew I never ne harde sey
that ever she was a destroyer of good knyghtes, but at all tymes,
as far as ever I coude know, she was a maynteyner of good
knyghtes; and ever she hath bene large and fre of hir goodis to all
good knyghtes, and the moste bownteuous lady of hir gyfftis and 305
her good grace that ever I saw other harde speke off. And therefore hit were shame to us all and to oure moste noble kynges
wyff whom we serve and we suffred her to be shamefully slayne.
And wete you well,' seyde Sir Bors, 'I woll nat suffir hit, for I dare
sey so much, for the quene ys nat gylty of Sir Patryseys dethe: 310
for she ought hym never none evyll wyll nother none of the four-
and-twenty knyghtes that were at that dyner, for I dare sey for
good love she bade us to dyner and nat for no male engyne. And
that, I doute nat, shall be preved hereafftir, for howsomever the
game goth, there was treson amonge us.'   315

Than some seyde to Bors, 'We may well belyve youre wordys.'
And so somme were well pleased and some were nat.

So the day com on faste untyll the evyn that the batayle sholde
be. Than the quene sente for Sir Bors and asked hym how he was
disposed.   320

'Truly, madame,' seyde he, 'I am disposed in lykewyse as I

293-4 *the man of most worship of the worlde and moste crystynde,* the most honourable man
in the world and the most [honourable man] christened (C)
300-15 See C.
300 *mesemyth,* it seems to me
301 *ne,* nor (C)   *harde sey,* heard it said
303 *maynteyner,* supporter (C)
304 *large,* generous   *of,* with
308 *and,* if
311 *ought,* owed
312-13 *for good love,* in all sincerity
313 *nat for no,* not for any   *male engyne,* evil machination (Fr. *mal engin*)
314 *preved,* found (lit. 'proved')
314-15 *howsomever the game goth* (C)
315 *treson,* deceit
318-19 *the evyn that the batayle sholde be,* the eve of battle, the evening before the day of
battle

promysed you, that ys to sey I shall natt fayle you onles there by
aventure com a bettir knyght than I am to do batayle for you.
Than, madam, I am of you discharged of my promyse.'

'Woll ye,' seyde the quene, 'that I telle my lorde the kyng   325
thus?'

'Doth as hit pleasith you, madam.'

Than the quene yode unto the kyng and tolde hym the
answere of Sir Bors.

'Well, have ye no doute,' seyde the kynge, 'of Sir Bors, for I   330
calle hym now that ys lyvynge one of the nobelyst knyghtes of the
worlde, and moste perfitist man.'

And thus hit paste on tylle the morne, and so the kynge and
the quene and all manner of knyghtes that were there at that
tyme drewe them unto the medow bysydys Wynchester where   335
the batayle shold be. And so whan the kynge was com with the
quene and many knyghtes of the Table Rounde, so the quene
was than put in the Conestablis awarde and a grete fyre made
aboute an iron stake, that an Sir Madore de la Porte had the
bettir, she sholde there be brente. For such custom was used in   340
tho dayes: for favoure, love, nother affinité there sholde be none
other but ryghtuous jugemente, as well uppon a kynge as uppon
a knyght, and as well uppon a quene as uppon another poure
lady.

So thys meanewhyle cam in Sir Madore de la Porte and toke   345
hys othe before the kynge, how that the quene ded thys treson
untill hys cosyn Sir Patryse, 'and unto myne othe I woll preve hit
with my body, honde for hande, who that woll sey the contrary.'

Ryght so cam in Sir Bors de Ganys and seyde that 'as for
Quene Gwenivere, she ys in the ryght, and that woll I make   350
good with my handes that she ys nat culpable of thys treson that
is put uppon her.'

'Than make the redy,' seyde Sir Madore, 'and we shall preve
whethir thou be in the ryght or I!'

---

327 *Doth*, Do
328 *yode*, went
331-2 See C.
338 *Conestablis*, Constable's (C)   *awarde*, ward, guard
339 *an*, if
341 *tho*, those   *nother*, nor   *affinité*, affinity, kinship
343-4 Understand: 'as well uppon a queen as uppon another lady, who was poor'
345 See C.
347 *untill*, unto   *unto*, according to
348 *who that*, whosoever
353 *the*, yourself

'Sir Madore,' seyde Sir Bors, 'wete you well, I know you for a 355
good knyght. Natforthan I shall nat feare you so gretly but I
truste to God I shall be able to withstonde youre malyce. But
thus much have I promised my lorde Arthure and my lady the
quene, that I shall do batayle for her in thys cause to the utter-
myste, onles that there com a bettir knyght than I am and dis- 360
charge me.'

'Is that all?' seyde Sir Madore. 'Othir com thou off and do
batayle with me, other elles sey nay.'

'Take youre horse,' seyde Sir Bors, 'and, as I suppose, I shall
nat tarry long but ye shall be answerde.' 365

Than ayther departed to their tentis and made hem redy to
horsebacke as they thought beste. And anone Sir Madore cam
into the fylde with hys shylde on hys shulder and hys speare in
hys honde, and so rode aboute the place cryyng unto Kyng
Arthure, 'Byd youre champyon com forthe and he dare!' 370

Than was Sir Bors ashamed, and toke hys horse and cam to the
lystis ende. And than was he ware where cam frome a woode
there fast by a knyght all armed uppon a whyght horse, with a
straunge shylde of straunge armys, and he cam dryvyng all that
hys horse myght renne. And so he cam to Sir Bors and seyd thus: 375
'Fayre knyght, I pray you be nat displeased, for here muste a
bettir knyght than ye ar have thys batayle. Therefore I pray you
withdraw you, for wyte you well I have had thys day a right
grete journey and thys batayle ought to be myne. And so I
promysed you whan I spake with you laste, and with all my herte 380
I thanke you of youre good wylle.'

Than Sir Bors rode unto Kynge Arthure and tolde hym how
there was a knyght com that wolde have the batayle to fyght for
the quene.

'What knyght ys he?' seyde the kyng. 385

'I wote nat,' seyde Sir Bors, 'but suche covenaunte he made
with me to be here thys day. Now, my lorde,' seyde Sir Bors, 'here
I am discharged.'

---

³⁵⁶ *Natforthan,* Nevertheless (lit. 'not for that')
³⁵⁷ *malyce,* hostility (without overtones of moral evil)
³⁶⁶ *ayther,* each (C)
³⁷² *lystis,* lists' (C)
³⁷³ *there fast by,* fast by that place, nearby   *all armed,* completely armed
³⁷⁴ *straunge,* unknown   *dryvyng,* spurring   *all that,* as fast as
³⁸¹ *wylle,* intention

Than the kynge called to that knyght and asked hym if he
wolde fyght for the quene. 390
Than he answerd and seyde, 'Sir, therefore com I hyddir.
And therefore, sir kynge,' he seyde, 'tarry me no lenger, for I may
not tarry, for anone as I have fynysshed thys batayle I muste
departe hens, for I have to do many batayles elswhere. For wyte
you well,' seyde that knyght, 'thys ys dishonoure to you and to all 395
knyghtes of the Rounde Table to se and know so noble a lady
and so curteyse a quene as Quene Gwenyvere ys, thus to be rebuked and shamed amongyst you.'
Than they all mervayled what knyght that myght be that so
toke the batayle uppon hym, for there was nat one that knew 400
hym but if hit were Sir Bors. Than seyde Sir Madore de la
Porte unto the kynge, 'Now lat me wete with whom I shall have
ado.'
And than they rode to the lystes ende, and there they cowched
their spearis and ran togydirs with all their myghtes. And anone 405
Sir Madors speare brake all to pecis, but the othirs speare hylde
and bare Sir Madors horse and all backwarde to the erthe a
grete falle. But myghtyly and delyverly he avoyded his horse
from hym and put hys shylde before hym and drew hys swerde
and bade the othir knyght alyght and do batayle with hym on 410
foote.
Than that knyght descended downe frome hys horse lyghtly
lyke a valyaunt man, and put hys shylde before hym and drew
hys swerde; and so they cam egirly unto batayle, and aythir gaff
othir many sadde strokes, trasyng and traversyng, racynge and 415
foynying, and hurtlyng togydir with their swerdis as hit were
wylde boorys. Thus were they fyghtyng nyghe an owre; for thys
Sir Mador was a stronge knyght and myghtyly preved in many

391 *hyddir*, here (lit. 'hither')
392 *tarry*, delay
393 *anone as*, as soon as
394 *hens*, from here (lit. 'hence')   *For*, And
397-8 *rebuked*, disgraced
401 *but if*, unless
402 *wete*, know
404 *cowched*, put into the rest (C)
406 *brake*, broke   *to*, into   *hylde*, held [firm]
408 *delyverly*, nimbly (C)   *avoyded*, free
414 *egirly*, fiercely
415 See C.   *sadde*, heavy (not 'sad')
417 *boorys*, boars
418 *preved*, proved, tested

stronge batayles. But at the laste thys knyght smote Sir Madore
grovelynge uppon the erthe, and the knyghte stepte nere hym to   420
have pulde Sir Madore flatlynge uppon the grounde. And therewith sodeynly Sir Madore arose, and in hys rysyng he smote that
knyght thorow the thyk of the thyghes, that the bloode braste
oute fyersly. And whan he felte hymself so wounded and saw hys
bloode, he lete hym aryse uppon hys feete; and than he gaff hym   425
such a buffette uppon the helme that he felle to the erthe flatlyng,
and therewith he strode to hym to have pulled of hys helme of
hys hede. And so Sir Madore prayde that knyght to save hys lyff.
And so he yeldyd hym as overcom, and releaced the quene of hys
quarell.   430

'I woll nat graunte the thy lyff,' seyde that knyght, 'only that
thou frely release the quene for ever, and that no mencion be
made uppon Sir Patryseys tombe that ever Quene Gwenyver consented to that treson.'

'All thys shall be done,' seyde Sir Madore. 'I clerely discharge   435
my quarell for ever.'

Than the knyghtes parters of the lystis toke up Sir Madore and
led hym tylle hys tente, and the othir knyght wente strayte to the
stayre-foote where sate Kynge Arthure. And by that tyme was the
quene com to the kyng and aythir kyssed othir hartely. And   440
whan the kynge saw that knyght he stowped downe to hym and
thanked hym, and in lyke wyse ded the quene; and the kynge
prayde hym to put of his helmet and to repose hym and to take
a soppe of wyne. And than he putte of hys helmette to drynke,
and than every knyght knew hym that hit was Sir Launcelot.   445
And anone as the kyng wyst that, he toke the quene in hys honde
and yode unto Sir Launcelot and seyde, 'Sir, grauntemercy of
youre grete travayle that ye have had this day for me and for my
quyene.'

---

419 *stronge*, fierce
420 *grovelynge*, on his hands and knees
421 *flatlynge*, on his stomach, prostrate
422 See C.
426 *buffette*, blow
427 *of*, off
428 *prayde*, begged (C)
431 *only that*, unless
437 *knyghtes parters of the lystis*, officers of the lists (C)
438 *tylle*, to
444 *soppe of wine* (C)
446 *anone as*, as soon as   *in hys*, understand 'by the'
447 *grauntemercy*, many thanks (Fr. *grand merci*) (C)

'My lorde,' seyde Sir Launcelot, 'wytte you well y ought of   450
ryght ever to be in youre quarell and in my ladyes the quenys
quarell to do batayle, for ye ar the man that gaff me the hygh
Order of Knyghthode, and that day my lady, youre quene, ded
me worshyp, and ellis had I bene shamed. For that same day
that ye made me knyght, thorow my hastynes I loste my swerde,   455
and my lady youre quene founde hit, and lapped hit in her
trayne, and gave me my swerde whan I had nede thereto; and
ells had I bene shamed amonge all knyghtes. And therefore, my
lorde Arthure, I promysed her at that day ever to be her knyght
in ryght othir in wronge.'   460
'Grauntemercy,' seyde the kynge, 'for this journey. And wete
you well,' seyde the kynge, 'I shall acquyte youre goodnesse.'
And evermore the quene behylde Sir Launcelot, and wepte so
tendirly that she sanke allmoste to the grownde for sorow that he
had done to her so grete kyndenes where she shewed hym grete   465
unkyndenesse. Than the knyghtes of hys bloode drew unto hym,
and there aythir of them made grete joy of othir. And so cam all
the knyghtes of the Table Rounde that were there at that tyme
and wellcommed hym.
And than Sir Madore was had to lechecrauffte, and Sir   470
Launcelot was heled of hys play. And so there was made grete
joy, and many merthys there was made in that courte.
And so hit befelle that the Damesell of the Lake that hyght
Nynyve, whych wedded the good knyght Sir Pelleas, and so she
cam to the courte, for ever she ded grete goodnes unto Kynge   475
Arthure and to all hys knyghtes thorow her sorsery and en-
chauntementes. And so whan she herde how the quene was
greved for the dethe of Sir Patryse, than she tolde hit opynly
that she was never gylty; and there she disclosed by whom hit

450-1 *of ryght,* in justice
451 *in youre quarell,* on your side
456 *lapped,* wrapped
457 *gave me my swerde* (C)
460 *in ryght othir in wronge* (C)
461 *journey,* day's work (i.e. in fighting; Fr. *journée*)
462 *acquyte,* requite, reward
470 *was had to lechecrauffte,* was given (lit. 'was had into') medical treatment (See C
and l. 804)
471 *play,* wound (Fr. *plaie*)
473 *hyght,* was called
474 *and so she* is redundant
476 *sorsery,* magic
478 *greved for,* harassed because of

was done, and named hym Sir Pynel; and for what cause he ded   480
hit, there hit was opynly knowyn and disclosed. And so the
quene was excused, and thys knyght Sir Pynell fledde unto hys
contrey, and was opynly knowyn that he enpoysynde the appyls
at that feste to that entente to have destroyed Sir Gawayne,
bycause Sir Gawayne and hys brethirne destroyed Sir Lamerok   485
de Galys which Sir Pynell was cosyn unto.

Than was Sir Patryse buryed in the chirche of Westemynster
in a towmbe, and thereuppon was wrytten: 'Here lyeth Sir
Patryse of Irelonde, slayne by Sir Pynell le Saveaige, that enpoysynde appelis to have slayne Sir Gawayne, and by mysse-   490
fortune Sir Patryse ete one of the applis, and than suddeynly he
braste.' Also there was wrytyn uppon the tombe that Quene
Gwenyvere was appeled of treson of the deth of Sir Patryse by
Sir Madore de la Porte, and there was made the mencion how
Sir Launcelot fought with hym for Quene Gwenyvere and over-   495
com hym in playne batayle. All thys was wretyn uppon the
tombe of Sir Patryse in excusyng of the quene.

And than Sir Madore sewed dayly and longe to have the
quenys good grace, and so by the meanys of Sir Launcelot he
caused hym to stonde in the quenys good grace, and all was for- 500
gyffyn.

II

Thus hit passed untyll Oure Lady Day of the Assumpcion.
Within a fiftene dayes of that feste the kynge lete crye a grete
justyse and a turnement that sholde be at that day at Camelott,
otherwyse callyd Wynchester, and the kyng lete cry that he and 505

482 *excused*, cleared of all guilt
483 See C.
492 *braste*, burst
496 *playne*, open
498 *sewed*, sought
499 *by the meanys of*, by the good offices of
499-500 *he* is Lancelot, *hym* Mador
502 *Oure Lady Day of the Assumpcion*, the Feast of the Assumption of the Blessed Virgin
Mary: 15th August
503 *a fiftene dayes*, a fortnight (C)   *lete crye*, had proclaimed
504 *a justyse*, a jousting (lit. 'a jousts') (C)   *sholde be*, would be
504-5 *Camelott otherwyse callyd Wynchester* (C)

the Kynge of Scottes wolde juste ayenst all that wolde come ageynst them. And whan thys cry was made, thydir cam many good knyghtes, that ys to sey the Kynge of North Galis, and Kynge Angwysh of Irelonde, and the Kynge with the Hondred Knyghtes, and Syr Galahalte the Haute Prynce, and the Kynge 510 of Northumbirlonde, and many other noble deukes and erlis of other dyverse contreyes.

So Kynge Arthure made hym redy to departe to hys justis, and wolde have had the quene with hym; but at that tyme she wolde nat, she seyde, for she was syke and myght nat ryde. 515

'That me repentith,' seyde the kynge, 'for thys seven yere ye saw nat such a noble felyship togydirs excepte the Whytsontyde whan Sir Galahad departed frome the courte.'

'Truly,' seyde the quene, 'ye muste holde me excused. Y may nat be there, and that me repentith.' 520

And many demed the quene wolde nat be there because of Sir Launcelot, for he wolde nat ryde with the kynge; for he seyde he was nat hole of the play of Sir Madore. Wherefore the kynge was hevy and passynge wroth, and so he departed towarde Wynchestir with hys felyship. And so by the way the kynge lodged at 525 a towne that was called Astolot, that ys now in Englysh callyd Gylforde, and there the kynge lay in the castell.

So whan the kynge was departed the quene called Sir Launcelot unto her and seyde thus: 'Sir, ye ar gretly to blame thus to holde you behynde my lorde. What, trowe ye, what woll youre 530 enemyes and myne sey and deme? Noughte else but "Se how Sir Launcelot holdith hym ever behynde the kynge, and so the quene doth also, for that they wolde have their plesure togydirs." And thus woll they sey,' seyde the quene.

---

[507] *cry*, proclamation
[508-12] See C.
[513] *justis*, jousting
[515] *syke*, sick
[516] *That me repentith*, I am sorry about that (lit. 'That causes regret to me'); cf. l. 166
[517-18] See C.
[522] *he seyde* (C)
[523] *hole*, whole, recovered   *play*, wound
[524] *hevy and passynge wroth* (C)
[526-7] *Astolot that ys now in Englysh callyd Gylforde* (C)
[527] See C.   *lay*, took up residence in
[529-34] See C.
[530] *holde you behynde*, stay behind   *trowe ye*, do you think

'Have ye no doute thereof, madame,' seyde Sir Launcelot.   535
'I alow youre witte. Hit ys of late com syn ye were woxen so
wyse! And therefore, madam, at thys tyme I woll be ruled by
youre counceyle, and thys nyght I woll take my reste, and to-
morow betyme I woll take my way towarde Wynchestir. But
wytte you well,' seyde Sir Launcelot unto the quene, 'at that   540
justys I woll be ayenste the kynge and ayenst all hys felyship.'

'Sir, ye may there do as ye lyste,' seyde the quene, 'but be my
counceyle ye shall nat be ayenste youre kynge and your felyshyp.
For there bene full many hardé knyghtes of youre bloode as ye
wote well ynough, hit nedeth not to reherce them.'   545

'Madame,' seyde Sir Launcelot, 'I praye you that ye be not
displeasyd with me, for I shall take the adventure that God woll
gyff me.'

And so uppon the morne erly he harde masse and brake hys
faste, and so he toke hys leve of the quene and departed. And than   550
he rode so muche unto the tyme he cam to Astolott, and there hit
happynd hym that in the evenyng-tyde he com to an olde barownes place that hyght Sir Barnarde of Astolot. And as Sir Launcelot entird into hys lodgynge, Kynge Arthure aspyed hym as he
dud walke in a gardeyne besyde the castell how he took hys   555
lodgynge: he knew hym welle inow.

'Well, sirs,' seyde Kynge Arthure unto hys knyghtes that were
with hym in that gardeyne besyde the castell, 'I have now aspyed
one knyght,' he seyde, 'that woll play hys play at the justys to
whiche we be gone towarde, I undirtake he wil do merveils.'   560

'Who ys that, we pray you telle us?' seyde many knyghtes that
were there at that tyme.

535-41 See C.
536 *alow*, praise   *witte*, wisdom (lit. 'intelligence')   *syn ye were*, understand
'that you are' (lit. 'since you were')   *woxen*, grown (lit. 'waxed')
539 *betyme*, early
542 *lyste*, wish   *be*, by
544 *hardé*, bold and enduring
545 *reherce them*, repeat their names
547-8 See C.
549 *harde*, heard
552-3 *an olde barownes place that hyght Sir Bernarde*, the house of an old baron who was
called Sir Bernard
554 *aspyed*, espied
556 *inow*, enough
559 *play his play*, play his game (metaphorical)
560 *I undirtake*, I assure you (lit. 'I take it upon myself')

'Ye shall nate wyte for me!' seyde the kynge, 'at thys tyme.'
And so the kynge smyled, and wente to hys lodgynge.

So whan Sir Launcelot was in hys lodgyng and unarmed in hys   565
chambir, the olde barown, Sir Barnarde, com to hym makynge
hys reverence and wellcomed hym in the beste maner. But he
knew nat Sir Launcelot.

'Fayre sir,' seyde Sir Launcelot tylle hys oste, 'I wolde pray
you to lende me a shylde that were nat opynly knowyn, for myne   570
ys well knowyn.'

'Sir,' seyde hys oste, 'ye shall have youre desire, for mesemyth
ye bene one of the lyklyest knyghtes that ever y sawe, and therefore, sir, I shall shew you freynship.' And he seyde, 'Sir, wyte
you well I have two sunnes that were but late made knyghtes.   575
and the eldist hyght Sir Tirry, and he was hurte that same day
he was made knyght, and he may nat ryde; and hys shylde ye
shalle have, for that ys nat knowyn, I dare sey, but here and in
no place else. And my yongest sonne hyght Sir Lavayne, and if
hit please you he shall ryde with you unto that justis, for he ys of   580
hys ayge stronge and wyght. For much my herte gyvith unto you,
that ye sholde be a noble knyght. And therefore I praye you to
telle me youre name,' seyde Sir Barnarde.

'As for that,' seyd Sir Launcelot, 'ye muste holde me excused
as at thys tyme, and if God gyff me grace to spede well at the   585
justis I shall com agayne and telle you my name. But I pray you
in ony wyse lete me have your sonne, Sir Lavayne, with me, and
that I may have hys brothers shylde.'

'Sir, all thys shall be done,' seyde Sir Barnarde.

So thys olde barown had a doughtir that was called that tyme   590
the Fayre Maydyn off Astolot, and ever she behylde Sir Launcelot wondirfully. And, as the booke sayth, she keste such a love
unto Sir Launcelot that she cowde never withdraw hir loove,
wherefore she dyed; and her name was Elayne le Blanke. So thus
as she cam to and fro, she was so hote in love that she besought   595

566-7 *makynge hys reverence*, bowing
570 *shylde*, shield
572 *mesemyth*, it seems to me
573 *lyklyest*, most promising
577 *may*, can
581 *wyght*, tough (C)   *my herte gyvith unto*, my heart inclines to
592 See C.   *wondirfully*, wonderingly   *keste*, gave (lit. 'cast')
594 *Elayne le Blanke*, Elaine la Blanche, Elaine the Fair (C)
595 *cam to and fro* (C)

Sir Launcelot to were uppon hym at the justis a tokyn of hers.

'Damesell,' seyde Sir Launcelot, 'and if I graunte you that, ye may sey that I do more for youre love than ever y ded for lady or jantillwoman.'

Than he remembird hymselff that he wolde go to the justis 600 disgysed, and because he had never aforne borne no maner of tokyn of no damesell, he bethought hym to bere a tokyn of hers, that none of hys bloode thereby myght know hym. And than he seyde, 'Fayre maydyn, I woll graunte you to were a tokyn of youres uppon myne helmet. And therefore what ys hit? Shewe 605 ye hit me.'

'Sir,' she seyde, 'hit ys a rede sleve of myne, of scarlet, well embrowdred with grete perelles.'

And so she brought hit hym. So Sir Launcelot resseyved hit and seyde, 'Never dud I erste so much for no damesell.' 610

Than Sir Launcelot betoke the fayre mayden hys shylde in kepynge, and prayde her to kepe hit untill tyme that he com agayne. And so that nyght he had myrry reste and grete chere, for thys damesell Elayne was ever aboute Sir Launcelot all the whyle she myght be suffirde. 615

So uppon a day, on the morne, Kynge Arthure and all hys knyghtis departed, for there the kyng had tarryed three dayes to abyde hys noble knyghtes. And so whan the kynge was rydden, Sir Launcelot and Sir Lavayne made them redy to ryde, and aythir of them had whyght shyldis, and the rede sleve Sir 620 Launcelot lete cary with hym. And so they toke their leve at Sir Barnarde, the olde barowne, and at hys doughtir, the Fayre Mayden of Astolat, and than they rode so longe tylle that they cam to Camelot, that tyme called Wynchester, and there was

596 *were*, wear   *tokyn*, token (C)
597 *and if*, if
598 *for your love*, for your sake (C)
600 *wolde*, intended to
601 *aforne*, before
601-2 *never ... no ... no*, never ... any ... any
602 *he bethought him to*, he made up his mind to, decided to
608 *perelles*, pearls
610 *erste*, before
611-12 *betoke ... in kepynge*, gave ... into [her] care
615 *suffirde*, allowed
617-18 *to abyde*, to wait for ... to arrive
618 *was rydden*, had ridden away
620 *whyght* (C)
621 *lete cary*, arranged to have carried
623 *tylle that*, until

grete pres of kyngis, deukes, erlis, and barownes, and many noble   625
knyghtes. But there Sir Launcelot was lodged pryvaly by the
meanys of Sir Lavayne with a ryche burgeyse, that no man in
that towne was ware what they were. And so they reposed them
there tyll Oure Lady Day of the Assumpcion that the grete justes
sholde be.   630

So whan trumpettis blew unto the fylde and Kynge Arthur was
sette on hyght uppon a chafflet to beholde who ded beste (but,
as the Freynshe booke seyth, the kynge wold nat suffir Sir
Gawayne to go frome hym, for never had Sir Gawayne the bettir
and Sir Launcelot were in the fylde, and many tymes was Sir   635
Gawayne rebuked so whan Sir Launcelot cam into ony justis
dysgysed), than som of the kyngis, as Kynge Angwysh of Irelonde
and the Kynge of Scottis, were that tyme turned to be uppon the
syde of Kynge Arthur. And than on the othir party was the
Kynge of North Galis, and the Kynge with the Hondred   640
Knyghtis, and the Kynge of Northumbirlonde, and Sir Galahalte the Halte Prynce. But thes three kyngis and thys duke was
passynge wayke to holde ayenste Kynge Arthurs party, for with
hym were the nobelyst knyghtes of the worlde. So than they
withdrew them, aythir party frome othir, and every man made   645
hym redy in his beste maner to do what he myght. Than Sir
Launcelot made hym redy and put the rede slyeve uppon hys
helmette and fastened hit faste.

And so Sir Launcelot and Sir Lavayne departed oute of
Wynchestir pryvayly and rode untyll a litill leved woode behynde   650
the party that hylde ayenste Kynge Arthurs party, and there
they hylde hem stylle tylle the partyes smote togydirs. And than
cam in the Kynge of Scottis and the Kynge of Irelonde on
Kynge Arthurs party, and ayenste them cam in the Kynge of
Northumbirlonde and the Kynge with the Hondred Knyghtes.   655

627 *burgeyse*, burgess
629 *that*, understand 'when'
632 *chafflet*, scaffold, platform
633 See C.
635 *and*, if
636 *rebuked so*, given such a setback
637 *as*, such as
642 *was*, were
643 *wayke*, weak
645 *aythir . . . othir*, each . . . the other
650 *leved*, leafy
652 See C.

And there began a grete medlé, and there the Kynge of
Scottis smote downe the Kynge of Northumbirlonde, and the
Kynge with the Hondred Knyghtes smote downe Kynge
Angwysh of Irelonde. Than Sir Palamydes, that was one Arthurs
party, he encountird with Sir Galahalte, and ayther of hem   660
smote downe othir, and aythir party halpe their lordys on horseback agayne. So there began a stronge assayle on bothe partyes.

And than com in Sir Braundyles, Sir Sagramoure le Desyrous,
Sir Dodynas le Saveayge, Sir Kay le Senesciall, Sir Gryffelet le
Fyze de Dieu, Sir Lucan de Butlere, Sir Bedwere, Sir Aggravayne,   665
Sir Gaherys, Sir Mordred, Sir Melyot de Logrys, Sir Ozanna le
Cure Hardy, Sir Saphyr, Sir Epynogrys, Sir Gallerowne of
Galeway. Alle thes fiftene knyghtes, that were knyghtes of the
Rounde Table, so thes with mo other cam in togydir and bete
abacke the Kynge off Northumbirlonde and the Kynge of North   670
Walys.

Whan Sir Launcelot saw thys, as he hoved in the lityll leved
wood, than he seyde unto Sir Lavayne, 'Se yondir ys a company
of good knyghtes, and they holde them togydirs as borys that
were chaced with doggis.'   675

'That ys trouth,' seyde Sir Lavayne.

'Now,' seyde Sir Launcelot, 'and ye woll helpe a lityll, ye shall
se yonder felyship that chacith now thes men on oure syde, that
they shall go as faste backwarde as they wente forewarde.'

'Sir, spare ye nat for my parte,' seyde Sir Lavayne, 'for I shall   680
do what I may.'

Than Sir Launcelot and Sir Lavayne cam in at the thyckyst
of the prees, and there Sir Launcelot smote downe Sir Brandeles,
Sir Sagramour, Sir Dodynas, Sir Kay, Sir Gryfflet, and all thys
he ded with one speare; and Sir Lavayne smote downe Sir Lucan   685
de Butlere and Sir Bedwere. And than Sir Launcelot gate another

---

656 *medlé*, melée, general engagement
659 *one*, on
661 *halpe*, helped
662 *assayle*, assault
668 *Galeway*, Galloway
669 *mo other*, others besides
670 *abacke*, backwarde
672 *hoved*, waited
674 See C.   *borys*, boars
676 *trouth*, true (lit. 'truth')
683 *prees*, crowd, crush
686 *gate*, got

grete speare, and there he smote downe Sir Aggravayne and Sir
Gaherys, Sir Mordred, Sir Melyot de Logrys; and Sir Lavayne
smote downe Sir Ozanna Le Cure Hardy. And than Sir Lancelot drew hys swerde, and there he smote on the ryght honde and   690
on the lyft honde, and by grete forse he unhorsed Sir Safir, Sir
Epynogrys, and Sir Galleron. And than the knyghtes of the Table
Rounde withdrew them abacke aftir they had gotyn their horsys
as well as they myght.

'A, mercy Jesu!' seyde Sir Gawayne. 'What knyght ys yondir   695
that doth so mervaylous dedys of armes in that fylde?'

'I wote what he ys,' seyde the kyng, 'but as at thys tyme I woll
nat name hym.'

'Sir,' seyde Sir Gawayne, 'I wolde sey hit were Sir Launcelot
by hys rydynge and hys buffettis that I se hym deale. But ever   700
mesemyth hit sholde nat be he, for that he beryth the rede slyve
uppon hys helmet; for I wyst hym never beare tokyn at no justys
of lady ne jantillwoman.'

'Lat hym be,' seyde Kynge Arthure, 'for he woll be bettir
knowyn and do more or ever he departe.'   705

Than the party that was ayenst Kynge Arthur were well com-
forted, and than they hylde hem togydirs that befornhande were
sore rebuked. Than Sir Bors, Sir Ector de Marys and Sir Lyonell, they called unto them the knyghtes of their blood, as Sir
Blamour de Ganys, Sir Bleoberys, Sir Alyduke, Sir Galyhud, Sir   710
Galyhodyn, Sir Bellyngere le Bewse. So thes nine knyghtes of Sir
Launcelottis kynne threst in myghtyly; for they were all noble
knyghtes, and they of grete hate and despite that they had unto
hym thought to rebuke that noble knyght Sir Launcelot and Sir
Lavayne, for they knew hem nat.   715

And so they cam hurlyng togydirs and smote downe many
knyghtes of North Walys and of Northumbirlonde. And whan
Sir Launcelot saw them fare so, he gate a grete speare in hys

---

693 *gotyn*, got (cf. American *gotten*)
695 See C.
697 *what*, who
701 *for that*, because
705 *or*, ere, before
712-16 See C.
712 *threst*, thrust
714 *rebuke*, shame
715 *hem*, them
716 *hurlyng*, hurtling

honde; and there encountird with hym all at onys, Sir Bors, Sir
Ector, and Sir Lyonell. And they alle three smote hym at onys   720
with their spearys, and with fors of themselff they smote Sir
Launcelottis horse revers to the erthe. And by myssefortune Sir
Bors smote Sir Launcelot thorow the shylde into the syde, and
the speare brake and the hede leffte stylle in the syde.

Whan Sir Lavayne saw hys mayster lye on the grounde he ran   725
to the Kynge of Scottis and smote hym to the erthe; and by
grete forse he toke hys horse and brought hym to Sir Launcelot,
and magré them all he made hym to mownte uppon that horse.
And then Sir Launcelot gate a speare in hys honde, and there he
smote Sir Bors, horse and man, to the erthe; and in the same   730
wyse he served Sir Ector and Sir Lyonell; and Sir Lavayne smote
downe Sir Blamour de Gaynys. And then Sir Launcelot drew hys
swerde, for he felte hymselff so sore hurte that he wente there to
have had hys deth. And than he smote Sir Bleoberis such a buffet
on the helmet that he felle downe to the erthe in a sowne, and in   735
the same wyse he served Sir Alyduke and Sir Galyhud; and Sir
Lavayne smote downe Sir Bellyngere, that was sone to Alysaunder le Orphelyn.

And by thys was done, was Sir Bors horsed agayne and in cam
with Sir Ector and Sir Lyonell, and all they three smote with their   740
swerdis uppon Sir Launcelottis helmet. And whan he felte their
buffettis, and with that hys wounde greved hym grevously, than
he thought to do what he myght whyle he cowde endure. And
than he gaff Sir Bors such a buffette that he made hym bowghe
hys hede passynge lowe; and therewithall he raced of hys helme,   745
and myght have slayne hym, but whan he saw his vysayge so
pulde hym downe. And in the same wyse he served Sir Ector and

---

719 *they encountird with hym all*, they all met with him
721 *with fors of themselff*, understand 'by their combined momentum'
722 *revers*, backwards
724 *brake*, broke   *leffte*, was left
725 *mayster*, lord (C)
728 *magré*, despite (Fr. *malgré*)   *made hym*, had him
731 *wyse*, manner
733 *wente*, expected (lit. 'weened')
735 *in a sowne*, unconscious (lit. 'in a swoon')
739 *by thys*, by [the time that] this
742 *with that*, besides   *than*, then
744 *bowghe*, bow
745 *raced of*, tore off
746–50 See C.
747 *downe*, i.e. off his horse

Sir Lyonell; for, as the booke seyth, he myght have slayne them, but whan he saw their visages hys herte myght nat serve hym thereto, but leffte hem there.

750

And than afterward he hurled into the thyckest prees of them alle, and dyd there the merveyloust dedes of armes that ever man sawe or herde speke of, and ever the good knyghte Sir Lavayne with hym. And there Sir Launcelot with hys swerde smote downe and pulled downe, as the Freynsh booke seyth, mo than thirty knyghtes, and the moste party were of the Table Rounde. And there Sir Lavayne dud full well that day, for he smote downe ten knyghtes of the Table Rounde.

755

'Mercy Jesu,' seyde Sir Gawayne unto Kynge Arthur, 'I mervayle what knyght that he ys with the rede sleve.'

760

'Sir,' seyde Kyng Arthure, 'he woll be knowyn or ever he departe.'

And than the kynge blew unto lodgynge, and the pryce was gyvyn by herowdis unto the knyght with the whyght shylde that bare the rede slyve. Than cam the Kynge of North Galys, and the Kynge of Northhumbirlonde, and the Kynge with the Hondred Knyghtes, and Sir Galahalte the Haute Prince, and seyde unto Sir Launcelot, 'Fayre knyght, God you blysse, for muche have ye done for us thys day. And therefore we pray you that ye woll com with us, that ye may resceyve the honour and the pryce as ye have worshypfully deserved hit.'

765

770

'Fayre lordys,' seyde Sir Launcelot, 'wete you well, gyff I have deserved thanke I have sore bought hit, and that me repentith, for I am never lyke to ascape with the lyff. Therefore, my fayre lordys, I pray you that ye woll suffir me to departe where me lykith, for I am sore hurte. And I take no forse of none honoure, for I had levir repose me than to be lorde of all the worlde.'

775

---

752 *merveyloust*, most marvellous
753 *herde speke of*, heard spoken of
755 *smote*, struck
763 *blew unto lodgynge*, gave orders to the trumpeters to sound the signal for the end of the sport   *pryce*, prize
764 *herowdis*, heralds
772 *gyff*, if
773 *thanke*, gratitude   *sore*, greviously, dearly   *that me repentith*, I regret it See C and cf. l. 166.
774 *ascape*, escape   *the*, understand 'my'
775–6 *me lykith*, I please (C)
776 *take no forse of none*, take no account of any
777 *had levir*, would rather   *repose me*, rest (lit. 'rest myself')

And therewithall he groned pyteuously and rode a grete walop
awaywarde from them untyll he cam undir a woodys evyse. And
whan he saw that he was frome the fylde nyghe a myle, that he   780
was sure he myght nat be seyne, than he seyde with an hyghe
voyce and with a grete grone, 'A, jantill knyght, Sir Lavayne!
Helpe me that thys truncheoune were oute of my syde, for hit
stykith so sore that hit nyghe sleyth me.'

'A, myne owne lorde,' seyde Sir Lavayne, 'I wolde fayne do   785
that myght please you, but I drede me sore, and I pulle oute the
truncheoune, that ye shall be in perelle of dethe.'

'I charge you,' seyde Sir Launcelot, 'as ye love me, draw hit oute.'

And therewithall he descended frome hys horse, and ryght so
ded Sir Lavayne. And forthwithall Sir Lavayne drew the trun-   790
cheoune oute of hys syde, and gaff a grete shryche and a gresly
grone, that the blood braste oute, nyghe a pynte at onys, that at
the laste he sanke downe uppon hys arse and so sowned downe,
pale and dedly.

Alas,' seyde Sir Lavayne, 'what shall I do?'   795

And than he turned Sir Launcelot into the wynde, and so he
lay there nyghe halff an owre as he had bene dede. And so at the
laste Sir Launcelot caste up hys yghen and seyde, 'A, Sir Lavayne,
helpe me that I were on my horse! For here ys faste by, within
thys two myle, a jantill ermyte that somtyme was a full noble   800
knyght and a grete lorde of possessyons, and for grete goodnes he
hath takyn hym to wyllfull poverté and forsakyn myghty londys.
And hys name ys Sir Bawdwyn of Bretayne, and he ys a full
noble surgeon and a good leche. Now lat se and helpe me up

---

778 *walop*, gallop (from obsolete Northern French *waloper* 'to gallop'; replaced in
16th cent. by present form based on standard French *galoper* 'to gallop')
779 *awaywarde*, away   *evyse*, eaves, foliage
783 *that thys truncheoune were* (C)   *truncheoune*, spear-shaft
784 *stykith*, is embedded
786 *and*, if
788 *charge*, command
789 *ryght so*, at once
790 *forthwithall*, forthwith, at once
790-1 See C.
791 *shryche*, cry (lit. 'shriek')   *gresly*, frightful (lit. 'grisly')
793-6 See C.
797 *as*, as if
798 *yghen*, eyes
801 *of*, as to [his]—therefore 'a lord of great possessions'
802 *wyllfull*, voluntary
804 *leche*, physician, doctor; cf. l. 470   *lat se*, see

that I were there, for ever my harte gyvith me that I shall never 805
dye of my cousyne jermaynes hondys.'

And than with grete payne Sir Lavayne holpe hym uppon hys
horse, and than they rode a grete walop togydirs, and ever Sir
Launcelot bled, that hit ran downe to the erthe. And so by fortune they cam to that ermytayge whiche was undir a woode, and 810
a grete clyff on the othir syde, and a fayre watir rennynge undir
hit. And than Sir Lavayne bete on the gate with the but of hys
speare and cryed faste, 'Lat in, for Jesus sake!'

And anone there cam a fayre chylde to hem and asked them
what they wolde. 815

'Fayre sonne,' seyde Sir Lavayne, 'go and pray thy lorde the
ermyte for Goddys sake to late in here a knyght that ys full sore
wounded. And thys day, telle thy lorde, I saw hym do more
dedys of armys than ever I herde sey that ony man ded.'

So the chylde wente in lyghtly, and than he brought the 820
ermyte, whych was a passynge lycly man. Whan Sir Lavayne
saw hym he prayed hym for Goddys sake of succour.

'What knyght ys he?' seyde the ermyte. 'Ys he of the house
of Kynge Arthure or nat?'

'I wote nat,' seyde Sir Lavayne, 'what he ys, nother what ys 825
hys name, but well I wote I saw hym do mervaylously thys day
as of dedys of armys.'

'On whos party was he? seyde the ermyte.

'Sir,' seyde Sir Lavayne, 'he was thys day ayenste Kynge
Arthure, and there he wanne the pryce of all the knyghtis of the 830
Rounde Table.'

'I have seyne the day,' seyde the ermyte, 'I wolde have
loved hym the worse bycause he was ayenste my lorde Kynge
Arthure, for sometyme I was one of the felyship, but now I
thanke God I am othirwyse disposed. But where ys he? Lat me 835
se hym.'

---

805 *gyvith*, tells
806 *cousyne jermayne* (C)
807 *holpe*, helped
808 *walop*, gallop; cf. l. 778
811 *watir*, stream
815 *wolde*, would, wanted
820 *lyghtly*, quickly
821 *passynge*, very   *lycly*, capable-looking
823–4 *of the house of Kynge Arthure*, one of King Arthur's men
825 *nother*, nor
830 *of all*, from all
832–6 See C.

Than Sir Lavayne brought the ermyte to hym. And whan the ermyte behylde hym as he sate leenynge uppon hys sadyll-bowe, ever bledynge spiteuously, and ever the knyght ermyte thought that he sholde know hym; but he coude nat brynge hym to knowlech bycause he was so pale for bledyng.

'What knyght ar ye?' seyde the ermyte, 'and where were ye borne?'

'My fayre lorde,' seyde Sir Launcelot, 'I am a straungere and a knyght aventures that laboureth thorowoute many realmys for to wynne worship.'

Than the ermyte avysed hym bettir, and saw by a wounde on hys chyeke that he was Sir Launcelot.

'Alas,' seyde the ermyte, 'myne owne lorde! Why layne you youre name from me? Perdeus, I ought to know you of ryght, for ye ar the moste nobelyst knyght of the worlde. For well I know you for Sir Launcelot.'

'Sir,' seyde he, 'syth ye know me helpe me, and ye may, for Goddys sake! For I wolde be oute of thys payne at onys, othir to deth othir to lyff.'

'Have ye no doute,' seyde the ermyte, 'for ye shall lyve and fare ryght well.'

And so the ermyte called to hym two of hys servauntes, and so he and hys servauntes bare hym into the ermytayge, and lyghtly unarmed hym and leyde hym in hys bedde. And than anone the ermyte staunched hys bloode and made hym to drynke good wyne, that he was well refygowred and knew hymselff. For in thos dayes hit was nat the gyse as ys nowadayes; for there were none ermytis in tho dayes but that they had bene men of worship and of prouesse, and tho ermytes hylde grete householdis and refreysshed people that were in distresse.

Now turne we unto Kynge Arthure and leve we Sir Launcelot in the ermytayge. So whan the kyngis were comen togydirs on

839 *spiteuously*, cruelly
841 *to knowlech*, to mind   *for*, from
844–6 See C.
845 *adventures*, adventurous
847 *avysed hym better*, considered again
849 *layne*, hide
850 *Perdeus*, By God
853 *syth*, since   *and*, if
862 *refygowred*, revived (lit. 're-vigoured')   *knew*, understand 'came to'
863 *gyse*, way
864–6 See C.

both partyes, and the grete feste sholde be holdyn, Kynge
Arthure asked the Kynge of North Galis and their felyshyp where   870
was that knyght that bare the rede slyve. 'Lat brynge hym before
me, that he may have hys lawde and honoure and the pryce, as
hit ys ryght.'

Than spake Sir Galahalte the Haute Prynce and the Kynge
with the Hondred Knyghtes, and seyde, 'We suppose that   875
knyght ys myscheved so that he ys never lyke to se you nother
none of us all. And that ys the grettyst pyté that ever we wyste of
ony knyght.'

'Alas,' seyde Kynge Arthure, 'how may thys be? Ys he so sore
hurte? But what is hys name?' seyde Kynge Arthure.   880

'Truly,' seyde they all, 'we know nat hys name, nother frome
whens he cam, nother whother he wolde.'

'Alas,' seyde the kynge, 'thys ys the warste tydyngis that cam
to me thys seven yere! For I wolde nat for all the londys I welde
to knowe and wyte hit were so that that noble knyght were   885
slayne.'

'Sir, knowe ye ought of hym?' seyde they all.

'As for that,' seyde Kynge Arthure, 'whethir I know hym
other none, ye shall nat know for me what man he ys. But Allmyghty Jesu sende me good tydyngis of hym.'   890

And so seyde they all.

'Be my hede,' seyde Sir Gawayne, 'gyff hit so be that the good
knyght be so sore hurte, hit ys grete damage and pité to all thys
londe, for he ys one of the nobelyst knyghtes that ever I saw in a
fylde handyll speare or swerde. And iff he may be founde I shall   895
fynde hym, for I am sure he ys nat farre frome thys contrey.'

'Sir, beare you well,' seyde Kynge Arthure, 'and ye maye
fynde hym, onles that he be in such a plyte that he may nat welde
hymselff.'

---

869 *sholde be holdyn*, was to be held
871 *Lat brynge hym*, Have him brought
872 *lawde*, praise
876 *myscheved*, hurt
882 *whother he wolde*, where (lit. 'whither') he intended [to go]
884 *welde*, rule (lit. 'wield')
887 *ought*, aught, anything
889 *for*, by
892 *gyff*, if   *so be*, be so
896 *contrey*, region, neighbourhood
897 *and*, if
897–9 See C.   *welde hymselffe*, control his limbs and faculties (lit. 'wield himself')

'Jesu defende!' seyde Sir Gawayne. 'But wyte well, I shall   900
know what he ys and I may fynde hym.'

Ryght so Sir Gawayne toke a squyre with hym uppon hakeneyes and rode all aboute Camelot within six or seven myle, but
so ne he com agayne and cowde here no worde of hym. Than
within two dayes Kynge Arthure and all the felyshyp returned   905
unto London agayne. And so as they rode by the way hyt happened Sir Gawayne at Astolot to lodge with Sir Barnarde thereas
was Sir Launcelot lodged. And so as Sir Gawayne was in hys
chamber to repose hym, Sir Barnarde, the olde barowne, cam in
to hym, and hys doughtir Elayne, to chere hym and to aske hym   910
what tydyngis, and who ded beste at the turnemente of Wynchester.

'So God me helpe,' seyde Sir Gawayne, 'there were two
knyghtes that bare two whyght shyldys, but one of them bare a
rede sleve uppon hys hede, and sertaynly he was the beste   915
knyght that ever y saw juste in fylde. For I dare sey,' seyde Sir
Gawayne, 'that one knyght with the rede slyve smote downe
fourty knyghtes of the Rounde Table, and his felow ded ryght
well and worshipfully.'

'Now blyssed be God,' seyde thys Fayre Maydyn of Astolate,   920
'that that knyght sped so welle! For he ys the man in the worlde
that I firste loved, and truly he shall be the laste that ever I shall
love.'

'Now, fayre maydyn,' seyde Sir Gawayne, 'ys that good
knyght youre love?'   925

'Sertaynly, sir,' she seyde, 'wyte you well he ys my love.'

'Than know ye hys name?' seyde Sir Gawayne.

'Nay, truly, sir,' seyde the damesell, 'I know nat hys name
nothir frome whens he com, but to sey that I love hym, I
promyse God and you I love hym.'   930

---

900 *Jesu defende!* God forbid! (cf. Fr. *défendre*)
902 *Ryght so,* At once
902-3 *hakeneyes,* hacks (i.e. horses of middling size and quality, used for ordinary
riding rather than for draught, hunting or war)
904 *com* came
906 *by the way* on their way
907 *thereas,* where
910 *chere,* welcome
914 *but,* and
920 See C.
921 *sped,* succeeded, did
929 *to sey that* ,as to saying that

'How had ye knowlecch of hym firste?' seyd Sir Gawayne.

Than she tolde hym as ye have harde before, and how hir fadir betoke hym her brother to do hym servyse, and how hir fadir lente hym her brothirs, Sir Tyrryes, shylde: 'and here with me he leffte hys owne shylde.'   935

'For what cause ded he so?' seyde Sir Gawayne.

'For thys cause,' seyde the damesell, 'for hys shylde was full well knowyn amonge many noble knyghtes.'

'A, fayre damesell,' seyde Sir Gawayne, 'please hit you to lette me have a syght of that shylde.'   940

'Sir,' she seyde, 'hit ys in my chambir, coverde wyth a case, and if ye woll com with me ye shall se hit.'

'Nat so,' seyde Sir Barnarde to hys doughter, 'but sende ye for that shylde.'

So whan the shylde was com Sir Gawayne toke of the case, and 945 whan he behylde that shylde he knew hyt anone that hit was Sir Launcelottis shylde and hys owne armys.

'A, Jesu mercy!' seyde Sir Gawayne, 'now ys my herte more hevyar than ever hit was tofore.'

'Why?' seyde thys mayde Elayne.   950

'For I have a grete cause,' seyde Sir Gawayne. 'Ys that knyght that owyth thys shylde youre love?'

'Yee truly,' she seyde, 'my love ys he: God wolde that I were hys love!'

'So God me spede,' seyde Sir Gawayne, 'fayre damesell, ye 955 have ryght, for and he be youre love, ye love the moste honorabelyst knyght of the worlde and the man of moste worship.'

'So methought ever,' seyde the damesell, 'for never ar that tyme, for no knyght that ever I saw, loved I never none arste.'

---

932 *harde*, heard
933 *betoke hym her brother*, sent her brother to him
939 *please it you*, may it please you, will you; cf. Fr. *s'il vous plaît*
941 *case*, covering (C)
943–4 See C.
945 *of*, off
947 *armys*, [coat of] arms
948–9 *more hevyar*, sadder
952 *owyth*, owns
953 *God wolde*, would God
955 *spede*, cause . . . to succeed, favour
956 *have*, are; modelled on Fr. *vous avez raison*
958 *methought*, it seemed to me (not 'I thought')   *ar*, ere, previously
959 See C.   *arste*, erst, before

'God graunte,' seyde Sir Gawayne, 'that aythir of you may 960
rejoyse othir, but that ys in a grete aventure. But truly,' seyde
Sir Gawayne unto the damesell, 'ye may sey ye have a fayre
grace, for why I have knowyn that noble knyght thys four-and-
twenty yere, and never or that day I nor none othir knyght, I
dare make good, saw never nother herde say that ever he bare 965
tokyn or sygne of no lady, jantillwoman, nor maydyn at no
justis nother turnemente. And therefore, fayre maydyn,' seyde
Sir Gawayne, 'ye ar much beholdyn to hym to gyff hym thanke.
    'But I drede me,' seyde Sir Gawayne, 'that ye shall never se
hym in thys worlde, and that ys as grete pité as ever was of ony 970
erthely man.'
    'Alas,' seyde she, 'how may thys be? Ys he slayne?'
    'I say nat so,' seyde Sir Gawayne, 'but wete you well he ys
grevously wounded, by all maner of sygnys, and by mens syght
more lycklyer to be dede than to be on lyve. And wyte you well 975
he ys the noble knyght Sir Launcelot, for by thys shylde I know
hym.'
    'Alas!' seyde thys Fayre Maydyn of Astolat, 'how may thys be?
And what was hys hurte?'
    'Truly,' seyde Sir Gawayne, 'the man in the worlde that 980
loved hym beste hurte hym so. And I dare sey,' seyde Sir Gawayne, 'and that knyght that hurte hym knew the verry sertaynté that he had hurte Sir Launcelot, hit were the moste
sorow that ever cam to hys herte.'
    'Now, fayre fadir,' seyde than Elayne, 'I requyre you gyff me 985
leve to ryde and seke hym, othir ellis I wote well I shall go oute
of my mynde. For I shall never stynte tyll that I fynde hym and
my brothir, Sir Lavayne.'
    'Do ye as hit lykith you,' seyde hir fadir, 'for sore me repentis
of the hurte of that noble knyght.'   990
    Ryght so the mayde made hyr redy and departed before Sir
Gawayne, makynge grete dole. Than on the morne Sir Gawayne

960-8 See C.
961 *rejoyse*, gladden   *in a grete aventure*, a very chancy thing
963 *grace*, fortune, blessing   *for why*, because
968 *beholdyn*, indebted
969 *drede me*, fear
982 *and*, if
987 *For*, And   *stynte*, stop
989-90 *me repentis of*, I am sorry for
992 *dole*, sorrow

com to Kynge Arthure and tolde hym all how he had founde
Sir Launcelottis shylde in the kepynge of the Fayre Mayden of
Astolat.   995

'All that knew I aforehande,' seyde Kynge Arthure, 'and that
caused me I wolde nat suffir you to have ado at the grete justis;
for I aspyed hym,' seyde Kynge Arthure, 'whan he cam untyll
hys lodgyng, full late in the evenyng, in Astolat. But grete mervayle have I,' seyde Kynge Arthure, 'that ever he wolde beare 1000
ony sygne of ony damesell, for ar now I never herde sey nor
knew that ever he bare ony tokyn of none erthely woman.'

'Be my hede, sir,' seyde Sir Gawayne, 'the Fayre Maydyn of
Astolat lovith hym mervaylously well. What hit meanyth I cannat sey. And she ys ryddyn aftir to seke hym.'   1005

So the kynge and all com to London, and there Gawayne all
opynly disclosed hit to all the courte that hit was Sir Launcelot
that justed beste. And whan Sir Bors harde that, wyte you well he
was an hevy man, and so were all hys kynnysmen. But whan the
quyene wyst that hit was Sir Launcelot that bare the rede slyve 1010
of the Fayre Maydyn of Astolat, she was nygh ought of her mynde
for wratthe. And than she sente for Sir Bors de Ganys in all
haste that myght be. So whan Sir Bors was com before the
quyene she seyde, 'A, Sir Bors! Have ye nat herde sey how
falsely Sir Launcelot hath betrayed me?'   1015

'Alas, madame,' seyde Sir Bors, 'I am aferde he hath betrayed
hymselff and us all.'

'No forse,' seyde the quene, 'though he be distroyed, for he ys
a false traytoure knyght.'

'Madame,' seyde Sir Bors, 'I pray you sey ye no more so, for 1020
wyte you well I may nat here no such langayge of hym.'

'Why so, Sir Bors?' seyde she. 'Shold I nat calle hym traytoure whan he bare the rede slyve uppon hys hede at Wynchester at the grete justis?'

'Madame,' seyde Sir Bors, 'that slyeve-berynge repentes me 1025
sore, but I dare say he dud beare hit to none evyll entent, but for
thys cause he bare the rede slyve: that none of hys blood shold

---

993 *all how*, everything about how
997 *the grete justis* (C)
1002 *none erthely woman* (C)
1006–7 *all opynly*, entirely openly
1014–44 See C.
1025 *repentes*, grieves
1026 *I dare say* In the literal, not in the weaker modern sense.

know hym. For or than we nother none of us all never knew that
ever he bare tokyn or sygne of maydyn, lady, nothir jantillwoman.'   1030

'Fy on hym!' seyde the quene. 'Yet for all hys pryde and bobbaunce, there ye proved youreselff better man than he.'

'Nay, madam, sey ye nevermore so, for he bete me and my
felowys, and myght have slayne us and he had wolde.'

'Fy on hym!' seyde the quene. 'For I harde Sir Gawayne say   1035
before my lorde Arthure that hit were mervayle to telle the grete
love that ys betwene the Fayre Maydyn of Astolat and hym.'

'Madam,' seyde Sir Bors, 'I may nat warne Sir Gawayne to
sey what hit pleasith him; but I dare sey, as for my lorde Sir
Launcelot, that he lovith no lady, jantillwoman, nother mayden, 1040
but as he lovith all inlyke muche. And therefore, madam,' seyde
Sir Bors, 'ye may sey what ye wyll, but wyte you well I woll hast
me to syke hym and fynde hym wheresumever he be, and God
sende me good tydyngis of hym!'

And so leve we them there, and speke we of Sir Launcelot,   1045
that lay in grete perell. And so as thys fayre madyn Elayne cam
to Wynchester she sought there all aboute, and by fortune Sir
Lavayne hir brothir was ryddyn to sporte hym, to enchaff hys
horse; and anone as thys maydyn Elayne saw hym she knew
hym, and than she cryed on-lowde tylle hym. And whan he   1050
herde her he com to her, and anone with that she asked hir
brother, 'How dothe my lorde Sir Launcelot?'

'Who tolde you, syster, that my lordys name was Sir Launcelot?'

Than she tolde hym how Sir Gawayne by hys shylde knew   1055
hym. So they rode togydirs tyll that they cam to the ermytayge,
and anone she alyght. So Sir Lavayne brought her in to Sir
Launcelot, and whan she saw hym ly so syke and pale in hys bed
she myght nat speke, but suddeynly she felle downe to the erthe
in a sowghe. And there she lay a grete whyle.   1060

1028 *or*, ere, before
1031 *Fy* (C)
1031-2 *bobbaunce*, showing off
1034 *and he had wolde*, if he had wanted to (lit. 'willed')
1038 *warne*, forbid
1041 *inlyke*, equally
1048 *enchaff*, exercise; cf. ll. 137-8n
1050 *on-lowde*, aloud   *tylle*, to
1060 *in a sowghe*, fainting

103

And when she was releved she shryked and seyde, 'My lord, Sir Launcelot? Alas, whyghe lye ye in thys plyte?' And than she sowned agayne.

And than Sir Launcelot prayde Sir Lavayne to take hir up, 'and brynge hir hydir to me.'   1065

And whan she cam to herselff Sir Launcelot kyste her and seyde, 'Fayre maydyn, why fare ye thus? For ye put me to more payne. Wherefore make ye no such chere, for and ye be com to comforte me ye be ryght wellcom; and of thys lytyll hurte that I have I shall be ryght hastely hole, by the grace of God. But I 1070 mervayle', seyde Sir Launcelot, 'who tolde you my name.'

And so thys maydyn tolde hym all how Sir Gawayne was lodged with hir fader, 'and there by youre shylde he dyscoverde youre name.'

'Alas!' seyde Sir Launcelot, 'that repentith me that my name 1075 ys knowyn, for I am sure hit woll turne untyll angir.'

And than Sir Launcelot compaste in hys mynde that Sir Gawayne wolde telle Quene Gwenyvere how he bare the rede slyve and for whom, that he wyst well wolde turne unto grete angur.   1080

So thys maydyn Elayne never wente frome Sir Launcelot, but wacched hym day and nyght, and dud such attendaunce to hym that the Freynshe booke seyth there was never woman dyd more kyndlyer for man than she. Than Sir Launcelot prayde Sir Lavayne to make aspyes in Wynchester for Sir Bors if he cam 1085 there, and tolde hym by what tokyns he sholde know hym: by a wounde in hys forehede.

'For I am sure,' seyde Sir Launcelot, 'that Sir Bors woll seke me, for he ys the same good knyght that hurte me.'

Now turne we unto Sir Bors de Ganys, that cam untyll Wyn- 1090 chestir to seke aftir hys cosyne Sir Launcelot. And whan he cam to Wynchester anone there were men that Sir Lavayne had made to lye in a wacche for suche a man, and anone Sir Lavayne had warnyng. And than Sir Lavayne cam to Wynchestir and

---

1061 *releved*, restored to herself
1066 See C.
1076 *turne untyll*, result in
1077 *compaste*, worked out
1079 *that*, which
1084 *prayde*, asked
1085 *make aspyes*, put watchers

founde Sir Bors, and there he told hym what he was and with 1095
whom he was, and what was hys name.

'Now, fayre knyght,' seyde Sir Bors, 'ye be wellcom, and I requyre you that ye woll brynge me to my lorde Sir Launcelot.'

'Sir,' seyde Sir Lavayne, 'take youre horse, and within thys
owre ye shall se hym.' 1100

So they departed and com to the ermytayge. And whan Sir
Bors saw Sir Launcelot lye in hys bedde, dede pale and discoloured, anone Sir Bors loste hys countenaunce, and for kyndenes and pité he myght nat speke but wepte tendirly a grete
whyle. But whan he myght speke he seyde thus: 'A, my lorde 1105
Sir Launcelot, God you blysse and sende you hasty recoveryng!
For full hevy am I of my mysfortune and of myne unhappynesse.
For now I may calle myselff unhappy, and I drede me that God
ys gretely displeasyd with me, that He wolde suffir me to have
such a shame for to hurte you that ar all oure ledar and all oure 1110
worship; and therefore I calle myselff unhappy. Alas, that ever
such a caytyff knyght as I am sholde have power by unhappines
to hurte the moste noblyst knyght of the worlde! Where I so
shamefully sette uppon you and overcharged you, and where ye
myght have slayne me, ye saved me; and so ded nat I, for I and 1115
all oure bloode ded to you their utteraunce. I mervayle', seyde
Sir Bors, 'that my herte or my bloode wolde serve me. Wherefore,
my lorde Sir Launcelot, I aske you mercy.'

'Fayre cousyn,' seyde Sir Launcelot, 'ye be ryght wellcom, and
wyte you well, overmuche ye sey for the plesure of me whych 1120
pleasith me nothynge, for why I have the same isought. For I
wolde with pryde have overcom you all, and there in my pryde I
was nere slayne, and that was in myne owne defaughte; for I
myght have gyffyn you warnynge of my beynge there, and than had
I had no hurte. For hit ys an olde-seyde sawe: there ys harde 1125

1095 *what*, who
1102–3 *discoloured*, pale (lit. 'without colour')
1103–4 *kyndenes*, natural feeling
1106 *hasty*, swift
1107 *unhappynesse*, ill luck (C)
1108 *unhappy*, unfortunate
1110 *for to*, understand 'as to'
1112 *caytyff*, wretched
1114 *overcharged*, charged with excessive (i.e. unfair) force against
1116 *utteraunce*, utmost
1123 *in myne owne defaughte*, my own fault
1125 *sawe*, proverb (C)

batayle thereas kynne and frendys doth batayle ayther ayenst
other, for there may be no mercy, but mortall warre. Therefore,
fayre cousyn,' seyde Sir Launcelot, 'lat thys langage overpasse,
and all shall be wellcom that God sendith. And latte us leve of
thys mater and speke of som rejoysynge, for thys that ys done may 1130
nat be undone; and lat us fynde a remedy how sone that I may
be hole.'

Than Sir Bors lenyd uppon hys beddys syde and tolde Sir
Launcelot how the quene was passynge wrothe with hym, 'because ye ware the rede slyve at the grete justes'. And there Sir 1135
Bors tolde hym all how Sir Gawayne discoverde hit 'by youre
shylde that ye leffte with the Fayre Madyn of Astolat.'

'Than ys the quene wrothe?' seyde Sir Launcelot. 'Therefore
am I ryght hevy; but I deserved no wrath, for all that I ded was
bycause I wolde nat be knowyn.'   1140

'Sir, ryght so excused I you,' seyde Sir Bors, 'but all was in
vayne, for she seyde more largelyer to me than I to you sey now.
But, sir, ys thys she,' seyde Sir Bors, 'that ys so busy aboute you,
that men calle the Fayre Maydyn of Astolat?'

'Forsothe, she hit ys,' seyde Sir Launcelot, 'that by no meanys 1145
I cannat put her fro me.'

'Why sholde ye put her frome you?' seyde Sir Bors. 'For she
ys a passyng fayre damesell, and well besayne and well taught.
And God wolde, fayre cousyn,' seyde Sir Bors, 'that ye cowde love
her, but as to that I may nat nother dare nat counceyle you. But 1150
I se well,' seyde Sir Bors, 'by her dyligence aboute you that she
lovith you intyerly.'

'That me repentis,' seyde Sir Launcelot.

'Well,' seyde Sir Bors, 'she ys nat the first that hath loste hir
payne uppon you, and that ys the more pyté.' And so they talked 1155
of many mo thynges.

And so within three or four dayes Sir Launcelot wexed bygge

1129 See C.
1130 *rejoysynge*, matter for rejoicing
1135 *ware*, wore
1142 *seyde*, spoke (intransitive)   *largelyer*, more at large, more sweepingly
1144 *that*, she whom
1145 *that* (C)
1148 *well besayne*, attractive   *well taught*, well-mannered, well-bred (not 'well taught')
1156 *mo* more
1157 *bygge*, strong

and lyght. Than Sir Bors tolde Sir Launcelot how there was sworne a grete turnement and justes betwyxt Kyng Arthure and the Kynge of North Galis, that sholde be uppon Allhalowmasse 1160 Day, besydes Wynchestir.

'Is that trouth?' seyde Sir Launcelot. 'Than shall ye abyde with me stylle a lityll whyle untyll that I be hole, for I fele myself resonabely bygge and stronge.'

'Blessed be God!' seyde Sir Bors.   1165

Than they were there nyghe a moneth togydirs, and ever thys maydyn Elayne ded ever hir dyligence and labour both nyght and day unto Sir Launcelot, that there was never chylde nother wyff more mekar tyll fadir and husbande than was thys Fayre Maydyn of Astolat; wherefore Sir Bors was gretly pleased with 1170 her.

So uppon a day, by the assente of Sir Lavayne, Sir Bors, and Sir Launcelot, they made the ermyte to seke in woodys for diverse erbys, and so Sir Launcelot made fayre Elayne to gadir erbys for hym to make hym a bayne. So in the meanewhyle Sir 1175 Launcelot made Sir Lavayne to arme hym at all pecis, and there he thought to assay hymselff uppon horsebacke with a speare, whether he myght welde hys armour and hys speare for hys hurte or nat.

And so whan he was uppon hys horse he steyrred hym freyshly, 1180 and the horse was passyng lusty and frycke because he was nat laboured of a moneth before. And than Sir Launcelot bade Sir Lavayne gyff hym that grete speare, and so Sir Launcelot cowchyd that speare in the reeste. The courser lepte myghtyly whan he felte the spurres, and he that was uppon hym, whiche 1185

----

¹¹⁵⁸ *lyght*, active

¹¹⁵⁸⁻⁹ *there was sworne*, it was sworn that there should be (C)

¹¹⁶⁰⁻¹ *Allhalowmasse Day*, All Saints' Day: 1st November

¹¹⁶⁹ *more mekar* (C)

¹¹⁷³⁻⁴ Translate 'they arranged for the hermit to search in the woods for various plants'; *made* here does not imply compulsion.

¹¹⁷⁵ *bayne*, bath (Fr. *bain*)

¹¹⁷⁶ *arme hym at all pecis*, arm him 'cap-a-pie', arm him from head to foot (C)

¹¹⁷⁷ *assay*, test

¹¹⁸⁰ *steyrred hym freyshly*, gathered the horse vigorously under him (lit. 'bestirred him [the horse] eagerly')

¹¹⁸¹ *lusty*, lively   *frycke*, fresh

¹¹⁸¹⁻² *was nat laboured*, had not been made to work

¹¹⁸² *of*, for

¹¹⁸³ *that*, the   *grete speare*, lance (C)

¹¹⁸⁴ *reeste*, rest

was the nobelyst horseman of the worlde, strayned hym myghtyly and stabely, and kepte stylle the speare in the reeste. And there-with Sir Launcelot strayned hymselff so straytly, with so grete fors, to gete the courser forewarde that the bottom of hys wounde braste both within and withoute, and therewithall the bloode cam 1190 oute so fyersely that he felte hymselff so feble that he myght nat sitte uppon hys horse. And than Sir Launcelot cryed unto Sir Bors,

'A, Sir Bors and Sir Lavayne, helpe! For I am com unto myne ende!' 1195

And therewith he felle downe on the one syde to the erth lyke a dede coorse. And than Sir Bors and Sir Lavayne cam unto hym with sorow-makynge oute of mesure. And so by fortune thys mayden, Elayne, harde their mournynge; and than she cam thyder, and whan she founde Sir Launcelot there armed in that 1200 place she cryed and wepte as she had bene wood. And than she kyssed hym and ded what she myght to awake hym, and than she rebuked her brothir and Sir Bors, and called hem false tray-tours, and seyde,

'Why wolde ye take hym oute of hys bed? For and he dye, I 1205 woll appele you of hys deth!'

And so with that cam the ermyte, Sir Bawdewyn of Bretayne, and whan he founde Sir Launcelot in that plyte he seyde but lityll, but wyte you well he was wroth. But he seyde, 'Lette us have hym in,' and anone they bare hym into the ermytage and unarm- 1210 ed hym, and leyde hym in hys bedde; and evermore hys wounde bled spiteuously, but he stirred no lymme off hym. Than the knyght armyte put a thynge in hys nose and a litill dele of watir in hys mowthe, and than Sir Launcelot waked of hys swowghe. And than the ermyte staunched hys bledyng, and whan Sir 1215

1186–7 *strayned hym myghtyly and stabely*, exerted himself strongly and steadily
1187 *stylle the speare*, the spear motionless
1188 *straytly*, severely   *with so*, with such
1197 *coorse*, corpse
1198 *oute of mesure* (C)
1199 *mournynge*, laments
1201 *wood*, mad
1206 *appele*, accuse
1209 *wyte you well*, have no doubt about it (lit. 'understand clearly')
1210 *bare*, bore
1212 *spiteuously*, cruelly
1213 *armyte*, hermit   *put a thynge in hys nose*, put something in his nose (C)   *dele*, quantity

Launcelot myght speke he asked why he put his lyff so in jouperté.

'Sir,' seyde Sir Launcelot, 'because I wente I had be stronge inowghe, and also Sir Bors tolde me there sholde be at Alhalowmasse a grete justis betwyxte Kynge Arthur and the Kynge of 1220 Northe Galys. And therefore I thought to assay myselff, whether I myght be there or not.'

'A, Sir Launcelot,' seyde the ermyte, 'youre harte and youre currayge woll never be done untyll youre laste day! But ye shall do now be my counceyle: lat Sir Bors departe frome you, and lat 1225 hym do at that turnemente what he may; and, by the grace of God,' seyde the knyght ermyte, 'be that the turnemente be done and he comyn hydir agayne, sir, ye shall be hole, so that ye woll be governed by me.'

Than Sir Bors made hym redy to departe frome hym, and Sir 1230 Launcelot seyde, 'Fayre cousyn, Sir Bors, recommaunde me unto all tho ye owght recommaunde me unto, and I pray you enforce youreselff at that justis that ye may be beste, for my love. And here shall I abyde you, at the mercy of God, tyll youre agaynecommynge.'   1235

And so Sir Bors departed and cam to the courte of Kynge Arthure, and tolde hem in what place he had leffte Sir Launcelot.

'That me repentis!' seyde the kynge. 'But syn he shall have hys lyff, we all may thanke God.'

And than Sir Bors tolde the quene what jouperté Sir Launcelot 1240 was in whan he wolde a asayde hys horse: 'And all that he ded, madame, was for the love of you, because he wolde a bene at thys turnemente.'

'Fy on hym, recreayde knyght!' seyde the quene. 'For wyte you well I am ryght sory and he shall have hys lyff.'   1245

'Madam, hys lyff shall he have,' seyde Sir Bors, 'and who that wolde otherwyse, excepte you, madame, we that ben of hys blood

---

1217 *jouperté*, jeopardy
1218 *wente*, thought (lit. 'weened')
1225 *be*, by   *lat*, let
1227 *be*, by [the time]
1228 *comyn*, come   *so that*, if
1231 *recommaunde me unto*, remember me to
1232 *tho*, those
1232-3 *enforce youreselff*, try hard
1233 *for my love*, for my sake
1237 *hem*, them
1241 *a*, have

wolde helpe to shortyn their lyves. But, madame,' seyde Sir Bors, 'ye have ben oftyntymes displeased with my lorde Sir Launcelot, but at all tymys at the ende ye founde hym a trew knyght.' And so he departed. 1250

And than every knyght of the Rounde Table that were there at that tyme presente made them redy to be at that justes at Allhalowmasse. And thidir drew many knyghtes of diverse contreyes. And as Allhalowmasse drew nere, thydir cam the Kynge of North Galis, and the Kynge with the Hondred Knyghtes, and Sir Galahalt the Haute Prynce of Surluse. And thider cam Kynge Angwysh of Irelonde, and the Kynge of Northumbirlonde, and the Kynge of Scottis. So these three kynges com to Kynge Arthurs party. 1255 1260

And so that day Sir Gawayne ded grete dedys of armys and began first; and the herowdis nombirde that Sir Gawayne smote downe twenty knyghtes. Than Sir Bors de Ganys cam in the same tyme, and he was numbirde that he smote downe twenty knyghtes; and therefore the pryse was gyvyn betwyxt them bothe, for they began firste and lengist endured. Also Sir Gareth, as the boke seyth, ded that day grete dedis of armys, for he smote downe and pulled downe thirty knyghtes; but whan he had done those dedis he taryed nat, but so departed, and therefore he loste hys pryse. And Sir Palamydes ded grete dedis of armys that day, for he smote downe twenty knyghtes; but he departed suddeynly, and men demed that he and Sir Gareth rode togydirs to som maner adventures. 1265 1270

So whan thys turnement was done Sir Bors departed, and rode tylle he cam to Sir Launcelot, hys cousyne, and than he founde hym walkyng on hys feete. And there aythir made grete joy of other, and so he tolde Sir Launcelot of all the justys, lyke as ye have herde. 1275

'I mervayle,' seyde Sir Launcelot, 'that Sir Gareth, whan he had done such dedis of armys, that he wolde nat tarry.' 1280

1252-3 *were . . . them*, was . . . him (because of the singular subject *every knyght*)
1254 *drew*, gathered
1260 *party*, side
1266-7 See C.
1269 *taryed*, remained (lit. 'tarried') (C)
1272-3 *to som maner adventures*, to adventures of some kind (C)
1277-8 *lyke as ye have herde* (C)
1280 *that he* is redundant

'Sir, thereof we mervayled all,' seyde Sir Bors, 'for but if hit were you, other the noble knyght Sir Trystram, other the good knyght Sir Lamorake de Galis, I saw never knyght bere downe so many knyghtes and smyte downe in so litill a whyle as ded Sir Gareth. And anone as he was gone we all wyst nat where he 1285 becom.'

'Be my hede,' seyde Sir Launcelot, 'he ys a noble knyght and a myghty man and well-brethed; and yf he were well assayed,' seyd Sir Launcelot, 'I wolde deme he were good inow for ony knyght that beryth the lyff. And he ys a jantill knyght, curteyse, 1290 trew, and ryght bownteuous, meke and mylde, and in hym ys no maner of male engynne, but playne, faythfull an trew.'

So than they made hem redy to departe frome the ermytayge. And so uppon a morne they toke their horsis, and this Elayne le Blanke with hem. And whan they cam to Astolat there were they 1295 well lodged and had grete chere of Sir Barnarde, the olde baron, and of Sir Tirré, hys sonne.

And so uppon the morne, whan Sir Launcelot sholde departe, fayre Elayne brought hir fadir with her, and Sir Lavayne, and Sir Tirré, and than thus she sayde: 'My lorde, Sir Launcelot, 1300 now I se ye woll departe frome me. Now, fayre knyght and cur-tayse knyght,' seyde she, 'have mercy uppon me, and suffir me nat to dye for youre lqve.'

'Why, what wolde ye that I dud?' seyde Sir Launcelot.

'Sir, I wolde have you to my husbande,' seyde Elayne.   1305

'Fayre damesell, I thanke you hartely,' seyde Sir Launcelot, 'but truly,' seyde he, 'I caste me never to be wedded man.'

'Than, fayre knyght,' seyde she, 'woll ye be my paramour?'

'Jesu deffende me!' seyde Sir Launcelot, 'for than I rewarded youre fadir and youre brothir full evyll for their grete goodnesse.' 1310

'Alas! than,' seyde she, 'I muste dye for youre love.'

1281 *but if*, unless
1282–3 See C.
1285 *anone as*, as soon as, when
1286 *becom*, went
1289 *deme*, judge
1290 *beryth the lyff*, lives
1291 *bownteuous*, generous
1292 *male engynne*, machinations, trickery   *playne*, straightforward, honest
1294 *le*, la
1298 *sholde*, was to
1307 *caste me never*, intend never

'Ye shall nat do so,' seyde Sir Launcelot, 'for wyte you well,
fayre mayden, I myght have bene maryed and I had wolde, but
I never applyed me yett to be maryed. But bycause, fayre damesell, that ye love me as ye sey ye do, I woll for youre good wylle 1315
and kyndnes shew to you som goodnesse; and that ys thys: that
wheresomever ye woll besette youre herte uppon som good
knyght that woll wedde you, I shall gyff you togydirs a thousand
pounde yerly, to you and to youre ayris. This muche woll I gyff
you, fayre mayden, for youre kyndnesse, and allweyes whyle I 1320
lyve to be youre owne knyght.'

'Sir, of all thys,' seyde the maydyn, 'I woll none, for but yff ye
woll wedde me, other to be my paramour at the leste, wyte you
well, Sir Launcelot, my good dayes ar done.'

'Fayre damesell,' seyde Sir Launcelot, 'of thes two thynges ye 1325
muste pardon me.'

Than she shryked shirly and felle downe in a sowghe; and than
women bare hir into her chambir, and there she made overmuche
sorowe. And than Sir Launcelot wolde departe, and there he
asked Sir Lavayne what he wolde do.   1330

'Sir, what sholde I do,' seyde Sir Lavayne, 'but folow you, but
if ye dryve me frome you or commaunde me to go frome you.'

Than cam Sir Barnarde to Sir Launcelot and seyde to hym,
'I cannat se but that my doughtir woll dye for youre sake.'

'Sir, I may nat do withall,' seyde Sir Launcelot, 'for all that 1335
that me sore repentith, for I reporte me to youreselff that my
profir ys fayre. And me repentith,' seyde Sir Launcelot, 'that she
lovith me as she dothe, for I was never the causer of hit; for I
reporte me unto youre sonne, I never erly nother late profirde
her bownté nother fayre behestes. And as for me,' seyde Sir 1340
Launcelot, 'I dare do all that a knyght sholde do, and sey that

1312–21 See C.
1313 *and I had wolde,* if I had wished
1317 *besette,* set
1319 *ayris,* heirs
1322 *but yff,* unless
1327 *shryked,* screamed   *shirly,* shrilly   *sowghe,* faint
1328–9 *overmuche sorowe* (C)
1331–2 See C.
1335 *I may nat do withall,* I cannot do anything about it (C)
1336 *reporte me to yourselff,* refer myself to you [as the judge]
1337 *profir,* offer
1338 *for,* and
1340 *bownté,* gifts   *behestes,* promises (not 'commands')

112

she ys a clene mayden for me, bothe for dede and wylle. And I
am ryght hevy of hir distresse, for she ys a full fayre maydyn,
goode and jentill, and well itaught.'

'Fadir,' seyde Sir Lavayne, 'I dare make good she ys a clene 1345
maydyn as for my lorde Sir Launcelot; but she doth as I do, for
sythen I saw first my lorde Sir Launcelot I cowde never departe
frome hym, nother nought I woll, and I may folow hym.'

Than Sir Launcelot toke hys leve, and so they departed and
cam to Wynchestir. And whan Kynge Arthur wyst that Sir 1350
Launcelot was com hole and sownde, the kynge made grete joy
of hym; and so ded Sir Gawayne and all the knyghtes of the
Rounde Table excepte Sir Aggravayne and Sir Mordred. Also
Quene Gwenyver was woode wrothe with Sir Launcelot, and
wolde by no meanys speke with hym, but enstraunged herselff 1355
frome hym. And Sir Launcelot made all the meanys that he
myght for to speke with the quene, but hit wolde nat be.

Now speke we of the Fayre Maydyn of Astolat, that made such
sorow day and nyght that she never slepte, ete, nother dranke,
and ever she made hir complaynte unto Sir Launcelot. So whan 1360
she had thus endured a ten dayes, that she fyebled so that she
muste nedis passe oute of thys worlde, than she shrove her clene
and resseyved hir Creature. And ever she complayned stylle
uppon Sir Launcelot.

Than hir gostly fadir bade hir leve such thoughtes. Than she 1365
seyde, 'Why sholde I leve such thoughtes? Am I nat an erthely
woman? And all the whyle the brethe ys in my body I may complayne me, for my belyve ys that I do none offence, though I love
an erthely man, unto God, for He fourmed me thereto, and all

1342 *for me*, as far as I am concerned
1343 *hevy*, sad
1344 *well itaught*, well-mannered, well-bred
1347 *sythen*, since
1348 *nother nought I woll*, and I will not [do so] either   *and*, if
1353 See C.
1354 *woode wrothe with*, out of her mind (more freely 'beside herself') with rage at (C)
1355 *by no meanys* (C)
1361 *a ten dayes*, see l. 503n   *fyebled*, became enfeebled
1362 *muste nedis*, must necessarily   *shrove her*, confessed her sins and was absolved
1363 *hir Creature*, her Creator, i.e. the Eucharist   *complayned . . . uppon*, lamented
1365 *gostly fadir*, spiritual father, confessor
1366–82 See C.
1367–8 *complayne me*, lament
1368 *belyve*, belief
1369 *fourmed*, formed, made

113

maner of good love comyth of God. And othir than good love 1370
loved I never Sir Launcelot du Lake. And I take God to recorde,
I loved never none but hym, nor never shall, of erthely creature;
and a clene maydyn I am for hym and for all othir. And sitthyn
hit ys the sufferaunce of God that I shall dye for so noble a
knyght, I beseche the Hyghe Fadir of Hevyn to have mercy 1375
uppon me and my soule, and uppon myne unnumerable paynys,
that that I suffer may be alygeaunce of parte of my synnes. For,
Swete Lorde Jesu,' seyde the fayre maydyn, 'I take God to recorde
I was never to The grete offenser nother ayenste Thy lawis but
that I loved thys noble knyght, Sir Launcelot, oute of mesure. 1380
And of myselff, Good Lorde, I had no myght to withstonde the
fervent love, wherefore I have my deth.'

And than she called hir fadir, Sir Bernarde, and hir brothir,
Sir Tirry, and hartely she prayd hir fadir that hir brothir
myght wryght a lettir lyke as she ded endite, and so hir fadir 1385
graunted her. And whan the lettir was wryten, worde by worde
lyke as she devised hit, than she prayde hir fadir that she myght
be wacched untylle she were dede. 'And whyle my body ys hote
lat thys lettir be put in my ryght honde, and my honde bounde
faste to the letter untyll that I be colde. And lette me be put in 1390
a fayre bed with all the rychyste clothys that I have aboute me,
and so lat my bed and all my rychyst clothis be ledde with me in
a charyat unto the nexte place where the Temmys ys. And there
lette me be put within a barget, and but one man with me, such
as ye truste, to stirre me thidir; and that my barget be coverde 1395
with blacke samyte over and over. And thus, fadir, I beseche you,
lat hit be done.'

So hir fadir graunted hit her faythfully: all thynge sholde be

1374 *the sufferaunce of God*, what God permits, God's will
1377 *alygeaunce*, remission
1379 *offenser*, offender   *nother ayenste*, neither [was I] against   *but*, except
1380 *oute of mesure*, excessively
1381 *the*, understand 'this'
1384 *hartely*, earnestly   *hir brothir* (C)
1385 *lyke as*, as   *endite*, dictate (not 'write')
1388 *hote*, warm
1388-90 See C.
1391 *clothys*, clothes and lengths of fabric (C)   *aboute*, on and around
1392 *ledde*, transported (C)
1393 *charyat*, cart   *next*, nearest (lit. 'nigh-est') (C)
1394 *barget*, boat (cf. *barge*)
1395 *stirre*, steer   *thidir*, there (C)
1396 *samyte*, a rich silk usually interwoven with gold thread
1398 *graunted her faythfully*, promised [it] faithfully to her

114

done lyke as she had devised. Than her fadir and hir brothir made grete dole for her. And whan thys was done, anone she 1400 dyed.

And whan she was dede the corse and the bedde all was lad the nexte way unto the Temmys, and there a man and the corse, and all thynge as she had devised, was put in the Temmys. And so the man stirred the bargett unto Westmynster, and there hit rubbed 1405 and rolled too and fro a grete whyle or ony man aspyed hit.

So by fortune Kynge Arthure and Quene Gwenyver were talkynge togydirs at a wyndow, and so as they loked into the Temmys they aspyed that blacke barget and had mervayle what hit mente. Than the kynge called Sir Kay and shewed hit him. 1410

'Sir,' seyde Sir Kay, 'wete you well, there ys som new tydynges.'

'Therefore go ye thidir,' seyde the kynge to Sir Kay, 'and take with you Sir Braundiles and Sir Aggravayne, and brynge me redy worde what ys there.'

Than thes three knyghtes departed and cam to the barget and 1415 wente in. And there they founde the fayryst corse lyyng in a ryche bed that ever they saw, and a poore man syttynge in the bargettis ende, and no worde wolde he speke. So thes three knyghtes returned unto the kynge agayne and tolde hym what they founde. 1420

'That fayre corse woll I se,' seyde the kynge.

And so the kynge toke the quene by the honde and wente thydir. Than the kynge made the barget to be holde faste, and than the kynge and the quene wente in with sertayne knyghtes with them, and there he saw the fayryst woman ly in a ryche bed, 1425 coverde unto her myddyll with many rych clothys, and all was of cloth of golde. And she lay as she had smyled.

Than the quene aspyed the lettir in hir ryght hande and tolde the kynge. Than the kynge toke hit and seyde, 'Now am I sure thys lettir woll telle us what she was, and why she ys com hyddir.' 1430

So than the kynge and the quene wente oute of the bargette, and so commaunded a sertayne to wayte uppon the barget. And

---

1400 *anone,* soon
1404 *was,* were
1405–6 *rubbed and rolled* (C)
1406 *or,* ere, before
1414 *redy,* swift
1423 *holde,* held
1425 See C.
1427 *as she had smyled,* as if she smiled
1432 *a sertayne,* a certain [number of attendants]

so whan the kynge was com to hys chambir, he called many knyghtes aboute hym and seyde that he wolde wete opynly what was wryten within that lettir.   1435

Than the kynge brake hit and made a clerke to rede hit, and thys was the entente of the lettir: 'Moste noble knyght, my lorde Sir Launcelot, now hath dethe made us two at debate for youre love. And I was youre lover, that men called the Fayre Maydyn of Astolate. Therefore unto all ladyes I make my mone that for 1440 my soule ye pray and bury me at the leste, and offir ye my masse-peny: thys ys my laste requeste. And a clene maydyn I dyed, I take God to wytnesse. And pray for my soule, Sir Launcelot, as thou arte pereles.'

Thys was all the substaunce in the lettir. And whan hit was 1445 rad the kynge, the quene and all the knyghtes wepte for pité of the dolefull complayntes. Than was Sir Launcelot sente for, and whan he was com Kynge Arthure made the lettir to be rad to hym.

And whan Sir Launcelot harde hit worde by worde, he seyde, 1450 'My lorde Arthur, wyte you well I am ryght hevy of the deth of thys fayre lady. And God knowyth I was never causar of her deth be my wyllynge, and that woll I reporte me unto her owne brothir that here ys, Sir Lavayne. I woll nat say nay,' seyde Sir Launcelot, 'but that she was both fayre and good, and much I 1455 was beholdyn unto her, but she loved me oute of mesure.'

'Sir,' seyde the quene, 'ye myght have shewd hir som bownté and jantilnes whych myght have preserved hir lyff.'

'Madame,' seyde Sir Launcelot, 'she wolde none other wayes be answerde but that she wolde be my wyff othir ellis my para- 1460 mour, and of thes two I wolde not graunte her. But I proffird her,

---

1434 *wete*, know
1436 *brake*, opened (i.e. broke the seal)
1437 *entente*, gist, purport
1438 *at debate*, at odds
1439 *I was your lover*, I loved you (not 'I was your mistress')
1440–2 Translate: 'I make my complaint to all ladies, that you [i.e. Lancelot] at least pray for my soul and have me buried, and make the offering at my Requiem' (C)
1444 *pereles*, peerless
1446 *rad*, read
1447 *dolefull*, pitiful
1452–3 Translate: 'I never wished to cause her death'
1453 *that*, in that   *reporte me*, refer myself
1454–5 *say nay ... but that*, deny that
1457 *bownté*, generosity   *jantilnes*, sympathy
1459 *none other wayes*, in no other way

for her good love that she shewed me, a thousand pound yerely to her and to her ayres, and to wedde ony maner of knyght that she coude fynde beste to love in her harte. For, madame,' seyde Sir Launcelot, 'I love nat to be constrayned to love, for love muste 1465 only aryse of the harte selff, and nat by none constraynte.'

'That ys trouth, sir,' seyde the kynge, 'and with many knyghtes love ys fre in hymselffe, and never woll be bonde; for where he ys bonden he lowsith hymselff.'

Than seyde the kynge unto Sir Launcelot, 'Sir, hit woll be 1470 youre worshyp that ye oversé that she be entered worshypfully.'

'Sir,' seyde Sir Launcelot, 'that shall be done as I can beste devise.'

And so many knyghtes yode thyder to beholde that fayre dede mayden. And so uppon the morn she was entered rychely; and 1475 Sir Launcelot offird her masse-peny, and all tho knyghtes of the Table Rounde that were there at that tyme offerde with Sir Launcelot. And than the poure man wente agayne wyth the barget.

Than the quene sent for Sir Launcelot and prayde hym of 1480 mercy for why that she had ben wrothe with hym causeles.

'Thys ys nat the firste tyme,' seyde Sir Launcelot, 'that ye have ben displesed with me causeles. But, madame, ever I muste suffir you, but what sorrow that I endure, ye take no forse.'

So thys passed on all that wynter, with all manner of huntynge 1485 and hawkynge; and justis and turneyes were many betwyxte many grete lordis. And ever in all placis Sir Lavayn gate grete worshyp, that he was nobely defamed amonge many knyghtis of the Table Rounde.

Thus hit past on tylle Crystemasse, and than every day there 1490 was justis made for a dyamonde: who that justed best shulde have a dyamounde. But Sir Launcelot wolde nat juste but if hit were

---

1464–9 See C.
1468 *hymselffe*, itself   *bonde*, bound
1471 *worshyp*, honour (C)   *entered*, interred, buried
1473 *devise*, think of
1474 *yode*, went
1476 *tho*, those
1480–1 *prayde hym of mercy*, asked his forgiveness
1481 *for why that*, because
1484 *suffir*, endure   *take no forse*, take no account [of it]
1487 *gate*, got
1488 *defamed*, reported (not 'defamed')
1492 *but if*, unless

a grete justes cryed; but Sir Lavayne justed there all the Crystemasse passyngly well, and was beste praysed, for there were but
feaw that ded so well. Wherefore all maner of knyghtes demed 1495
that Sir Lavayn sholde be made knyght of the Table Rounde at
the next feste of Pentecoste.

III

So at afftir Crystemas Kynge Arthure lete calle unto hym many
knyghtes, and there they avysed togydirs to make a party and a
grete turnemente and justis. And the Kynge of North Galys seyde 1500
to Kynge Arthure he wolde have on hys party Kyng Angwysh of
Irelonde and the Kynge wyth the Hondred Knyghtes and the
Kynge of Northhumbirlonde and Sir Galahalt the Haute Prynce.
So thes four kynges and this myghty deuke toke party ayenste
Kynge Arthure and the knyghtes of the Rounde Table. And the 1505
cry was made that the day off justys shulde be besydes Westemynster, upon Candylmasse day, whereof many knyghtes
were glad and made them redy to be at that justys in the freysshyste maner.

Than Quene Gwenyver sente for Sir Launcelot and seyd thus: 1510
'I warne you that ye ryde no more in no justis nor turnementis
but that youre kynnesmen may know you. And at thys justis that
shall be ye shall have of me a slyeve of golde; and I pray you for
my sake to force yourselff there, that men may speke you worshyp; but I charge you, as ye woll have my love, that ye warne 1515
your kynnesmen that ye woll beare that day the slyve of golde
uppon your helmet.'

'Madame,' seyde Sir Launcelot, 'hit shall be done.'

1493 *cryed*, proclaimed
1495 *demed*, thought
1498 *lete calle*, ordered to be called
1499 *avysed*, consulted   *party*, side, team (as in sport)
1500 *justis*, series of jousts (C)
1508-9 *freysshyste* (C)
1511 *warne*, forbid (C)
1513 *slyeve*, sleeve (C)
1514 *force*, exert
1515 *warne*, warn

And aythir made grete joy of othir. And whan Sir Launcelot saw hys tyme he tolde Sir Bors that he wolde departe, and no mo 1520 wyth hym but Sir Lavayne, unto the good ermyte that dwelled in the foreyst of Wyndesore, whos name was Sir Brastias. And there he thought to repose hym and to take all the reste that he myght, because he wolde be freysh at that day of justis.

So Sir Launcelot and Sir Lavayne departed, that no creature 1525 wyste where he was becom but the noble men of hys blood. And whan he was come to the ermytayge, wyte you well he had grete chyre. And so dayly Sir Launcelot used to go to a welle faste by the ermytage, and there he wolde ly downe and se the well sprynge and burble, and somtyme he slepte there. 1530

So at that tyme there was a lady that dwelled in that foreyste, and she was a grete hunteresse, and dayly she used to hunte, and ever she bare her bowghe with her. And no men wente never with her, but allwayes women, and they were all shooters and cowde well kylle a dere, bothe at the stalke and at the treste. And 1535 they dayly beare bowys and arowis, hornys and wood-knyves, and many good doggis they had, bothe for the strenge and for a bate.

So hit happed the lady, the huntresse, had abated her dogge for the bowghe at a barayne hynde, and so this barayne hynde 1540 toke the flyght over hethys and woodis. And ever thys lady and parte of her women costed the hynde, and checked hit by the noyse of the hounde to have mette with the hynde at som watir. And so hit happened that that hynde cam to the same welle thereas Sir Launcelot was slepynge and slumberynge. 1545

And so the hynde, whan he cam to the welle, for heete she

1519 *aythir*, each
1521 *ermyte*, hermit
1524 *wolde*, wished to
1526 *wyste*, knew
1527 *wyte you well*, cf. l. 104*n*
1528 *chyre*, cheer, welcome
1533 *bowghe*, bow   *no ... never*, no ... ever
1535 *cowde*, could   *at the stalke*, by stalking [it]   *at the treste*, by ambush (C)
1537 *for the strenge*, for use in hunting on a leash (cf. *string*)
1537-8 *for a bate*, for releasing for free pursuit and attack
1539-40 Translate: 'had unleashed her dog at a barren hind to get a shot at it.' Cf. prec.
1542 *costed*, outflanked [the hind] to prevent it from turning (cf. *coast*, vb.)
1542-3 Translate: 'and discovered from the cry of the hound that it had come upon the hind at some stretch of water' (Malory's syntax is confused and the sense of *check* disputed)
1546 *he*, she; from Old English *heo*, 'she'; cf. l. 2662 and 'Morte' l. 1344

wente to soyle, and there she lay a grete whyle. And the dogge
cam aftir and unbecaste aboute, for she had lost the verray parfyte fewte of the hynde. Ryght so cam that lady, the hunteres,
that knew by her dogge that the hynde was at the soyle by that 1550
welle, and thyder she cam streyte and founde the hynde. And
anone as she had spyed hym she put a brode arow in her bowe
and shote at the hynde, and so she overshotte the hynde, and so
by myssefortune the arow smote Sir Launcelot in the thycke of
the buttok over the barbys. 1555

Whan Sir Launcelot felte hym so hurte he whorled up woodly,
and saw the lady that had smytten hym. And whan he knew she
was a woman he sayde thus: 'Lady, or damesell, whatsomever
ye be, in an evyll tyme bare ye thys bowe. The devyll made you
a shoter!' 1560

'Now, mercy, fayre sir!' seyde the lady, 'I am a jantillwoman
that usyth here in thys foreyste huntynge, and God knowyth I
saw you nat, but as here was a barayne hynde at the soyle in thys
welle. And I wente I had done welle, but my hande swarved.'

'Alas,' seyde Sir Launcelot, 'ye have myscheved me.' 1565

And so the lady departed; and Sir Launcelot, as he myght,
pulled oute the arow and leffte the hede stylle in hys buttok. And
so he wente waykely unto the ermytayge, evermore bledynge as
he wente. And whan Sir Lavayne and the ermyte aspyed that Sir
Launcelot was so sore hurte, wyte you well they were passyng 1570
hevy. But Sir Lavayne wyst nat how that he was hurte nothir by
whom. And than were they wrothe oute of mesure. And so wyth
grete payne the ermyte gate oute the arow-hede oute of Sir

[1547] *wente to soyle*, took to the water (C)
[1548] *unbecaste*, cast round (i.e. for the quarry)
[1548-9] *verray parfyte fewte*, true, clear trail
[1550] *was at the soyle*, had gone to ground, was hidden
[1552] *brode*, broad (C)
[1555] *barbys*, barbs
[1556] *woodly*, fierce (lit. 'madly')
[1557] *smytten*, hit
[1561] *mercy* (C)
[1562] *usyth . . . huntynge*, is accustomed to hunt
[1563] *as*, understand 'that'
[1564] *wente*, weened, thought
[1565] *myscheved*, injured
[1566] *as he myght*, as best he might
[1568] *wente*, walked (lit. 'went')　　*waykely*, weakly
[1569] *aspyed*, espied, saw
[1571] *hevy*, downcast
[1571-2] See C.

Launcelottis buttoke, and muche of hys bloode he shed; and the wounde was passynge sore and unhappyly smytten, for hit was 1575 on such a place that he myght nat sytte in no sadyll.

'A, mercy Jesu!' seyde Sir Launcelot, 'I may calle myselff the moste unhappy man that lyvyth, for ever whan I wolde have faynyst worshyp there befallyth me ever som unhappy thynge. Now, so Jesu me helpe,' seyde Sir Launcelot, 'and if no man 1580 wolde but God, I shall be in the fylde on Candilmas day at the justys, whatsomever falle of hit.'

So all that myght be gotyn to hele Sir Launcelot was had. So, whan the day was come, Sir Launcelot lat devise that he was arayed, and Sir Lavayne and their horsis, as they had ben Sara- 1585 syns. And so they departed and cam nyghe to the fylde.

So the Kynge of North Galys he had an hondred knyghtes with hym, and the Kynge of Northehumbirlonde brought with hym an hondred good knyghtes, and Kynge Angwysh of Irelonde brought with hym an hondred good knyghtes redy to juste. And 1590 Sir Galahalte the Haute Prynce brought with hym an hondred good knyghtes, and the Kynge wyth the Hondred Knyghtes brought with hym as many, and all these were proved good knyghtes.

Than cam in Kynge Arthurs party, and in cam wyth hym the 1595 Kynge of Scottes, and an hondred knyghtes with hym, and Kynge Uryence of Goore brought with hym an hondred knyghtes, and Kynge Howell of Bretayne he brought wyth hym an hondred knyghtes, and Deuke Chalaunce of Claraunce brought with hym an hondred knyghtes. And Kynge Arthure 1600 hymselff cam into the fylde with two hondred knyghtes, and the moste party were knyghtes of the Rounde Table that were all proved noble men. And there were olde knyghtes set on skaffoldys for to jouge with the quene who ded beste.

Than they blew unto the fylde. And there the Kynge off 1605

1574 *hys . . . he.* Lancelot's . . . the hermit
1575 *sore* serious   *unhappyly,* unfortunately (cf. *hap,* 'chance')
1578–9 *wolde have faynyst,* want most eagerly to have
1580–1 *if no man wolde but God,* if no man wishes it but God [does wish it] (C)
1582 *falle of,* befall as a result of
1584 *lat devise,* had [it] brought about
1585 *arayed,* equipped   *as they had ben,* as if they were
1587–1602 See C.
1593 *proved,* tested, experienced
1602 *moste party,* largest part
1603 *skaffoldys,* platforms raised on scaffolding

North Galis encountred wyth the Kynge of Scottes, and there
the Kynge of Scottis had a falle; and the Kynge of Irelonde
smote downe Kynge Uryence, and the Kynge of Northhumbirlonde smote downe Kynge Howell of Bretayne, and Sir Galahalte the Haute Prynce smote downe Deuke Chalaunce of 1610
Claraunce. And than Kynge Arthure was wood wrothe, and
ran to the Kynge wyth the Hondred Knyghtes, and so Kynge
Arthure smote hym downe. And aftir wyth that same speare he
smote downe other three knyghtes, and than hys speare brake,
and ded passyngly well. So therewith cam in Sir Gawayne and 1615
Sir Gaherys, Sir Aggravayne and Sir Mordred, and there
everych of them smote downe a knyght and Sir Gawayne smote
downe four knyghtes. And than there began a grete medlé, for
than cam in the knyghtes of Sir Launcelottys blood, and Sir
Gareth and Sir Palomydes wyth them, and many knyghtes of the 1620
Rounde Table; and they began to holde the four kynges and the
myghty deuke so harde that they were ny discomfyte. But thys
Sir Galahalte the Haute Prynce was a noble knyght, and by hys
myghty proues of armys he hylde the knyghtes of the Rounde
Table strayte ynough.   1625
   So all thys doynge saw Sir Launcelot, and than he cam into
the fylde wyth Sir Lavayne with hym, as hit had bene thunder.
And than anone Sir Bors and the knyghtes of hys bloode aspyed
Sir Launcelot anone and seyde unto them all, 'I warne you, be-
ware of hym with the slyve of golde uppon hys hede, for he ys 1630
hymselff my lorde Sir Launcelot.'
   And for grete goodnes Sir Bors warned Sir Gareth. 'Sir, I am
well payde,' seyde Sir Gareth, 'that I may know hym.'
   'But who ys he,' seyde they all, 'that rydith with hym in the
same aray?'   1635

1606 *encountred*, met, i.e. jousted
1608 *smote*, struck
1611 *wood wrothe*, mad with rage (C)
1614 *other three*, three other
1614-15 See C.
1615 *passyngly*, very
1618 *medlé*, mêlée
1621 *holde*, press
1622 *ny discomfyte*, nearly put to the worse
1624-5 *hylde . . . strayte*, held . . . in check (lit. 'strait')
1629 *anone*, anon, at once   See C.
1631 *hymselff my lorde Sir Launcelot*, my lord Sir Lancelot himself
1632 *for grete goodnes*, because of his generous nature
1633 *payde*, pleased

'Sir, that ys the good and jantyll knyght Sir Lavayne,' seyde Sir Bors.

So Sir Launcelot encountred with Sir Gawayne, and there by force Sir Launcelot smote downe Sir Gawayne and his horse to the erthe. And so he smote downe Sir Aggravayne and Sir 1640 Gaherys, and also he smote downe Sir Mordred, and all this was wyth one speare. Than Sir Lavayne mette with Sir Palomydes, and aythir mette other so harde and so fersely that both theire horsis felle to the erthe. And than were they horsed agayne; and than mette Sir Launcelot with Sir Palomydes, and there Sir 1645 Palomydes had a falle. And so Sir Launcelot, or ever he stynte, and as faste as he myght gete spearys, he smote downe thirty knyghtes, and the moste party were knyghtes of the Rounde Table. And ever the knyghtes of hys bloode wythdrew them, and made hem ado in othir placis where Sir Launcelot cam nat.   1650

And than Kynge Arthure was wrotthe whan he saw Sir Launcelot do suche dedis, and than the kynge called unto hym Sir Gawayne, Sir Gaherys, Sir Aggravayne, Sir Mordred, Sir Kay, Sir Gryfflet, Sir Lucan de Butlere, Sir Bedyvere, Sir Palomydes and Sir Safyre, hys brothir. And so the kynge wyth thes 1655 ten knyghtes made them redy to sette uppon Sir Launcelot and uppon Sir Lavayne.

And all thys aspyed Sir Bors and Sir Gareth. 'Now I drede me sore,' seyde Sir Bors, 'that my lorde Sir Launcelot woll be harde macched.'   1660

'Now, be my hede,' seyde Sir Gareth, 'I woll ryde unto my lorde Sir Launcelot for to helpe hym, whatsomever me betyde; for he ys the same man that made me knyght.'

'Sir, ye shall nat do so,' seyde Sir Bors, 'be my counceyle, onles that ye were disgysed.'   1665

'Sir, ye shall se me sone disgysed,' seyde Sir Gareth.

And therewithall he had aspyed a Waylshe knyght where he was to repose hym, for he was sore hurte before of Sir Gawayne.

1646 *stynte*, stinted, stopped
1650 *made hem ado*, kept themselves busy
1651 *wrotthe*, angry
1664-5 See C.
1666 *sone*, soon
1667 *Waylshe*, Welsh
1667-8 See C.
1668 *of*, by

And unto hym Sir Gareth rode and prayde hym of hys knyght-
hode to lende hym hys shylde for hys.   1670

'I woll well,' seyde the Waylshe knyght.

And whan Sir Gareth had hys shylde—the booke seythe hit
was gryne, wyth a maydyn whych semed in hit—than Sir
Gareth cam dryvynge unto Sir Launcelot all that ever he myght,
and seyde, 'Sir knyght, take kepe to thyselff, for yondir com-   1675
myth Kynge Arthur with ten noble knyghtes wyth hym, to put
you to rebuke. And so I am com to beare you felyshyp for the
olde love ye have shewed unto me.'

'Grauntemercy,' seyde Sir Launcelot.

'But, sir,' seyde Sir Gareth, 'encountir ye with Sir Gawayne,   1680
and I shall encountir with Sir Palomydes, and lat Sir Lavayne
macche with the noble Kynge Arthur. And whan we have delyverde them lat us three holde us sadly togydirs.'

So than cam in Kynge Arthure wyth hys ten knyghtes with
hym, and Sir Launcelot encountred with Sir Gawayne and gaff   1685
hym suche a buffette that the arson of hys sadyll braste, and Sir
Gawayne felle to the erthe. Than Sir Gareth encountred with
the good knyght Sir Palomydes, and he gaff hym such a buffet
that bothe hys horse and he daysshed to the erthe. Than encountred Kynge Arthure wyth Sir Lavayne, and there aythir of   1690
them smote other to the erthe, horse and all, that they lay bothe
a grete whyle. Than Sir Launcelot smote downe Sir Aggravayne
and Sir Gaherys and Sir Mordred; and Sir Gareth smote downe
Sir Kay, Sir Safir and Sir Gryfflet.

And than Sir Lavayne was horsed agayne, and he smote   1695
downe Sir Lucan de Butlere and Sir Bedyvere, and than there
began grete thrange of good knyghtes. Than Sir Launcelot

1669 *of*, by
1671 *I woll well*, very willingly (lit. 'I will it gladly')
1672 *seythe*, says (C)
1673 *gryne*, green   *maydyn*, maiden   *semed*, seemed (C)
1674 *dryvynge*, riding hard   *all that*, with all the speed that
1675 *take kepe to*, take care of
1676–7 *put . . . to rebuke*, give a setback
1677 *felyshyp*, fellowship
1679 *Grauntemercy*, Many thanks (Fr. *grand merci*)
1682–3 *delyverde*, dealt with
1683 *sadly*, firmly (not 'sadly')
1686 *arson*, cantle (Fr. *arçon*)   *braste*, burst
1689 *daysshed*, was dashed, was hurled
1691 *that*, so that
1697 *thrange*, throng, press [of people]

hurled here and there, and raced and pulled of helmys, that at
that tyme there myght none sytte hym a buffette with speare nothir
with swerde. And Sir Gareth ded such dedys of armys that all 1700
men mervayled what knyght he was with the gryne shylde, for he
smote downe that day and pulled downe mo than thirty
knyghtes. And, as the Freynshe booke sayth, Sir Launcelot mervayled, whan he behylde Sir Gareth do such dedis, what knyght
he myght be. And Sir Lavayne smote downe and pulled downe 1705
mo than twenty knyghtes. And yet, for all thys, Sir Launcelot
knew nat Sir Gareth; for and Sir Trystram de Lyones other Sir
Lamorak de Galys had ben on lyve, Sir Launcelot wolde have
demed he had bene one of them twayne.

So ever as Sir Launcelot, Sir Gareth and Sir Lavayne fought 1710
on the tone syde, Sir Bors, Sir Ector de Marys, Sir Lyonell, Sir
Bleoberys, Sir Galyhud, Sir Galyhodyn and Sir Pelleas and
many mo other of Kynge Banys blood faught uppon another
party and hylde the Kynge wyth the Hondred Knyghtes and
the Kynge of Northhumbirlonde ryght strayte. So thys turne- 1715
mente and justis dured longe tylle hit was nere nyght, for the
knyghtes of the Rounde Table releved ever unto Kynge Arthure;
for the kyng was wrothe oute of mesure that he and hys knyghtes
myght nat prevayle that day.

Than sayde Sir Gawayne to the kynge, 'Sir, I mervayle where 1720
ar all thys day Sir Bors de Ganys and hys felyshyp of Sir Launcelottis blood, that of all thys day they be nat aboute you. And
therefore I deme hit ys for som cause,' seyde Sir Gawayne.

---

¹⁶⁹⁸ *hurled,* rushed   *raced . . . of,* tore off
¹⁶⁹⁹ *sytte hym,* withstand from him   *nothir,* nor
¹⁷⁰² *mo,* more
¹⁷⁰³ See C.
¹⁷⁰⁵⁻⁶ See C.
¹⁷⁰⁷ *for and,* because if (C)
¹⁷⁰⁸ *on lyve,* alive
¹⁷⁰⁹ *demed,* deemed, judged
¹⁷¹⁰ *ever as,* all the time that
¹⁷¹¹ *the tone,* the one, one
¹⁷¹³ *Kynge Banys blood* (C)
¹⁷¹⁴⁻¹⁵ *hylde . . . strayte,* held . . . firmly in check
¹⁷¹⁶ *dured longe,* lasted (lit. 'endured') for a long time
¹⁷¹⁷ *releved ever unto,* continually reinforced
¹⁷¹⁸ *wrothe oute of mesure,* cf. l. 1198n
¹⁷²² *of,* during   *be nat,* have not been
¹⁷²³ *deme,* judge, suspect

'Be my hede,' seyde Sir Kay, 'Sir Bors ys yondir all thys day
uppon the ryght honde of thys fylde, and there he and his blood 1725
dothe more worshypfully than we do.'

'Hit may well be,' seyde Sir Gawayne, 'but I drede me ever
of gyle. For on payne of my lyff,' seyde Sir Gawayne, 'that same
knyght with the rede slyve of golde ys hymselff Sir Launcelot, for
I se well by hys rydynge and by hys greate strokis. And the othir 1730
knyght in the same colowres ys the good yonge knyght Sir
Lavayne. And that knyght with the grene shylde ys my brothir
Sir Gareth, and yet he hath disgysed hymselff, for no man shall
make hym be ayenste Sir Launcelot, bycause he made hym
knyght.' 1735

'By my hede,' seyde Kynge Arthure, 'neveaw, I belyeve you.
And therefore now telle me what ys youre beste counceyle.'

'Sir,' seyde Sir Gawayne, 'my counceile ys to blow unto lodgynge. For and he be Sir Launcelot du Lake and my brothir Sir
Gareth wyth hym, wyth the helpe of that goode yonge knyght 1740
Sir Lavayne, truste me truly, hit woll be no boote to stryve wyth
them but if we sholde falle ten or twelve uppon one knyght, and
that were no worshyp, but shame.'

'Ye say trouthe,' seyde the kynge. 'And for to sey sothe,' seyde
the kynge, 'hit were shame for us, so many as we be, to sette 1745
uppon them ony more. For wyte you well,' seyde Kynge Arthure,
'they be three good knyghtes, and namely that knyght with the
slyve of golde.'

And anone they blew unto lodgyng, but furthwithall Kynge
Arthure lete sende unto the four kyngis and to the myghty deuke 1750
and prayde hem that the knyght with the slyve of golde departe
nat frome them but that the kynge may speke with hym. Than

1724 *Be, By   ys,* has been (C)
1726 *dothe,* do
1728 *gyle,* guile, trickery
1730 *I se well,* I see [it] well
1734 *ayenste,* against
1737 *counceyle,* counsel
1739 *and . . . and,* if . . . and if
1739–43 See C.
1741 *boote,* use (lit. 'reward')
1742 *but if,* unless
1744 *sothe,* truly (lit. 'truth')
1747 *namely,* especially
1749 *furthwithall,* forthwith, at once
1750 *lete sende,* had [a message] sent

furthwithall Kynge Arthur alyght and unarmed hym and toke
a lytyll hakeney and rode after Sir Launcelot, for ever he had a
spy uppon hym. And so he founde hym amonge the four kyngis 1755
and the deuke, and there the kynge prayde hem all unto suppere,
and they seyde they wolde with good wyll. And whan they were
unarmed Kynge Arthure knew Sir Launcelot, Sir Gareth, and
Sir Lavayne.

'A, Sir Launcelot,' seyde Kynge Arthure, 'thys day ye have 1760
heted me and my knyghtes!'

And so they yode unto Kynge Arthurs lodgynge all togydir,
and there was a grete feste and grete revell. And the pryce was
yevyn unto Sir Launcelot, for by herowdys they named hym that
he had smytten downe fifty knyghtys, and Sir Gareth five-and- 1765
thirty knyghtes, and Sir Lavayne four-and-twenty. Than Sir
Launcelot tolde the kynge and the quene how the lady hunteras
shotte hym in the Foreyste of Wyndesore in the buttok wyth a
brode arow, and how the wounde was at that tyme six inchys
depe and inlyke longe.   1770

Also Kynge Arthure blamed Sir Gareth because he leffte hys
felyshyp and hylde with Sir Launcelot.

'My lorde,' seyde Sir Garethe, 'he made me knyght, and whan
I saw hym so hard bestad, methought hit was my worshyp to
helpe hym. For I saw hym do so muche dedis of armys, and so 1775
many noble knyghtes ayenste hym, that whan I undirstode that
he was Sir Launcelot du Lake I shamed to se so many good
knyghtes ayenste hym alone.'

'Now, truly,' seyde Kynge Arthur unto Sir Gareth, 'ye say
well, and worshypfully have ye done, and to youreselff grete 1780
worshyp. And all the dayes of my lyff,' seyde Kynge Arthure
unto Sir Gareth, 'wyte you well I shall love you and truste you

[1753] *hym,* himself
[1754] *hakeney,* hack, comfortable ambler
[1756] *prayde hem . . . unto,* asked them . . . to
[1761] *heted,* warmed
[1762] *yode,* went
[1763] *pryce,* prize
[1764] *yevyn,* given   *herowdys,* heralds
[1767] *hunteras,* huntress
[1770] *inlyke,* similarly
[1772] *hylde with,* held with, supported
[1773-8] See C.
[1774] *bestad,* pressed   *methought,* it seemed to me (not 'I thought')
[1775] *so muche,* such great
[1777] *I shamed,* I was ashamed

the more bettir. For ever hit ys,' seyde Kynge Arthure, 'a worshypfull knyghtes dede to help and succoure another worshypfull knyght whan he seeth hym in daungere; for ever a worshyp- 1785
full man woll be lothe to se a worshypfull man shamed. And he
that ys of no worshyp and medelyth with cowardise, never shall
he shew jantilnes nor no maner of goodnes where he seeth a man
in daungere, for than woll a cowarde never shew mercy. And allwayes a good man woll do ever to another man as he wolde be 1790
done to hymselff.'

So than there were made grete festis unto kyngis and deukes;
and revell, game, and play, and all maner of nobeles was used.
And he that was curteyse, trew, and faythefull to hys frynde was
that tyme cherysshed.   1795

IV

And thus hit passed on frome Candylmas untyll after Ester, that
the moneth of May was com, whan every lusty harte begynnyth
to blossom and to burgyne. For, lyke as trees and erbys burgenyth
and florysshyth in May, in lyke wyse every lusty harte that ys ony
maner of lover spryngith, burgenyth, buddyth, and florysshyth 1800
in lusty dedis. For hit gyvyth unto all lovers corrayge, that lusty
moneth of May, in somthynge to constrayne hym to som maner
of thynge more in that moneth than in ony other monethe, for
dyverce causys: for than all erbys and treys renewyth a man and
woman, and in lyke wyse lovers callyth ageyne to their mynde 1805

[1783] *the more bettir,* the better (C)
[1786] *lothe,* unwilling
[1787] *medelyth with,* is a prey to (lit. 'mixes with')
[1789-91] See C.
[1792] *festis,* feasts
[1793] *nobeles was used,* behaviour proper for noble men was the custom
[1796] *Candlemas,* the popular name, because church candles were blessed then, of
the Feast of the Purification of the Blessed Virgin Mary: 2nd February (C)
[1797] *moneth,* month
[1798] *burgyne* burgeon   *erbys,* plants (lit. 'herbs')
[1801] *corrayge,* vital force, energy   *lusty,* lively
[1802-3] Translate: 'to compel them in some way more in that month than in any
other month [to do] something'.
[1804] See C.

128

olde jantylnes and olde servyse, and many kynde dedes that was
forgotyn by neclygence.

For, lyke as wynter rasure dothe allway arace and deface
grene summer, so faryth hit by unstable love in man and woman,
for in many persones there ys no stabylité. For we may se all day, 1810
for a lytyll blaste of wyntres rasure, anone we shall deface and lay
aparte trew love, for lytyll or nowght, that coste muche thynge.
Thys ys no wysedome nother no stabylité, but hit ys fyeblenes of
nature and grete disworshyp, whosomever usyth thys.

Therefore, lyke as May moneth flowryth and floryshyth in 1815
every mannes gardyne, so in lyke wyse lat every man of worshyp
florysh hys herte in thys worlde: firste unto God, and nexte unto
the joy of them that he promysed hys feythe unto. For there was
never worshypfull man nor worshypfull woman but they loved
one bettir than anothir, and worshyp in armys may never be 1820
foyled. But firste reserve the honoure to God, and secundely thy
quarell muste com of thy lady. And such love I calle vertuouse
love.

But nowadayes men can nat love sevennyght but they muste
have all their desyres. That love may nat endure by reson, for 1825
where they bethe sone accorded and hasty, heete sone keelyth.
And ryght so faryth the love nowadayes, sone hote sone colde.
Thys ys no stabylyté. But the olde love was nat so; for men and
women coude love togydirs seven yerys, and no lycoures lustis was
betwyxte them; and than was love trouthe and faythefulnes. And 1830
lo, in lyke wyse was used such love in Kynge Arthurs dayes.

Wherefore I lykken love nowadayes unto sommer and wynter:
for, lyke as the tone ys colde and the othir ys hote, so faryth love
nowadayes. And therefore all ye that be lovers, calle unto youre
remembraunce the monethe of May, lyke as ded Quene Gweny- 1835

1806 *jantylnes and . . . servyse* (C)   *was,* were
1808 *For,* But   *rasure,* obliteration   *arace,* erase   *deface,* blot out
1809 *by,* with
1815–23 See C.
1817 *florysh hys herte,* make his heart bloom
1820 *one bettir than anothir,* one [person] better than any other
1821 *foyled,* frustrated
1824 *sevennyght,* a week (cf. *fortnight*)
1826 *bethe,* are   *accorded,* agreed   *hasty,* hastily   *heete sone keelyth,* heat soon
cools (C)
1829 *lycoures lustis,* lustful desires   *was,* were
1830 Translate: 'then love was loyalty and faithfulness' (C)
1833 *so* (C)
1835 *ded,* did

129

ver, for whom I make here a lytyll mencion, that whyle she lyved she was a trew lover, and therefor she had a good ende.

So hit befelle in the moneth of May, Quene Gwenyver called unto her ten knyghtes of the Table Rounde, and she gaff them warnynge that early uppon the morn she wolde ryde on-mayynge 1840 into woodis and fyldis besydes Westemynster: 'And I warne you that there be none of you but he be well horsed, and that ye all be clothed all in gryne, othir in sylke othir in clothe. And I shall brynge with me ten ladyes, and every knyght shall have a lady be hym. And every knyght shall have a squyar and two yo- 1845 men, and I woll that all be well horsed.'

So they made hem redy in the freysshyst maner, and thes were the namys of the knyghtes: Sir Kay le Senesciall, Sir Aggravayne, Sir Braundyles, Sir Sagramour le Desyrous, Sir Dodynas le Savayge, Sir Ozanna le Cure Hardy, Sir Ladynas of the Foreyst 1850 Savayge, Sir Persaunte of Inde, Sir Ironsyde that was called the Knyght of the Rede Laundes, and Sir Pelleas the Lovear. And thes ten knyghtes made them redy in the freysshyste maner to ryde wyth the quyne.

And so uppon the morne or hit were day, in a May mornynge, 1855 they toke their horsys wyth the quene and rode on-mayinge in wodis and medowis as hit pleased hem, in grete joy and delytes; for the quene had caste to have bene agayne with Kynge Arthur at the furthest by ten of the clok, and so was that tyme her purpose. 1860

Than there was a knyght whych hyght Sir Mellyagaunce and he was sonne unto Kynge Bagdemagus, and this knyght had at that tyme a castell of the gyffte of Kynge Arthure within seven myle of Westemynster. And thys knyght Sir Mellyagaunce loved passyngly well Quene Gwenyver, and so had he done longe and 1865 many yerys. And the booke seyth he had layn in awayte for to stele away the quene, but evermore he forbare for bycause of Sir Launcelot; for in no wyse he wolde meddyll with the quene and

---

1837 See C.
1840 *wolde*, intended [to]   *on-mayynge*, a-Maying, celebrating the coming of May
1843 *othir . . . othir*, either . . . or
1845 *be*, by
1847 *freysshyst*, gayest
1852 *Lovear*, Lover
1855 *or*, ere, before
1858 *for*, and   *caste*, planned
1863 *of the gyffte*, in the gift, at the disposal (i.e. Arthur had given it to him)
1866 See C.
1868 *and*, if

Sir Launcelot were in her company, othir ellys and he were
nerehonde her.   1870
    And that tyme was such a custom that the quene rode never
wythoute a grete felyshyp of men of armys aboute her. And they
were many good knyghtes, and the moste party were yonge men
that wolde have worshyp, and they were called the Quenys
Knyghtes. And never in no batayle, turnement, nother justys 1875
they bare none of hem no maner of knowlecchynge of their own
armys but playne whyght shyldis, and thereby they were called
the Quenys Knyghtes. And whan hit happed ony of them to be of
grete worshyp by hys noble dedis, than at the nexte feste of
Pentecoste, gyff there were ony slayne or dede (as there was none 1880
yere that there fayled but there were som dede), than was there
chosyn in hys stede that was dede the moste men of worshyp that
were called the Quenys Knyghtes. And thus they cam up alle
firste or they were renowmed men of worshyp, both Sir Launcelot and all the remenaunte of them.   1885
    But thys knyght Sir Mellyagaunce had aspyed the quene well
and her purpose, and how Sir Launcelot was nat wyth her, and
how she had no men of armys with her but the ten noble knyghtis
all rayed in grene for maiynge. Than he purveyde hym a twenty
men of armys and·an hondred archars for to destresse the quene 1890
and her knyghtes; for he thought that tyme was beste seson to
take the quene.
    So as the quene was oute on mayynge wyth all her knyghtes
whych were bedaysshed wyth erbis, mossis, and floures in the
beste maner and freysshyste, ryght so there cam oute of a wood 1895
Sir Mellyagaunte with an eyght score men, all harneyst as they

1869 *and,* if
1870 *nerehonde,* near
1872 *men of armys,* men-at-arms
1873 *party,* part
1874 *wolde have,* wanted to have
1876 *they bare none of hem,* none of them bore   *knowlecchynge,* cognizance (C)
1879 *worshyp,* honour, reputation
1880 *ony,* any [of the Knights of the Round Table]   *none,* to
1881 *fayled but there were som,* understand 'failed to be some'
1882 *in hys stede that was,* in their places who were
1884 *renowmed,* renowned, famous
1889 *rayed,* arrayed
1890 *destresse,* overwhelm (not 'distress')
1891 *seson,* time (lit. 'season', perhaps as in hunting)
1894 *bedaysshed,* adorned
1895 *ryght so,* all at once
1896 *harneyst,* armed

shulde fyght in a batayle of areste, and bade the quene and her
knyghtis abyde, for magré their hedis they shulde abyde.

'Traytoure knyght,' seyd Quene Gwenyver, 'what caste thou
to do? Wolt thou shame thyselff? Bethynke the how thou arte a 1900
kyngis sonne and a knyght of the Table Rounde, and thou thus
to be aboute to dishonoure the noble kyng that made the
knyght! Thou shamyst all knyghthode and thyselffe and me.
And I lat the wyte thou shalt never shame me, for I had levir kut
myne owne throte in twayne rather than thou sholde dishonoure 1905
me!'

'As for all thys langayge,' seyde Sir Mellyagaunte, 'be as hit be
may. For wyte you well, madame, I have loved you many a yere,
and never ar now cowde I gete you at such avayle, and therefore
I woll take you as I fynde you.' 1910

Than spake all the ten noble knyghtes at onys and seyde, 'Sir
Mellyagaunte, wyte thou well thou arte aboute to jouparté thy
worshyp to dishonoure, and also ye caste to jouparté oure persones. Howbehit we be unarmed and ye have us at a grete
avauntayge—for hit semyth by you that ye have layde wacche 1915
uppon us—but rather than ye shulde put the quene to a shame
and us all, we had as lyff to departe frome owre lyvys, for and we
othyrwayes ded we were shamed for ever.'

Than seyde Sir Mellyagaunt, 'Dresse you as well as ye can,
and kepe the quene!' 1920

Than the ten knyghtis of the Rounde Table drew their swerdis,
and thes othir lat ren at them wyth their spearys. And the ten
knyghtis manly abode them and smote away their spearys, that
no speare ded them no harme. Than they laysshed togydirs wyth
swerdis, and anone Sir Kay, Sir Sagramoure, Sir Aggravayne, 1925
Sir Dodynas, Sir Ladynas, and Sir Ozanna were smytten to the
erthe with grymly woundis. Than Sir Braundiles and Sir Per-

1897 *batayle of areste*, battle in which there would be no direct contact with the enemy
1898 *magré their hedis*, willy-nilly (lit. 'in spite of their heads')
1900 *Bethynke the*, Consider
1904 *lat the wyte*, let you know   *had levir*, would rather
1907–10 See C.
1909 *ar*, before   *avayle*, advantage
1912 *jouparté*, [put in . . .] jeopardy
1914 *Howbehit*, although
1915 *by you*, by you [being here at this time]
1916 See C.
1919 *Dresse you*, Form up, Position yourselves
1922 *lat ren*, ran
1923 *manly*, like men (adverb)

saunte, Sir Ironsyde and Sir Pelleas faught longe, and they were sore wounded, for thes ten knyghtes, or ever they were leyde to the grounde, slew fourty men of the boldyste and the beste of 1930 them.

So whan the quene saw her knyghtes thus dolefully wounded and nedys muste be slayne at the laste, than for verry pyté and sorow she cryed and seyde, 'Sir Mellyagaunte, sle nat my noble knyghtes and I woll go with the uppon thys covenaunte: that thou 1935 save them and suffir hem no more to be hurte, wyth thys that they be lad with me wheresomever thou ledyst me. For I woll rather sle myselff than I woll go wyth the, onles that thes my noble knyghtes may be in my presence.'

'Madame,' seyde Sir Mellyagaunt, 'for your sake they shall be 1940 lad wyth you into myne owne castell, with that ye woll be reuled and ryde with me.'

Than the quene prayde the four knyghtes to leve their fyghtynge, and she and they wolde nat departe.

'Madame,' seyde Sir Pelleas, 'we woll do as ye do, for as for me, 1945 I take no force of my lyff nor deth.' For, as the Freynshe booke seyth, Sir Pelleas gaff such buffettis there that none armoure myght holde hym.

Than by the quenys commaundemente they leffte batayle and dressed the wounded knyghtes on horsebak, som syttyng and 1950 som overtwarte their horsis, that hit was pité to beholde. And than Sir Mellyagaunt charged the quene and all her knyghtes that none of al hir felyshyp shulde departe frome her, for full sore he drad Sir Launcelot du Lake, laste he shulde have ony knowlecchynge. And all this aspyed the quene, and pryvaly she called 1955 unto her a chylde of her chambir whych was swyfftely horsed of a grete avauntayge.

1933 *and nedys muste*, and [that they] needs must
1936 *wyth thys that*, with this [condition] that
1941 *with that*, on [condition] that   *reuled*, governed, sensible (C)
1944 *departe*, depart from one another, separate
1946-7 See C.
1948 *holde*, withstand
1950 *dressed*, arranged
1951 *overtwarte*, across
1952 *charged*, commanded
1954 *drad*, dreaded   *laste*, lest
1954-5 *knowlecchynge*, knowledge
1956 *chylde*, boy, page
1956-7 *of a grete avauntayge*, to [his] great advantage

'Now go thou,' seyde she, 'whan thou seyst thy tyme, and
beare thys rynge unto Sir Launcelot du Laake, and pray hym as
he lovythe me that he woll se me and rescow me, if ever he woll 1960
have joy of me. And spare nat thy horse,' seyde the quyene,
'nother for watir nother for londe.'

So thys chyld aspyed hys tyme, and lyghtly he toke hys horse
with the spurres and departed as faste as he myght. And wan Sir
Mellyagaunte saw hym so fle, he undirstood that hit was by the 1965
quyenys commaundemente for to warne Sir Launcelot. Than
they that were beste horsed chaced hym and shotte at hym, but
frome hem all the chylde wente delyverly.

And than Sir Mellyagaunte sayde unto the quyne, 'Madame,
ye ar aboute to betray me, but I shall ordayne for Sir Launcelot 1970
that he shall nat com lyghtly at you.'

And than he rode wyth her and all the felyshyp to his castell
in all the haste that they myght. And so by the way Sir Mellyagaunte layde in buyshemente of the beste archars that he
myghte gete in his countré to the numbre of a thirty to awayte 1975
uppon Sir Launcelot, chargynge them that yf they saw suche a
maner of a knyght com by the way uppon a whyght horse, 'that
in ony wyse ye sle hys horse, but in no maner have ye ado wyth
hym bodyly, for he ys over hardé to be overcom'. So thys was
done, and they were com to hys castell; but in no wyse the quene 1980
wolde never lette none of the ten knyghtes and her ladyes oute
of her syght, but allwayes they were in her presence. For the
booke sayth Sir Mellyagaunte durste make no mastryes for drede
of Sir Launcelot, insomuche he demed that he had warnynge.

So whan the chylde was departed fro the felyshyp of Sir 1985
Mellyagaunte, wythin a whyle he cam to Westemynster, and
anone he founde Sir Launcelot. And whan he had tolde hys
messayge and delyverde hym the quenys rynge, 'Alas!' seyde Sir

1960-1 *if ever he woll have joy of me* (C)
1962 *nother for watir nother for londe* (C)
1963 *lyghtly*, swiftly
1963-4 *toke hys horse with the spurres*, took spurs to his horse
1968 *delyverly*, adroitly
1970 *ordayne*, make arrangements
1971 *lyghtly*, easily
1974 *in buyshemente*, in ambush   *of*, some of
1976-7 *a maner of*, a kind of
1978 *in ony wyse*, in any way [you can]
1982-3 See C.
1983 *make no mastryes*, make use of his greater power (lit. 'make any masteries')

Launcelot, 'now am I shamed for ever, onles that I may rescow that noble lady frome dishonour!' Than egirly he asked hys 1990 armys.

And ever the chylde tolde Sir Launcelot how the ten knyghtes faught mervaylously, and how Sir Pelleas, Sir Ironsyde, Sir Braundyles and Sir Persaunte of Inde fought strongely, but namely Sir Pelleas, that there myght none harneys holde hym; 1995 and how they all faught tylle at the laste they were layde to the erthe, and how the quene made apoyntemente for to save their lyvys and to go wyth Sir Mellyagaunte.

'Alas!' seyed Sir Launcelot, 'that moste noble lady, that she shulde be so destroyed! I had lever', seyde Sir Launcelot, 'than 2000 all Fraunce that I had bene there well armed.'

So whan Sir Launcelot was armed and uppon hys horse he prayde the chylde of the quynys chambir to warne Sir Lavayne how suddeynly he was departed and for what cause. 'And pray hym, as he lovyth me, that he woll hyghe hym aftir me, and that 2005 he stynte nat untyll he com to the castell where Sir Mellyagaunt abydith, for there', seyde Sir Launcelot, 'he shall hyre of me, and I be a man lyvynge! Than shall I rescow the quene and the ten knyghtes, the whyche he traytorously hath taken, and that shall I prove upon his hede and all them that holde wyth hym.' 2010

Than Sir Launcelot rode as faste as he myght, and the booke seyth he toke the watir at Westmynster Brydge and made hys horse swymme over the Temmys unto Lambyth. And so within a whyle he cam to the same place thereas the ten noble knyghtes fought with Sir Mellyagaunte. And than Sir Launcelot folowed 2015 the trak untyll that he cam to a woode, and there was a strayte way, and there the thirty archers bade Sir Launcelot turne agayne and folow no longer that trak.

'What commaundemente have ye thereto,' seyde Sir Launce-lot, 'to cause me, that am a knyght of the Rounde Table, to 2020 leve my ryght way?'

1990 *asked*, asked for
1995 *namely*, especially   *harneys*, armour
1997 *apoyntement*, agreement
2000–1 See C.
2004 *how*, why
2005 *hyghe hym*, come quickly
2006 *stynte*, stop
2007 *hyre*, hear
2011–13 See C.
2016 *strayte*, narrow (lit. 'strait')

'Thys way shalt thou leve, othir ellis thou shalte go hit on thy foote, for wyte thou well thy horse shall be slayne.'

'That ys lytyll maystry,' seyde Sir Launcelot, 'to sle myne horse! But as for myselff, whan my horse ys slayne I gyff ryght nought of you, nat and ye were fyve hundred mo!' 2025

So than they shotte Sir Launcelottis horse and smote hym with many arowys. And than Sir Launcelot avoyded hys horse and wente on foote, but there were so many dychys and hedgys betwyxte hem and hym that he myght nat meddyll with none of hem. 2030

'Alas, for shame!' seyde Sir Launcelot, 'that ever one knyght shulde betray anothir knyght! But hyt ys an olde-seyde saw: "A good man ys never in daungere but whan he ys in the daungere of a cowhard".' 2035

Than Sir Launcelot walked on a whyle, and was sore acombird of hys armoure, hys shylde, and hys speare, and all that longed unto hym. Wyte you well he was full sore anoyed. And full lothe he was for to leve onythynge that longed unto hym, for he drad sore the treson of Sir Mellyagaunce. 2040

Than by fortune there cam by hym a charyote that cam thydir to feche wood.

'Say me, carter,' seyde Sir Launcelot, 'what shall I gyff the to suffir me to lepe into thy charyote, and that thou wolte brynge me unto a castell within thys two myle?' 2045

'Thou shalt nat entir into thys charyot,' seyde the carter, 'for I am sente for to fecche wood.'

'Unto whom?' seyde Sir Launcelot.

'Unto my lorde, Sir Mellyagaunce,' seyde the carter.

'And with hym wolde I speke,' seyde Sir Launcelot. 2050

'Thou shalt nat go with me!' seyde the carter.

Whan Sir Launcelot lepe to hym and gaff hym backwarde

2024 *That is lytyll maystry,* That is [a thing needing] little skill
2025-6 *gyff ryght nought of you,* won't give a damn for you (lit. 'give nothing at all for you')
2026 *and,* if   *mo,* more
2028 *avoyded,* got clear of
2033 *saw,* proverb
2034 *daungere,* danger   *daungere,* power
2035 *cowhard,* coward (cf. *cowherd*)
2036 *acombird of,* encumbered by (C)
2041 *charyote,* cart
2044 *suffir,* allow
2045 *thys two myle* (C)

with hys gauntelet a reremayne, that he felle to the erthe starke
dede, than the tothir carter, hys felow, was aferde and wente to
have gone the same way. And than he sayde, 'Fayre lorde, sauff 2055
my lyff, and I shall brynge you where ye woll.'

'Than I charge the,' seyde Sir Launcelot, 'that thou dryve me
and thys charyote unto Sir Mellyagaunce yate.'

'Than lepe ye up into the charyotte,' seyde the carter, 'and ye
shall be there anone.'   2060

So the carter drove on a grete walop, and Sir Launcelottes hors
folowed the charyot, with mo than a forty arowys brode and
rough in hym.

And more than an owre and an halff Quene Gwenyver was a-
waytyng in a bay-wyndow. Than one of hir ladyes aspyed an 2065
armed knyght stondyng in a charyote.

'A! se, madam,' seyde the lady, 'where rydys in a charyot a
goodly armed knyght, and we suppose he rydyth unto hangynge.'

'Where?' seyde the quene.

Than she aspyed by hys shylde that he was there hymself Sir 2070
Launcelot du Lake, and than was she ware where cam hys horse
after the charyotte, and ever he trode hys guttis and hys paunche
undir hys feete.

'Alas!' seyde the quene, 'now I may preve and se that well ys
that creature that hath a trusty frynde. A ha, moste noble knyght!' 2075
seyde Quene Gwenyver, 'I se well that ye were harde bestad
whan ye ryde in a charyote.' And than she rebuked that lady that
lykened Sir Launcelot to ryde in a charyote to hangynge: 'Forsothe hit was fowle-mowthed,' seyde the quene, 'and evyll lykened, so for to lyken the moste noble knyght of the worlde unto such 2080
a shamefull dethe. A! Jesu deffende hym and kepe hym', sayde
the quene, 'frome all myschevous ende!'

So by thys was Sir Launcelot comyn to the gatis of that castell,
and there he descended down and cryed, that all the castell

2053 *reremayne*, backhander (C)
2054 *tothir*, other   *felow*, companion   *wente*, thought
2058 *yate*, gate
2061 *a grete walop*, [at] a tremendous gallop
2071 *was she ware*, she became aware
2074–5 See C.
2074 *preve*, know [by experience] (lit. 'prove')
2076 *harde bestad*, hard pressed
2078 *to ryde*, understand 'to one riding'
2080 *unto such*, understand 'to someone going to such'

myght rynge: 'Where arte thou, thou false traytoure Sir Melly- 2085
agaunte, and knyght of the Table Rounde? Now com forth here,
thou traytour knyght, thou and all thy felyshyp with the, for here I
am, Sir Launcelot du Lake, that shall fyght with you all!'

And therewithall he bare the gate wyde opyn uppon the
porter, and smote hym undir the ere wyth hys gauntelet, that hys 2090
nekke braste in two pecis. Whan Sir Mellyagaunce harde that
Sir Launcelot was comyn he ranne unto the quene and felle
uppon hys kne and seyde, 'Mercy, madame, for now I putte me
holé in your good grace.'

'What ayles you now?' seyde Quene Gwenyver. 'Pardé, I 2095
myght well wete that some good knyght wolde revenge me,
thoughe my lorde Kynge Arthure knew nat of thys your worke.'

'A, madame,' seyde Sir Mellyagaunte, 'all thys that ys amysse
on my party shall be amended ryght as yourselff woll devyse, and
holy I put me in youre grace.' 2100

'What wolde ye that I ded?' seyde the quene.

'Madame, I wolde no more,' seyde Sir Mellyagaunt, 'but that
ye wolde take all in youre owne hondys, and that ye woll rule my
lorde Sir Launcelot. And such chere as may be made hym in
thys poure castell ye and he shall have untyll to-morn, and than 2105
may ye and all they returne ayen unto Westmynster; and my
body and all that I have I shall put in youre rule.'

'Ye sey well,' seyde the quene, 'and bettir ys pees than evermore warre, and the lesse noyse the more ys my worshyp.'

Than the quene and hir ladyes wente downe unto Sir Launcelot 2110
that stood wood wrothe oute of mesure in the inner courte to abyde
batayle, and ever he seyde, 'Thou traytour knyght, com forthe!'

Than the quene cam unto hym and seyde, 'Sir Launcelot, why
be ye so amoved?'

'A, madame,' seyde Sir Launcelot, 'why aske ye me that 2115
questyon? For mesemyth,' seyde Sir Launcelot, 'ye oughte to be
more wrotther than I am, for ye have the hurte and the dis-

2092-3 *felle uppon hys kne*, knelt down
2094 *holé*, wholly
2095 *ayles*, ails
2103 *rule*, make [Lancelot] be sensible (cf. l. 1942*n*)
2104 *chere . . . made*, hospitality . . . given
2108-9 See C.
2114 *amoved*, upset (C)
2117 *more wrotther*, more angry (C)

honour. For wyte you well, madame, my hurte ys but lytyll in
regard for the sleyng of a marys sonne, but the despite grevyth me
much more than all my hurte.'   2120

'Truly,' seyde the quene, 'ye say trouthe, but hartely I thanke
you,' seyde the quene; 'but ye muste com in with me pesyblé, for
all thynge ys put in myne honde, and all that ys amysse shall be
amended, for the knyght full sore repentys hym of thys mysadventure that ys befallyn hym.'   2125

'Madame,' seyde Sir Launcelot, 'syth hit ys so that ye be
accorded with hym, as for me I may nat agaynesay hit, howbehit
Sir Mellyagaunte hath done full shamefully to me and cowardly.
And, madame,' seyde Sir Launcelot, 'and I had wyste that ye
wolde have bene so lyghtly accorded with hym I wolde nat a   2130
made such haste unto you.'

'Why say ye so?' seyde the quene. 'Do ye forthynke youreselff
of youre good dedis? Wyte you well,' seyde the quene, 'I accorded never with hym for no favoure nor love that I had unto hym,
but of every shameful noyse of wysedom to lay adoune.'   2135

'Madame,' seyde Sir Launcelot, 'ye undirstonde full well I
was never wyllynge nor glad of shamefull sclaundir nor noyse;
and there ys nother kynge, quene ne knyght that beryth the
lyffe, excepte my lorde Kynge Arthur and you, madame, that
shulde lette me but I shulde make Sir Mellyagaunte harte full   2140
colde or ever I departed frome hense.'

'That wote I well,' seyde the quene, 'but what woll ye more?
Ye shall have all thynge ruled as ye lyste to have hit.'

'Madame,' seyde Sir Launcelot, 'so ye be pleased, I care not.
As for my parte, ye shall sone please me.'   2145

Ryght so the quene toke Sir Launcelot by the bare honde, for
he had put of hys gauntelot, and so she wente wyth hym tyll her
chambir, and than she commanded hym to be unarmed.

2118–19 *in regard for*, in regard to
2119 *marys*, mare's
2119–20 *despite . . . hurte*, insult ·. . injury
2122 *pesyblé*, peaceably
2126 *syth*, since
2127 *accorded*, agreed   *agaynesay*, gainsay, contradict   *howbehit*, although
2130 *a*, have
2132 *forthynke yourselff*, repent (C)
2135 Translate: 'but in order to put down by wisdom every scandalous rumour'
2138–9 *beryth the lyffe*, lives
2140 *lette me*, stop me

And than Sir Launcelot asked the quene where were hir ten knyghtes that were wounded with her. Than she shewed them 2150 unto hym, and there they made grete joy of the comyng of Sir Launcelot, and he made grete dole of their hurtis, and bewayled them gretely. And there Sir Launcelot tolde them how cowardly and traytourly Sir Mellyagaunt sette archers to sle hys horse, and how he was fayne to put hymselff in a charyotte. And thus they 2155 complayned everyche to other, and full fayne they wolde have ben revenged, but they kepte the pees bycause of the quene.

Than, as the Freynsh booke saythe, Sir Launcelot was called many dayes aftyr 'le Shyvalere de Charyotte', and so he ded many dedys and grete adventures he had. And so we leve of here 2160 of le Shyvalere le Charyote, and turne we to thys tale.

So Sir Launcelot had grete chere with the quene. And than he made a promyse with the quene that the same nyght he sholde com to a wyndow outewarde towarde a gardyne, and that wyndow was barred with iron, and there Sir Launcelot promysed 2165 to mete her whan all folkes were on slepe.

So than cam Sir Lavayne dryvynge to the gatis, seyyng, 'Where ys my lorde Sir Launcelot?' And anone he was sente fore, and whan Sir Lavayne saw Sir Launcelot, he seyde, 'A, my lorde! I founde howe ye were harde bestadde, for I have founde 2170 your hors that ys slayne with arowys.'

'As for that,' seyde Sir Launcelot, 'I praye you, Sir Lavayne, speke ye of othir maters and lat thys passe, and we shall ryght hit anothir tyme and we may.'

Than the knyghtes that were hurt were serched, and soffte 2175 salves were layde to their woundis, and so hit passed on tyll souper-tyme. And all the chere that myght be made them there was done unto the quene and all her knyghtes. And whan season was they wente unto their chambirs, but in no wyse the quene wolde nat suffir her wounded knyghtes to be fro her, but that 2180

2155 *fayne*, compelled (C)
2156 *full fayne*, very willingly
2158–9 *le Shyvalere de Charyotte*, le Chevalier du Chariot, the Knight of the Cart (C)
2160 *leve of here of*, depart here from
2164 *outewarde*, facing out
2166 *on slepe*, asleep
2167 *dryvynge to the gatis*, to the gates, riding hard
2174 *and*, if
2175 *were searched*, had their wounds probed [and cleaned]
2180 *fro*, away from

they were layde in wythdraughtes by hir chambir, uppon beddis and paylattes, that she myght herselff se unto them that they wanted nothynge.

So whan Sir Launcelot was in hys chambir whych was assygned unto hym, he called unto hym Sir Lavayne and tolde hym that nyght he must go speke with hys lady, Quene Gwenyver. 2185

'Sir,' seyde Sir Lavayne, 'let me go with you, and hyt please you, for I drede me sore of the treson of Sir Mellyagaunte.'

'Nay,' seyde Sir Launcelot, 'I thanke you, but I woll have nobody wyth me.' 2190

Than Sir Launcelot toke hys swerde in hys honde and prevaly wente to the place where he had spyed a ladder toforehande, and that he toke undir hys arme, and bare hit thorow the gardyne and sette hit up to the wyndow. And anone the quene was there redy to mete hym. 2195

And than they made their complayntes aythir to othir of many dyverce thyngis, and than Sir Launcelot wysshed that he myght have comyn in to her.

'Wyte you well,' seyde the quene, 'I wolde as fayne as ye that ye myght com in to me.' 2200

'Wolde ye so, madame,' seyde Sir Launcelot, 'wyth youre harte that I were with you?'

'Ye, truly,' seyde the quene.

'Than shall I prove my myght,' seyde Sir Launcelot, 'for youre love.' 2205

And than he sette hys hondis uppon the barrys of iron and pulled at them with suche a myght that he braste hem clene oute of the stone wallys. And therewithall one of the barres of iron kutte the brawne of hys hondys thorowoute, to the bone. And than he lepe into the chambir to the quene. 2210

'Make ye no noyse,' seyde the quene, 'for my wounded knyghtes lye here fast by me.'

So, to passe uppon thys tale, Sir Launcelot wente to bedde with the quene and toke no force of hys hurte honde, but toke hys

---

[2181] *wythdraughtes*, closets, small private rooms communicating with the main one
[2182] *paylattes*, pallets, mattresses
[2191] *prevaly*, secretly
[2198] *comyn*, come
[2199] *fayne*, willingly
[2203] *Ye*, yes (lit. 'yea')
[2210] *lepe*, leapt

pleasaunce and hys lykynge untyll hit was the dawnyng of the 2215
day; for wyte you well he slept nat, but wacched. And whan he
saw hys tyme that he myght tary no lenger, he toke hys leve and
departed at the wyndowe, and put hit togydir as well as he
myght agayne, and so departed untyll hys owne chambir. And
there he tolde Sir Lavayne how that he was hurte. Than Sir 2220
Lavayne dressed hys honde and staunched hit, and put uppon hit
a glove, that hit sholde nat be aspyed.

And so the quene lay longe in her bed in the mornynge tylle
hit was nine of the clok. Than Sir Mellyagaunte wente to the
quenys chambir and founde her ladyes there redy clothed.   2225

'A, Jesu mercy!' seyde Sir Mellyagaunte, 'what ayles you,
madame, that ye slepe thys longe?'

And therewithall he opened the curtayn for to beholde her. And
than was he ware where she lay, and all the hede-sheete, pylow,
and over-shyte was all bebled of the bloode of Sir Launcelot and 2230
of hys hurte honde. Whan Sir Mellyagaunt aspyed that blood,
than he demed in her that she was false to the kynge, and that
som of the wounded knyghtes had lyene by her all that nyght.

'A ha, madame!' seyde Sir Mellyagaunte, 'now I have founde
you a false traytouras unto my lorde Arthur, for now I preve well 2235
hit was nat for nought that ye layde thes wounded knyghtis
within the bondys of youre chambir. Therefore I woll calle you of
tresoun afore my lorde Kynge Arthure. And now I have proved
you, madame, wyth a shamefull dede; and that they bene all false,
or som of them, I woll make hit good, for a wounded knyght 2240
thys nyght hath layne by you.'

2215 *pleasaunce*, pleasure
2216 *wacched*, waked, remained awake
2217 *tary*, tarry, remain
2218 *at*, by
2219 *untyll*, unto
2223 See C.
2226 *Jesu mercy!* (C)
2228 *for to*, to
2229 *hede-sheete*, headsheet (C)
2230 *was*, were
2232 *in*, of
2233 *som*, one   *lyene*, lain
2235 *traytouras*, traitress   *preve*, find by [my own] experience
2237 *bondys*, bounds, walls   *calle*, accuse (C)
2238 *proved you*, tested you (i.e. in your honesty)
2239 *wyth*, by means of   *bene*, be
2240 *som*, one

'That ys false,' seyde the quene, 'that I woll report me unto them.'

But whan the ten knyghtes harde Sir Mellyagaunteys wordys, than they spake all at onys and seyd, 'Sir Mellyagaunte, thou 2245 falsely belyest my lady the quene, and that we woll make good uppon the, any of us. Now, chose whych thou lyste of us whan we are hole of the woundes thou gavyst us.'

'Ye shall nat!' seyde Sir Mellyagaunte, 'Away with youre proude langayge! For here ye may all se,' seyde Sir Mellyagaunte, 2250 'that a wounded knyght thys nyght hath layne by the quene.'

Than they all loked and were sore ashamed whan they saw that bloode. And wyte you well Sir Mellyagaunte was passyng glad that he had the quene at suche avauntayge, for he demed by that to hyde hys owne treson. 2255

And so with thys rumour com in Sir Launcelot and fownde them at a grete affray.

'What aray ys thys?' seyde Sir Launcelot.

Than Sir Mellyagaunce tolde hem what he had founde, and so he shewed hym the quenys bed. 2260

'Now truly,' seyde Sir Launcelot, 'ye ded nat youre parte nor knyghtly, to touche a·quenys bed whyle hit was drawyn and she lyyng therein. And I daresay,' seyde Syr Launcelot, 'my lorde Kynge Arthur hymselff wolde nat have displayed hir curtaynes, she beyng within her bed, onles that hit had pleased hym to have 2265 layne hym downe by her. And therefore, Sir Mellyagaunce, ye have done unworshypfully and shamefully to youreselff.'

'Sir, I wote nat what ye meane,' seyde Sir Mellyagaunce, 'but well I am sure there hath one of hir hurte knyghtes layne with her thys nyght. And that woll I prove with myne hondys, that 2270 she ys a traytoures unto my lorde Kynge Arthur.'

'Beware what ye do,' seyde Sir Launcelot, 'for and ye say so and wyll preve hit, hit woll be takyn at youre handys.'

2242 *report me*, refer myself
2247 *lyste*, want
2248 *hole*, whole, recovered
2256 *rumour*, uproar, tumult
2257 *affray*, disturbance
2258 *aray*, trouble (lit. 'situation', cf. *array*)
2261 *youre parte*, what was proper for you
2261-2 *nor knyghtly*, nor [did you behave] in a knightly way
2262 *hit was drawyn*, the curtains were shut
2264 *displayed*, opened
2273 *hit*, it (i.e. your implied challenge)

'My lorde Sir Launcelot,' seyde Sir Mellyagaunce, 'I rede you beware what ye do; for thoughe ye ar never so good a knyght, as 2275 I wote well ye ar renowned the beste knyght of the worlde, yet shulde ye be avysed to do batayle in a wronge quarell, for God woll have a stroke in every batayle.'

'As for that,' seyde Sir Launcelot, 'God ys to be drad! But as to that I say, I say nay playnly, that thys nyght there lay none of 2280 thes ten knyghtes wounded with my lady, Quene Gwenyver. And that woll I prove with myne hondys, that ye say untrewly in that. Now, what sey ye?' seyde Sir Launcelot.

'Thus I say,' seyde Sir Mellyagaunce, 'here ys my glove that she ys a traytoures unto my lorde Kynge Arthur, and that thys 2285 nyght one of the wounded knyghtes lay wyth her.'

'Well, sir, and I resceyve youre glove,' seyde Sir Launcelot.

And anone they were sealed with their synattes, and de lyverde unto the ten knyghtes.

'At what day shall we do batayle togydirs?' seyde Sir Launce- 2290 lot.

'Thys day eyght dayes,' seyde Sir Mellyagaunce, 'in the fylde besydys Westemynster.'

'I am agreed,' seyde Sir Launcelot.

'But now,' seyde Sir Mellyagaunce, 'sytthyn hit ys so that we 2295 muste nedys fyght togydirs, I pray you, as ye betthe a noble knyghte, awayte me wyth no treson nother no vylany the meane- whyle, nother I none for you.'

'So God me helpe,' seyde Sir Launcelot, 'ye shall ryght well wyte that I was never of no such condysions. For I reporte me to 2300 all knyghtes that ever have knowyn me, I fared never wyth no treson, nother I loved never the felyshyp of hym that fared with treson.'

2274 *rede*, advise
2276 *wote*, know
2277 See C.   *be avysed*, reconsider (lit. 'be advised')   *wronge quarell*, unjust cause
2284 See C.
2288 *they*, they (i.e. the articles of their agreement)   *synattes*, signet rings
2293 *besydys*, beside
2295 *sytthyn*, since
2296 *betthe*, be
2297 *awayte*, lie in wait for   *nother*, nor
2298 *nother I none for you*, and I [will] not [lie in wait with] any for you
2300 *wyte*, know   *never of no such condysions*, never given to that kind of thing
2301 *fared*, behaved, acted

'Than lat us go unto dyner,' seyde Sir Mellyagaunce, 'and aftir dyner the quene and ye may ryde all unto Westemynster.'   2305

'I woll well,' seyde Sir Launcelot.

Than Sir Mellyagaunce seyde unto Sir Launcelot, 'Sir, pleasyth you to se the esturys of thys castell?'

'With a good wyll,' seyde Sir Launcelot.

And than they wente togydir frome chambir to chambir, for 2310 Sir Launcelot drad no perellis: for ever a man of worshyp and of proues dredis but lytyll of perels, for they wene that every man be as they bene. But ever he that faryth with treson puttyth oftyn a trew man in grete daungere. And so hit befelle uppon Sir Launcelot that no perell dred: as he wente with Sir Mellyagaunce he 2315 trade on a trappe, and the burde rolled, and there Sir Launcelot felle downe more than ten fadom into a cave full off strawe.

And than Sir Mellyagaunce departed and made no fare, no more than he that wyste nat where he was. And whan Sir Launcelot was thus myssed they mervayled where he was be 2320 comyn, and than the quene and many of them demed that he was departed, as he was wonte to do, suddaynly. For Sir Mellyagaunce made suddaynly to put on syde Sir Lavaynes horse, that they myght all undirstonde that Sir Launcelot were departed suddaynly.   2325

So than hit passed on tyll afftir dyner, and than Sir Lavayne wolde nat stynte untyll that he had horse-lytters for the wounded knyghtes, that they myght be caryed in them; and so with the quene and them all, bothe ladyes and jantylwomen and other, rode unto Westemynster. And there the knyghtes tolde Kynge 2330 Arthure how Sir Mellyagaunce had appeled the quene of hyghe treson, and how Sir Launcelot had resceyved the glove of hym, 'and thys day eyght dayes they shall do batayle before you.'

2306 *I woll well,* willingly
2308 *esturys,* fishponds
2311 *perellis,* perils, dangers
2312 *proues,* prowess   *wene,* think
2315 *that,* who
2316 *trade,* trod   *burde,* trapdoor (cf. *board*)   *rolled,* fell open (lit. 'turned on its hinge')
2317 *fadom,* fathoms
2318 *made no fare,* made no fuss, behaved naturally
2319 *he that wyste,* one who knew
2323 *to put on syde,* to be put aside, to be hidden
2327 *lytters,* litters
2331 *appeled,* accused

'Be my hede,' seyde Kynge Arthure, 'I am aferde Sir Mellyagaunce hath charged hymselff with a grete charge. But where is 2335
Sir Launcelot?' seyde the kynge.

'Sir,' seyde they all, 'we wote nat where he ys, but we deme he
ys ryddyn to som adventure, as he ys offtyntymes wonte to do,
for he hath Sir Lavaynes horse.'

'Lette hym be,' seyde the kynge, 'for he woll be founden but if 2340
he be betrapped wyth som treson.'

Thus leve we Sir Launcelot liyng within that cave in grete
payne. And every day there cam a lady and brought hym hys
mete and hys drynke, and wowed hym every day to have layne
by her, and ever the noble knyght Sir Launcelot seyde her nay.   2345

Than seyde she, 'Sir, ye ar nat wyse, for ye may never oute of
this preson but if ye have my helpe. And also youre lady, Quene
Gwenyver, shall be brente in youre defaute onles that ye be there
at the day of batayle.'

'God deffende,' seyde Sir Launcelot, 'that she shulde be brente 2350
in my defaught! And if hit be so,' seyde Sir Launcelot, 'that I may
nat be there, hit shall be well undirstonde, bothe at the kynge and
the quene and with all men of worship, that I am dede, syke, othir in preson. For all men that know me woll say for me that I am
in som evyll case and I be nat that day there. And thus well I un- 2355
dirstonde that there ys som good knyght, othir of my blood other
som other that lovys me, that woll take my quarell in honde.
And therefore,' seyde Sir Launcelot, 'wyte you well, ye shall nat
feare me; and if there were no mo women in all thys londe but ye,
yet shall nat I have ado with you.'   2360

'Than ar ye shamed,' seyde the lady, 'and destroyed for ever.'

'As for worldis shame, now Jesu deffende me! And as for my
distresse, hit ys welcom, whatsomever hit be that God sendys me.'

2334 *aferde*, afraid (lit. 'afeared)
2335 *charged*, burdened
2337 *wote . . . deme*, know . . . think
2340 *but if*, unless
2344 *mete*, food   *wowed*, wooed   *layne by*, slept with
2346 *may never oute*, can never get out
2348 *in*, by
2350 *deffende*, forbid
2352 *undirstonde*, understood (lit. 'understand[ed]')   *at*, by
2355 *case*, situation   *and*, if
2358-9 *ye shall nat feare me*, you will not frighten me (C)
2359-60 *and if . . . shall*, If . . . would

146

So she cam to hym agayne the same day that the batayle
shulde be and seyde, 'Sir Launcelot, bethynke you, for ye ar to 2365
hard-harted. And therefore, and ye wolde but onys kysse me, I
shulde delyver you and your armoure, and the beste horse that
was within Sir Mellyagaunce stable.'

'As for to kysse you,' seyde Sir Launcelot, 'I may do that and
lese no worshyp. And wyte you well, and I undirstood there were 2370
ony disworshyp for to kysse you, I wold nat do hit.'

And than he kyssed hir. And anone she gate hym up untyll
hys armour, and whan he was armed she brought hym tylle a
stable where stoode twelve good coursers, and bade hym to chose
of the beste. Than Sir Launcelot loked uppon a whyght courser 2375
and that lyked hym beste, and anone he commaunded the kepers
faste to sadle hym with the beste sadyll of warre that there was,
and so hit was done as he badde. Than he gate hys owne speare
in hys honde and hys swerde by hys syde, and than he commaunded the lady unto God and sayde, 'Lady, for thys dayes dede 2380
I shall do you servyse, if ever hit lye in my power.'

Now leve we here Sir Launcelot, all that ever he myght walop,
and speke we of Quene Gwenyver that was brought tyll a fyre to
be brente; for Sir Mellyagaunce was sure, hym thought, that
Sir Launcelotte sholde nat be at that batayle, and therefore he 2385
ever cryed uppon Kynge Arthur to do hym justyse othir ellys
brynge forth Sir Launcelot. Than was the kynge and all the
courte full sore abaysshed and shamed that the quene shulde have
be brente in the defaute of Sir Launcelot.

'My lorde Kynge Arthur,' seyde Sir Lavayne, 'ye may undir- 2390
stonde that hit ys nat well with my lorde Sir Launcelot, for and
he were on lyve, so he be nat syke other in preson, wyte you well
he wolde have bene here. For never harde ye that ever he fayled

2364 *the same day*, on the same day
2365 *bethynke you*, reconsider   *to*, too (C)
2366 *onys*, once
2370 *lese no worshyp*, not do anything shameful (C)
2372 *gate*, got, brought
2376 *lyked him*, pleased him
2377 *sadyll of war*, war-saddle (C)
2379-80 *commaunded*, commended
2382 *walop*, gallop
2384 *hym thought*, [it] seemed to him
2386 *cryed*, called   *othir ellys*, or else
2387 *was*, were
2391 *hit ys*, things are   *and*, if
2392 *be*, were   *syke*, sick

yet hys parte for whom he sholde do batayle fore. And therefore,'
seyde Sir Lavayne, 'my lorde Kynge Arthur, I beseche you that 2395
ye will gyff me lycence to do batayle here thys day for my lorde
and mayster, and for to save my lady the quene.'

'Grauntemercy, jantill Sir Lavayne,' seyde Kynge Arthur, 'for
I dare say all that Sir Mellyagaunce puttith uppon my lady the
quene ys wronge. For I have spokyn with all the ten wounded 2400
knyghtes, and there ys nat one of them, and he were hole and
able to do batayle, but he wolde prove uppon Sir Mellyagaunce
body that it is fals that he puttith uppon my lady.'

'And so shall I,' seyde Sir Lavayne, 'in the deffence of my
lorde Sir Launcelot, and ye woll gyff me leve.' 2405

'And I gyff you leve,' seyde Kynge Arthur, 'and do youre beste,
for I dare well say there ys som treson done to Sir Launcelot.'

Than was Sir Lavayn armed and horsed, and delyverly at the
lystes ende he rode to perfourme hys batayle. And ryght as the
herrowdis shuld cry: 'Lechés les alere!' ryght so com Sir Launce- 2410
lot dryvyng with all the myght of hys horse. And than Kynge
Arthure cryed: 'Whoo!' and 'Abyde!'

And than was Sir Launcelot called on horseback tofore Kynge
Arthur, and there he tolde opynly tofor the kynge all how that
Sir Mellyagaunce had served hym firste and laste. And whan the 2415
kynge and quene and all the lordis knew off the treson of Sir
Mellyagaunte, they were all ashamed on hys behalffe. Than was
the quene sente fore and sette by the kynge in the grete truste of
hir champion.

And than there was no more els to say, but Sir Launcelot and 2420
Sir Mellyagaunte dressed them unto batayle and toke their
spearys, and so they com togydirs as thunder, and there Sir
Launcelot bare hym quyte over hys horse croupe. And than Sir
Launcelot alyght and dressed hys shylde on hys shuldir and toke

2394 *for whom*, for them for whom   *fore* is redundant (repetition of the previous *for*).
2399 *I dare say* is to be taken literally   *puttith uppon*, alleges against
2408 *delyverly*, swiftly and skilfully
2410 *Lechés les alere*, laissez-les aller, let them go (C)   *ryght so*, all at once
2411 *dryvyng*, riding hard
2413 *tofore*, before
2416 *off*, of
2418 *by*, next to (C)   *truste of*, confidence in
2421 *dressed*, rode
2423 *croupe*, croup, rump
2424 *alyght* alighted   *dressed*, positioned

hys swerde in hys honde, and so they dressed to eche other and 2425
smote many grete strokis togydir. And at the laste Sir Launcelot
smote hym suche a buffet uppon the helmet that he felle on the
tone syde to the erthe.

And than he cryed uppon hym lowde and seyde, 'Moste noble
knyght, Sir Launcelot, save my lyff! For I yelde me unto you, and 2430
I requyre you, as ye be a knyght and felow of the Table Rounde,
sle me nat, for I yelde me as overcomyn, and whethir I shall lyve
or dey, I put me in the kynges honde and youres.'

Than Sir Launcelot wyst nat what to do, for he had lever than
all the good in the worlde that he myght be revenged uppon 2435
hym. So Sir Launcelot loked uppon the quene, gyff he myght
aspye by ony sygne or countenaunce what she wolde have done.
And anone the quene wagged hir hede uppon Sir Launcelot, as
ho seyth 'sle hym'. And full well knew Sir Launcelot by her
sygnys that she wolde have hym dede.   2440

Than Sir Launcelot bade hym, 'Aryse, for shame, and perfourme thys batayle with me to the utteraunce!'

'Nay,' seyde Sir Mellyagaunce, 'I woll never aryse untyll that
ye take me as yolden and recreaunte.'

'Well, I shall proffir you a large proffir,' seyde Sir Launcelot, 2445
'that ys for to say I shall unarme my hede and my lyffte quarter
of my body, all that may be unarmed as for that quarter; and I
woll lette bynde my lyfft honde behynde me there hit shall nat
helpe me; and ryght so I shall do batayle with you.'

Than Sir Mellyagaunce sterte up upon hys legges and seyde 2450
on hyght, 'Take hede, my lorde Arthur, of thys proffir, for I woll
take hit. And lette hym be dissarmed and bounden accordyng
to hys proffir.'

2428 *tone*, one
2429 *lowde*, loudly
2430 *yelde*, yield
2436 *gyff*, if
2437 *countenaunce*, expression   *wolde*, wanted [to]
2438 *anone*, at once   *wagged*, nodded
2438–9 *as ho seyth*, like [one] who said (lit. 'says'), cf. the archaic *as who should say*
2442 *to the utteraunce*, to the utmost, to the death
2444 *yolden*, yielded   *recreaunte*, overcome (not 'recreant') (C)
2446 *lyffte*, left
2447 *quarter*, part, see l. 2459
2448 *lette bynde*, have ... bound   *there*, where
2449 *ryght so*, just like that
2450–1 *sterte ... seyde on hyght*, jumped ... cried aloud

'What sey ye?' seyde Kynge Arthur unto Sir Launcelot. 'Woll
ye abyde by youre proffir?'   2455
'Ye, my lorde,' seyde Sir Launcelot, 'for I woll never go fro
that I have onys sayde.'

Than the knyghtes parters of the fylde disarmed Sir Launcelot,
firste hys hede and than hys lyffte arme and hys lyffte syde, and
they bounde his lyffte arme to hys lyffte syde fast behynde hys 2460
bak, withoute shylde or onythynge. And anone they yode
togydirs.

Wyte you well there was many a lady and many a knyght mervayled of Sir Launcelot that wolde jouparté hymselff in suche
wyse.   2465

Than Sir Mellyagaunce com wyth swerde all on hyght, and
Sir Launcelot shewed hym opynly hys bare hede and the bare
lyffte syde. And whan he went to have smytten hym uppon the
bare hede, than lyghtly he devoyded the lyffte legge and the
lyffte syde and put hys ryght honde and hys swerde to that stroke, 2470
and so put hit on syde wyth grete slyght. And than with grete
force Sir Launcelot smote hym on the helmet such a buffett that
the stroke carved the hed in two partyes.

Than there was no more to do, but he was drawyn oute of the
fylde, and at the grete instaunce of the knyghtes of the Table 2475
Rounde the kynge suffird hym to be entered, and the mencion
made uppon hym who slewe hym and for what cause he was
slayne.

And than the kynge and the quene made more of Sir Launce-
lot, and more was he cherysshed than ever he was aforehande.   2480

---

²⁴⁵⁶ *Ye*, yes
²⁴⁵⁸ *knyghtes parters of the fylde*, officers of the lists (C)
²⁴⁶¹ *yode*, went (lit. 'walked')
²⁴⁶⁶ *on hyght*, raised high (lit. 'on high')
²⁴⁶⁹ *devoyded*, slipped aside
²⁴⁷¹ *slyght*, dexterity (cf. *sleight-of-hand*)
²⁴⁷³ *partyes*, parts
²⁴⁷⁶ *suffird*, allowed   *entered*, buried (C)
²⁴⁷⁷ *hym*, him (i.e. his tomb)

The Healing of Sir Urry

V

Than, as the Freynshe boke makith mencion, there was a good knyght in the londe of Hungré whos name was Sir Urré. And he was an adventurys knyght, and in all placis where he myght here ony adventures dedis and of worshyp, there wold he be.

So hit happened in Spayne there was an erle, and hys sunnes name was called Sir Alpheus. And at a grete turnemente in Spayne thys Sir Urry, knyght of Hungré, and Sir Alpheus of Spayne encountred togydirs for verry envy, and so aythir undirtoke other to the utteraunce. And by fortune thys Sir Urry slew Sir Alpheus, the erlys son of Spayne. But thys knyght that was slayne had yevyn Sir Urry, or ever he were slayne, seven grete woundis: three on the hede, and three on hys body, an one uppon hys lyffte honde. And thys Sir Alpheus had a modir whiche was a grete sorseras; and she, for the despyte of hir sunnes deth, wrought by her suttyle craufftis that Sir Urry shulde never be hole, but ever his woundis shulde one tyme fester and another tyme blede, so that he shulde never be hole untyll the beste knyght of the worlde had serched hys woundis. And thus she made her avaunte, wherethorow hit was knowyn that this Sir Urry sholde never be hole.

Than hys modir lete make an horse-lytter and put hym therein with two palfreyes caryyng hym. And than she toke wyth hym hys syster, a full fayre damesell whose name was Fyleloly, and a payge wyth hem to kepe their horsis, and so they lad Sir Urry thorow many contreyes. For, as the Freynshe booke saythe, she lad hym so seven yere thorow all londis crystened and never cowde fynde no knyght that myght ease her sunne.

So she cam unto Scotlonde and into the bondes of Inglonde.

2485

2490

2495

2500

2505

2481 *Than,* Then *the Freynshe boke* (C)
2483 *here,* hear of
2488 *for verry envy,* out of sheer hatred
2491 *yevyn,* given *or,* before
2492 *an,* and
2494 *sorceras,* sorceress *for the despyte,* because of the injury
2495 *suttyle craufftis,* subtle skills
2496 *hole,* whole, recovered
2498 *serched,* probed
2499 *avaunte* boast *wherethorow* whereby, through which
2501 *lete make,* had made
2505 See C.
2506 *londis crystened,* Christian (lit. 'christened') lands
2508 *bondes,* bounds

And by fortune she com nyghe the feste of Pentecoste untyll
Kynge Arthurs courte, that at that tyme was holdyn at Carlehylle. 2510
And whan she cam there she made hit to be opynly knowyn how
that she was com into that londe for to hele her sonne. Than
Kynge Arthur lette calle that lady and aske her the cause why she
brought that hurte knyght into that londe.

'My moste noble kynge,' seyde that lady, 'wyte you well I 2515
brought hym hyddir to be heled of hys woundis, that of all thys
seven yere myght never be hole.'

And thus she tolde the kynge, and where he was wounded and
with whom, and how hys modir discoverde hit in her pryde how
she had wrought by enchauntemente that he sholde never be hole 2520
untyll the beste knyght of the worlde had serched hys woundis.

'And so I have passed all the londis crystynde thorow to have
hym healed excepte thys londe, and gyff I fayle to hele him here
in thys londe I woll never take more payne uppon me. And that
ys grete pité, for he was a good knyghte and of grete nobeles.' 2525

'What ys hys name?' seyde King Arthure.

'My good and gracious lorde,' she seyde, 'his name ys Sir Urré
of the Mounte.'

'In good tyme,' seyde the kynge, 'ye ar com into thys londe,
and sythyn ye ar com into thys londe, ye ar ryght wellcom. And 2530
wyte you welle, here shall youre son be healed and ever ony
Crystyn man may heale hym. And for to gyff all othir men off
worshyp a currayge, I myselff woll asay to handyll your sonne,
and so shall all the kynges, dukis, and erlis that ben here presente
at thys tyme with me. Thereto woll I commaunde them, and 2535
well I wote they shall obey and do after my commaundement.
And wyte you well,' seyde Kynge Arthure unto Sir Urrés syster, 'I
shall begynne to handyll hym and serche hym unto my power, nat
presumyng uppon me that I am so worthy to heale youre son be my
dedis, but I woll corrayge othir men of worshyp to do as I woll do.' 2540

2510 *holdyn*, held   *Carlehylle*, Carlisle
2512 *that londe* (C)
2519 *hys modir* (C)   *discoverde*, revealed (lit. 'uncovered')
2530 *sythyn*, since
2531 *wyte*, know   *and*, if
2533 *asay*, essay, try
2536 *after*, according to
2539 *presumyng uppon me*, being so presumptious about myself [as to assume]   *be*,
by
2540 *corrayge*, encourage

152

And than the kynge commaunded all the kynges, dukes and erlis, and all noble knyghtes of the Rounde Table that were there that tyme presente to com into the medow of Carlehyll.

And so at that tyme there were but an hondred an ten of the Rounde Table, for forty knyghtes were that tyme away. And so 2545 here we muste begynne at Kynge Arthur, as is kyndely to begynne at hym that was that tyme the moste man of worshyp crystynde.

Than Kynge Arthur loked uppon Sir Urré, and he thought he was a full lykly man whan he was hole. And than the kynge made to take hym downe of the lyttar and leyde hym uppon the 2550 erth, and anone there was layde a cussheon of golde that he shulde knele uppon. And than Kynge Arthur sayde, 'Fayre knyght, me rewyth of thy hurte, and for to corrayge all other noble knyghts I woll pray the sofftely to suffir me to handyll thy woundis.'

'My moste noble crystynd kynge, do ye as ye lyste,' seyde Sir 2555 Urré, 'for I am at the mercy of God and at youre commaunde-mente.'

So than Kynge Arthur softely handeled hym. And than som of hys woundis renewed uppon bledynge.

Than Kynge Claryaunce of Northumbirlonde serched, and hit 2560 wolde nat be. And than Sir Barraunte le Apres, that was called the Kynge with the Hundred Knyghtes, he assayed and fayled.

So ded Kynge Uryence of the londe of Gore. So ded Kynge Angwysh of Irelonde, and so ded Kynge Newtrys of Garloth. So ded Kynge Carydos of Scotlonde. So ded the duke Sir Galahalt 2565 the Haute Prynce. So ded Sir Constantyne that was Kynge Cadors son of Cornwayle. So ded Duke Chalaunce of Claraunce. So ded the Erle of Ulbawys. So ded the Erle Lambayle. So ded the Erle Arystanse.

Than cam in Sir Gawayne wyth hys three sunnes, Sir Gyn- 2570 galyn, Sir Florence, and Sir Lovell (thes two were begotyn uppon Sir Braundeles syster), and all they fayled. Than cam in Sir Aggravayne, Sir Gaherys, and Sir Mordred, and the good knyght

---

2546 *kyndely*, natural
2547 See C.
2549 *lykly*, promising
2550 *made to take hym*, had him taken
2552–3 *me rewyth of*, I am sorry about (lit. '[it] causes me pity about')
2554 *sofftely to suffir me*, to allow me gently
2555 *lyste*, wish
2556 *at the*, under the

153

Sir Gareth that was of verry knyghthod worth all the brethirn.

So cam in the knyghtes of Sir Launcelottis kyn, but Sir 2575
Launcelot was nat that tyme in the courte, for he was that tyme
uppon hys adventures. Than Sir Lyonell, Sir Ector de Marys,
Sir Bors de Ganys, Sir Blamoure de Ganys, Sir Bleoberys de
Gaynys, Sir Gahalantyne, Sir Galyhodyn, Sir Menaduke, Sir
Vyllars the Valyaunte, Sir Hebes le Renowné, all thes were of 2580
Sir Launcelottis kynne, and all they fayled.

Than cam in Sir Sagramour le Desyrus, Sir Dodynas le
Saveage, Sir Dynadan, Sir Brewne le Noyre that Sir Kay named
La Cote Male Tayle, and Sir Kay le Senesciall, Sir Kay d'Es-
traunges, Sir Mellyot de Logris, Sir Petipace of Wynchylsé, Sir 2585
Galleron of Galoway, Sir Melyon of the Mountayne, Sir Car-
doke, Sir Uwayne les Avoutres, and Sir Ozanna le Cure Hardy.
Than cam in Sir Ascamour, and Sir Grummor Grummorson,
Sir Crosseleme, Sir Severause le Brewse that was called a pass-
ynge stronge knyght.   2590

For, as the booke seyth, the chyff lady of the Lady off the Lake
fested Sir Launcelot and Sir Severause le Brewse, and whan she
had fested them both at sundry tymes, she prayde hem to gyff her
a done, and anone they graunted hit her. And than she prayde Sir
Severause that he wolde promyse her never to do batayle ayenste 2595
Sir Launcelot, and in the same wyse she prayde Sir Launcelot
never to do batayle ayenste Sir Severause, and so aythir promysed
her. (For the Freynshe booke sayth that Sir Severause had never
corayge nor grete luste to do batayle ayenste no man but if hit
were ayenste gyauntis and ayenste dragons and wylde bestis.)   2600

So leve we thys mater and speke we of them that at the kynges
rekeyste were there at the hyghe feste, as knyghtes of the Rounde
Table, for to serche Sir Urré. And to thys entente the kynge ded
hit: to wyte whych was the moste nobelyste knyght amonge them
all.   2605

2574 *verry*, true   *the*, understand 'his'
2581 *all they*, they all
2585-9 See C.
2589-90 *passynge*, very
2591 See C.   *chyff*, chief
2592 *fested*, feasted, entertained
2594 *done*, gift (cf. Fr. *donner*)   *anone*, at once
2599 *corayge*, enthusiasm   *luste*, wish   *no*, understand 'any'
2602 *rekeyste*, request
2603 *entente*, intent, purpose
2604 *wyte*, know

Than cam in Sir Agglovale, Sir Durnor, and Sir Tor that was begotyn uppon the cowardis wyff (but he was begotyn afore Aryes wedded her). And Kynge Pellynore begate them all: firste Sir Tor, Sir Agglovale, Sir Durnor, Sir Lamorak, the moste nobeleste knyght one of them that ever was in Kynge Arthurs 2610 dayes as for a wordly knyght, and Sir Percivale that was pyerles, excepte Sir Galahad, in holy dedis (but they dyed in the queste of the Sangreall).

Than cam in Sir Gryfflet le Fyze de Du, Sir Lucan the Butlere, Sir Bedyvere hys brothir, Sir Braundeles, Sir Constantyne Sir 2615 Cadors son of Cornwayle that was kynge aftir Arthurs dayes, and Sir Clegis, Sir Sadok, Sir Dynas le Senesciall de Cornwayle, Sir Fergus, Sir Dryaunte, Sir Lambegus, Sir Clarrus off Cleremownte, Sir Cloddrus, Sir Hectymere, Sir Edwarde of Carnarvan, Sir Dynas, Sir Pryamus whych was crystynde by the meanys 2620 of Sir Trystram the noble knyght, and thes three were brethirn; Sir Helayne le Blanke that was son unto Sir Bors, for he begate hym uppon Kynge Brandygorys doughter, and Sir Bryan de Lystenoyse; Sir Gauter, Sir Raynolde, Sir Gyllymere, whych were three brethirn whych Sir Launcelot wan uppon a brydge in 2625 Sir Kayes armys; Sir Gwyarte le Petite, Sir Bellyngere le Bewse that was son to the good knyght Sir Alysaundir le Orphelyn that was slayne by the treson of Kynge Marke.

Also that traytoure kynge slew the noble knyght Sir Trystram as he sate harpynge afore hys lady, La Beall Isode, with a tren- 2630 chaunte glayve, for whos dethe was the moste waylynge of ony knyght that ever was in Kynge Arthurs dayes, for there was never none so bewayled as was Sir Trystram and Sir Lamerok, for they were with treson slayne: Sir Trystram by Kynge Marke, and Sir Lamorake by Sir Gawayne and hys brethirn.   2635

And thys Sir Bellynger revenged the deth of hys fadir Sir Alysaundir, and Sir Trystram, for he slewe Kynge Marke. And

---

2607 *eowardis*, cowherd's
2609–10 *the moste nobeleste knyght one of them*, one of the noblest knights
2611 *wordly*, earthly (lit. 'worldly') (C)   *pyerles*, peerless
2612 they (C)
2615 *Sir Constantyne* (C)
2621 *Sir Trystram* (C)
2625 *wan*, won, took prisoner
2626 *armys*, armour
2630–1 *trenchaunte*, trenchant, sharp
2631 *glayve*, spear

La Beall Isode dyed sownyng uppon the crosse of Sir Trystram, whereof was grete pité. And all that were with Kynge Marke whych were of assente of the dethe of Sir Trystram were slayne, 2640 as Sir Andred and many othir.

Than cam Sir Hebes, Sir Morganoure, Sir Sentrayle, Sir Suppynabiles, Sir Belyaunce le Orgulus that the good knyght Sir Lamorak wan in playne batayle, Sir Neroveus and Sir Plenoryus, two good knyghtes that Sir Launcelot wanne; Sir Darras, Sir 2645 Harry le Fyze Lake, Sir Ermynde brother to Kyng Hermaunce, for whom Sir Palomydes faught at the Rede Cité with two brethirn; and Sir Selyses of the Dolerous Towre, Sir Edward of Orkeney, Sir Ironsyde that was called the noble knyght of the Rede Laundis, that Sir Gareth wan for the love of dame Lyones; Sir 2650 Arrok, Sir Degrevaunt, Sir Degrave Saunze Vylony that faught wyth the gyaunte of the Blak Lowe; Sir Epynogrys that was the kynges son of Northumbirlonde, Sir Pelleas that loved the Lady Ettarde (and he had dyed for her sake, had nat bene one of the ladyes of the lake whos name was Dame Nynyve; and she wedde 2655 Sir Pelleas, and she saved hym ever aftir, that he was never slayne by her dayes—and he was a full noble knyght); and Sir Lamyell of Cardyff that was a grete lovear, Sir Playne de Fors, Sir Melyaus de Lyle, Sir Boarte le Cure Hardy that was Kynge Arthurs son, Sir Madore de la Porte, Sir Collgrevaunce, Sir 2660 Hervyse de la Foreyst Saveayge, Sir Marrok the good knyght that was betrayed with his wyff, for he made hym seven yere a warwolff; Sir Persaunt, Sir Pertolope hys brothir, that was called the Grene Knyght, and Sir Perymones, brother unto them bothe, whych was called the Rede Knyght, that Sir Gareth wanne whan 2665 he was called Bewmaynes.

All thes hondred knyghtes and ten serched Sir Urryes woundis by the commaundemente of Kynge Arthur.

'Mercy Jesu!' seyde Kynge Arthur, 'where ys Sir Launcelot du Lake, that he ys nat here at thys tyme?'   2670

2638 *sownyng,* fainting   *the crosse* (C)
2639 *whereof was,* understand 'which was a'
2640 *whyche were of assent of,* who agreed to
2654 *had nat bene,* understand 'but for' (C)
2655 *wedde,* wedded
2657 *by,* in
2658 *lovear,* lover
2662 *he,* she (cf. l. 1546 & n)
2667 *hondred knyghtes and ten* (C)

And thus as they stood and spake of many thyngis, there one aspyed Sir Launcelot that com rydynge towarde them, and anone they tolde the kynge.

'Pees,' seyde the kynge, 'lat no man say nothyng untyll he be com to us.'   2675

So whan Sir Launcelot had aspyed Kynge Arthur he descended downe frome hys horse and cam to the kynge and salewed hym and them all.

And anone as the damesell, Sir Urryes syster, saw Sir Launcelot, she romed to her brothir thereas he lay in hys lyttar and 2680 seyde, 'Brothir, here ys com a knyght that my harte gyveth gretly unto.'

'Fayre syster,' seyde Sir Urré, 'so doth my harte lyghte gretly ayenste hym, and certaynly I hope now to be heled, for my harte gyvith me more unto hym than to all thes that have serched me.'   2685

Than seyde Kynge Arthur unto Sir Launcelot, 'Sir, ye muste do as we have done,' and tolde hym what they had done and shewed hym them all that had serched hym.

'Jesu defende me,' seyde Sir Launcelot, 'whyle so many noble kyngis and knyghtes have assayde and fayled, that I shulde pre- 2690 sume uppon me to enchyve that all ye, my lordis, myght nat enchyve.'

'Ye shall nat chose,' seyde Kynge Arthur, 'for I commaunde you to do as we all have done.'

'My moste renowmed lorde,' seyde Sir Launcelot, 'Ye know 2695 well I dare nat, nor may nat, disobey you. But, and I myght or durste, wyte you well I wolde nat take uppon me to towche that wounded knyght in that entent that I shulde passe all othir knyghtes. Jesu deffende me frome that shame!'

'Sir, ye take hit wronge,' seyde Kynge Arthur, 'for ye shall nat 2700 do hit for no presumpcion, but for to beare us felyshyp, inso-muche as ye be a felow of the Rounde Table. And wyte you well,'

2677 *salewed*, greeted
2680 *romed*, went over (lit. 'roamed')
2681–2, 2684–5 *my harte gyveth (me) unto*, my heart inclines to
2683 *lyghte*, lighten
2684 *ayenste hym*, in his presence
2689 *Jesu defende me*, God forbid (lit. 'May Jesus forbid me')
2691 *enchyve*, achieve
2696 *and*, if
2698 *in that entente*, with the intention, with the idea
2699 *deffende*, defend

seyde Kynge Arthur, 'and ye prevayle nat and heale hym, I dare
sey there ys no knyght in thys londe that may hele hym. And
therefore I pray you do as we have done.'   2705

And than all the kyngis and knyghtes for the moste˙party
prayed Sir Launcelot to serche hym. And than the wounded
knyght, Sir Urré, set hym up waykely and seyde unto Sir
Launcelot, 'Now, curteyse knyght, I requyre the, for Goddis sake,
heale my woundis! For methynkis ever sytthyn ye cam here my 2710
woundis grevyth me nat so muche as they ded.'

'A, my fayre lorde,' seyde Sir Launcelot, 'Jesu wolde that I
myght helpe you! For I shame sore with myselff that I shulde be
thus requyred, for never was I able in worthynes to do so hyghe
a thynge.'   2715

Than Sir Launcelot kneled downe by the wounded knyght,
saiyng, 'My lorde Arthure, I muste do youre commaundemente,
whych ys sore ayenste my harte.' And than he hylde up hys
hondys and loked unto the este, saiynge secretely unto hymselff,
'Now, Blyssed Fadir and Son and Holy Goste, I beseche The of 2720
Thy mercy that my symple worshyp and honesté be saved, and
Thou Blyssed Trynyté, Thou mayste yeff me power to hele thys
syke knyght by the grete vertu and grace of The, but, Good
Lorde, never of myselff.'

And than Sir Launcelot prayde Sir Urré to lat hym se hys 2725
hede; and than, devoutly knelyng, he ransaked the three woundis, that they bled a lytyll; and forthwithall the woundis fayre
heled and semed as they had bene hole a seven yere. And in lyke
wyse he serched hys body of othir three woundis, and they healed
in lyke wyse. And than the laste of all he serched hys honde, and 2730
anone hit fayre healed.

Than Kynge Arthur and all the kynges and knyghtes kneled
downe and gave thankynges and lovynges unto God and unto Hys

2706 Translate: 'the greater part of all the kings and knights asked',·
2708 *set hym up waykely*, sat himself up weakly
2713 *shame*, am embarrassed   *with*, in
2719 *este*, east
2722 *yeff*, give
2726 *ransaked*, thoroughly probed . . . with his fingers
2727 *forthwithall*, forthwith, at once
2729 Translate: 'he probed [the] three other wounds in his body' (*of* = 'with
regard to').
2733 *lovynges*, praise

Blyssed Modir. And ever Sir Launcelote wepte, as he had bene
a chylde that had bene beatyn.   2735
    Than Kyng Arthure lat ravyshe prystes and clarkes in the
moste devoutiste wyse to brynge in Sir Urré into Carlyle with
syngyng and lovyng to God. And whan thys was done the kynge
lat clothe hym in the rychest maner that coude be thought, and
than was there but feaw bettir made knyghtes in all the courte, 2740
for he was passyngly well made and bygly.
    Than Kynge Arthur asked Sir Urré how he felte hymselff.
    'A! my good and gracious lorde, I felte myselffe never so lusty.'
    'Than woll ye juste and do dedys of armys?' seyd Kynge
Arthur.   2745
    'Sir, and I had all that longed unto justis, I wolde be sone redy.'
    Than Kynge Arthur made a party of a hondred knyghtes to be
ayenste an hondred, and so uppon the morn they justed for a
dyamounde, but there justed none of the daungerous knyghtes.
And so for to shortyn this tale, Sir Urré and Sir Lavayne justed 2750
beste that day, for there was none of them but he overthrew and
pulled down a thirty knyghtes. And than by assente of all the
kynges and lordis Sir Urré and Sir Lavayne were made knyghtes
of the Table Rounde.
    And than Sir Lavayne keste hys love unto Dame Fyleloly, Sir 2755
Urré syster, and than they were wedded with grete joy, and so
Kynge Arthur gaff to every of them a barony of londis. And this
Sir Urré wolde never go frome Sir Launcelot, but he and Sir
Lavayne awayted evermore uppon hym, and they were in all the
courte accounted for good knyghtes and full desyrous in armys. 2760
And many noble dedis they ded, for they wolde have no reste but
ever sought uppon their dedis.
    Thus they lyved in all that courte wyth grete nobeles and joy

---

2734-5 See C.
2736 *lat ravyshe*, had fetched   *clarkes*, clerks, i.e. clerics
2739 See C.
2740 *was*, were
2741 *bygly*, big
2743 *lusty*, vigorous
2746 *longed*, belonged
2751 *none*, neither
2755 *keste*, gave (lit. 'cast')
2757 *every*, each
2760 *desyrous*, eager
2762 *sought uppon their dedis*, pursued [honour] by their actions (C)

longe tymes. But every nyght and day Sir Aggravayne, Sir Gawaynes brother, awayted Quene Gwenyver and Sir Launcelot 2765 to put hem bothe to a rebuke and a shame.

And so I leve here of this tale, and overlepe grete bookis of Sir Launcelot, what grete adventures he ded whan he was called 'le Shyvalere de Charyot'. For, as the Freynshe booke sayth, because of dispyte that knyghtes and ladyes called hym 'the Knyght that rode in the Charyot' lyke as he were 2770 *juged to the jybett, therefore, in the despite of all them that named hym so, he was caryed in a charyotte a twelve-monethe; for, but lytill aftir that he had slayne Sir Mellyagaunte in the quenys quarell, he never of a twelve-moneth com on horsebak. And, as the Freynshe booke sayth, he ded that twelve-moneth more than forty batayles.* 2775

And bycause I have loste the very mater of le Shevalere de Charyot I departe frome the tale of Sir Launcelot; and here I go unto the Morte Arthur, and that caused Sir Aggravayne.

And here on the othir syde folowyth 'The Moste Pyteuous Tale of the Morte Arthure saunz Gwerdon' par le Shyvalere Sir Thomas Malleorré, 2780 *Knyght.*

Jesu, ayé de ly pitié
Pur voutre bone mercy! Amen.

2768-75 See C.
2769 *dispyte*, resentment
2771 *juged*, condemned   *jybett*, gibbet, gallows   *in the despite of*, in scorn of
2772-4 See C.
2773 *quarell*, cause
2776 *very mater*, true story
2779 *here on the other side*, over the page (C)
2780 *saunz Gwerdon*, without reward   *par le Shyvalere*, by the knight
2782-3 *Jesu ayé de ly pitié pur voutre bone mercy*, Jesus, have pity on him through your gracious (lit. 'good') mercy (C)

Le Morte Darthur

I

In May, whan every harte floryshyth and burgenyth (for, as the
season ys lusty to beholde and comfortable, so man and woman re-
joysyth and gladith of somer commynge with his freyshe floures,
for wynter wyth hys rowghe wyndis and blastis causyth lusty men
and women to cowre and to syt by fyres), so thys season hit befelle   5
in the moneth of May a grete angur and unhappe that stynted
nat tylle the floure of chyvalry of alle the worlde was destroyed
and slayne.

And all was longe upon two unhappy knyghtis whych were
named Sir Aggravayne and Sir Mordred, that were brethirn   10
unto Sir Gawayne. For thys Sir Aggravayne and Sir Mordred had
ever a prevy hate unto the quene, Dame Gwenyver, and to Sir
Launcelot; and dayly and nyghtly they ever wacched uppon Sir
Launcelot.

So hyt myssefortuned Sir Gawayne and all hys brethirne were   15
in Kynge Arthurs chambir, and than Sir Aggravayne seyde thus,
opynly and nat in no counceyle, that manye knyghtis myght here:
'I mervayle that we all be nat ashamed bothe to se and to know
how Sir Launcelot lyeth dayly and nyghtly by the quene. And
all we know well that hit ys so, and hit ys shamefully suffird of us   20
all that we shulde suffir so noble a kynge as Kynge Arthur ys to be
shamed.'

Than spake Sir Gawayne and seyde, 'Brothir Sir Aggravayne,
I pray you and charge you, meve no such maters no more afore
me, for wyte you well,' seyde Sir Gawayne, 'I woll nat be of youre   25
counceyle.'

'So God me helpe,' seyde Sir Gaherys and Sir Gareth, 'we woll
nat be knowyn, brothir Aggravayne, of your dedis.'

'Than woll I!' seyde Sir Mordred.

---

¹ *burgenyth*, burgeons
² *lusty*, invigorating *comfortable*, comforting
⁵ *cowre*, cower
⁵⁻⁶ All *so . . . May*, except *befelle*, is superfluous repetition.
⁶ *unhappe*, misfortune
⁹ *longe uppon*, because of *unhappy*, wretched (C)
¹⁷ *counceyle*, council
¹⁹ *lyeth . . . by*, sleeps with
²⁴ *meve*, start (lit. 'move')
²⁵⁻⁶ *of your counceyle*, privy to this (C)
²⁸ *knowyn . . . of*, [to be involved] in

161

'I lyve you well,' seyde Sir Gawayne, 'for ever unto all un- 30
happynes, brothir Sir Mordred, ye woll graunte. And I wolde
that ye leffte all thys, and made you nat so bysy, for I know,'
seyde Sir Gawayne, 'what woll falle of hit.'

'Falle whatsumever falle may,' seyde Sir Aggravayne, 'I woll
disclose hit to the kynge!' 35

'Nat be my counceyle,' seyde Sir Gawayne, 'for, and there
aryse warre and wrake betwyxte Sir Launcelot and us, wyte you
well, brothir, there woll many kynges and grete lordis holde with
Sir Launcelot. Also, brothir Sir Aggravayne,' seyde Sir Gawayne,
'ye muste remembir how oftyntymes Sir Launcelot hath rescowed 40
the kynge and the quene; and the beste of us all had bene full
colde at the harte-roote had nat Sir Launcelot bene bettir than
we, and that hathe he preved hymselff full ofte. And as for my
parte,' seyde Sir Gawayne, 'I woll never be ayenste Sir Launcelot for one dayes dede, that was whan he rescowed me frome 45
Kynge Carados of the Dolerous Towre and slew hym and saved
my lyff. Also, brother Sir Aggravayne, and Sir Mordred, in lyke
wyse Sir Launcelot rescowed you bothe and three score and two
frome Sir Tarquyne. And therefore, brothir, methynkis suche
noble dedis and kyndnes shulde be remembirde.' 50

'Do ye as ye lyste,' seyde Sir Aggravayne, 'for I woll layne hit
no lenger.'

So wyth thes wordis cam in Sir Arthur.

'Now, brothir,' seyde Sir Gawayne, 'stynte youre stryff.'

'That woll I nat,' seyde Sir Aggravayne and Sir Mordred. 55

'Well, woll ye so?' seyde Sir Gawayne. 'Than God spede you,
for I woll nat here of youre talis, nothir be of youre counceile.'

'No more woll I,' seyde Sir Gaherys.

'Nother I,' seyde Sir Gareth, 'for I shall never say evyll by that
man that made me knyght.' 60

And therewythall they three departed makynge grete dole.

'Alas!' seyde Sir Gawayne and Sir Gareth, 'now ys thys realme

---

30 *lyve*, believe
30–1 *unhappynes*, mischief
31 *graunte*, accede to
36 *counceyle*, counsel
37 *wrake*, destruction (cf. *rack and ruin*)
45–9 See C.
51 *lyste*, wish   *layne*, hide
57 *here of*, hear   *talis*, words (*lit.* 'tales')

holy destroyed and myscheved, and the noble felyshyp of the
Rounde Table shall be disparbeled.'

So they departed, and than Kynge Arthure asked them what   65
noyse they made.

'My lorde,' seyde Sir Aggravayne, 'I shall telle you, for I may
kepe hit no lenger. Here ys I and my brothir Sir Mordred brake
unto my brothir Sir Gawayne, Sir Gaherys, and to Sir Gareth—
for thys ys all, to make hit shorte—how we know all that Sir   70
Launcelot holdith youre quene, and hath done longe, and we be
your syster sunnes: we may suffir hit no lenger. And all we wote
that ye shulde be above Sir Launcelot, and ye ar the kynge that
made hym knyght, and therefore we woll preve hit that he is a
traytoure to youre person.'   75

'Gyff hit be so,' seyde the kynge, 'wyte you well, he ys none
othir. But I wolde be lothe to begyn such a thynge but I myght
have prevys of hit, for Sir Launcelot ys an hardy knyght, and all
ye know that he ys the beste knyght amonge us all, and but if he be
takyn with the dede he woll fyght with hym that bryngith up the   80
noyse, and I know no knyght that ys able to macch hym. Therefore, and hit be sothe as ye say, I wolde that he were takyn with
the dede.'

For, as the Freynshe booke seyth, the kynge was full lothe that
such a noyse shulde be uppon Sir Launcelot and his quene; for the   85
kynge had a demyng of hit, but he wold nat here thereoff, for Sir
Launcelot had done so much for hym and for the quene so many
tymes that wyte you well the kynge loved hym passyngly well.

'My lorde,' seyde Sir Aggravayne, 'ye shall ryde to-morne an-
huntyng, and doute ye nat, Sir Launcelot woll nat go wyth you.   90
And so whan hit drawith towarde nyght ye may sende the quene
worde that ye woll ly oute all that nyght, and so may ye sende for
your cookis. And than, uppon payne of deth, that nyght we shall

---

⁶⁴ *disparbeled*, scattered
⁶⁸ *Mordred brake*, Mordred [who] disclosed
⁷¹ *holdith*, holds, i.e. sexually
⁷² *syster sunnes* (C)
⁷⁶ *Gyff*, If
⁷⁷ *but*, unless
^{79–80} See C.   *but if*, unless
⁸¹ *noyse*, rumour
⁸⁴ See C.
⁸⁶ *demyng*, suspicion
⁸⁸ *passyngly*, exceedingly

take hym wyth the quene; and we shall brynge hym unto you, quycke or dede.'   95

'I woll well,' seyde the kynge. 'Than I counceyle you to take with you sure felyshyp.'

'Sir,' seyde Sir Aggravayne, 'my brothir Sir Mordred and I woll take wyth us twelve knyghtes of the Rounde Table.'

'Beware,' seyde Kynge Arthure, 'for I warne you, ye shall   100
fynde hym wyght.'

'Lat us deale!' seyde Sir Aggravayne and Sir Mordred.

So on the morne Kynge Arthure rode an-huntyng and sente worde to the quene that he wolde be oute all that nyght. Than Sir Aggravayne and Sir Mordred gate to them twelve knyghtes and   105
hyd hemselff in a chambir in the castell of Carlyle. And thes were their namys: Sir Collgrevaunce, Sir Mador de la Porte, Sir Gyngalyne, Sir Mellyot de Logris, Sir Petipace of Wynchylsé, Sir Galleron of Galoway, Sir Melyon de la Mountayne, Sir Asco- more, Sir Gromore Somer Joure, Sir Curselayne, Sir Florence,   110
and Sir Lovell. So thes twelve knyghtes were with Sir Mordred and Sir Aggravayne, and all they were of Scotlonde, other ellis of Sir Gawaynes kynne, other well-wyllers to hys brothir.

So whan the nyght cam Sir Launcelot tolde Sir Bors how he wolde go that nyght and speke wyth the quene.   115

'Sir,' seyde Sir Bors, 'ye shall nat go thys nyght be my coun- ceyle.'

'Why?' seyde Sir Launcelot.

'Sir,' seyde Sir Bors, 'for I drede me ever of Sir Aggravayne that waytith uppon you dayly to do you shame and us all. And   120
never gaff my harte ayenste no goynge that ever ye wente to the quene so much as now, for I mystruste that the kynge ys oute thys nyght frome the quene bycause peradventure he hath layne som wacche for you and the quene. Therefore I drede me sore of som treson.'   125

'Have ye no drede,' seyde Sir Launcelot, 'for I shall go and com agayne and make no taryynge.'

---

96 *woll well*, agree (lit. 'will [it] well')
101 *wyght*, formidable
107–11 See C.
119 *I drede me*, I am afraid
120 *waytith*, lies in wait
121 See C.
123 *peradventure*, perhaps   *layne*, laid

'Sir,' seyde Sir Bors, 'that me repentis, for I drede me sore that youre goyng thys nyght shall wratth us all.'

'Fayre neveawe,' seyd Sir Launcelot, 'I mervayle me much 130
why ye say thus, sytthyn the quene hath sente for me. And wyte you well, I woll nat be so much a cowarde, but she shall undirstonde I woll se her good grace.'

'God spede you well,' seyde Sir Bors, 'and sende you sounde and sauff agayne!' 135

So Sir Launcelot departed and toke hys swerde undir hys arme, and so he walked in hys mantell, that noble knyght, and put hymselff in grete jouparté. And so he past on tylle he cam to the quenys chambir; and so lyghtly he was had into the chambir. For, as the Freynshhe booke seyth, the quene and Sir Launcelot were 140
togydirs. And whether they were abed other at other maner of disportis, me lyste nat thereof make no mencion, for love that tyme was nat as love ys nowadayes.

But thus as they were togydir there cam Sir Aggravayne and Sir Mordred wyth twelve knyghtes with them of the Rounde 145
Table, and they seyde with grete cryyng and scaryng voyce, 'Thou traytoure, Sir Launcelot, now arte thou takyn!'

And thus they cryed wyth a lowde voyce, that all the courte myght hyre hit. And thes fourtene knyghtes all were armed at all poyntis, as they shulde fyght in a batayle. 150

'Alas!' seyde Quene Gwenyver, 'now ar we myscheved bothe!'

'Madame,' seyde Sir Launcelot, 'ys there here ony armour within youre chambir that I myght cover my poure body wythall? And if there be ony, gyff hit me and I shall sone stynte their malice, by the grace of God!' 155

'Now, truly,' seyde the quyne, 'I have none armour, nother helme, shylde, swerde, nother speare; wherefore I dred me sore oure longe love ys com to a myschyvus ende. For I here by their noyse there be many noble knyghtes, and well I wote they be surely armed, and ayenst them ye may make no resistence. Where- 160
fore ye ar lykly to be slayne, and than shall I be brente! For and

129 *wratth*, injure
130 *nevaewe*, nephew
139–41 See C.
142 *disportis*, pastime
146 *scaryng*, frightening
151 *myscheved*, ruined
154–5 *stynte their malice*, put an end to their hostility
160 *surely*, well (lit. 'reliably')
161 *For and*, For if

ye myght ascape them,' seyde the quene, 'I wolde nat doute but
that ye wolde rescowe me in what daunger that I ever stood in.'

'Alas!' seyde Sir Launcelot, 'in all my lyff thus was I never
bestad that I shulde be thus shamefully slayne, for lake of myne   165
armour.'

But ever in one Sir Aggravayne and Sir Mordred cryed, 'Traytour knyght, com oute of the quenys chambir! For wyte thou well
thou arte besette so that thou shalt nat ascape.'

'A, Jesu mercy!' seyd Sir Launcelot, 'thys shamefull cry and   170
noyse I may nat suffir, for better were deth at onys than thus to
endure thys payne.'

Than he toke the quene in hys armys and kyssed her and seyde,
'Moste nobelest Crysten quene, I besech you, as ye have ben
ever my speciall good lady, and I at all tymes your poure knyght   175
and trew unto my power, and as I never fayled you in ryght nor
in wronge sytthyn the firste day Kynge Arthur made me knyght,
that ye woll pray for my soule if that I be slayne. For well I am
assured that Sir Bors, my nevewe, and all the remenaunte of my
kynne, with Sir Lavayne and Sir Urré, that they woll nat fayle   180
you to rescow you from the fyer. And therfore, myne owne lady,
recomforte youreselff, whatsomever com of me, that ye go with
Sir Bors, my nevew, and Sir Urré; and they all woll do you all
the plesure that they can or may, and ye shall lyve lyke a quene
uppon my londis.'   185

'Nay, Sir Launcelot, nay!' seyde the quene. 'Wyte thou well
that I woll never lyve longe aftir thy dayes. But and ye be slayne
I woll take my dethe as mekely as ever ded marter take hys dethe
for Jesu Crystes sake.'

'Well, madame,' seyde Sir Launcelot, 'syth hit ys so that the   190
day ys com that oure love muste departe, wyte you well I shall
selle my lyff as dere as I may. And a thousandfolde', seyde Sir
Launcelot, 'I am more hevyar for you than for myselff! And now
I have levir than to be lorde of all Crystendom that I had sure
armour uppon me, that men myght speke of my dedys or ever I   195
were slayne.'

---

163 *in what daunger that I ever*, whatever danger I
165 *bestad*, [hard]-pressed   *that*, so that
167 *in one*, with one [voice]
176–7 *in ryght nor in wronge* (C)
182 *recomforte*, comfort   *com*, become   *that*, so that
186 *thou* (C)
191 *departe*, part, divide
195 *or*, before

'Truly,' seyde the quene, 'and hit myght please God, I wolde that they wolde take me and sle me and suffir you to ascape.'

'That shall never be,' seyde Sir Launcelot. 'God deffende me frome such a shame! But, Jesu Cryste, be Thou my shylde and myne armoure!'   200

And therewith Sir Launcelot wrapped hys mantel aboute hys arme well and surely; and by than they had getyn a grete fourme oute of the halle, and therewith they all russhed at the dore.

'Now, fayre lordys,' seyde Sir Launcelot, 'leve youre noyse and   205
youre russhynge, and I shall sette opyn thys dore, and than may
ye do with me what hit lykith you.'

'Com of, than,' seyde they all, 'and do hit, for hit avaylyth the nat to stryve ayenste us all! And therefore lat us into thys chambir, and we shall save thy lyff untyll thou com to Kynge Arthur.'   210

Than Sir Launcelot unbarred the dore, and with hys lyffte honde he hylde hit opyn a lytyll, that but one man myght com in at onys. And so there cam strydyng a good knyght, a much man and a large, and hys name was called Sir Collgrevaunce of Goore. And he wyth a swerde strake at Sir Launcelot myghtyly,   215
and so he put asyde the stroke, and gaff hym such a buffette uppon the helmet that he felle grovelyng dede wythin the chambir dore.

Than Sir Launcelot with grete myght drew that dede knyght within the chambir dore. And than Sir Launcelot, wyth helpe   220
of the quene and her ladyes, he was lyghtly armed in Collgre- vaunce armoure. And ever stood Sir Aggravayne and Sir Mor- dred, cryyng, 'Traytoure knyght! Come forthe oute of the quenys chambir!'

'Sires, leve youre noyse,' seyde Sir Launcelot, 'for wyte you   225
well, Sir Aggravayne, ye shall nat preson me thys nyght! And therefore, and ye do be my counceyle, go ye all frome thys chambir dore and make you no suche cryyng and such maner of sclaundir as ye do. For I promyse you be my knyghthode, and ye woll departe and make no more noyse, I shall as to-morne   230
appyere afore you all and before the kynge, and than lat hit be sene whych of you all, other ellis ye all, that woll deprave me of

---

²⁰³ *getyn,* got (cf. American *gotten*)   *fourme,* form, bench
²⁰⁸ *Com of,* Come on
^{208–9} *avaylyth . . . nat,* is no use to
^{213–14} *much . . . large,* big . . . broad
²²¹ *lyghtly,* swiftly
²²⁶ *preson,* imprison
²³² *deprave,* accuse

167

treson. And there shall I answere you, as a knyght shulde, that hydir I cam to the quene for no maner of male engyne, and that woll I preve and make hit good uppon you wyth my hondys.'   235

'Fye uppon the, traytour,' seyde Sir Aggravayne and Sir Mordred, 'for we woll have the magré thyne hede and sle the, and we lyste! For we let the wyte we have the choyse of Kynge Arthure to save the other sle the.'

'A, sirres,' seyde Sir Launcelot, 'ys there none other grace with   240
you? Than kepe youreselff!'

And than Sir Launcelot sette all opyn the chambir dore, and myghtyly and knyghtly he strode in amonge them. And anone at the firste stroke he slew Sir Aggravayne, and anone aftir eleven of hys felowys. Within a whyle he had layde them down colde to   245
the erthe, for there was none of the twelve knyghtes myght stonde Sir Launcelot one buffet. And also he wounded Sir Mordred, and therewithall he fled with all hys myght.

And than Sir Launcelot returned agayne unto the quene and seyde, 'Madame, now wyte you well, all oure trew love ys brought   250
to an ende, for now wyll Kyng Arthur ever be my foo. And there-fore, madam, and hit lyke you that I may have you with me, I shall save you frome all maner adventures daungers.'

'Sir, that ys nat beste,' seyde the quene, 'mesemyth, for now ye have don so much harme hit woll be beste that ye holde you   255
styll with this. And if ye se that as to-morne they woll putte me unto dethe, than may ye rescowe me as ye thynke beste.'

'I woll well,' seyde Sir Launcelot, 'for have ye no doute, whyle I am a man lyvyng I shall rescow you.'

And than he kyste her, and ayther of hem gaff othir a rynge,   260
and so the quene he leffte there and wente untyll hys lodgynge.

Whan Sir Bors saw Sir Launcelot he was never so glad of hys home-comynge as he was than.

'Jesu mercy!' seyde Sir Launcelot, 'why be ye all armed? What meanyth thys?'   265

---

234 *male engyne*, wicked subterfuge
235 *preve*, prove
236 *Fye*, Shame (cf. 'Lancelot and Guenivere', l. 1031*n*)
237 *magré thyne hede*, willy nilly (lit. 'in spite of your head')
238 *of* from
248 *he*, i.e. Mordred
251 *foo*, foe, enemy
253 *adventures*, fortuitous, unlucky (lit. 'adventurous')
254–7 See C.
262 *was never*, had never been

'Sir,' seyde Sir Bors, 'aftir ye were departed frome us, we all
that ben of youre blood and youre well-wyllars were so adretched
that som of us lepe oute of oure beddis naked and som in their
dremys caught naked swerdys in their hondis. And therefore,'
seyde Sir Bors, 'we demed there was som grete stryff on honde,   270
and so we all demed that ye were betrapped with som treson; and
therefore we made us thus redy, what nede that ever ye were in.'

'My fayre nevew,' seyde Sir Launcelot unto Sir Bors, 'now shall
ye wyte all that thys nyght I was more harde bestad than ever I
was dayes of my lyff. And thanked be God, I am myselff ascaped   275
their daungere.' And so he tolde them all how and in what maner,
as ye have harde toforehande. 'And therefore, my felowys,' seyde
Sir Launcelot, 'I pray you all that ye woll be of harte good, and
helpe me in what nede that ever I stonde, for now ys warre
comyn to us all.'   280

'Sir,' seyde Sir Bors, 'all ys wellcom that God sendyth us, and
as we have takyn much weale with you and much worshyp, we
woll take the woo with you as we have takyn the weale.'

And therefore they seyde all, the good knyghtes, 'Loke ye take
no discomforte, for there ys no bondys of knyghtes undir hevyn but 285
we shall be able to greve them as much as they may us; and
therefore discomforte nat youreselff by no maner. And we shall
gadir togyder all that we love and that lovyth us, and what that
ye woll have done shall be done. And therefore, Sir Launcelot,'
seyde they, 'we woll take the wo with the weale.'   290

'Grauntmercy,' seyde Sir Launcelot, 'of youre good comforte;
for in my grete distresse, fayre nevew, ye comforte me gretely,
and much am I beholdynge unto you. But thys, my fayre nevew,
I wolde that ye ded, in all haste that ye may, or hit ys far dayes
paste: that ye woll loke in their lodgynge that ben lodged nyghe   295
here aboute the kynge, whych woll holde with me and whych

---

²⁶⁷ *ben,* are   *adretched,* troubled in [our] sleep
²⁶⁸ *lepe,* leapt
²⁷⁰ *demed,* suspected
²⁷⁴ *ye wyte all,* you all know
²⁷⁵ *dayes of my lyff,* understand 'in my life' (cf. l. 294)
²⁷⁶ *their daungere,* their (i.e. Mordred's company's) power
^{281–3} See C.
²⁸⁵ *bondys,* company (lit. 'bands')
²⁹³ *beholdynge,* beholden
^{294–5} *far dayes paste,* far on in (lit. 'of', cf. l. 275) the day
^{295–6} *loke . . . whych,* look . . . [to see] who

169

woll nat. For now I wolde know whych were my frendis fro
my fooes.'

'Sir,' seyde Sir Bors, 'I shall do my payne, and or hit be seven
of the clok I shall wyte of such as ye have dout fore, who that woll   300
holde with you.'

Than Sir Bors called unto hym Sir Lyonel, Sir Ector de Marys,
Sir Blamour de Ganys, Sir Bleoberys de Ganys, Sir Gahalantyne,
Sir Galyhodyn, Sir Galyhud, Sir Menaduke, Sir Vyllyers the
Valyaunte, Sir Hebes le Renowné, Sir Lavayne, Sir Urré of   305
Hungry, Sir Neroveus, Sir Plenoryus (for thes two were knyghtes
that Sir Launcelot wan uppon a brydge, and therefore they wolde
never be ayenst hym), and Sir Harry le Fyz Lake, and Sir
Selyses of the Dolerous Towre; Sir Mellyas de Lyle, and Sir
Bellangere le Bewse that was Sir Alysaundir le Orphelyne sone   310
(bycause hys modir was Alys la Beale Pelleryn, and she was kyn
unto Sir Launcelot, he hylde wyth hym). So cam Sir Palomydes
and Sir Saphir, hys brothir; Sir Clegis, Sir Sadok, Sir Dynas and
Sir Clarryus of Cleremount.

So thes five-and-twenty knyghtes drew hem togydirs, and by   315
than they were armed and on horsebak they promysed Sir
Launcelot to do what he wolde. Than there felle to them, what
of Northe Walys and of Cornwayle, for Sir Lamorakes sake and
for Sir Trystrames sake, to the numbir of a seven score knyghtes.

Than spake Sir Launcelot: 'Wyte you well, I have bene ever   320
syns I cam to thys courte well-wylled unto my lorde Arthur and
unto my lady Quene Gwenyver unto my power. And thys nyght
bycause my lady the quene sente for me to speke with her (I suppose hit was made by treson—howbehit I dare largely excuse her
person natwithstondynge) I was there be a forecaste nerehonde   325
slayne. But as Jesu provyded for me, I ascaped all their malice
and treson.'

---

²⁹⁹ *do my payne*, do my best   *or*, ere, before
³⁰⁰⁻¹ Translate: 'I shall know who, among those you have doubts of, will hold
with you'
³⁰⁶⁻⁸ See C.
³⁰⁸ *Harry le Fyz Lake*, Harry the son of Lac (Fr. *le fils*)
³¹⁵⁻¹⁶ *by than*, when
³¹⁷⁻¹⁸ *what of*, what [with those] of
³¹⁸ See C.
³²³⁻⁴ *suppose*, believe
³²⁴ *largely*, thoroughly   *excuse*, defend
³²⁴⁻⁵ *her person*, her
³²⁵ *be a forecaste*, by a plot   *nerehonde*, nearly
³²⁷ *treson*, treachery (not 'treson' in the legal sense)

And than that noble knyght Sir Launcelot tolde hem how he
was harde bestad in the quenys chambir, and how and in what
maner he ascaped from them.   330

'And therefore,' seyde Sir Launcelot, 'wyte you well, my fayre
lordis, I am sure there nys but warre unto me and to myne. And
for cause I have slayne thys nyght Sir Aggravayne, Sir Gawaynes
brothir, and at the leste twelve of hys felowis, and for thys cause
now am I sure of mortall warre. For thes knyghtes were sente and 335
ordayned by Kynge Arthur to betray me, and therefore the kyng
woll in thys hete and malice jouge the quene unto brennyng, and
that may nat I suffir that she shulde be brente for my sake. For
and I may be harde and suffirde and so takyn, I woll feyght for
the quene, that she ys a trew lady untyll her lorde. But the kynge 340
in hys hete, I drede, woll nat take me as I ought to be takyn.'

'My lorde, Sir Launcelot,' seyde Sir Bors, 'be myne advyce, ye
shall take the woo wyth the weall, and take hit in pacience and
thank God of hit. And sytthyn hit ys fallyn as hit ys, I counceyle
you to kepe youreselff, for and ye woll youreselffe, there ys no fely- 345
shyp of knyghtes crystynde that shall do you wronge. And also I
woll counceyle you, my lorde, that my lady Quene Gwenyver, and
she be in ony distres, insomuch as she ys in payne for youre sake,
that ye knyghtly rescow her; for and ye ded ony other wyse all
the worlde wolde speke of you shame to the worldis ende. Inso- 350
much as ye were takyn with her, whether ye ded ryght othir
wronge, hit ys now youre parte to holde wyth the quene, that she
be nat slayne and put to a myschevous deth. For and she so dye,
the shame shall be evermore youres.'

'Now Jesu deffende me from shame,' seyde Sir Launcelot, 'and 355
kepe and save my lady the quene from vylany and shamefull
dethe, and that she never be destroyed in my defaute! Wherefore,

---

332 *nys but*, is nothing but
333 *for cause*, because
334 *and for thys cause* is redundant
336 *ordayned*, arranged   *betray*, trap
337 *hete*, anger   *malice*, enmity   *brennyng*, the stake
339 Translate: 'For if I am allowed to speak, and what I say (lit. 'thus') is accepted'
344 *sytthyn*, since   *ys fallyn*, has happened
345 *kepe*, guard   *woll youreselffe*, will [guard] yourself
347 *and*, if
350 *worldis ende* (C)
353 *myschevous*, wretched (not 'mischievous')
357 *in*, by

171

my fayre lordys, my kyn and my fryndis,' seyde Sir Launcelot, 'what woll ye do?'

And anone they seyde all with one voyce, 'We woll do as ye woll do.'

'Than I put thys case unto you,' seyde Sir Launcelot, 'that my lorde Kynge Arthure, by evyll counceile, woll tomorn in hys hete put my lady the quene unto the fyre and there to be brente. Than, I pray you, counceile me what ys beste for me to do.'

Than they seyde all at onys with one voice, 'Sir, us thynkis beste that ye knyghtly rescow the quene. Insomuch as she shall be brente, hit ys for youre sake; and hit ys to suppose, and ye myght be handeled, ye shulde have the same dethe, othir ellis a more shamefuller dethe. And, sir, we say all that ye have rescowed her frome her deth many tymys for other mennes quarels; therefore us semyth hit ys more youre worshyp that ye rescow the quene from thys peryll, insomuch that she hath hit for your sake.'

Than Sir Launcelot stood stylle and sayde, 'My fayre lordis, wyte you well I wolde be lothe to do that thynge that shulde dishonour you or my bloode; and wyte you well I wolde be full lothe that my lady the quene shulde dye such a shameful deth.

'But and hit be so that ye woll counceyle me to rescow her, I must do much harme or I rescow her, and peradventure I shall there destroy som of my beste fryndis, and that shold moche repente me. And peradventure there be som, and they coude wel bryng it aboute or disobeye my lord Kynge Arthur, they wold sone come to me, the whiche I were loth to hurte. And if so be that I may wynne the quene away, where shall I kepe her?'

'Sir, that shall be the leste care of us all,' seyde Sir Bors, 'for how ded the moste noble knyght Sir Trystram? By youre good wyll, kept nat he with hym La Beall Isode nere three yere in Joyous Garde, the whych was done by youre althers avyce? And that same place ys youre owne, and in lyke wyse may ye do and

360

365

370

375

380

385

364 *fyre and there*, understand 'fire, there'
366-73 See C.
366 *us thynkis*, [it] seems to us
367-8 Translate: 'In so far as she is to be burnt at all, it is on your account'
368 *to suppose*, to be supposed
368-9 *and ye myght be handeled*, if they could get their hands on you
372 *us semyth*, it [seems] to us
376 *bloode*, blood (C)
380-1 *repente*, grieve
385 *leste*, least
388 *youre althers*, of you all

172

ye lyst, and take the quene knyghtly away with you, if so be that   390
the kynge woll jouge her to be brente. And in Joyous Garde may
ye kepe her longe inowe untyll the hete be paste of the kynge, and
than hit may fortune you to brynge the quene agayne to the kynge
with grete worshyp, and peradventure ye shall have than thanke
for youre bryngyng home where othir may happyn to have magré.'   395

'That ys hard for to do,' seyde Sir Launcelot, 'for by Sir Trystram I may have a warnynge; for whan by meanys of tretyse Sir
Trystram brought agayne La Beall Isode unto Kynge Marke
from Joyous Garde, loke ye now what felle on the ende: how
shamefully that false traytour Kyng Marke slew hym as he sate   400
harpynge afore hys lady, La Beall Isode. Wyth a grounden
glayve he threste hym in behynde to the harte, whych grevyth sore
me,' seyde Sir Launcelot, 'to speke of his dethe, for all the worlde
may nat fynde such another knyght.'

'All thys ys trouthe,' seyde Sir Bors, 'but there ys one thyng   405
shall corrayge you and us all: ye know well that Kynge Arthur
and Kynge Marke were never lyke of condycions, for there was
never yet man that ever coude preve Kynge Arthure untrew of hys
promyse.'

But so, to make shorte tale, they were all condiscended that,   410
for bettir othir for wars, if so were that the quene were brought on
that morne to the fyre, shortely they all wolde rescow her. And so
by the advyce of Sir Launcelot they put hem all in an enbusshement in a wood as nyghe Carlyle as they myght, and there they
abode stylle to wyte what the kynge wold do.   415

Now turne we agayne unto Sir Mordred that whan he was
ascaped frome the noble knyght Sir Launcelot, anone he gate hys
horse and mounted upon hym, and cam to Kynge Arthur sore

---

392 *inowe*, enough
395 *have magré*, be looked on with displeasure (C)
397 *tretyse*, tretyse, [a] formal agreement
399 *felle*, befell   *on*, in
400 See C.
401 *grounden*, sharpened
402 *glayve*, spear (C)   *threste hym in*, stabbed him   *behynde*, from behind, **in**
the back
406 *corrayge*, give . . . confidence
407 *lyke of*, alike in   *condycions*, character (cf. 'conditioning')
410 *make shorte tale*, make [this] tale short   *condiscended*, agreed
411 *wars*, worse
412 *shortely* (C)
413–14 *enbusshement*, ambush

173

wounded and all forbled; and there he tolde the kynge all how hit
was, and how they were all slayne save hymselff alone.   420

'A, Jesu mercy! How may thys be?' seyde the kynge. 'Toke ye
hym in the quenys chambir?'

'Yee, so God me helpe,' seyde Sir Mordred, 'there we founde
hym unarmed, and anone he slew Sir Collgrevaunce and armed
hym in hys armour.' And so he tolde the kynge frome the be-   425
gynnyng to the endynge.

'Jesu mercy!' seyde the kynge, 'he ys a mervaylous knyght of
proues. And alas,' seyde the kynge, 'me sore repentith that ever
Sir Launcelot sholde be ayenste me, for now I am sure the noble
felyshyp of the Rounde Table ys brokyn for ever, for wyth hym   430
woll many a noble knyght holde. And now hit ys fallen so,' seyde
the kynge, 'that I may nat with my worshyp but my quene muste
suffir dethe,' and was sore amoved.

So than there was made grete ordynaunce in thys ire, and the
quene muste nedis be jouged to the deth. And the law was such   435
in tho dayes that whatsomever they were, of what astate or degré,
if they were founden gylty of treson there shuld be none other
remedy but deth, and othir the menour other the takynge wyth
the dede shulde be causer of their hasty jougement. And ryght so
was hit ordayned for Quene Gwenyver: bycause Sir Mordred   440
was ascaped sore wounded, and the dethe of thirtene knyghtes of
the Rounde Table, thes previs and experyenses caused Kynge
Arthure to commaunde the quene to the fyre and there to be
brente.

Than spake Sir Gawayn and seyde, 'My lorde Arthure, I   445
wolde counceyle you nat to be over hasty, but that ye wolde put
hit in respite, thys jougemente of my lady the quene, for many

---

419 *forbled*, bleeding badly (lit. 'very-much-bled')
424 *unarmed*, without armour (not 'without weapons')
428 *proues*, prowess
432–3 Translate: 'I cannot honourably [do anything] other than [see that] my queen is executed'
433 *amoved*, angered
434 *grete ordynaunce*, a great fuss (lit. 'a great deal of administrative activity') *ire*, angry mood
436 *what*, whatever
437–8 *none other remedy but*, no alternative to
438 *the menour*, the mainour, being caught with incriminating evidence upon one (C)
438–9 *wyth the dede*, in the act
439 *hasty jougement*, summary condemnation
440 *ordayned*, decreed
442 *experyenses*, this evidence
446–7 *put hit in respite*, postpone it

causis. One ys thys, thoughe hyt were so that Sir Launcelot were
founde in the quenys chambir, yet hit myght be so that he cam
thydir for none evyll. For ye know, my lorde,' seyde Sir Gawayne,   450
'that my lady the quene hath oftyntymes ben gretely beholdyn
unto Sir Launcelot, more than to ony othir knyght; for oftyntymes he hath saved her lyff and done batayle for her whan all
the courte refused the quene. And peradventure she sente for
hym for goodnes and for none evyll, to rewarde hym for his good   455
dedys that he had done to her in tymes past. And peravnenture my
lady the quene sente for hym to that entente, that Sir Launcelot
sholde a com to her good grace prevaly and secretly, wenyng to
her that hyt had be beste so to do in eschewyng and dredyng of
slaundir; for oftyntymys we do many thynges that we wene for   460
the beste be, and yet peradventure hit turnyth to the warste. For I
dare sey,' seyde Sir Gawayne, 'my lady your quene ys to you both
good and trew. And as for Sir Launcelot,' seyde Sir Gawayne,
'I dare say he woll make hit good uppon ony knyght lyvyng that
woll put uppon hym vylany or shame, and in lyke wyse he woll   465
make good for my lady the quene.'

'That I beleve well,' seyde Kynge Arthur, 'but I woll nat that
way worke with Sir Launcelot, for he trustyth so much uppon
hys hondis and hys myght that he doutyth no man. And therefore for my quene he shall nevermore fyght, for she shall have the   470
law. And if I may gete Sir Launcelot, wyte you well he shall have
as shamefull a dethe.'

'Jesu defende me,' seyde Sir Gawayne, 'that I never se hit nor
know it.'

'Why say you so?' seyde Kynge Arthur. 'For, perdé, ye have   475
no cause to love hym! For thys nyght last past he slew youre
brothir Sir Aggravayne, a full good knyght, and allmoste he had
slayne youre othir brother, Sir Mordred, and also there he slew
thirtene noble knyghtes. And also remembir you, Sir Gawayne,
he slew two sunnes of youres, Sir Florens and Sir Lovell.'   480

'My lorde,' seyde Sir Gawayne, 'of all thys I have a knowleche,

---

455 *for goodnes,* for an honourable motive (lit. 'because of [her] goodness')
457 *entente,* intent, purpose (C)
458 *a,* have   *wenyng,* thinking (lit. 'weening')
459-60 *in eschewyng and dredyng of slaundir* (C)
468 *worke with,* deal with   *uppon,* in
469 *doutyth,* fears
475 *perdé,* by God
480 *two* (C)

whych of her dethis sore repentis me. But insomuch as I gaff hem
warnynge and tolde my brothir and my sonnes aforehonde what
wolde falle on the ende, and insomuche as they wolde nat do be
my counceyle, I woll nat meddyll me thereoff, nor revenge me   485
nothynge of their dethys; for I tolde them there was no boote to
stryve with Sir Launcelot. Howbehit I am sory of the deth of my
brothir and of my two sunnes, but they ar the causars of their owne
dethe; for oftyntymes I warned my brothir Sir Aggravayne, and
I tolde hym of the perellis the which ben now fallen.'   490

Than seyde Kynge Arthur unto Sir Gawayne,
'Make you redy, I pray you, in youre beste armour, wyth youre
brethirn, Sir Gaherys and Sir Gareth, to brynge my quene to
the fyre and there to have her jougement.'

'Nay, my moste noble kynge,' seyde Sir Gawayne, 'that woll I   495
never do, for wyte you well I woll never be in that place where so
noble a quene as ys my lady Dame Gwenyver shall take such a
shamefull ende. For wyte you well,' seyde Sir Gawayne, 'my harte
woll nat serve me for to se her dye, and hit shall never be seyde
that ever I was of youre counceyle for her deth.'   500

'Than,' seyde the kynge unto Sir Gawayne, 'suffir your
brethirn Sir Gaherys and Sir Gareth to be there.'

'My lorde,' seyde Sir Gawayne, 'wyte you well they wyll be
lothe to be there present bycause of many adventures that ys lyke
to falle, but they ar yonge and full unable to say you nay.'   505

Than spake Sir Gaherys and the good knyght Sir Gareth unto
Kynge Arthur,
'Sir, ye may well commande us to be there, but wyte you well
hit shall be sore ayenste oure wyll. But and we be there by youre
strayte commaundement, ye shall playnly holde us there excused: 510
we woll be there in pesyble wyse, and beare none harneyse of
warre uppon us.'

'In the name of God,' seyde the kynge, 'than make you redy,
for she shall have sone her jugemente.'

484 on, in   be, by
486-7 no boote to stryve, nothing to be gained by fighting
494 have her jougement, have her sentence carried out
499 serve me, render me its normal service, allow me
500 of youre counceyle, see p. ll. 25-6
504 adventures, unpredictable things (cf. advent)   ys, are
509 and, if
510 strayte, strict   playnly, fully (not 'plainly')
511 pesyble, peaceful   harneyse, equipment
514 sone, soon

176

'Alas,' seyde Sir Gawayne, 'that ever I shulde endure to se 515
this wofull day!'

So Sir Gawayne turned hym and wepte hartely, and so he
wente into hys chambir. And so the quene was lad furthe withoute Carlyle, and anone she was dispoyled into her smokke. And
than her gostely fadir was brought to her to be shryven of her 520
myssededis. Than was there wepyng and waylynge and wryngyng of hondis, of many lordys and ladyes; but there were but feaw
in comparison that wolde beare ony armoure for to strengthe the
dethe of the quene.

Than was there one that Sir Launcelot had sente unto that 525
place, whych wente to aspye what tyme the quene shulde go unto
her deth. And anone as he saw the quene dispoyled into her smok
and so shryvyn, than he gaff Sir Launcelot warnynge anone. Than
was there but spurryng and pluckyng up of horse, and ryght so
they cam unto the fyre. And who that stoode ayenste them, there 530
were they slayne; there myght none withstande Sir Launcelot.

So all that bare armes and withstoode them, there were they
slayne, full many a noble knyght. For there was slayne Sir
Bellyas le Orgulus, Sir Segwarydes, Sir Gryfflet, Sir Braundyles,
Sir Agglovale, Sir Tor; Sir Gauter, Sir Gyllymer, Sir Raynold 535
(three brethirn); and Sir Damas, Sir Priamus, Sir Kay le
Straunge, Sir Dryaunt, Sir Lambegus, Sir Hermynde; Sir
Pertolyp, Sir Perymones (two brethren whych were called the
Grene Knyght and the Rede Knyght).

And so in thys russhynge and hurlynge, as Sir Launcelot 540
thrange here and there, hit mysfortuned hym to sle Sir Gaherys
and Sir Gareth, the noble knyght, for they were unarmed and
unwares. As the Freynshe booke sayth, Sir Launcelot smote Sir
Gaherys and Sir Gareth uppon the brayne-pannes, wherethorow

515 *endure*, continue living
519 *dispoyled*, stripped   *into*, down to   *smokke*, petticoat
520 *gostely fadir*, spiritual father, confessor   *to her to be*, to her for her to be
shryven, confessed and absolved
523 *to strengthe*, to further
526 *whych*, who   *aspye*, espy
529 *but*, nothing but   *horse* (C)
540 *hurlynge*, tumult
541 *thrange*, thrust
543 See C.   *unwares*, caught unaware
544-5 *brayne-pannes*, skulls   *wherethorow that*, through which

177

that they were slayne in the felde. Howbehit in very trouth Sir   545
Launcelot saw them nat. And so were they founde ded amonge
the thyckyste of the prees.

Than Sir Launcelot, whan he had thus done, and slayne and
put to flyght all that wolde wythstonde hym, than he rode streyt
unto Quene Gwenyver and made caste a kurdyll and a gown   550
uppon her, and than he made her to be sette behynde hym and
prayde her to be of good chere. Now wyte you well the quene was
glad that she was at that tyme ascaped frome the deth, and than
she thanked God and Sir Launcelot.

And so he rode hys way wyth the quene, as the Freynshe booke   555
seyth, unto Joyous Garde, and there he kepte her as a noble
knyght shulde. And many grete lordis and some kynges sente Sir
Launcelot many good knyghtes, and many full noble knyghtes
drew unto hym. Whan this was knowen openly, that Kynge
Arthure and Sir Launcelot were at debate, many knyghtes were   560
glad, and many were sory of their debate.

II

Now turne we agayne unto Kynge Arthure, that whan hit was
tolde hym how and in what maner the quene was taken away
frome the fyre, and whan he harde of the deth of his noble
knyghtes, and in especiall Sir Gaherys and Sir Gareth, than he   565
sowned for verry pure sorow.

And whan he awooke of hys swoughe, than he sayde, 'Alas,
that ever I bare crowne uppon my hede! For now have I loste
the fayryst felyshyp of noble knyghtes that ever hylde Crystyn
kynge togydirs. Alas, my good knyghtes be slayne and gone   570

545–6 See C.
547 *prees*, crush
550 *a kurdyll and a gown*, a dress and a coat (C)
555–6 See C.
560 *at debate*, at odds
561 *their debate*, their conflict
564 *harde*, heard
566 *sowned*, fainted   *verry*, true (cf. Fr. *vrai*)
569–70 See C.

away fro me, that now within thys two dayes I have loste nygh forty knyghtes, and also the noble felyshyp of Sir Launcelot and hys blood, for now I may nevermore holde hem togydirs with my worshyp. Now, alas, that ever thys warre began!

'Now, fayre felowis,' seyde the kynge, 'I charge you that no man telle Sir Gawayne of the deth of hys two brethirne; for I am sure,' seyde the kynge, 'whan he hyryth telle that Sir Gareth ys dede, he wyll go nygh oute of hys mynde. Merci Jesu,' seyde the kynge, 'why slew he Sir Gaherys and Sir Gareth? For I dare sey, as for Sir Gareth, he loved Sir Launcelot of all men erthly.'   580

'That ys trouth,' seyde som knyghtes, 'but they were slayne in the hurlynge, as Sir Launcelot thrange in the thyckyst of the prees. And as they were unarmed, he smote them and wyst nat whom that he smote, and so unhappely they were slayne.'

'Well,' seyde Arthure, 'the deth of them woll cause the grettist mortall warre that ever was, for I am sure that whan Sir Gawayne knowyth hereoff, that Sir Gareth ys slayne, I shall never have reste of hym tyll I have destroyed Sir Launcelottys kynne and hymselff bothe, othir ellis he to destroy me. And therefore,' seyde the kynge, 'wyte you well, my harte was never so hevy as hit ys now. And much more I am soryar for my good knyghtes losse than for the losse of my fayre quene; for quenys I myght have inow, but such a felyship of good knyghtes shall never be togydirs in no company. And now I dare sey,' seyde Kynge Arthur, 'there was never Crystyn kynge that ever hylde such a felyshyp togydyrs. And alas, that ever Sir Launcelot and I shulde be at debate! A, Aggravayne Aggravayne!' seyde the kynge, 'Jesu forgyff hit thy soule, for thyne evyll wyll that thou haddist and Sir Mordred, thy brothir, unto Sir Launcelot hath caused all this sorrow.' And ever amonge thes complayntes the kynge wepte and sowned.   600

Than cam there one to Sir Gawayne and tolde hym how the quene was lad away with Sir Launcelot, and nygh a four-and-twenty knyghtes slayne.

'A, Jesu, save me my two brethirn!' seyde Sir Gawayne, 'For   605

573-4 *with my worshyp,* in honour
580 *of,* more than (lit. 'among')   *erthly,* on earth
582 *hurlynge,* hurly-burly
584 *unhappely,* unluckily
601 *sowned,* fainted
603 *lad,* led

full well wyst I,' sayde Sir Gawayne, 'that Sir Launcelot wolde
rescow her, othir ellis he wolde dye in that fylde; and to say the
trouth he were nat of worshyp but if he had rescowed the quene,
insomuch as she shulde have be brente for his sake. And as in
that,' seyde Sir Gawayne, 'he hath done but knyghtly, and as I   610
wolde have done myselff and I had stonde in lyke case. But
where ar my brethirn?' seyde Sir Gawayne, 'I mervayle that I
here nat of them.'

Than seyde that man, 'Truly, Sir Gaherys and Sir Gareth be
slayne.'   615

'Jesu deffende!' seyd Sir Gawayne. 'For all thys worlde I
wolde nat that they were slayne, and in especiall my good brothir
Sir Gareth.'

'Sir,' seyde the man, 'he ys slayne, and that ys grete pité.'

'Who slew hym?' seyde Sir Gawayne.   620

'Sir Launcelot,' seyde the man, 'slew hem both.'

'That may I nat beleve,' seyde Sir Gawayne, 'that ever he
slew my good brother Sir Gareth, for I dare say my brothir
loved hym bettir than me and all hys brethirn and the kynge
bothe. Also I dare say, an Sir Launcelot had desyred my brothir   625
Sir Gareth with hym, he wolde have ben with hym ayenste the
kynge and us all. And therefore I may never belyeve that Sir
Launcelot slew my brethern.'

'Veryly, sir,' seyde the man, 'hit ys noysed that he slew hym.'

'Alas,' seyde Sir Gawayne, 'now ys my joy gone!'   630

And than he felle downe and sowned, and longe he lay there
as he had ben dede. And whan he arose oute of hys swoughe
he cryed oute sorowfully and seyde, 'Alas!' And forthwith he ran
unto the kynge, criyng and wepyng, and seyde, 'A, myne uncle
Kynge Arthur! My good brothir Sir Gareth ys slayne, and so ys   635
my brothir Sir Gaherys, whych were two noble knyghtes.'

Than the kynge wepte and he bothe, and so they felle on
sownynge. And whan they were revyved, than spake Sir Gawayne
and seyde, 'Sir, I woll goo and se my brother Sir Gareth.'

---

607 *othir ellis,* or else   *fylde,* battle-field
611 *stonde,* stood
616 *Jesu deffende,* God forbid (Fr. *défendre*)
617 *in especiall,* especially
625 *an,* if
625–6 *desyred ... with,* asked ... [to be] with
626 See C.
629 *Veryly,* Truly   *noysed,* reported, said

'Sir, ye may nat se hym,' seyde the kynge, 'for I caused hym 640
to be entered and Sir Gaherys bothe, for I well undirstood that
ye wolde make overmuche sorow, and the syght of Sir Gareth
shulde have caused youre double sorrow.'

'Alas, my lorde,' seyde Sir Gawayne, 'how slew he my brothir
Sir Gareth? Myn own good lorde, I pray you telle me.' 645

'Truly,' seyde the kynge, 'I shall tell you as hit hath bene tolde
me: Sir Launcelot slew hym and Sir Gaherys both.'

'Alas,' seyde Sir Gawayne, 'they beare none armys ayenst hym,
neyther of them bothe.'

'I wote nat how hit was,' seyde the kynge, 'but as hit ys sayde, 650
Sir Launcelot slew them in the thyk prees and knew tham nat.
And therefore lat us shape a remedy for to revenge their dethys.'

'My kynge, my lorde, and myne uncle,' seyde Sir Gawayne,
'wyte you well, now I shall make you a promyse whych I shall
holde be my knyghthode, that frome thys day forewarde I shall 655
never fayle Sir Launcelot untyll that one of us have slayne that
othir. And therefore I requyre you, my lorde and kynge, dresse
you unto the warres, for wyte you well, I woll be revenged uppon
Sir Launcelot; and therefore, as ye woll have my servyse and my
love, now haste you thereto and assay youre frendis. For I 660
promyse unto God,' seyde Sir Gawayn, 'for the deth of my
brothir Sir Gareth, I shall seke Sir Launcelot thorowoute seven
kynges realmys, but I shall sle hym, other ellis he shall sle me.'

'Sir, ye shall nat nede to seke hym so far,' seyde the kynge, 'for
as I here say, Sir Launcelot woll abyde me and us all wythin the 665
castell of Joyous Garde. And muche peple drawyth unto hym, as
I here say.'

'That may I ryght well belyve,' seyde Sir Gawayne; 'but my
lorde,' he sayde, 'assay your fryndis and I woll assay myne.'

'Hit shall be done,' seyde the kynge, 'and as I suppose I shall 670
be bygge inowghe to dryve hym oute of the bygyst toure of hys
castell.'

So than the kynge sente lettirs and wryttis thorowoute all

---

641 *entered*, buried (lit. 'interred')
648 *beare*, bore
656–7 *that one*, 'one', contrasts with *that other*, 'the other'
657–8 *dresse you unto*, prepare yourself for (cf. Fr. *dresser*)
659–60 See C.
660 *assay*, try
666 *muche*, many
671 *bygge*, strong
673 *wryttis*, writs

Inglonde, both the lengthe and the brede, for to assomon all hys
knyghtes. And so unto Kynge Arthure drew many knyghtes,   675
deukes, and erlis, that he had a grete oste; and whan they were
assembeled the kynge enfourmed hem how Sir Launcelot had
beraffte hym hys quene. Than the kynge and all hys oste made hem
redy to ley syege aboute Sir Launcelot where he lay within
Joyous Garde.   680

And anone Sir Launcelot harde thereof and purveyde hym
off many good knyghtes; for with hym helde many knyghtes,
som for hys owne sake and som for the quenys sake. Thus they
were on bothe partyes well furnysshed and garnysshed of all maner of thynge that longed unto the warre. But Kynge Arthurs oste   685
was so grete that Sir Launcelottis oste wolde nat abyde hym in
the fylde, for he was full lothe to do batayle ayenste the kynge;
but Sir Launcelot drew hym unto hys stronge castell with all
maner of vytayle plenté, and as many noble men as he myght
suffyse within the towne and the castell.   690

Than cam Kynge Arthure with Sir Gawayne wyth a grete oste
and leyde syge all aboute Joyus Garde, both the towne and the
castell, and there they made stronge warre on bothe partyes.
But in no wyse Sir Launcelot wolde ryde oute nor go oute of the
castell of longe tyme; and nother he wold nat suffir none of hys   695
good knyghtes to issew oute, nother of the towne nother of the
castell, untyll fiftene wykes were paste.

So hit felle uppon a daye in hervest tyme that Sir Launcelot
loked over the wallys and spake on hyght unto Kynge Arthure
and to Sir Gawayne: 700

'My lordis bothe, wyte you well all thys ys in vayne that ye
make at thys syge, for here wynne ye no worshyp, but magré and

---

674 *brede*, breadth   *assomon*, summon
678 *beraffte*, deprived (lit. 'bereft')
681-2 *purveyde hym off*, got, recruited
684 *garnysshed of*, supplied with   *longed*, belonged
685-7 See C.
688 *drew hym*, betook himself [and his army], went
689 *vytayle*, food   *plenté*, in plenty
690 *suffyse*, maintain
691 *oste*, host, army
693 *partyes*, sides
694 See C.
695 *of longe tyme*, for [a] long time
696 *nother ... nother*, neither ... nor
699 *spake on hyght*, called out loudly
702 *magré*, shame (C)

182

dishonoure. For and hit lyste me to com myselff oute and my
good knyghtes, I shulde full sone make an ende of thys warre.'

'Com forth,' seyde Kynge Arthur unto Sir Launcelot, 'and   705
thou darste, and I promyse the I shall mete the in myddis of thys
fylde.'

'God deffende me,' seyde Sir Launcelot, 'that ever I shulde
encounter wyth the moste noble kynge that made me knyght.'

'Now, fye upon thy fayre langayge!' seyde the kynge, 'for   710
wyte thou well and truste hit, I am thy mortall foo and ever woll
to my deth-day; for thou haste slayne my good knyghtes and full
noble men of my blood, that shall I never recover agayne. Also
thou haste layne be my quene, and holdyn her many wynters,
and sytthyn lyke a traytoure taken her away fro me by fors.'   715

'My moste noble lorde and kynge,' seyde Sir Launcelot, 'ye
may sey what ye woll, for ye wote well wyth youreselff I woll nat
stryve. But thereas ye say that I have slayne youre good knyghtes,
I wote well that I have done so, and that me sore repentith; but
I was forced to do batayle with hem in savyng of my lyff, othir   720
ellis I muste have suffirde hem to have slayne me.

'And as for my lady Quene Gwenyver, excepte youre person of
your hyghnes and my lorde Sir Gawayne, there nys no knyght undir hevyn that dare make hit good uppon me that ever I was
traytour unto youre person. And where hit please you to say that   725
I have holdyn my lady youre quene, yerys and wynters; unto
that I shall ever make a large answere, and prove hit uppon ony
knyght that beryth the lyff, excepte your person and Sir Gawayne,
that my lady Quene Gwenyver ys as trew a lady unto youre
person as ys ony lady lyvynge unto her lorde, and that woll I   730
make good with my hondis. Howbehyt hit hath lyked her good
grace to have me in favoure and cherysh me more than ony other
knyght, and unto my power agayne I have deserved her love;

706 *in myddis of,* in [the] midst of
711 *woll,* will [be]
713 *that shall I,* whom I shall
714 *holdyn,* possessed (sexually)
718 *thereas,* whereas
719 *that me sore repentith,* that grieves me very much
721 *suffirde,* allowed
722–3 *youre person of your hyghnes* (C)
723 *nys no,* is no
724 *hevyn,* heaven
726 *yerys and wynters,* for years and years
727 See C.
728 *beryth the lyff,* lives

for oftyntymes, my lorde, ye have concented that she sholde have
be brente and destroyed in youre hete, and than hit fortuned me   735
to do batayle for her, and or I departed from her adversary they
confessed there untrouthe, and she full worsshypfully excused.

'And at suche tymes, my lorde Arthur,' seyde Sir Launcelot,
'ye loved me and thanked me whan I saved your quene frome
the fyre, and than ye promysed me for ever to be my good lorde.   740
And now methynkith ye rewarde me full evyll for my good servyse. And, my lorde, mesemyth I had loste a grete parte of my
worshyp in my knyghthod and I had suffird my lady youre
quene to have ben brente, and insomuche as she shulde have
bene brente for my sake; for sytthyn I have done batayles for   745
youre quene in other quarels than in myne owne quarell, mesemyth now I had more ryght to do batayle for her in her ryght
quarell. And therefore, my good and gracious lorde,' seyde Sir
Launcelot, 'take your quene unto youre good grace, for she ys
both tru and good.'   750

'Fy on the, false recreayed knyght!' seyde Sir Gawayn. 'For I
lat the wyte: my lorde, myne uncle Kynge Arthur shall have hys
quene and the bothe magré thy vysayge, and sle you bothe and
save you, whether hit please hym.'

'Hit may well be,' seyde Sir Launcelot, 'but wyte you well,   755
my lorde Sir Gawayne, and me lyste to com oute of thys castell
ye shuld wyn me and the quene more harder than ever ye wan a
stronge batayle.'

'Now, fy on thy proude wordis!' seyde Sir Gawayne. 'As for
my lady the quene, wyte thou well, I woll never say of her shame.   760
But thou, false and recrayde knyght,' seyde Sir Gawayne, 'what
cause haddist thou to sle my good brother Sir Gareth, that loved
the more than me and all my kynne? And alas, thou madist hym
knyght thyne owne hondis! Why slewest thou hym that loved
the so well?'   765

[735-7] See C.
[735-6] hit fortuned me to do batayle, I happened to fight
[736-7] they . . . there, he . . . his
[740] to be my good lorde (C)
[743] worshyp in my knyghthod, honour as a knight   and, if
[751] the, you (lit. 'thee')   recreayed, craven (C)
[753] magré thy vysayge, despite you
[754] whether, whichever
[760] of her shame, shame of her
[764] thyne owne hondis, with your own hands

'For to excuse me,' seyde Sir Lancelot, 'hit boteneth me nat, but by Jesu, and by the feyth that I owghe unto the hyghe Order of Knyghthode, I wolde with as a good a wyll have slayne my nevew Sir Bors de Ganys, at that tyme. And alas, that ever I was so unhappy', seyde Sir Launcelot, 'that I had nat seyne Sir Gareth and Sir Gaherys!'   770

'Thou lyest, recrayed knyght,' seyde Sir Gawayne, 'thou slew-yste hem in the despite of me. And therefore wyte thou well, Sir Launcelot, I shall make warre upon the, and all the whyle that I may lyve be thyne enemy!'   775

'That me repentes,' seyde Sir Launcelot, 'for well I undir-stonde hit boteneth me nat to seke none accordemente whyle ye, Sir Gawayne, ar so myschevously sett. And if ye were nat, I wolde nat doute to have the good grace of my lorde Kynge Arthure.'   780

'I leve well, false recrayed knyght,' seyde Sir Gawayne, 'for thou haste many longe dayes overlad me and us all, and de-stroyed many of oure good knyghtes.'

'Sir, ye say as hit pleasith you,' seyde Sir Launcelot, 'yet may hit never be seyde on me and opynly preved that ever I be fore-   785
caste of treson slew no goode knyght as ye, my lorde Sir Gawayne, have done; and so ded I never but in my deffence, that I was dryven thereto in savyng of my lyff.'

'A, thou false knyght,' seyde Sir Gawayne, 'that thou menyst by Sir Lamorak. But wyte thou well, I slew hym!'   790

'Sir, ye slew hym nat youreselff,' seyde Sir Launcelot, 'for hit had ben overmuch on honde for you to have slayne hym, for he was one of the beste knyghtes crystynde of his ayge. And hit was grete pité of hys deth!'

'Well, well, Sir Launcelot,' seyde Sir Gawayne, 'sytthyn thou   795
enbraydyst me of Sir Lamorak, wyte thou well I shall never leve

---

766 *For to excuse me*, To make excuses for myself   *hit boteneth me nat*, it is no use (lit. 'it profits me not')
773 *in the despite of*, in order to spite (C)
777 *accordemente*, settlement
778 *myschevously sett*, determined on disaster
781 *leve*, believe [it]
782 *overlad*, oppressed
785-6 *be forecaste of treson*, by [a] treacherous plot
789-90 *that thou menyst by*, by that you mean
792 *overmuch on honde*, too much of a handful (lit. 'in hand')
793-4 Translate: 'his death was a great pity'
795-6 *thou enbraydyst*, you upbraid   *of*, with

185

the tyll I have the at suche avayle that thou shalt nat ascape my hondis.'

'I truste you well inowgh,' seyde Sir Launcelot. 'And ye may gete me, I gett but lytyll mercy.'   800

But as the Freynsh booke seyth, Kynge Arthur wolde have takyn hys quene agayne and to have bene accorded with Sir Launcelot, but Sir Gawayne wolde nat suffir hym by no maner of meane. And so Sir Gawayne made many men to blow uppon Sir Launcelot, and so all at onys they called hym 'false recrayed   805 knyght'.

But whan Sir Bors de Ganys, Sir Ector de Marys, and Sir Lyonell harde thys outecry, they called unto them Sir Palomydes Sir Safirs brothir and Sir Lavayne an Sir Urré, wyth many mo knyghtes of their bloode, and all they wente unto Sir   810 Launcelot and seyde thus: 'My lorde, wyte you well we have grete scorne of the grete rebukis that we have harde Sir Gawayne sey unto you; wherefore we pray you and charge you as ye woll have oure servyse, kepe us no lenger wythin thys wallis, for we lat you wete playnly we woll ryde into the fylde and do batayle wyth   815 hem. For ye fare as a man that were aferde, and for all your fayre speche hit woll nat avayle you, for wyte you well Sir Gawayne woll nevir suffir you to accorde wyth Kynge Arthur. And therefore fyght for youre lyff and ryght, and ye dare.'

'Alas,' seyde Sir Launcelot, 'for to ryde oute of thys castell and   820 to do batayle I am full lothe.'

Than Sir Launcelot spake on hyght unto Kyng Arthur and Sir Gawayne: 'My lorde, I requyre you and beseche you, sytthyn that I am thus requyred and conjoured to ryde into the fylde, that neyther you, my lorde Kyng Arthur, nother you, Sir   825 Gawayne, com nat into the fylde.'

'What shall we do than?' seyde Sir Gawayne. 'Is nat thys the kynges quarell to fyght wyth the? And also hit ys my quarell to fyght wyth the because of the dethe of my brothir Sir Gareth.'

---

797 *at such avayle*, at such [a] disadvantage
799 *truste*, believe
801 See C.
804 *blow*, i.e. trumpets
805 *and so*, and then
812 *rebukis*, insults
813–16 See C.
814 *thys*, these
816 *fare as*, behave like   *aferde*, frightened
824 *thus* (C)   *conjoured*, solemnly appealed to

'Than muste I nedys unto batayle,' seyde Sir Launcelot. 'Now 830
wyte you well, my lorde Arthur and Sir Gawayne, ye woll repent
hit whansomever I do batayle wyth you.'

And so than they departed eythir frome othir; and than aythir
party made hem redy on the morne for to do batayle, and grete
purveyaunce was made on bothe sydys. And Sir Gawayne lat 835
purvey many knyghtes for to wayte uppon Sir Launcelot for to
oversette hym and to sle hym.

And on the morn at underne Kynge Arthure was redy in the
fylde with three grete ostys. And than Sir Launcelottis felyshyp
com oute at the three gatis in full good aray; and Sir Lyonell cam 840
in the formyst batayle, and Sir Launcelot cam in the myddyll,
and Sir Bors com oute at the thirde gate. And thus they cam in
order and rule as full noble knyghtes. And ever Sir Launcelot
charged all hys knyghtes in ony wyse to save Kynge Arthure and
Sir Gawayne. 845

Than cam forth Sir Gawayne frome the kyngis oste, and he
cam before and profirde to juste. And Sir Lyonel was a fyers knyght,
and lyghtly he encountred with hym, and there Sir Gawayne
smote Sir Lyonell thorowoute the body, that he daysshed to the
erth lyke as he had ben dede. And than Sir Ector de Marys and 850
other mo bare hym into the castell.

And anone there began a grete stowre and much people were
slayne; and ever Sir Launcelot ded what he myght to save the
people on Kynge Arthurs party. For Sir Bors and Sir Palomydes
and Sir Saffir overthrew many knyghts, for they were dedely 855
knyghtes, and Sir Blamour de Ganys and Sir Bleoberys de
Ganys wyth Sir Bellyngere le Bewse, thes six knyghtes ded much
harme. And ever was Kynge Arthur nyghe aboute Sir Launcelot

830 *must I nedys unto*, I must go to
832 *whansomever*, whensoever, when
833 *eythir*, each
834 *hem*, itself (lit. 'them')
835 *purveyaunce*, preparation
835-6 *lat purvey*, had ... provided
836 *wayte uppon*, watch for
837 *oversette*, unhorse
838 *underne*, about 9.00 a.m.
840 *aray*, array, order
841 *formyst batayle*, first division, vanguard (C)
844 *in ony wyse*, whatever happened
847 *profirde*, offered *fyers*, fierce
848 *lyghtly*, swiftly
849 *daysshed*, was dashed
852 *stowre*, battle *much*, many

to have slayne hym, and ever Sir Launcelot suffird hym and
wolde nat stryke agayne. So Sir Bors encountirde wyth Kynge   860
Arthur, and there wyth a spere Sir Bors smote hym downe, and
so he alyght and drew hys swerde and seyd to Sir Launcelot, 'Sir,
shall I make an ende of thys warre?' (For he mente to have slayne
hym.)

'Nat so hardy,' seyde Sir Launcelot, 'uppon payne of thy hede,   865
that thou touch hym no more! For I woll never se that moste
noble kynge that made me knyght nother slayne nor shamed.'

And therewithall Sir Launcelot alyght of hys horse and toke
up the kynge and horsed hym agayne, and seyd thus: 'My lorde
the kynge, for Goddis love, stynte thys stryff, for ye gette here no   870
worshyp and I wolde do myne utteraunce. But allwayes I forbeare you, and ye nor none off youres forberyth nat me. And
therefore, my lorde, I pray you remembir what I have done in
many placis, and now am I evyll rewarded.'

So whan Kynge Arthur was on horsebak he loked on Sir   875
Launcelot; than the teerys braste oute of hys yen, thynkyng of
the grete curtesy that was in Sir Launcelot more than in ony other
man. And therewith the kynge rod hys way and myght no lenger
beholde hym, saiyng to hymselff, 'Alas, alas, that ever yet thys
warre began!'   880

And than aythir party of the batayles wythdrew them to repose them, and buryed the dede, and serched the wounded men
and leyde to their woundes soffte salves; and thus they endured
that nyght tylle on the morne. And on the morne by undirn they
made them redy to do batayle, and than Sir Bors lad the vawarde.   885

So uppon the morn there cam Sir Gawayne, as brym as ony
boore, wyth a grete spere in hys honde. And whan Sir Bors saw
hym he thought to revenge hys brother Sir Lyonell of the despite
Sir Gawayne gaff hym the other day. And so, as they that knew

---

⁸⁶⁶ *that thou touch*, touch (C)
⁸⁶⁷ *nother*, either (lit. 'neither')
⁸⁶⁸ *alyght*, alighted, dismounted   *of*, from
⁸⁷⁰ *love*, sake   *stynte*, stop
⁸⁷¹ *utteraunce*, utmost
⁸⁷¹⁻² *forbeare*, hold off from
⁸⁷⁶ *braste*, burst   *yen*, eyes
⁸⁷⁸ *rod*, rode   *myght no lenger*, could not any longer bring [himself] to
⁸⁸¹ *aythir party of the batayles*, each party in the fighting
⁸⁸² *serched*, treated (lit. 'probed')
⁸⁸⁵ *vawarde*, first division, vanguard
⁸⁸⁶ *brym*, fierce
⁸⁸⁸⁻⁹ *despite . . . gaff*, insult . . . done to

aythir other, feautred their spearis, and with all their myght of 890
their horsis and themselff so fyersly they mette togydirs and so
felonsly that aythir bare other thorow, and so they felle bothe to
the bare erthe.

And than the batayle joyned, and there was much slaughter on
bothe partyes. Than Sir Launcelot rescowed Sir Bors and sent 895
hym into the castell, but neyther Sir Gawayne nother Sir Bors
dyed nat of their woundis, for they were well holpyn.

Than Sir Lavayne and Sir Urré prayde Sir Launcelot to do hys
payne and feyght as they do: 'For we se that ye forbeare and
spare, and that doth us much harme. And therefore we pray you 900
spare nat youre enemyes no more than they do you.'

'Alas,' seyde Sir Launcelot, 'I have no harte to fyght ayenste my
lorde Arthur, for ever mesemyth I do nat as me ought to do.'

'My lorde,' seyde Sir Palomydes, 'thoughe ye spare them
never so much all thys day, they woll never can you thanke; and 905
yf they may gete you at avayle ye ar but a dede man.'

So than Sir Launcelot undirstoode that they seyde hym
trouthe. Than he strayned hymselff more than he ded toforehonde, and bycause of hys nevew, Sir Bors, who was sore wounded, he payned hymselff the more. And so within a lytyll whyle, 910
by evynsong tyme, Sir Launcelottis party the bettir stood, for
their horsis wente in blood paste the fyttlokkes, there were so
many people slayne. And than for verry pité Sir Launcelot with-
hylde hys knyghtes and suffird Kynge Arthurs party to withdraw
them on syde. And so he withdrew hys meyny into the castell, 915
and aythir partyes buryed the dede and put salve unto the wounded men. So whan Sir Gawayne was hurte, they on Kynge
Arthurs party were nat so orgulus as they were toforehonde to do
batayle.

So of thys warre that was betwene Kynge Arthure and Sir 920
Launcelot hit was noysed thorow all Crystyn realmys, and so hit

---

⁸⁹⁰ *featured*, [they] put . . . in the rests
⁸⁹² *felonsly*, murderously   *bare . . . thorow*, transfixed
⁸⁹⁴ *joyned*, was joined
⁸⁹⁷ *well holpyn*, cured by skilful treatment
^{898–9} *do hys payne*, do his part
⁹⁰⁵ *can you thanke*, give you thanks
⁹⁰⁶ *at avayle*, at a disadvantage
⁹¹² *fyttlokkes*, fetlocks
^{913–14} *withhylde*, held . . . back
⁹¹⁵ *on syde*, out of range (lit. 'aside')
⁹¹⁶ *aythir*, both (lit. 'each')
⁹¹⁸ *orgulus*, arrogantly determined   *toforehonde*, beforehand

cam at the laste by relacion unto the Pope. And than the Pope
toke a consideracion of the grete goodnes of Kynge Arthur and of
the hygh proues off Sir Launcelot, that was called the moste
nobelyst knyght of the worlde. Wherefore the Pope called unto   925
hym a noble clerke that at that tyme was there presente (the
Freynshe boke seyth hit was the Bysshop of Rochester), and the
Pope gaff hym bulles undir leade and sente hem unto the kynge,
chargyng hym uppon payne of entirdytynge of all Inglonde
that he take hys quene agayne and accorde with Sir Launcelot.   930

So whán thys Bysshop was com unto Carlyle he shewed the
kynge hys bullys, and whan the kynge undirstode them he wyste
nat what to do: but full fayne he wolde have bene acorded with
Sir Launcelot, but Sir Gawayn wolde nat suffir hym; but to have
the quene he thereto agreed. But in no wyse Sir Gawayne wolde   935
suffir the kynge to accorde with Sir Launcelot; but as for the
quene, he consented. So the Bysshop had of the kynge hys grete
seale and hys assuraunce, as he was a trew and anoynted kynge,
that Sir Launcelot shulde go sauff and com sauff, and that the
quene shulde nat be seyde unto of the kynge, nother of none   940
other, for nothynge done of tyme paste. And of all thes appoyntementes the Bysshop brought with hym sure wrytynge to shew
unto Sir Launcelot.

So whan the Bysshop was com to Joyous Garde, there he
shewed Sir Launcelot how he cam frome the Pope with wryt-   945
ynge unto Kyng Arthur and unto hym. And there he tolde hym
the perelis, gyff he wythhelde the quene frome the kynge.

'Sir, hit was never in my thought,' seyde Sir Launcelot, 'to
withholde the quene frome my lorde Arthur. But I kepe her for
thys cause: insomuche as she shulde have be brente for my sake,   950
mesemed hit was my parte to save her lyff and put her from that
daungere tyll bettir recover myght com. And now I thanke God,'
seyde Sir Launcelot, 'that the Pope hathe made her pease. For

922 *by relacion*, by report
927 See C.
928 *bulles*, bulls, edicts   *leade*, seal (C)
929 *entirdytynge*, putting under interdict
937–8 *hys grete seale*, a written agreement under his Great Seal
940 *seyde unto*, reproached
940–1 *nother of none other*, nor by anyone else
941–2 *appoyntementes*, decisions
942 *sure*, trustworthy
947 *perelis*, dangers   *gyff*, if
951–2 *her from that daungere*, that danger from her
952 *recover*, way out of it

God knowyth,' seyde Sir Launcelot, 'I woll be a thousandefolde
more gladder to brynge her agayne than ever I was of her takyng   955
away, wyth thys: I may be sure to com sauff and go sauff, and that
the quene shall have her lyberté as she had before, and never for
nothyng that hath be surmysed afore thys tyme that she never
frome thys stonde in no perell. For ellis,' seyde Sir Launcelot, 'I
dare adventure me to kepe her frome an harder showre than   960
ever yet I had.'

'Sir, hit shall nat nede you,' seyde the Bysshop, 'to drede thus
muche; for wyte yow well, the Pope muste be obeyed, and hit
were nat the Popis worshyp nother my poure honesté to know
you distressed nother the quene: nother in perell nother shamed.'   965
And than he shewed Sir Launcelot all hys wrytynge bothe
frome the Pope and Kynge Arthure.

'Thys ys sure ynow,' seyde Sir Launcelot. 'For full well I dare
truste my lordys owne wrytyng and hys seale, for he was never
shamed of hys promyse. Therefore,' seyde Sir Launcelot unto the   970
Bysshop, 'ye shall ryde unto the kynge afore; and recommaunde
me unto hys good grace, and lat hym have knowlecchynge that
this same day eyght dayes, by the grace of God, I myselff shall
brynge the quene unto hym. And than sey ye to my moste redouted kynge that I woll sey largely for the quene, that I shall   975
none excepte for drede nother for feare but the kynge hymselff
and my lorde Sir Gawayne; and that ys for the kyngis love more
than for hymselff.'

So the Bysshop departed and cam to the kynge to Carlehyll,
and tolde hym all how Sir Launcelot answerd hym; so that   980
made the teares falle oute at the kyngis yen. Than Sir Launcelot
purveyed hym an hondred knyghtes, and all were well clothed

956 *wyth thys*, provided that
958-9 *that* and *frome thys* are redundant
959 *ellis*, otherwise
960 *adventure me*, take my chance   *showre*, assault
962 *hit shall nat nede you*, you shall not need (C)
970 *shamed of*, disgraced by [breaking]
971 *afore*, before [me]
971-2 *recommaunde me to his good grace*, commend me to His Majesty (C)
972 *have knowlecchynge*, know
973 *by the grace of God*, God willing
974-5 *redouted kynge*, dread sovereign
975 *sey largely for the quene*, speak freely on the queen's behalf (C)
977 *that*, i.e. making an exception of Gawain   *love*, sake
978 *hymselff*, i.e. Gawain himself
979 *Carlehyll*, Carlisle
981 *yen*, eyes (*eye* with *-n* plural, cf. *oxen*)

in grene velvet, and their horsis trapped in the same to the heelys, and every knyght hylde a braunche of olyff in hys honde in tokenyng of pees. And the quene had four-and-twenty jantill- 985 women folowyng her in the same wyse. And Sir Launcelot had twelve coursers folowyng hym, and on every courser sate a yonge jantylman; and all they were arayed in whyght velvet with sarpis of golde aboute their neckys, and the horse trapped in the same wyse down to the helys, wyth many owchys, isette with 990 stonys and perelys in golde, to the numbir of a thousande. And in the same wyse was the quene arayed, and Sir Launcelot in the same, of whyght clothe of golde tyssew.

And ryght so as ye have harde, as the Freynshe booke makyth mencion, he rode with the quene frome Joyus Garde to Carlehyll. 995 And so Sir Launcelot rode thorowoute Carlehylle, and so into the castell, that all men myght beholde hem. And wyte you well, there was many a wepyng ien. And than Sir Launcelot hym- selff alyght and voyded hys horse, and toke adowne the quene, and so lad her where Kyng Arthur was in hys seate; and Sir 1000 Gawayne sate afore hym, and many other grete lordys.

So whan Sir Launcelot saw the kynge and Sir Gawayne, than he lad the quene by the arme, and than he kneled downe and the quene bothe. Wyte you well, than was there many a bolde knyght wyth Kynge Arthur that wepte as tendirly as they had 1005 seyne all their kynne dede afore them.

So the kynge sate stylle and seyde no worde. And whan Sir Launcelot saw hys countenaunce he arose up and pulled up the quene with hym, and thus he seyde full knyghtly: 'My moste redouted kynge, ye shall undirstonde, by the Popis commaunde- 1010 mente and youres I have brought to you my lady the quene, as ryght requyryth. And if there be ony knyght, of what degré that ever he be off, except your person, that woll sey or dare say but that she ys trew and clene to you, I here myselff, Sir Launcelot du

---

984 *olyff*, olive
989 *sarpis*, neck-rings, torques
990 *owchys*, clasps, pendants, and other decorations worked in precious metals and jewels   *isette*, set
991 *perelys*, pearls
993 *whyght clothe of golde tyssew*, white cloth with gold thread woven into it (C)
994 See C.
997 See C.
998 *ien*, eye (lit. 'eyes')
1012 *ryght*, justice

Lake, woll make hit good uppon hys body that she ys a trew lady 1015
unto you.

'But, sir, lyars ye have lystened, and that hath caused grete
debate betwyxte you and me. For tyme hath bene, my lorde
Arthur, that ye were gretly pleased with me whan I ded batayle
for my lady youre quene; and full well ye know, my moste noble 1020
kynge, that she hathe be put to grete wronge or thys tyme. And
sytthyn hyt pleased you at many tymys that I shulde feyght for
her, therefore mesemyth, my good lorde, I had more cause to
rescow her from the fyer whan she sholde have ben brente for my
sake.   1025

'For they that tolde you tho talys were lyars, and so hit felle
uppon them: for by lyklyhode, had nat the myght of God bene
with me, I myght never have endured with fourtene knyghtes, and
they armed and afore purposed, and I unarmed and nat purposed. For I was sente for unto my lady youre quyne, I wote nat 1030
for what cause, but I was nat so sone within the chambir dore but
anone Sir Aggravayne and Sir Mordred called me traytoure and
false recrayed knyght.'

'Be my fayth, they called the ryght!' seyde Sir Gawayne.

'My lorde Sir Gawayne,' seyde Sir Launcelot, 'in their quarell 1035
they preved nat hemselff the beste, nother in the ryght.'

'Well, well, Sir Launcelot,' seyde the kynge, 'I have gyvyn you
no cause to do to me as ye have done, for I have worshipt you and
youres more than ony othir knyghtes.'

'My good lorde,' seyde Sir Launcelot, 'so ye be nat displeased, 1040
ye shall undirstonde that I and myne have done you oftyntymes
bettir servyse than ony othir knyghtes have done, in many dyverce
placis; and where ye have bene full hard bestadde dyvers tymes,
I have myself rescowed you frome many daungers; and ever unto
my power I was glad to please you and my lorde Sir Gawayne. 1045
Bothe in justis and in turnementis and in batayles set, bothe on
horsebak and on foote, I have oftyn rescowed you, and you, my

---

¹⁰¹⁷ *lystened*, listened to
¹⁰²¹ *be*, been
¹⁰²⁶ *tho*, those   *hit*, i.e. their wickedness, which recoiled upon themselves
¹⁰²⁷ *by lyklyhode*, in all probability
¹⁰²⁸ *myght*, could   *with*, against
¹⁰²⁹ *afore purposed*, acting with premeditation (cf. *malice aforethought*)
¹⁰³¹ *sone*, soon
¹⁰³⁸ *worshipt*, honoured
¹⁰⁴⁰ *so*, so long as, if
¹⁰⁴³ *hard bestadde*, hard pressed   *dyvers tymes*, at various times

lorde Sir Gawayne, and many mo of youre knyghtes in many dyvers placis.

'For now I woll make avaunte,' seyde Sir Launcelot. 'I woll 1050 that ye all wyte that as yet I founde never no maner of knyght but that I was over harde for hym and I had done myne utteraunce, God graunte mercy! Howbehit I have be macched with good knyghtes, as Sir Trystram and Sir Lamorak, but ever I had a favoure unto them and a demyng what they were. And I take 1055 God to recorde,' seyde Sir Launcelot, 'I never was wrothe nor gretly hevy wyth no good knyght and I saw hym besy and aboute to wyn worshyp; and glad I was ever whan I founde a good knyght that myght onythynge endure me on horsebak and on foote. Howbehit Sir Carados of the Dolerous Toure was a full 1060 noble knyght and a passynge stronge man, and that wote ye, my lorde Sir Gawayne; for he myght well be called a noble knyght whan he be fyne fors pulled you oute of your sadyll and bounde you overthwarte afore hym to hys sadyll-bow. And there, my lorde Sir Gawayne, I rescowed you and slew hym afore your 1065 syght. Also I founde youre brothir, Sir Gaherys, and Sir Terquyn ledyng hym bounden afore hym; and there also I rescowed youre brothir and slew Sir Terquyn and delyverde three score and four of my lorde Arthurs knyghtes oute of hys preson. And now I dare sey,' seyde Sir Launcelot, 'I mette never wyth so stronge a knyght 1070 nor so well-fyghtyng as was Sir Carados and Sir Tarquyn, for they and I faught to the uttermest.

'And therefore,' seyde Sir Launcelot unto Sir Gawayne, 'mesemyth ye ought of ryght to remembir this; for, and I myght have youre good wyll, I wold truste to God for to have my lorde 1075 Arthurs good grace.'

'Sir, the kynge may do as he wyll,' seyde Sir Gawayne, 'but wyte thou well, Sir Launcelot, thou and I shall never be accorded whyle we lyve, for thou hast slayne three of my brethyrn; and two of hem thou slew traytourly and piteuously, for they bare none 1080 harneys ayenste the, nother none wold do.'

1050 *make avaunte*, make [my] boast
1052 *over harde*, too tough   *and*, if
1053 *God graunte mercy*, thanks (lit. 'great thanks') be to God   *howbehit*, although
1055 *demyng*, suspicion
1056 *to recorde*, as [my] witness
1063 *be fyne fors*, by main force
1064 *overthwarte*, cross-ways
1078 *accorded*, reconciled
1080 *piteuously*, pitiably
1081 *nother none wold do*, translate: ' and were determined not to'

194

'Sir, God wolde they had ben armed,' seyde Sir Launcelot, 'for than had they ben on lyve. And wete you well, Sir Gawayne, as for Sir Gareth, I loved no kynnesman I had more than I loved hym, and ever whyle I lyve,' seyde Sir Launcelot, 'I woll bewayle 1085 Sir Gareth hys dethe, nat all only for the grete feare I have of you, but for many causys whych causyth me to be sorowfull. One is that I made hym knyght; another ys, I wote well he loved me aboven all othir knyghtes; and the third ys, he was passyng noble and trew, curteyse and jantill and well-condicionde. The fourthe 1090 ys, I wyste well, anone as I harde that Sir Gareth was dede, I knew well that I shulde never aftir have youre love, my lorde Sir Gawayne, but everlastyng warre betwyxt us. And also I wyste well that ye wolde cause my noble lorde Kynge Arthur for ever to be my mortall foo. And as Jesu be my helpe, and be my 1095 knyghthode,' seyde Sir Launcelot, 'I slewe never Sir Gareth nother hys brother be my wyllynge, but alas that ever they were unarmed that unhappy day!

'But this much I shall offir me to you,' seyde Sir Launcelot, 'if hit may please the kyngis good grace and you, my lorde Sir 1100 Gawayn: I shall firste begyn at Sandwyche, and there I shall go in my shearte, bare-foote; and at every ten myles ende I shall founde and gar make an house of relygion, of what order that ye woll assygne me, with an hole covente, to synge and rede day and nyght in especiall for Sir Gareth sake and Sir Gaherys. And 1105 thys shall I perfourme from Sandwyche unto Carlyle; and every house shall have suffycyent lyvelod. And thys shall I perfourme whyle that I have ony lyvelod in Crystyndom, and there ys none of all thes religious placis but they shall be perfourmed, furnysshed and garnysshed with all thyngis as an holy place ought to 1110 be, I promyse you faythfully. And thys, Sir Gawayne, me thynketh were more fayrar and more holyar and more perfyte to their soulis than ye, my moste noble kynge, and you, Sir Gawayne, to warre uppon me, for thereby shall ye gete none avayle.'

1083 *on lyve*, alive
1086 *Gareth hys*, Gareth's   *all only*, alone (adv.; lit. 'alonely')
1090 *jantil and well-condicionde*, chivalrous and true-hearted
1095–6 *be my knyghthode*, by my knighthood
1102 *in my shearte*, in my shirtsleeves (C)
1103 *gar make*, have made (C)   *what*, whatever
1104 *hole covente*, whole community of religious (cf. *convent*)
1107 *lyvelod*, livelihood
1109 *perfourmed*, completed
1114 *shall ye gete none avayle*, you shall get no advantage

Than all the knyghtes and ladyes that were there wepte as they 1115
were madde, and the tearys felle on Kynge Arthur hys chekis.

'Sir Launcelot,' seyde Sir Gawayne, 'I have ryght well harde
thy langayge and thy grete proffirs. But wyt thou well, lat the
kynge do as hit pleasith hym, I woll never forgyff the my brothirs
dethe, and in especiall the deth of my brothir Sir Gareth. And if 1120
myne uncle Kynge Arthur wyll accorde wyth the, he shall loose
my servys, for wyte thou well,' seyde Sir Gawayne, 'thou arte
bothe false to the kynge and to me.'

'Sir,' seyde Sir Launcelot, 'he beryth nat the lyff that may
make hit good. And ye, Sir Gawayne, woll charge me with so 1125
hyghe a thynge, ye muste pardone me, for than nedis must I
answere you.'

'Nay, nay,' seyde Sir Gawayne, 'we ar paste that as at thys
tyme, and that causyth the Pope, for he hath charged myne uncle
the kynge that he shall take agayne his quene and to accorde wyth 1130
the, Sir Launcelot, as for thys season, and therefore thou shalt go
sauff as thou com. But in this londe thou shalt nat abyde paste a
fiftene dayes, such somons I gyff the, for so the kynge and we
were condescended and accorded ar thou cam. And ellis,' seyde
Sir Gawayn, 'wyte thou well, thou shulde nat a comyn here but 1135
if hit were magré thyne hede. And if hit were nat for the Popis
commaundement,' seyde Sir Gawayne, 'I shulde do batayle with
the myne owne hondis, body for body, and preve hit uppon the
that thou haste ben both false unto myne uncle Kynge Arthur,
and to me bothe; and that shall I preve on thy body, whan thou 1140
arte departed fro hense, wheresomever that I fynde the!'

Than Sir Launcelotte syghed, and therewith the tearys felle
on hys chekys, and than he seyde thus: 'Alas, most nobelyst
Crysten realme, whom I have loved aboven all othir realmys!
And in the I have gotyn a grete parte of my worshyp; and now 1145
that I shall departe in thys wyse, truly me repentis that ever I

---

¹¹¹⁹ *brothirs*, brothers'
¹¹²¹ *loose*, lose
¹¹²⁶ *nedis must I*, I must of necessity
¹¹³¹ See C.
¹¹³³ *somons*, summons, notice (C)
¹¹³⁴ *condescended*, agreed
¹¹³⁵ *a*, have
¹¹³⁵⁻⁶ See C.
¹¹³⁹ One or other *both* is redundant, and modern English demands *false both*, not
both false.
¹¹⁴⁴ *whom*, which

cam in thys realme, that I shulde be thus shamefully banysshyd,
undeserved and causeles. But fortune ys so varyaunte, and the
wheele so mutable, that there ys no constaunte abydynge. And
that may be preved by many olde cronycles, as of noble Ector of 1150
Troy and Alysaunder, the myghty conquerroure, and many mo
other; whan they were moste in her royalté, they alyght passyng
lowe. And so faryth hit by me,' seyde Sir Launcelot, 'for in thys
realme I had worshyp, and be me and myne all the hole Rounde
Table hath bene encreced more in worshyp, by me and myne, 1155
than ever hit was by ony of you all.

'And therefore wyte thou well, Sir Gawayne, I may lyve uppon
my londis as well as ony knyght that here ys. And yf ye, my moste
redoutted kynge, woll com uppon my londys with Sir Gawayne to
warre uppon me, I muste endure you as well as I may. But as to 1160
you, Sir Gawayne, if that ye com there, I pray you charge me
nat wyth treson nother felony, for and ye do, I muste answere
you.'

'Do thou thy beste,' seyde Sir Gawayne, 'and therefore hyghe
the faste that thou were gone! And wyte thou well we shall sone 1165
com aftir, and breke the strengyst castell that thou hast, uppon
thy hede!'

'Hyt shall nat nede that,' seyde Sir Launcelot, 'for and I were
as orgulous sette as ye ar, wyte you well I shulde mete you in
myddys of the fylde.'   1170

'Make thou no more langayge,' seyde Sir Gawayne, 'but
delyvir the quene from the, and pyke the lyghtly oute of thys
courte!'

'Well,' seyde Sir Launcelot, 'and I had wyste of thys shortecomyng, I wolde a advysed me twyse or that I had com here. For 1175
and the quene had be so dere unto me as ye noyse her, I durste
have kepte her frome the felyshyp of the beste knyghtes undir
hevyn.'

1148-9 *the wheel*, the Wheel of Fortune (C)
1151 *Alysaunder*, Alexander [the Great]
1152 *her*, their
1153 *faryth . . . by* goes . . . with
1162 *treson . . . felony* (C)
1164-5 *hyghe the*, get yourself moving, get going
1169 *orgulous sette*, proudly determined, full of arrogance (cf. Fr. *orgueilleux*)
1172 *pyke the*, be off   *lyghtly*, quickly
1174-5 *shortecomyng* (C)
1175 *advysed me twyse*, thought twice about it   *or that*, before
1175-6 *For and*, And if
1176 *noyse*, allege

197

And than Sir Launcelot seyde unto Quene Gwenyver in
hyryng of the kynge and hem all, 'Madame, now I muste departe 1180
from you and thys noble felyshyp for ever. And sytthyn hit ys so,
I besech you to pray for me, and I shall pray for you. And telle
ye me, and if ye be harde bestad by ony false tunges: but lyghtly,
my good lady, sende me worde, and if ony knyghtes hondys undir
the hevyn may delyver you by batayle, I shall delyver you.'   1185
And therewithall Sir Launcelot kyssed the quene, and than he
seyde all opynly, 'Now lat se whatsomever he be in thys place
that dare sey the quene ys nat trew unto my lorde Arthur! Lat se
who woll speke and he dare speke!'
And therewith he brought the quene to the kynge, and than 1190
Sir Launcelot toke hys leve and departed. And there was nother
kynge, duke nor erle, barowne nor knyght, lady nor jantyll-
woman, but all they wepte as people oute of their mynde, excepte
Sir Gawayne. And whan thys noble knyght Sir Launcelot toke
his horse to ryde oute of Carlehyll, there was sobbyng and 1195
wepyng for pure dole of hys departynge. And so he toke his way
to Joyous Garde, and than ever afftir he called hit the Dolerous
Towre. And thus departed Sir Launcelot frome the courte for
ever.
And so whan he cam to Joyous Garde he called hys felyshyp 1200
unto hym and asked them what they wolde do. Than they
answerde all holé togydirs with one voyce, they wold do as he
wolde do.
'Than, my fayre felowys,' seyde Sir Launcelot, 'I muste departe oute of thys moste noble realme. And now I shall departe, 1205
hit grevyth me sore, for I shall departe with no worship; for a
fleymed man departith never oute of a realme with no worship.
And that ys to me grete hevynes, for ever I feare aftir my dayes
that men shall cronycle uppon me that I was fleamed oute of thys
londe. And ellis, my fayre lordis, be ye sure, and I had nat drad 1210
shame, my lady Quene Gwenyvere and I shulde never have
departed.'
Than spake noble knyghtes, as Sir Palomydes and Sir Saffyr

1182-5 See C.
1187 *lat se*, let [it] be seen, let us see   *whatsomever*, who
1193 *mynde*, minds
1196 *dole*, sorrow   *of*, at
1197 See C.
1207 *fleymed*, banished
1210-12 See C.   *ellis*, otherwise

hys brothir, and Sir Bellynger le Bewse, and Sir Urré with Sir
Lavayne, with many other: 'Sir, and ye woll so be disposed to 1215
abyde in thys londe we woll never fayle you; and if ye lyste nat
abyde in thys londe, there ys none of the good knyghtes that here
be that woll fayle you, for many causis. One ys, all we that be nat
of your bloode shall never be wellcom unto the courte. And
sytthyn hit lyked us to take a parte with you in youre distres in 1220
this realme, wyte you well hit shall lyke us all as well to go in
othir contreyes with you and there to take suche parte as ye do.'

'My fayre lordys,' seyde Sir Launcelot, 'I well undirstond you,
and as I can, I thanke you. And ye shall undirstonde, suche
lyvelode as I am borne unto I shall departe with you in thys maner 1225
of wyse: that ys for to say, I shall departe all my lyvelode and all
my londis frely amonge you, and I myselff woll have as lytyll as
ony of you; for, have I sufficiaunte that may longe unto my person, I woll aske none other ryches nother aray. And I truste to
God to maynteyne you on my londys as well as ever ye were 1230
maynteyned.'

Than spake all the knyghtes at onys: 'Have he shame that woll
leve you! For we all undirstonde, in thys realme woll be no
quyett but ever debate and stryff, now the felyshyp of the Rounde
Table ys brokyn. For by the noble felyshyp of the Rounde Table 1235
was Kynge Arthur upborne, and by their nobeles the kynge and
all the realme was ever in quyet and reste. And a grete parte',
they sayde all, 'was because of youre moste nobeles, Sir Launcelot.'

'Now, truly,' seyde Sir Launcelot, 'I thanke you all of youre good
sayinge! Howbehit I wote well that in me was nat all the stabilité 1240
of thys realme, but in that I myght I ded my dever. And well I
am sure I knew many rebellyons in my dayes that by me and
myne were peased; and that I trow we all shall here of in shorte
space, and that me sore repentith. For ever I drede me,' seyde
Sir Launcelot, 'that Sir Mordred woll make trouble, for he ys 1245
passyng envyous and applyeth hym muche to trouble.'

1218-19 See C.
1220 *sytthyn*, since   *lyked*, pleased
1226 *departe*, part, divide
1228-9 *sufficiaunte that may longe unto my person*, enough for my bodily needs
1229 *aray*, dress (lit. 'array')
1238 *youre moste nobeles*, your supreme knightliness (C)
1239-40 *good sayinge*, praise
1241 *dever*, duty (cf. Fr. *devoir*)
1243 *peased*, pacified   *that*, i.e. rebellion
1244 *drede me*, dread

199

And so they were accorded to departe wyth Sir Launcelot to
hys landys. And to make shorte thys tale, they trussed and payed
all that wolde aske them; and holé an hondred knyghtes departed with Sir Launcelot at onys, and made their avowis they 1250
wolde never leve hym for weale ne for woo.

And so they shypped at Cardyff, and sayled unto Benwyke:
som men calle hit Bayan and som men calle hit Beawme, where
the wyne òf Beawme ys. But to say the sothe, Sir Launcelott and
hys neveawis were lordes of all Fraunce and of all the londis that 1255
longed unto Fraunce; he and hys kyndrede rejoysed hit all
thorow Sir Launcelottis noble proues.

And than he stuffed and furnysshed and garnysshed all his
noble townys and castellis. Than all the people of tho landis
cam unto Sir Launcelot on foote and hondis. And so whan he had 1260
stabelysshed all those contreyes, he shortly called a parlement;
and there he crowned Sir Lyonell Kynge off Fraunce, and Sir
Bors he crowned hym Kynge of all Kyng Claudas londis, and
Sir Ector de Marys, Sir Launcelottis yonger brother, he crowned
hym Kynge of Benwyke and Kynge of all Gyaṇ, whych was Sir 1265
Launcelottis owne londys. And he made Sir Ector prynce of them
all.

And thus he departed hys londis and avaunced all hys noble
knyghtes. And firste he avaunced them off hys blood, as Sir Blamour, he made hym Duke of Lymosyn in Gyan, and Sir Bleoberys, 1270
he made hym Duke of Payters. And Sir Gahalantyne, he made
hym Deuke of Overn; and Sir Galyodyn, he made hym Deuke of
Sentonge; and Sir Galyhud, he made hym Erle of Perygot; and
Sir Menaduke, he made hym Erle of Roerge; and Sir Vyllars
the Valyaunt, he made hym Erle of Bearne; and Sir Hebes le 1275
Renownes, he made hym Erle of Comange; and Sir Lavayne, he
made hym Erle of Armynake; and Sir Urré, he made hym Erle
of Estrake; and Sir Neroveus, he made hym Erle of Pardyak; and
Sir Plenoryus, he made hym Erle of Foyse; and Sir Selyses of the
Dolerous Toure, he made hym Erle of Marsank; and Sir Melyas 1280

1248 *trussed*, packed (lit. 'tied')
1250 *made their avowis*, took oaths, swore
1253 *Bayan*, Bayonne   *Beawme*, Beaune (C)
1256 *rejoysed*, enjoyed
1260 *on foote and hondis*, making their submission (C)
1261 *stabélysshed*, settled [affairs in]
1262–7 See C.
1268 *departed*, divided   *avaunced*, promoted
1270–87 See C.

de le Ile, he made hym Erle of Tursanke; and Sir Bellyngere le
Bewse, he made hym Erle of the Lauwndis; and Sir Palomydes,
he made hym Deuke of Provynce; and Sir Saffir, he made hym
Deuke of Landok. And Sir Clegys, he gaff hym the erledom of
Agente; and Sir Sadok, he gaff hym the erledom of Sarlat; and 1285
Sir Dynas le Senesciall, he made hym Deuke of Angeoy; and Sir
Clarrus, he made hym Duke of Normandy.

Thus Sir Launcelot rewarded hys noble knyghtes, and many
mo that mesemyth hit were to longe to rehers.

III

So leve we Sir Launcelot in hys londis and hys noble knyghtes 1290
with hym, and returne we agayne unto Kynge Arthure and unto
Sir Gawayne, that made a grete oste aredy to the numbir of
three score thousande. And all thynge was made redy for shyp-
pyng to passe over the see, to warre uppon Sir Launcelot and
uppon hys londis. And so they shypped at Cardyff.   1295

And there Kynge Arthur made Sir Mordred chyeff ruler of
all Ingelonde, and also he put the quene undir hys governaunce:
bycause Sir Mordred was Kynge Arthurs son, he gaff hym the
rule off hys londe and off hys wyff.

And so the kynge passed the see and landed uppon Sir Launce- 1300
lottis londis, and there he brente and wasted, thorow the ven-
geaunce of Sir Gawayne, all that they myght overrenne. So whan
thys worde was com unto Sir Launcelot, that Kynge Arthur and
Sir Gawayne were landed uppon hys londis and made full grete
destruccion and waste, than spake Sir Bors and seyde, 'My lorde 1305
Sir Launcelot, hit is shame that we suffir hem thus to ryde over
oure londys. For wyte you well, suffir ye hem as longe as ye wyll,
they woll do you no favoure and they may handyll you.'

Than seyde Sir Lyonell that was ware and wyse, 'My lorde

---

¹²⁹⁶ *chyeff ruler*, Regent
¹³⁰¹ *brente*, burned (C)
¹³⁰⁸ *and*, if
¹³⁰⁹ *ware*, wary   *wyse*, shrewd

Sir Launcelot, I woll gyff you thys counceyle: lat us kepe oure 1310
stronge walled townys untyll they have hunger and colde, and
blow on their nayles; and than lat us fresshly set uppon them and
shrede hem downe as shepe in a folde, that ever aftir alyauntis
may take ensample how they lande uppon oure londys!'

Than spake Kynge Bagdemagus to Sir Launcelot and seyde, 1315
'Sir, youre curtesy woll shende us all, and youre curtesy hath
waked all thys sorrow; for and they thus overryde oure londis,
they shall by proces brynge us all to nought whyle we thus in
holys us hyde.'

Than seyde Sir Galyhud unto Sir Launcelot, 'Sir, here bene 1320
knyghtes com of kyngis blod that woll nat longe droupe and dare
within thys wallys. Therefore gyff us leve, lyke as we ben knyghtes,
to mete hem in the fylde, and we shall slee them and so deale
wyth them that they shall curse the tyme that ever they cam into
thys contrey.'   1325

Than spake seven brethirn of Northe Walis whych were seven
noble knyghtes, for a man myghte seke seven kyngis londis or he
myght fynde such seven knyghtes. And thes seven noble knyghtes
seyde all at onys, 'Sir Launcelot, for Crystis sake, late us ryde oute
with Sir Galyhud, for we were never wonte to coure in castels 1330
nother in noble townys.'

Than spake Sir Launcelot, that was mayster and governoure
of hem all, and seyde, 'My fayre lordis, wyte you well I am full
lothe to ryde oute with my knyghtes, for shedynge of Crysten
blood; and yet my londis I undirstonde be full bare for to sus- 1335
tayne any oste awhyle, for the myghty warris that whylom made
Kyng Claudas uppon thys contrey and uppon my fadir Kyng Ban,
and on myne uncle Kynge Bors. Howbehit we woll as at this tyme
kepe oure stronge wallis. And I shall sende a messyngere unto my
lorde Arthur a tretyse for to take, for better ys pees than allwayes 1340
warre.'

1310 *kepe*, defend
1313 See C.   *shrede downe*, cut ... down   *alyauntis*, aliens
1314 *ensample*, example, warning
1316 *shende*, ruin
1318 *by proces*, by degrees
1318–19 *in holys us hyde*, hide ourselves in holes
1321 *dare*, lie terror-stricken
1330 *coure*, cower
1331 *townys* (C)
1336 *for*, because of
1340 *a tretyse for to take*, in order to make an agreement
1340–1 See C.

So Sir Launcelot sente forthe a damesel wyth a dwarff with her, requyryng Kynge Arthur to leve hys warryng uppon hys londys. And so he starte uppon a palferey, and the dwarffe ran by her syde, and whan she cam to the pavelon of Kynge Arthur, there 1345 she alyght. And there mette her a jantyll knyght, Sir Lucan the Butlere, and seyde, 'Fayre damsell, com ye frome Sir Launcelot du Lake?'

'Yee, sir,' she seyde, 'therefore cam I hyddir to speke with my lorde the kynge.'   1350

'Alas,' seyde Sir Lucan, 'my lorde Arthure wolde accorde with Sir Launcelot, but Sir Gawayne woll nat suffir hym.' And than he seyde, 'I pray to God, damesell, that ye may spede well, for all we that bene aboute the kynge wolde that Launcelot ded beste of ony knyght lyvynge.'   1355

And so with thys Sir Lucan lad the damesell to the kynge, where he sate with Syr Gawayne, for to hyre what she wolde say. So whan she had tolde her tale the watir ran oute of the kyngis yen, and all the lordys were full glad for to advyce the kynge to be accorded with Sir Launcelot, save all only Sir Gawayne. And 1360 he seyde, 'My lorde, myne uncle, what woll ye do? Woll ye now turne agayne, now ye ar paste thys farre uppon youre journey? All the worlde woll speke of you vylany and shame.'

'Now,' seyde Kynge Arthur, 'wyte you well, Sir Gawayne, I woll do as ye advyse me; and yet mesemyth', seyde Kynge Arthur, 1365 'hys fayre proffers were nat good to be reffused. But sytthyn I am com so far uppon thys journey, I woll that ye gyff the damesell her answere, for I may nat speke to her for pité, for her profirs ben so large.'

Than Sir Gawayne seyde unto the damesell thus: 'Damesell, 1370 sey ye to Sir Launcelot that hyt ys waste laboure now to sew to myne uncle. For telle hym, and he wolde have made ony laboure for pease, he sholde have made hit or thys tyme, for telle hym now hit ys to late. And say to hym that I, Sir Gawayne, so sende hym word, that I promyse hym by the faythe that I owghe to God 1375

1344 *he,* she cf. 'Lancelot', l. 1546n   *palferey,* palfrey (a small saddle-horse for ladies)
1345 *pavelon,* tent (cf. *pavilion*)
1353 *spede well,* succeed
1356 *lad,* led
1358 See C.
1362 *ar paste,* have gone (lit. 'passed')
1369 *large,* generous
1371 *sew to,* sue to, seek the favour of

and to knyghthode, I shall never leve hym tylle he hathe slayne
me or I hym!'

So the damesell wepte and departed, and so there was many a
wepyng yghe. And than Sir Lucan brought the damesell to her
palffrey; and so she cam to Sir Launcelot, where he was amonge 1380
all hys knyghtes, and whan Sir Launcelot had harde hir answere,
than the tearys ran downe by hys chekys.

And than hys noble knyghtes strode about hym and seyde,
'Sir Launcelot, wherefore make ye suche chere? Now thynke
what ye ar and what men we ar, and lat us noble knyghtis macche 1385
hem in myddis of the fylde.'

'That may be lyghtly done,' seyde Sir Launcelot, 'but I was
never so lothe to do batayle. And therefore I pray you, fayre
sirres, as ye love me, be ruled at thys tyme as I woll have you.
For I woll allwayes fle that noble kynge that made me knyght; 1390
and whan I may no farther, I muste nedis deffende me. And that
woll be more worshyp for me and us all than to compare with
that noble kynge whom we have all served.'

Than they hylde their langayge, and as that nyght they toke
their reste. And uppon the mornyng erly, in the dawnynge of the 1395
day, as knyghtes loked oute they saw the cité of Benwyke besyged
rounde aboute, and gan faste to sette up laddirs. And they within
kepte them oute of the towne and bete hem myghtyly frome the
wallis.

Than cam forthe Sir Gawayne, well armede, uppon a styff 1400
steede, and he cam before the chyeff gate with hys speare in hys
honde, cryynge: 'Where art thou, Sir Launcelot? Ys there none
of all your proude knyghtes that dare breake a speare with me?'

Than Sir Bors made hym redy and cam forth oute of the
towne. And there Sir Gawayne encountred with Sir Bors, and 1405
at that tyme he smote hym downe frome hys horse, and allmoste
he had slayne hym. And so Sir Bors was rescowed and borne into
the towne. Than cam forthe Sir Lyonell, brother unto Sir Bors,

---

1379 *yghe*, eye
1382 *by*, along
1383 *strode* (C)
1386 *in myddis of*, in the midst of
1387 *lyghtly*, easily
1392 *compare*, vie with
1394 *as*, on(lit. 'as to')
1397 *gan . . . laddirs*, [they] began . . . scaling ladders (C)
1400 *styff*, strong

and thoughte to revenge hym; and aythir feawtred their spearys and so ran togydirs, and there they mette spiteously, but Sir 1410 Gawayne had such a grace that he smote Sir Lyonell downe and wounded hym there passyngly sore. And than Sir Lyonell was rescowed and borne into the towne.

And thus Sir Gawayne com every day, and fayled nat but that he smote downe one knyght or othir. So thus they endured halff 1415 a yere, and much slaughter was of people on bothe partyes.

Than hit befelle uppon a day that Sir Gawayne cam afore the gatis, armed at all pecis, on a noble horse, with a greate speare in hys honde, and than he cryed with a lowde voyce and seyde, 'Where arte thou now, thou false traytour, Sir Launcelot? Why 1420 holdyst thou thyselff within holys and wallys lyke a cowarde? Loke oute now, thou false traytoure knyght, and here I shall revenge uppon thy body the dethe of my three brethirne!'

And all thys langayge harde Sir Launcelot every deale. Than hys kynne and hys knyghtes drew aboute hym, and all they 1425 seyde at onys unto Sir Launcelot, 'Sir, now muste you deffende you lyke a knyght, othir ellis ye be shamed for ever, for now ye be called uppon treson, hit ys tyme for you to styrre! For ye have slepte over longe, and suffirde overmuche.'

'So God helpe,' seyde Sir Launcelot, 'I am ryght hevy at Sir 1430 Gawaynes wordys, for now he chargith me with a grete charge. And therefore I wote as well as ye I muste nedys deffende me, other ellis to be recreaunte.'

Than Sir Launcelot bade sadyll hys strongest horse and bade let fecche hys armys and brynge all to the towre of the gate. And 1435 than Sir Launcelot spake on hyght unto the kynge and seyde, 'My lorde Arthur, and noble kynge that made me knyght! Wyte you well I am ryght hevy for youre sake that ye thus sewe uppon me. And allwayes I forbeare you, for and I wolde be vengeable I myght have mette you in myddys the fylde or thys tyme, and 1440

1409 *feawtred*, put . . . in the rests, settled
1410 *spiteously*, fiercely
1418 *at all pecis*, completely, cap-à-pie
1421 *holys*, windows (C)
1426 *at onys*, together (not 'at once')
1428 *called uppon*, accused of
1432 *me*, myself
1435 *the towre of the gate* (C)
1436 *on hyght*, loudly
1438 *sewe uppon*, pursue
1439 *wolde be vengeable*, wanted to be revengeful

thereto have made your boldiste knyghtes full tame. And now I
have forborne you and suffirde you halff a yere, and Sir Gawayne,
to do what ye wolde do. And now I may no lenger suffir to endure, but nedis I muste deffende myselff, insomuch as Sir
Gawayn hathe becalled me of treson; whych ys gretly ayenste 1445
my wyll that ever I shulde fyghte ayenste ony of youre blood,
but now I may nat forsake hit: for I am dryvyn thereto as beste
tylle a bay.'

Than Sir Gawayne seyde unto Sir Launcelotte, 'And thou
darste do batayle, leve thy babelynge and com off, and lat us 1450
ease oure hartis!'

Than Sir Launcelot armed hym lyghtely and mownted uppon
hys horse, and aythir of them gate great spearys in their hondys.
And so the oste withoute stoode stylle all aparte, and the noble
knyghtes of the cité cam oute by a greate numbir, that whan 1455
Kynge Arthur saw the numbir of men and knyghtes he mer-
vaylde and seyde to hymself, 'Alas, that ever Sir Launcelot was
ayenst me; for now I se that he hath forborne me.'

And so the covenaunte was made, there sholde no man nyghe
hem nother deale wyth them tylle the tone were dede other 1460
yolden.

Than Sir Launcelot and Sir Gawayne departed a greate way
in sundir, and than they cam togydirs with all their horse
myghtes as faste as they myght renne, and aythir smote othir in
myddis of their shyldis. But the knyghtes were so stronge and 1465
their spearys so bygge that their horsis myght nat endure their
buffettis, and so their horsis felle to the erthe. And than they
avoyded their horsys and dressed their shyldis afore them; than
they strode togydirs and gaff many sad strokis on dyverse placis
of their bodyes, that the bloode braste oute on many sydis. 1470

1443-4 *suffir to endure*, submit to endure [it patiently]
1445 *becalled*, accused
1447 *forsake*, avoid
1447-8 *as beste tyll a bay*, like a beast at bay (lit. 'to a bay')
1450 *com off*, come on
1455 *by a greate numbir*, in great numbers
1459-60 *nyghe hem nother deale wyth them*, come near them nor have anything to do with them
1460 *the tone*, one [of them]
1461 *yolden*, had yielded
1463 *in sundir*, apart
1466-7 *their buffettis*, the impact (lit. 'their blows')
1468 *avoyded*, freed themselves of   *dressed*, positioned
1469 *sad*, heavy (not 'sad')

Than had Sir Gawayne suche a grace and gyffte that an holy
man had gyvyn hym, that every day in the yere, frome undern
tyll hyghe noone, hys myght encresed tho three owres as much
as thryse hys strength. And that caused Sir Gawayne to wynne
grete honoure. And for hys sake Kynge Arthur made an ordy- 1475
naunce that all maner off batayles for ony quarels that shulde be
done afore Kynge Arthur shulde begynne at undern; and all was
done for Sir Gawaynes love, that by lyklyhode, if Sir Gawayne
were on the tone parté, he shulde have the bettir in batayle whyle
hys strengthe endured three owrys. But there were that tyme but 1480
feaw knyghtes lyvynge that knewe thys advauntayge that Sir
Gawayne had, but Kynge Arthure all only.

So Sir Launcelot faught wyth Sir Gawayne, and whan Sir
Launcelot felte hys myght evermore encrese, Sir Launcelot
wondred and drad hym sore to be shamed; for, as the Freynshe 1485
booke seyth, he wende, whan he felte Sir Gawayne double hys
strengthe, that he had bene a fyende and none earthely man.
Wherefore Sir Launcelot traced and traverced, and coverde
hymselff with hys shylde, and kepte hys myght and hys brethe
duryng three owrys. And that whyle Sir Gawayne gaff hym many 1490
sad bruntis and many sad strokis, that all the knyghtes that behylde Sir Launcelot mervayled how he myght endure hym, but
full lytyll undirstood they that travayle that Sir Launcelot had to
endure hym.

And than whan hit was paste noone Sir Gawaynes strengthe 1495
was gone and he had no more but hys owne myght. Whan Sir
Launcelot felte hym so com downe, than he strecched hym up
and strode nere Sir Gawayne and seyde thus: 'Now I fele ye have
done youre warste! And now, my lorde Sir Gawayn, I muste do

1471 *Than*, Now (C)
1473 *tho*, those
1474 *hys strength*, his [natural] strength
1478 *love*, sake
1485 *drad hym*, feared (reflexive)
1485-6 See C.
1486 *wende*, thought (lit. 'weened')
1487 *fyende*, fiend
1488 *traced and traverced*, see 'Lancelot', l. 415
1489 *kepte*, saved
1490 *that whyle*, [all] that while
1491 *sad bruntis*, heavy blows
1497-8 *strecched hym up and strode* (C)
1499 *warste*, worst

my parte, for many grete and grevous strokis I have endured you thys day with greate payne.' 1500

And so Sir Launcelot doubled hys strokis and gaff Sir Gawayne suche a buffet uppon the helmet that sydelynge he felle downe uppon hys one syde. And Sir Launcelot withdrew hym frome hym. 1505

'Why wythdrawyst thou the?' seyde Sir Gawayne. 'Turne agayne, false traytoure knyght, and sle me oute! For and thou leve me thus, anone as I am hole I shall do batayle with the agayne.'

'Sir,' seyde Sir Launcelot, 'I shall endure you, be Goddis 1510 grace! But wyte thou well, Sir Gawayne, I woll never smyte a felde knyght.'

And so Sir Launcelot departed and wente unto the cité. And Sir Gawayne was borne unto Kynge Arthurs pavylon, and anone lechys were brought unto hym of the beste, and serched 1515 and salved hym with souffte oynementis.

And than Sir Launcelot seyde, 'Now have good day, my lorde the kynge! For wyte you welle ye wynne no worshyp at thes wallis, for and I wolde my knyghtes outebrynge, there shulde many a douty man dye. And therefore, my lorde Arthur, remem- 1520 bir you of olde kyndenes, and howsomever I fare, Jesu be youre gyde in all placis.'

'Now, alas,' seyde the kynge, 'that ever thys unhappy warre began! For ever Sir Launcelot forbearyth me in all placis, and in lyke wyse my kynne, and that ys sene well thys day, what curtesy 1525 he shewed my neveawe Sir Gawayne.'

Than Kynge Arthur felle syke for sorow of Sir Gawayne, that he was so sore hurte, and bycause of the warre betwyxte hym and Sir Launcelot. So aftir that they on Kynge Arthurs party kepte the sege with lytyll warre wythouteforthe, and they withinforthe 1530 kepte their wallys and deffended them whan nede was. Thus Sir Gawayne lay syke and unsounde three wykes in hys tentis with all maner of lechecrauffte that myght be had.

[1503] *sydelynge*, sidelong, sideways
[1507] *oute*, outright
[1511-12] See C.
[1512] *felde*, fallen
[1515] *lechys*, surgeons (cf. 'Lancelot', l. 470 n)
[1515-16] *serched and salved hym*, probed and anointed his wounds
[1520] *douty*, doughty
[1527] *for sorow of*, of sorrow for
[1530] *wythouteforthe*, outside

And as sone as Sir Gawayne myght go and ryde, he armed hym
at all poyntis and bestroode a styff courser and gate a grete speare 1535
in hys honde, and so he cam rydynge afore the chyeff gate of
Benwyke. And there he cryed on hyght and seyde, 'Where arte
thou, Sir Launcelot? Com forth, thou false traytoure knyght and
recrayed, for I am here, Sir Gawayne, that woll preve thys that
I say uppon the!' 1540
And all thys langayge Sir Launcelot harde and sayde thus:
'Sir Gawayne, me repentis of youre fowle sayinge, that ye woll
nat cease of your langayge. For ye wote well, Sir Gawayne, I
know youre myght and all that ye may do, and well ye wote,
Sir Gawayne, ye may nat greatly hurte me.' 1545
'Com downe, traytoure knyght,' seyde he, 'and make hit good
the contrary wyth thy hondys! For hit myssehapped me the laste
batayle to be hurte of thy hondis, therefore, wyte thou well, I am
com thys day to make amendis, for I wene this day to ley the as
low as thou laydest me.' 1550
'Jesu deffende me,' seyde Sir Launcelot, 'that ever I be so farre
in youre daunger as ye have bene in myne, for than my dayes
were done. But, Sir Gawayne,' seyde Sir Launcelot, 'ye shall nat
thynke that I shall tarry longe, but sytthyn that ye unknyghtly
calle me thus of treson, ye shall have bothe youre hondys fulle of 1555
me.'
And than Sir Launcelot armed hym at all poyntis, and mounted uppon his horse and gate a grete speare in hys honde and rode
oute at the gate. And bothe their ostis were assembled, of them
withoute and within, and stood in aray full manly, and bothe 1560
partyes were charged to holde hem style to se and beholde the
batayle of thes two noble knyghtes.
And than they layde their spearys in their restis and so cam
togydir as thundir. And Sir Gawayne brake hys speare in an
hondred peces unto hys honde, and Sir Launcelot smote hym 1565
with a gretter myght, that Sir Gawaynes horse feete reysed, and
so the horse and he felle to the erthe.

1534 *go*, walk
1539 *recrayed*, recreant
1547-8 *hit myssehapped me . . . to be*, it happened by bad luck . . . that I was
1552 *in youre daunger*, in your power (not 'danger'; from Lat. *dominiarium*)
1555 *calle . . . of*, accuse . . . of
1560 *stood in aray*, were drawn up in order
1565 *unto*, as far back as
1566 *horse*, horse's   *reysed*, went up (lit. 'raised')

Than Sir Gawayne delyverly devoyded hys horse and put hys shylde afore hym, and egirly drew hys swerde and bade Sir Launcelot, 'Alyght, traytoure knyght!' and seyde, 'Gyff a marys 1570 sonne hath fayled me, wyte thou well a kyngis sonne and a quenys sonne shall nat fayle the!'

Than Sir Launcelot devoyded hys horse and dressed hys shylde afore hym and drew hys swerde, and so strode egirly to-gydirs and gaff many sad strokis, that all men on bothe partyes 1575 had thereof passyng grete wondir.

But whan Sir Launcelot felte Sir Gawaynes myght so mer-vaylously encres, he than wythhylde hys corayge and hys wynde; and so he kepte hym undir coverte of hys myght, and under hys shylde he traced and traverced here and there, to breake Sir 1580 Gawaynys strokys and hys currayge. And ever Sir Gawayne en-forced hymselff wyth all hys myght and power to destroy Sir Launcelot, for, as the Freynshe booke saythe, ever as Sir Gawaynes myght encresed, ryght so encreced hys wynde and hys evyll wyll. And thus he ded grete payne unto Sir Launcelot three 1585 owres, that he had much ado to defende hym.

And whan the three owres were paste, that he felte Sir Gawayne was com home to his owne propir strengthe, than Sir Launcelot sayde, 'Sir, now I have preved you twyse that ye ar a full daungerous knyght and a wondirfull man of your myght! 1590 And many wondir' dedis have ye done in youre dayes, for by youre myght encresyng ye have desceyved many a full noble knyght. And now I fele that ye have done youre myghty dedis, now, wyte you well, I muste do my dedis!'

And than Sir Launcelot strode nere Sir Gawayne and doubled 1595 hys strokis, and ever Sir Gawayne deffended hym myghtyly, but nevertheles Sir Launcelot smote such a stroke uppon hys helme and uppon the olde wounde that Sir Gawayne sanke downe upon hys one syde in a swounde. And anone as he ded awake he waved

---

1568 *delyverly*, swiftly and skilfully   *devoyded*, freed himself from
1570 *Gyff*, If
1573 *devoyded*, dismounted from
1574 *strode*, [they] strode
1578 *encres*, increase   *wythhylde*, husbanded   *corayge*, energy   *wynde*, breath, stamina
1579 *hym*, himself   *undir coverte of*, under the protection of
1583 See C.
1584 *ryght so*, even thus, in proportion   *wynde*, stamina (C)
1585 *evyll wyll*, hostility
1591 *wondir*, wonderful

210

and foyned at Sir Launcelot as he lay, and seyde, 'Traytoure 1600
knyght, wyte thou well I am nat yet slayne. Therefore com thou
nere me and performe thys batayle to the utteraunce!'

'I woll no more do than I have done,' seyde Sir Launcelot. 'For
whan I se you on foote I woll do batayle uppon you all the whyle
I se you stande uppon youre feete; but to smyte a wounded man 1605
that may nat stonde, God defende me from such a shame!'

And than he turned hym and wente hys way towarde the cité,
and Sir Gawayne evermore callyng hym 'traytoure knyght' and
seyde, 'Traytoure knyght! Wyte thou well, Sir Launcelot, whan
I am hole I shall do batayle with the agayne, for I shall never 1610
leve the tylle the tone of us be slayne!'

Thus as thys syge endured and as Sir Gawayne lay syke
nerehande a moneth, and whan he was well recovirde and redy
within three dayes to do batayle agayne with Sir Launcelot,
ryght so cam tydyngis unto Kynge Arthur frome Inglonde that 1615
made Kynge Arthur and all hys oste to remeve.

IV

As Sir Mordred was rular of all Inglonde, he lete make lettirs as
thoughe that they had com frome beyonde the see, and the lettirs
specifyed that Kynge Arthur was slayne in batayle with Sir
Launcelot. Wherefore Sir Mordred made a parlemente, and 1620
called the lordys togydir, and there he made them to chose hym
kynge. And so was he crowned at Caunturbyry, and hylde a feste
there fiftene dayes.

And aftirwarde he drew hym unto Wynchester, and there he
toke Quene Gwenyver, and seyde playnly that he wolde wedde 1625
her (which was hys unclys wyff and hys fadirs wyff). And so he
made redy for the feste, and a day prefyxte that they shulde be
wedded; wherefore Quene Gwenyver was passyng hevy. But she

1600 *foyned*, thrust
1613 *nerehande*, nearly
1617 *As*, When   *lete make*, had made
1621 See C.
1627 *prefyxte*, appointed

211

durst nat discover her harte, but spake fayre, and aggreed to Sir
Mordredys wylle.   1630

And anone she desyred of Sir Mordred to go to London to
byghe all maner thynges that longed to the brydale. And bycause
of her fayre speche Sir Mordred trusted her well ynough and gaff
her leve to go; and so whan she cam to London she toke the
Towre of London, and suddeynly in all haste possyble she stuffed 1635
hit with all maner of vytayle, and well garnysshed hit with men,
and so kepte hit.

And whan Sir Mordred wyst and understode how he was
begyled he was passynge wrothe oute of mesure. And shorte tale to
make, he layde a myghty syge aboute the Towre and made many   1640
grete assautis thereat, and threw many grete engynnes unto
them, and shotte grete gunnes. But all myght nat prevayle, for
Quene Gwenyver wolde never, for fayre speache nother for foule,
never to truste unto Sir Mordred to com in hys hondis agayne.

Than cam the Bysshop of Caunturbyry, whych was a noble   1645
clerke and an holy man, and thus he seyde unto Sir Mordred:
'Sir, what woll ye do? Woll ye firste displease God and sytthyn
shame youreselff and all knyghthode? For ys nat Kynge Arthur
youre uncle, and no farther but youre modirs brothir, and uppon
her he hymselffe begate you, uppon hys owne syster? Therefore   1650
how may ye wed youre owne fadirs wyff? And therefor, sir,'
seyde the bysshop, 'leve thys opynyon, other ellis I shall curse you
with booke, belle and candyll.'

'Do thou thy warste,' seyde Sir Mordred, 'and I defyghe the!'

'Sir,' seyde the bysshop, 'wyte you well I shall nat feare me to   1655
do that me ought to do. And also ye noyse that my lorde Arthur ys
slayne, and that ys nat so, and therefore ye woll make a foule
warke in thys londe!'

'Peas, thou false pryste!' seyde Sir Mordred, 'for and thou
chauffe me ony more, I shall make stryke of thy hede!'   1660

1629 *discover*, reveal
1632 *byghe*, buy
1634 *leve*, leave
1636 *vytayle*, provisions
1640–2 See C.
1652 *curse*, excommunicate
1655–6 Translate: 'I shall not be afraid to do what is right for me to do'
1656 *noyse*, put it about
1656–7 *make a foule warke*, do a wicked thing
1659 *Peas*, Silence
1660 *chauffe*, anger (lit. heat')

So the bysshop departed, and ded the cursynge in the moste orguluste wyse that myght be done. And than Sir Mordred sought the Bysshop off Caunturbyry for to have slayne hym. Than the bysshop fledde, and tooke parte of hys good with hym, and wente nyghe unto Glassyngbyry. And there he was a preste-ermyte in a chapel, and lyved in poverté and in holy prayers; for well he undirstood that myschevous warre was at honde. 1665

Than Sir Mordred soughte uppon Quene Gwenyver by lettirs and sondis, and by fayre meanys and foule meanys, to have her to com oute of the Towre of London; but all thys avayled nought, 1670 for she answered hym shortely, opynly and pryvayly, that she had levir sle herselff than to be maryed with hym.

Than cam there worde unto Sir Mordred that Kynge Arthure had areysed the syge frome Sir Launcelot and was commynge homwarde wyth a greate oste to be avenged uppon Sir Mordred, 1675 wherefore Sir Mordred made wryte wryttes unto all the baronny of thys londe. And muche people drew unto hym; for than was the comyn voyce amonge them that with Kynge Arthur was never othir lyff but warre and stryff, and with Sir Mordrede was grete joy and blysse. Thus was Kynge Arthur depraved, and evyll seyde 1680 off; and many there were that Kynge Arthur had brought up of nought, and gyffyn them londis, that myght nat than say hym a good worde.

Lo ye all Englysshemen, se ye nat what a myschyff here was? For he that was the moste kynge and nobelyst knyght of the 1685 worlde, and moste loved the felyshyp of noble knyghtes, and by hym they all were upholdyn, and yet myght nat thes Englyshe-men holde them contente with hym. Lo thus was the olde custom and usayges of thys londe, and men say that we of thys londe have nat yet loste ne foryetyn that custom and usage. Alas! thys ys a 1690 greate defaughte of us Englysshemen, for there may no thynge us please no terme.

1662 *orguluste*, fearsome
1664–7 See C.
1664 *hys good*, his belongings
1665 *Glassyngbyry*, Glastonbury
1669 *sondis*, messages (cf. *sendings*)
1674 *areysed*, raised
1676 *made wryte wryttes*, had writs made out and sent
1680 *depraved*, denigrated
1685 *moste*, greatest
1686 *moste*, most
1689 *usayges*, usage
1691 *defaughte*, fault   See C.

And so fared the peple at that tyme: they were better pleased
with Sir Mordred than they were with the noble Kynge Arthur,
and muche people drew unto Sir Mordred and seyde they wold 1695
abyde wyth hym for bettir and for wars. And so Sir Mordred
drew with a greate oste to Dovir, for there he harde sey that
Kyng Arthur wolde aryve, and so he thought to beate hys owne
fadir fro hys owne londys. And the moste party of all Inglonde
hylde wyth Sir Mordred, for the people were so new-fangill.   1700

And so as Sir Mordred was at Dovir with hys oste, so cam
Kyng Arthur wyth a greate navy of shyppis and galyes and
carykes, and there was Sir Mordred redy awaytyng uppon hys
londynge, to lette hys owne fadir to londe uppon the londe that
he was kynge over.   1705

Than there was launchyng of greate botis and smale, and full
of noble men of armys; and there was muche slaughtir of jantyll
knyghtes, and many a full bolde barown was layde full lowe, on
bothe partyes. But Kyng Arthur was so currageous that there
myght no maner of knyght lette hym to lande, and hys knyghtes 1710
fyersely folowed hym. And so they londed magré Sir Mordredis
hede and all hys power, and put Sir Mordred abak, that he
fledde and all hys people.

So whan thys batayle was done, Kynge Arthure let serche hys
people that were hurte and dede. And than was noble Sir 1715
Gawayne founde in a greate boote, liynge more than halff dede.
Whan Kyng Arthur knew that he was layde so low he wente unto
hym and so fownde hym. And there the kynge made greate
sorow oute of mesure, and toke Sir Gawayne in hys armys, and
thryse he there sowned.   1720

And than whan he was waked, Kyng Arthur seyde, 'Alas! Sir
Gawayne, my syster son, here now thou lyghest, the man in the
worlde that I loved moste. And now ys my joy gone! For now,
my nevew, Sir Gawayne, I woll discover me unto you, that in
youre person and in Sir Launcelot I moste had my joy and myne 1725

1693 *fared*, went
1695 *drew unto*, went over to (C)
1700 *new-fangill*, eager for novelty, fickle
1702–3 *galyes and carykes*, galleys and carracks (C)
1704 *lette . . . to londe*, stop . . . landing
1706 *botis*, boats
1709 *currageous*, fierce and brave (C)
1712 *power*, force (in both senses, 'strength' and 'army')   *put*, drove
1716 *boote*, boat
1722 See C.

214

affyaunce. And now have I loste my joy of you bothe, wherefore
all myne erthely joy ys gone fro me!'

'A, myn uncle,' seyde Sir Gawayne, 'now I woll that ye wyte
that my deth-dayes be com. And all I may wyte myne owne
hastynes and my wylfulnesse, for thorow my wylfulnes I was 1730
causer of myne owne dethe. For I was thys day hurte and smytten
uppon myne olde wounde that Sir Launcelot gaff me, and I fele
myselff that I muste nedis be dede by the owre of noone. And
thorow me and my pryde ye have all thys shame and disease, for
had that noble knyght, Sir Launcelot, ben with you, as he was and 1735
wolde have ben, thys unhappy warre had never ben begunne; for
he, thorow hys noble knyghthode and hys noble bloode, hylde all
youre cankyrde enemyes in subjeccion and daungere. And now,'
seyde Sir Gawayne, 'ye shall mysse Sir Launcelot. But alas that I
wolde nat accorde with hym! And therefore, fayre unkle, I pray 1740
you that I may have paupir, penne, and inke, that I may wryte
unto Sir Launcelot a sedull wrytten with myne owne honde.'

So whan pauper, penne and inke was brought, than Sir
Gawayne was sette up waykely by Kynge Arthure, for he was
shryven a lytyll afore. And than he toke hys penne and wrote 1745
thus, as the Freynshe booke makith mencion: 'Unto the, Sir
Launcelot, floure of all noble knyghtes that ever I harde of or saw
be my dayes, I, Sir Gawayne, Kynge Lottis sonne of Orkeney,
and systirs sonne unto the noble Kynge Arthur, sende the gretynge,
lattynge the to have knowlecche that the tenth day of May I was 1750
smytten uppon the olde wounde that thou gaff me afore the cité
of Benwyke, and thorow the same wounde that thou gaff me I
am com to my dethe-day. And I woll that all the worlde wyte
that I, Sir Gawayne, knyght of the Table Rounde, soughte my
dethe, and nat thorow thy deservynge, but myne owne sekynge. 1755
Wherefore I beseche the, Sir Launcelot, to returne agayne unto
thys realme and se my toumbe and pray som prayer more other
les for my soule. And thys same day that I wrote this same sedull

---

1726 *affyaunce*, trust
1729-30 Translate: 'And I can see [that] all [this is the result of] my own rashness
and obstinacy'
1734 *disease*, trouble ('not disease')
1737 *bloode*, kinsmen
1738 *cankyred*, malignant   *in . . . daungere*, in [his] power
1742 *sedull*, letter
1746 See C.
1748 *be*, in (lit. 'by')
1755 *and nat*, i.e. and [got it] not   *deservynge* (C)
1757-8 *more other les*, longer or shorter

I was hurte to the dethe in the same wounde, whych wounde was fyrste gyffyn of thyn honde, Sir Launcelot; for of a more nobelar 1760 man myght I nat be slayne.

'Also, Sir Launcelot, for all the love that ever was betwyxte us, make no taryyng, but com over the see in all the goodly haste that ye may, wyth youre noble knyghtes, and rescow that noble kynge that made the knyght, that ys my lorde Arthure for he ys 1765 full straytely bestad wyth an false traytoure, whych ys my halff-brothir, Sir Mordred. For he hath crowned hymselff kynge, and wolde have wedded my lady, Quene Gwenyver; and so had he done, had she nat kepte the Towre of London with stronge honde. And so the tenth day of May last paste my lorde Kynge Arthur 1770 and we all londed uppon them at Dover, and there we put that false traytoure, Sir Mordred, to flyght. And so hit there mys-fortuned me to be smytten uppon the strooke that ye gaff me of olde.

'And the date of thys lettir was wrytten but two owrys and an 1775 halff afore my dethe, wrytten with myne owne honde and sub-scrybed with parte of my harte blood. And therefore I requyre the, moste famous knyght of the worlde, that thou wolte se my tumbe.'

And than he wepte and Kynge Arthur both, and sowned. And 1780 whan they were awaked bothe, the kynge made Sir Gawayne to resceyve hys Saveour, and than Sir Gawayne prayde the kynge for to sende for Sir Launcelot and to cherysshe hym aboven all othir knyghtes. And so at the owre of noone Sir Gawayne yelded up the goste. And than the kynge lat entere hym in a chapell 1785 within Dover Castell. And there yet all men may se the skulle of hym, and the same wounde is sene that Sir Launcelot gaff hym in batayle.

Than was hit tolde the kynge that Sir Mordred had pyght a new fylde uppon Bareon Downe. And so uppon the morne 1790 Kynge Arthur rode thydir to hym, and there was a grete batayle

---

1766 *straytely bestad wyth*, hard pressed by
1771 *londed uppon*, translate 'landed into'
1773 *strooke*, wound
1776–7 *subscrybed*, signed
1782 *hys Saveour*, the Eucharist, Communion
1784–5 *yelded up the goste*, died (C)
1785 *lat entere hym*, had him buried
1786–8 See C.
1789–90 *pyght a new field*, drawn up his army in a new position
1790 *Bareon Downe*, Barham Down (C)

betwyxt hem, and muche people were slayne on bothe partyes. But at the laste Kynge Arthurs party stoode beste, and Sir Mordred and hys party fledde unto Caunturbyry. And than the kynge let serche all the downys for hys knyghtes that were slayne, 1795 and entered them; and salved them with soffte salvys that full sore were wounded. Than much people drew unto Kynge Arthur, and than they sayde that Sir Mordred warred uppon Kynge Arthure wyth wronge.

And anone Kynge Arthure drew hym wyth his oste downe by 1800 the seesyde westewarde, towarde Salusbyry. And there was a day assygned betwyxte Kynge Arthur and Sir Mordred, that they shulde mete uppon a downe besyde Salesbyry and nat farre frome the seesyde. And thys day was assygned on Monday aftir Trynyté Sonday, whereof Kynge Arthur was passyng glad, that 1805 he myght be avenged uppon Sir Mordred.

Than Sir Mordred araysed muche people aboute London, for they of Kente, Southsex and Surrey, Esax, Suffolke and Northe-folke helde the moste party with Sir Mordred. And many a full noble knyght drew unto hym and also to the kynge; but they that 1810 loved Sir Launcelot drew unto Sir Mordred.

So uppon Trynyté Sunday at nyght Kynge Arthure dremed a wondirfull dreme, and in hys dreme hym semed that he saw uppon a chafflet a chayre, and the chayre was faste to a whele, and thereuppon sate Kynge Arthure in the rychest clothe of golde 1815 that myght be made. And the kynge thought there was undir hym, farre from hym, an hydeous depe blak watir, and therein was all maner of serpentis and wormes and wylde bestis fowle and orryble. And suddeynly the kynge thought that the whyle turned up-so-downe, and he felle amonge the serpentis, and every beste 1820 toke hym by a lymme.

And than the kynge cryed as he lay in hys bed, 'Helpe! helpe!' And than knyghtes, squyars, and yomen awaked the kynge, and than he was so amased that he wyste nat where he was. And than

---

1800 *by*, along
1803 *downe*, hill (cf. *dune*)
1804 *thys day was assygned on*, it was arranged that this day should be [the]
1807 *araysed*, raised (C)
1809 *the moste party*, for the most part
1812–21 See C.
1814 *chafflet*, scaffold, framework   *faste to*, made fast to
1818 *wormes*, snakes, reptiles and dragons
1821 *toke*, seized
1824 *amased*, bemused

so he awaked untylle hit was nyghe day, and than he felle on 1825
slumberynge agayne, nat slepynge nor thorowly wakynge.

So the kyng semed verryly that there cam Sir Gawayne unto
hym with a numbir of fayre ladyes wyth hym. So whan Kyng
Arthur saw hym he seyde, 'Wellcom, my systers sonne, I wende
thou haddest bene dede. And now I se the on lyve, much am I be- 1830
holdyn unto Allmyghty Jesu. A, fayre nevew, what bene thes
ladyes that hyder be com with you?'

'Sir,' seyde Sir Gawayne, 'all thes be ladyes for whom I have
foughten for, whan I was man lyvynge. And all thes ar tho that I
ded batayle fore in ryghteuous quarels, and God hath gyvyn hem 1835
that grace at their grete prayer, bycause I ded batayle for them
for their ryght, that they shulde brynge me hydder unto you. Thus
much hath gyvyn me leve God for to warne you of youre dethe:
for and ye fyght as to-morne with Sir Mordred, as ye bothe have
assygned, doute ye nat ye shall be slayne, and the moste party of 1840
youre people on bothe partyes. And for the grete grace and goodnes that Allmyghty Jesu hath unto you, and for pyté of you and
many mo other good men there shall be slayne, God hath sente
me to you of Hys speciall grace to gyff you warnyng that in no
wyse ye do batayle as to-morne, but that ye take a tretyse for a 1845
moneth-day. And proffir you largely, so that to-morne ye put in
a delay. For within a moneth shall com Sir Launcelot with all
hys noble knyghtes, and rescow you worshypfully, and sle Sir
Mordred and all that ever wyll holde wyth hym.'

Than Sir Gawayne and all the ladyes vanysshed, and anone 1850
the kynge called uppon hys knyghtes, squyars, and yomen, and
charged them wyghtly to fecche hys noble lordis and wyse bysshoppis unto hym. And whan they were com the kynge tolde hem
of hys avision: that Sir Gawayne had tolde hym and warned hym
that and he fought on the morn, he sholde be slayne. Than the 1855
kynge commaunded Sir Lucan the Butlere and hys brothir Sir

1827 *the kyng semed verryly*, [to] the king [it] seemed truly
1836 *at their grete prayer*, at their urgent request
1837-8 Translate: 'God has given me this much freedom, to warn'
1839 *and*, if   *as*, on
1841 *grace*, favour
1843 *men there*, men [who] there
1844-5 *in no wyse ye do*, whatever happens you do not do   *take a tretyse*, arrange
terms
1846 *moneth-day*, a month-long respite   *so that*, provided that, so long as   *put in*,
put in for
1852 *wyghtly*, strictly
1854 *avision*, vision (C)

Bedyvere the Bolde, with two bysshoppis wyth hem, and charged
them in ony wyse, and they myght, to take a tretyse for a moneth-
day wyth Sir Mordred: 'And spare nat, proffir hym londys and
goodys as much as ye thynke resonable.'   1860

So than they departed and cam to Sir Mordred where he had
a grymme oste of an hondred thousand men, and there they
entretyd Sir Mordred longe tyme. And at the laste Sir Mordred
was aggreed for to have Cornwale and Kente by Kynge Arthurs
dayes; and afftir that all Inglonde, after the dayes of Kynge 1865
Arthur.

Than were they condescende that Kynge Arthure and Sir
Mordred shulde mete betwyxte bothe their ostis, and everych of
them shulde brynge fourtene persons. And so they cam wyth thys
worde unto Arthur. Than seyde he, 'I am glad that thys ys done'; 1870
and so he wente into the fylde. And whan Kynge Arthur shulde
departe he warned all hys hoost that and they se ony swerde
drawyn, 'loke ye com on fyersely and sle that traytoure, Sir
Mordred, for I in no wyse truste hym'.

In lyke wyse Sir Mordred warned hys oste that 'and ye se ony 1875
maner of swerde drawyn, loke that ye com on fyersely and so sle all
that ever before you stondyth, for in no wyse I woll nat truste for
thys tretyse.' And in the same wyse seyde Sir Mordred unto hys
oste: 'for I know well my fadir woll be avenged uppon me.'

And so they mette as their poyntemente was, and were agreed 1880
and accorded thorowly. And wyne was fette, and they dranke
togydir. Ryght so cam oute an addir of a lytyll hethe-buysshe,
and hit stange a knyght in the foote. And so whan the knyght
felte hym so stonge, he loked downe and saw the adder; and
anone he drew hys swerde to sle the addir, and thought none othir 1885
harme. And whan the oste on bothe partyes saw that swerde
drawyn, than they blewe beamys, trumpettis, and hornys, and
shoutted grymly, and so bothe ostis dressed hem togydirs. And

---

[1863] *entretyd*, treated with
[1864] *by*, in, during
[1867] *condescende*, agreed
[1868] *everych*, each (cf. *every*)
[1871-2] See C.   *shulde*, was about to
[1880] *poyntemente*, agreement
[1881] *fette*, fetched
[1882] *Ryght so*, At once, Even at that moment   *of*, from   *hethe-buysshe*, a clump
of heather
[1887] *beamys*, bugles

Kynge Arthur toke hys horse and seyde, 'Alas, this unhappy day!' and so rode to hys party; and Sir Mordred in lyke wyse. 1890

And never syns was there seyne a more dolefuller batayle in no Crysten londe, for there was but russhynge and rydynge, foynynge and strykynge, and many a grym worde was there spokyn of aythir to othir, and many a dedely stroke. But ever Kynge Arthure rode thorowoute the batayle of Sir Mordred many tymys and ded 1895 full nobely, as a noble kynge shulde do, and at all tymes he faynted never. And Sir Mordred ded hys devoure that day and put hymselffe in grete perell.

And thus they fought all the longe day, and never stynted tylle the noble knyghtes were layde to the colde erthe. And ever they 1900 fought stylle tylle hit was nere nyght, and by than was there an hondred thousand leyde dede uppon the erthe. Than was Kynge Arthure wode wroth oute of mesure, whan he saw hys people so slayne frome hym.

And so he loked aboute hym and cowde se no mo of all hys oste 1905 and good knyghtes leffte, no mo on lyve but two knyghtes: the tone was Sir Lucan de Buttler, and the tother was hys brother Sir Bedwere; and yette they were full sore wounded.

'Jesu mercy!' seyde the kynge, 'where ar all my noble knyghtes becom? Alas, that ever I shulde se thys doleful day! For now', 1910 seyde Kynge Arthur, 'I am com to myne ende. But wolde to God', seyde he, 'that I wyste now where were that traytoure Sir Mordred that hath caused all thys myschyff.'

Than Kynge Arthur loked aboute and was ware where stood Sir Mordred leanyng uppon hys swerde amonge a grete hepe of 1915 dede men.

'Now, gyff me my speare,' seyde Kynge Arthure unto Sir Lucan, 'for yondir I have aspyed the traytoure that all thys woo hath wrought.'

'Sir, latte hym be,' seyde Sir Lucan, 'for he ys unhappy; and 1920 yf ye passe this unhappy day ye shall be ryght well revenged upon

---

[1891] *syns*, since
[1897] *faynted*, relaxed his efforts   *devoure*, duty
[1903] *wood wroth oute of mesure*, mad with uncontrollable rage
[1907] *de Buttler* (C)
[1908] *yette*, even
[1909]–10 *where ar . . . becom*, what has become of . . .
[1914] *was ware*, became aware of
[1915] *leanyng uppon hys swerde*, i.e. from extreme exhaustion
[1920] *latte*, let   *unhappy*, accursed (C)
[1921] *passe*, survive   *unhappy*, unlucky

hym. And, good lord, remembre ye of your nyghtes dreme and
what the spyryte of Sir Gawayne tolde you tonyght, and yet God
of Hys grete goodnes hath preserved you hyddirto. And for
Goddes sake, my lorde, leve of thys, for, blyssed be God, ye have 1925
won the fylde: for yet we ben here three on lyve, and with Sir
Mordred ys nat one on lyve. And therefore if ye leve of now, thys
wycked day of Desteny ys paste.'

'Now tyde me dethe, tyde me lyff,' seyde the kyng, 'now I se
hym yondir alone, he shall never ascape myne hondes! For at a 1930
bettir avayle shall I never have hym.'

'God spyede you well!' seyde Sir Bedyvere.

Than the kynge gate his speare in bothe hys hondis, and ran
towarde Sir Mordred, cryyng and saying, 'Traytoure, now ys thy
dethe-day com!'   1935

And whan Sir Mordred saw Kynge Arthur he ran untyll hym
with hys swerde drawyn in hys honde; and there Kyng Arthur
smote Sir Mordred undir the shylde, with a foyne of hys speare,
thorowoute the body more than a fadom. And whan Sir Mordred
felte that he had hys dethys wounde he threste hymselff with the 1940
myght that he had upp to the burre of Kyng Arthurs speare, and
ryght so he smote hys fadir, Kynge Arthure, with hys swerde
holdynge in both hys hondys, uppon the syde of the hede, that the
swerde perced the helmet and the tay of the brayne. And therewith Mordred daysshed downe starke dede to the erthe.   1945

And noble Kynge Arthure felle in a swoughe to the erthe, and
there he sowned oftyntymys, and Sir Lucan and Sir Bedwere
offtetymys hove hym up. And so waykly betwyxte them they
lad hym to a lytyll chapell nat farre frome the see syde, and whan
the kyng was there, he thought hym resonabely eased.   1950

1925 *leve of*, stop (lit. 'leave off')
1925–6 See C.
1929 *tyde me dethe, tyde me lyff*, whether I live or die (lit. 'betide me death ...')(C)
1930–1 *at a bettir avayle*, at more of a disadvantage
1934 *cryying*, shouting
1936 *untyll*, towards
1938 *foyne*, thrust
1939 *a fadom*, six feet (lit. 'fathom')
1940–1 *the myght*, [all] the strength
1941 *burre*, burr (C)
1943 *holdynge*, being held   *that*, so that
1944 *tay*, outer membrane
1945 *dayshed*, collapsed
1948 *hove*, lifted
1949 See C.

Than harde they people crye in the fylde. 'Now go thou, Sir Lucan,' seyde the kyng, 'and do me to wyte what betokyns that noyse in the fylde.'

So Sir Lucan departed, for he was grevously wounded in many placis; and so as he yode he saw and harkened by the moonelyght 1955 how that pyllours and robbers were com into the fylde to pylle and to robbe many a full noble knyght of brochys and bees and of many a good rynge and many a ryche juell. And who that were nat dede all oute, there they slewe them for their harneys and their ryches.   1960

Whan Sir Lucan undirstood thys warke he cam to the kynge as sone as he myght, and tolde hym all what he had harde and seyne. 'Therefore be my rede,' seyde Sir Lucan, 'hit ys beste that we brynge you to som towne.'

'I wolde hit were so,' seyde the kynge, 'but I may nat stonde, 1965 my hede worchys so. A, Sir Launcelot!' seyde Kynge Arthure, 'thys day have I sore myssed the! And alas, that ever I was ayenste the; for now have I my dethe, whereof Sir Gawayne me warned in my dreame.'

Than Sir Lucan toke up the kynge the tone party and Sir 1970 Bedwere the othir parté, and in the lyfftyng up the kynge sowned. And in the lyfftynge Sir Lucan felle in a sowne, that parte of hys guttis felle oute of hys bodye, and therewith the noble knyght hys harte braste. And whan the kynge awoke he behylde Sir Lucan, how he lay fomyng at the mowth and parte of his guttes lay at hys 1975 fyete.

'Alas,' seyde the kynge, 'thys ys to me a fulle hevy syght, to se thys noble deuke so dye for my sake, for he wold have holpyn me that had more nede of helpe than I. Alas, that he wolde nat complayne hym, for hys harte was so sette to helpe me. Now Jesu 1980 have mercy uppon hys soule!'

Than Sir Bedwere wepte for the deth of hys brothir.

1951 *crye*, call out
1954 *for*, although
1955 *yode*, went   *harkened*, heard
1956 *pyllours*, pillagers
1957 *brochys*, ornaments (lit. 'brooches')   *bees*, torques (i.e. neck-rings), or arm-rings, or both
1963 *rede*, advice
1966 *worchys*, is working, is going round
1970 *the tone party*, [on] the one side

'Now leve thys mournynge and wepyng, jantyll knyght,' seyde
the kyng, 'for all thys woll nat avayle me. For wyte thou well, and
I myght lyve myselff, the dethe of Sir Lucan wolde greve me 1985
evermore. But my tyme hyeth faste,' seyde the kynge. 'Therefore,'
seyde Kynge Arthur unto Sir Bedwere, 'take thou here Excaliber,
my good swerde, and go wyth hit to yondir watirs syde; and whan
thou commyste there, I charge the throw my swerde in that water,
and com agayne and telle me what thou syeste there.'   1990
'My lorde,' seyde Sir Bedwere, 'youre commaundement shall
be done, and lyghtly brynge you worde agayne.'
So Sir Bedwere departed. And by the way he behylde that
noble swerde, and the pomell and the hauffte was all precious
stonys. And than he seyde to hymselff, 'If I throw thys ryche 1995
swerde in the water, thereof shall never com good, but harme and
losse.' And than Sir Bedwere hyd Excalyber undir a tre, and so
as sone as he myght he cam agayne unto the kynge and seyde he
had bene at the watir and had throwen the swerde into the watir.
'What sawe thou there?' seyde the kynge.   2000
'Sir,' he seyde, 'I saw nothyng but wawis and wyndys.'
'That ys untruly seyde of the,' seyde the kynge. 'And therefore
go thou lyghtly agayne, and do my commaundemente; as thou
arte to me lyff and dere, spare nat, but throw hit in.'
Than Sir Bedwere returned agayne and toke the swerde in hys 2005
honde; and yet hým thought synne and shame to throw away
that noble swerde. And so effte he hyd the swerde, and returned
agayne and tolde the kynge that he had bene at the watir and done
hys commaundement.
'What sawist thou there?' seyde the kynge.   2010
'Sir,' he seyde, 'I sy nothynge but watirs wap and wawys
wanne.'
'A, traytour unto me and untrew,' seyde Kyng Arthure, 'now
hast thou betrayed me twyse! Who wolde wene that thou that

1983-4 See C.
1984 *avayle*, help   *and*, if
1990 *syeste*, saw
1992 *brynge*, [I shall] bring (C)
1993 *by*, on
1994 *hauffte*, half   *was*, were
2001 *wawis*, waves
2003-4 *as thou arte to me lyff and dere*, as I have loved and valued you (C)
2006 *hym thought*, [it] seemed to him
2007 *effte*, again
2011-12 *watirs wap and wawys wanne*, the waters toss and the waves grow dark (C)

hast bene to me so leve and dere, and also named so noble a 2015
knyght, that thou wolde betray me for the ryches of thys swerde?
But now go agayn lyghtly; for thy longe taryynge puttith me in
grete jouperté of my lyff, for I have takyn colde. And but if thou
do now as I bydde the, if ever I may se the, I shall sle the myne
owne hondis, for thou woldist for my rych swerde se me dede.'   2020

Than Sir Bedwere departed and wente to the swerde and
lyghtly toke hit up, and so he wente unto the watirs syde. And
there he bounde the gyrdyll aboute the hyltis, and threw the
swerde as farre into the watir as he myght. And there cam an
arme and an honde above the watir, and toke hit and cleyght hit, 2025
and shoke hit thryse and braundysshed hit, and than vanysshed
with the swerde into the watir.

So Sir Bedyvere cam agayne to the kynge and tolde hym what
he saw.

'Alas,' seyde the kynge, 'helpe me hens, for I drede me I have 2030
taryed over longe.'

Than Sir Bedwere toke the kynge uppon hys bak and so wente
with hym to the watirs syde. And whan they were there, evyn
faste by the banke hoved a lytyll barge wyth many fayre ladyes
in hit, and amonge hem all was a quene, and all they had blak 2035
hoodis. And all they wepte and shryked whan they saw Kynge
Arthur.

'Now put me into that barge,' seyde the kynge.

And so he ded sofftely, and there resceyved hym three ladyes
with grete mournyng. And so they sette hem downe, and in one 2040
of their lappis Kyng Arthure layde hys hede.

And than the quene seyde, 'A, my dere brothir, why have ye
taryed so longe frome me? Alas, thys wounde on youre hede hath
caught overmuch coulde!'

And anone they rowed fromward the londe, and Sir Bedyvere 2045
behylde all tho ladyes go frowarde hym.

Than Sir Bedwere cryed and seyde, 'A, my lorde Arthur, what
shall becom of me, now ye go frome me and leve me here alone
amonge myne enemyes?'

2018 *jouperté*, jeopardy   *but if*, unless
2019-20 *myne owne hondis*, with my own hands
2023 *gyrdyll*, sword-belt
2025 *cleyght*, grasped . . . firmly
2030 *hens*, away (lit. 'hence')
2033-4 *evyn faste by*, right there by
2034 *hoved*, waited   *barge*, boat
2045 *fromward*, away from (cf. *towards*)

'Comforte thyselff,' seyde the kynge, 'and do as well as thou 2050
mayste, for in me ys no truste for to truste in. For I muste into the
vale of Avylyon to hele me of my grevous wounde. And if thou
here nevermore of me, pray for my soule!'

But ever the quene and ladyes wepte and shryked, that hit was
pité to hyre. And as sone as Sir Bedwere had loste the syght of the 2055
barge he wepte and wayled, and so toke the foreste and wente all
that nyght.

And in the mornyng he was ware, betwyxte two holtis hore, of
a chapell and an ermytage. Than was Sir Bedwere fayne, and
thyder he wente, and whan he cam into the chapell he saw where 2060
lay an ermyte grovelynge on all four, faste there by a tumbe was
newe gravyn. Whan the ermyte saw Sir Bedyvere he knewe hym
well, for he was but lytyll tofore Bysshop of Caunturbery that Sir
Mordred fleamed.

'Sir,' seyde Sir Bedyvere, 'what man ys there here entyred that 2065
ye pray so faste fore?'

'Fayre sunne,' seyde the ermyte, 'I wote nat veryly but by
demynge. But thys same nyght, at mydnyght, here cam a numbir
of ladyes and brought here a dede corse and prayde me to entyre
hym. And here they offird an hondred tapers, and they gaff me a 2070
thousande besauntes.'

'Alas!' seyde Sir Bedyvere, 'that was my lorde Kynge Arthur,
whych lyethe here gravyn in thys chapell.'

Than Sir Bedwere sowned, and whan he awooke he prayde
the ermyte that he myght abyde with hym stylle, there to lyve 2075
with fastynge and prayers. 'For from hens woll I never go,' seyde
Sir Bedyvere, 'be my wyll, but all the dayes of my lyff here to pray
for my lorde Arthur.'

'Sir, ye ar wellcom to me,' seyde the ermyte, 'for I know you
bettir than ye wene that I do: for ye ar Sir Bedwere the Bolde, 2080

2052 *Avylyon*, Avalon (C)
2056 *toke*, took to   *wente*, walked (C)
2058 *was ware*, became aware of   *holtis hore*, bare gray woods
2059 *fayne*, glad (C)
2061 *there by*, where by   *tumbe*, grave
2062 *new gravyn*, newly dug
2064 *fleamed*, put to flight, made go into hiding
2067-8 *by demynge*, by guess-work
2069 *entyre*, bury
2070 *hym*, it   *tapers*, candles
2071 *besauntes*, bezants (C)
2073 *gravyn*, buried
2077 *lyff here to pray*, life [will remain] here to pray: the verb is understood.

and the full noble duke Sir Lucan de Butlere was your brother.'

Than Sir Bedwere tolde the ermyte all as ye have harde tofore, and so he belaffte with the ermyte that was beforehande Bysshop of Caunturbyry. And there Sir Bedwere put uppon hym poure clothys, and served the ermyte full lowly in fastyng and in prayers. 2085

Thus of Arthur I fynde no more wrytten in bokis that bene auctorysed, nothir more of the verry sertaynté of hys dethe harde I never rede, but thus was he lad away in a shyp wherein were three quenys: that one was Kynge Arthur syster, Quene Morgan le Fay, the tother was the Quene of North Galis, and the thirde 2090 was the Quene of the Waste Londis. Also there was Dame Nynyve, the chyff lady of the laake, whych had wedded Sir Pellyas, the good knyght; and thys lady had done muche for Kynge Arthure. (And thys Dame Nynyve wolde never suffir Sir Pelleas to be in no place where he shulde be in daungere of hys 2095 lyff, and so he lyved unto the uttermuste of hys dayes with her in grete reste.)

Now more of the deth of Kynge Arthur coude I never fynde, but that thes ladyes brought hym to hys grave and such one was entyred there, whych the ermyte bare wytnes of that sometyme was 2100 Bysshop of Caunturbyry; but yet the ermyte knew nat in sertayne that he was veryly the body of Kynge Arthur. For thys tale Sir Bedwere, a knyght of the Table Rounde, made hit to be wrytten. 2105

Yet som men say in many partys of Inglonde that Kynge Arthure ys nat dede, but had by the wyll of Oure Lorde Jesu into another place; and men say that he shall com agayne, and he shall wynne the Holy Crosse. Yet I woll nat say that hit shall be so, but rather I wolde sey: here in thys worlde he chaunged hys 2110 lyff. And many men say that there ys wrytten uppon the tumbe thys vers: 'Hic iacet Arthurus, Rex quondam Rexque futurus.'

And thus leve I here Sir Bedyvere with the ermyte that dwelled

---

2083 belaffte, remained
2088 auctorysed, authorised, authoritative
2088-9 harde I never rede, I never heard . . . read (C)
2090-5 See C.
2101 whych, understand 'as'
2103 he, it   thys tale (C)   For, But
2109 wynne the Holy Crosse, recapture the True Cross (C)
2112 Hic iacet Arthurus, Rex quondam Rexque futurus, Here lies Arthur, the once and future king

that tyme in a chapell besydes Glassynbyry, and there was hys
ermytage. And so they lyved in prayers and fastynges and grete 2115
abstynaunce.

And whan Quene Gwenyver undirstood that Kynge Arthure
was dede and all the noble knyghtes, Sir Mordred and all the remanaunte, than she stale away with fyve ladyes with her, and so
she wente to Amysbyry. And there she lete make herselff a nunne, 2120
and wered whyght clothys and blak, and grete penaunce she toke
uppon her, as ever ded synfull woman in thys londe. And never
creature coude make her myry, but ever she lyved in fastynge,
prayers, and almes-dedis, that all maner of people mervayled
how vertuously she was chaunged.   2125

V

Now leve we the quene in Amysbery, a nunne in whyght clothys
and blak—and there she was abbas and rular, as reson wolde—
and now turne we from her and speke we of Sir Launcelot du
Lake, that whan he harde in hys countrey that Sir Mordred was
crowned kynge in Inglonde and made warre ayenst Kyng Arthur, 2130
hys owne fadir, and wolde lette hym to londe in hys owne londe
(also hit was tolde hym how Sir Mordred had leyde a syge aboute
the Towre of London, bycause the quene wold nat wedde hym),
than was Sir Launcelot wrothe oute of mesure and seyde to hys
kynnesmen, 'Alas! that double traytoure, Sir Mordred, now me 2135
repentith that ever he escaped my hondys, for much shame hath
he done unto my lorde Arthure. For I fele by thys dolefull letter
that Sir Gawayne sente me, on whose soule Jesu have mercy,
that my lorde Arthur ys full harde bestad. Alas,' seyde Sir Launcelot, 'that ever I shulde lyve to hyre of that moste noble kynge 2140

2118-19 *remanaunte*, rest
2119 *stale*, stole
2120 *lete make herse lff*, had herself made
2121 *wered*, wore   *whyght clothys and blak* (C)
2123 *myry*, merry (C)
2127 *abbas*, abbes   *as reson wolde*, naturally
2131 *lette hym to londe*, prevent him from landing   *hys owne*, i.e. Arthur's
2134 *wrothe oute of mesure*, furiously angry
2135 *double traytoure* (C)

that made me knyght thus to be oversette with hys subjette in hys owne realme!

'And this dolefull lettir that my lorde Sir Gawayne hath sente me afore hys dethe, praynge me to se hys tumbe, wyte you well hys doleffull wordes shall never go frome my harte. For he was a 2145 full noble knyght as ever was born! And in an unhappy owre was I born that ever I shulde have that myssehappe to sle firste Sir Gawayne, Sir Gaherys, the good knyght, and myne owne frynde Sir Gareth that was a full noble knyght. Now, alas, I may sey I am unhappy that ever I shulde do thus; and yet, alas, myght I never 2150 have hap to sle that traytoure, Sir Mordred!'

'Now leve youre complayntes,' seyde Sir Bors, 'and firste revenge you of the dethe of Sir Gawayne, on whos soule Jesu have mercy! And hit woll be well done that ye se hys tumbe, and secundly that ye revenge my lorde Arthur and my lady Quene 2155 Gwenyver.'

'I thanke you,' seyde Sir Launcelot, 'for ever ye woll my worshyp.'

Than they made hem redy in all haste that myght be, with shyppis and galyes, with hym and hys oste to pas in to Inglonde. 2160 And so he passyd over the see tyl he cam to Dover, and there he landed with seven kyngis, and the numbir was hedeous to beholde.

Than Sir Launcelot spyrred of men of Dover where was the kynge becom. And anone the people tolde hym how he was slayne and Sir Mordred to, with an hondred thousand that dyed uppon 2165 a day; and how Sir Mordred gaff Kynge Arthur the first batayle there at hys londynge, and there was good Sir Gawayne slayne; and uppon the morne Sir Mordred faught with the kynge on Baram Downe, and there the kyng put Sir Mordred to the wars.

'Alas,' seyde Sir Launcelot, 'thys is the hevyest tydyngis that 2170 ever cam to my harte! Now, fayre sirres,' seyde Sir Launcelot, 'shew me the tumbe of Sir Gawayne.'

And anone he was brought into the Castel of Dover, and so

2141 *with*, by
2143 *doleful*, sad
2146 *unhappy*, unfortunate
2147 *firste*, in the first place (i.e. on this list, not chronologically)
2157 *woll*, think of (lit. 'wish')
2162 *hedeous*, hideous
2163 *spyrred*, asked
2163–4 *where was . . . becom*, where . . . had got to
2164 *anone*, at once
2169 See C.

they shewed hym the tumbe. Than Sir Launcelot kneled downe
by the tumbe and wepte, and prayde hartely for hys soule. And 2175
that nyght he lete make a dole, and all that wolde com of the
towne or of the contrey they had as much fleyssh and fysshe and
wyne and ale, and every man and woman he dalt to twelve pence,
com whoso wolde. Thus with hys owne honde dalte he thys
money, in a mournyng gown; and ever he wepte hartely and 2180
prayde the people to pray for the soule of Sir Gawayne.

And on the morn all the prystes and clarkes that myght be
gotyn in the contrey and in the town were there, and sange
Massis of Requiem. And there offird first Sir Launcelot, and he
offird an hondred pounde, and than the seven kynges offirde, and 2185
every of them offirde fourty pounde. Also there was a thousand
knyghtes, and every of them offirde a pounde; and the offeryng
dured fro the morne to nyght. And there Sir Launcelot lay two
nyghtes uppon hys tumbe in prayers and in dolefull wepynge.

Than on the thirde day Sir Launcelot called the kyngis, deukes, 2190
and erlis, with the barownes and all hys noble knyghtes, and seyde
thus: 'My fayre lordis, I thanke you all of youre comynge into
thys contrey with me. But wyte you well all, we are com to late,
and that shall repente me whyle I lyve, but ayenste deth may no
man rebell. But sytthyn hit ys so,' seyde Sir Launcelot, 'I woll my- 2195
selffe ryde and syke my lady Quene Gwenyver. For, as I here sey,
she hath had grete payne and muche disease, and I here say that
she ys fledde into the weste. And therefore ye all shall abyde me
here, and but if I com agayne within thes fyftene dayes, take youre
shyppis and youre felyship and departe into youre countrey, for I 2200
woll do as I sey you.'

Than cam Sir Bors and seyde, 'My lorde, Sir Launcelot, what

---

²¹⁷⁵ *hartely*, earnestly
²¹⁷⁶ *lete make a dole*, gave alms (C)
²¹⁷⁶⁻⁸ See C.
²¹⁷⁸ *dalt*, gave
²¹⁷⁹ *whoso*, whosoever
²¹⁸² *clarkes*, clerks (i.e. clerics; see C)
²¹⁸⁴ *Massis of Requiem*, Requiem Masses (C)
²¹⁸⁹ *hys*, i.e. Gawain's
²¹⁹² *of*, for
²¹⁹⁴⁻⁵ See C.
²¹⁹⁶ *here*, hear
²¹⁹⁷ *disease*, trouble (not 'disease')
²¹⁹⁹ *but if*, unless

thynke ye for to do, now for to ryde in thys realme? Wyte you well ye shall do fynde feaw fryndis.'

'Be as be may as for that,' seyde Sir Launcelot, 'kepe you stylle 2205 here, for I woll furthe on my journey, and no man nor chylde shall go with me.'

So hit was no boote to stryve, but he departed and rode west-irly; and there he sought a seven or eyght dayes. And at the laste he cam to a nunry, and anone Quene Gwenyver was ware of Sir 2210 Launcelot as he walked in the cloyster. And anone as she saw hym there, she sowned thryse, that all ladyes and jantyllwomen had worke inowghe to hold the quene frome the erthe.

So whan she myght speke she called her ladyes and jantill-women to her, and than she sayde thus: 'Ye mervayle, fayre 2215 ladyes, why I make thys fare. Truly,' she seyde, 'hit ys for the syght of yondir knyght that yondir stondith. Wherefore I pray you alle calle hym hyddir to me.'

Than Sir Launcelot was brought before her; than the quene seyde to all tho ladyes, 'Thorow thys same man and me hath all 2220 thys warre be wrought, and the deth of the moste nobelest knyghtes of the worlde; for thorow oure love that we have loved togydir ys my moste noble lorde slayne. Therefore, Sir Launcelot, wyte thou well I am sette in suche a plyght to gete my soule hele. And yet I truste, thorow Goddis grace and thorow Hys Passion 2225 of Hys woundis wyde, that aftir my deth I may have a syght of the blyssed face of Cryste Jesu, and on Doomesday to sytte on Hys ryght syde; for as synfull as ever I was, now ar seyntes in hevyn. And therefore, Sir Launcelot, I requyre the and beseche the hartily, for all the love that ever was betwyxt us, that thou never 2230 se me no more in the visayge; and I commaunde the, on Goddis behalff, that thou forsake my company. And to thy kyngedom

---

2204 *fryndis*, friends
2205 Translate: 'Be that as it may' (C)
2206 *woll furthe*, will [go] off
2206-7 Translate: 'neither man nor boy shall'
2208 *boote*, use (lit. 'profit')
2210 *nunry*, convent
2213 *worke* (C)
2216 *make thys fare*, am behaving like this
2224 *plyght*, situation   *to*, understand 'as will'
2225 *yet*, even as late as this (C)
2227 *Doomesday*, the Day of Judgement
2228 *as synfull*, [people] as sinful
2231 *in the visayge*, face to face (lit. 'in the face')
2231-2 *on Goddis behalff*, in the name of God (C)

loke thou turne agayne, and kepe well thy realme frome warre
and wrake, for as well as I have loved the heretofore, myne harte
woll nat serve now to se the; for thorow the and me ys the floure 2235
of kyngis and knyghtes destroyed. And therefore, Sir Launcelot,
go thou to thy realme, and there take the a wyff, and lyff with hir
wyth joy and blys. And I pray the hartely to pray for me to the
Everlastynge Lorde that I may amende my mysselyvyng.'

'Now, my swete madame,' seyde Sir Launcelot, 'wolde ye that 2240
I shuld turne agayne unto my contrey and there to wedde a
lady? Nay, madame, wyte you well that shall I never do, for I
shall never be so false unto you of that I have promysed. But the
selff-same desteny that ye have takyn you to, I woll take me to,
for to please Jesu, and ever for you I caste me specially to pray.' 2245

'A, Sir Launcelot, if ye woll do so and holde thy promyse! But
I may never beleve you,' seyde the quene, 'but that ye woll turne
to the worlde agayne.'

'Well, madame,' seyde he, 'ye say as hit pleasith you, for yet
wyste ye me never false of my promyse. And God deffende but that 2250
I shulde forsake the worlde as ye have done! For in the queste of
the Sankgreall I had that tyme forsaykyn the vanytees of the
worlde, had nat youre love bene. And if I had done so at that tyme
with my harte, wylle, and thought, I had passed all the knyghtes
that ever were in the Sankgreall excepte Syr Galahad, my sone. 2255
And therfore, lady, sythen ye have taken you to perfeccion, I
must nedys take me to perfection, of ryght. For I take recorde of
God, in you I have had myn erthly joye, and yf I had founden
you now so dysposed, I had caste me to have had you into myn
owne royame. But sythen I fynde you thus desposed, I ensure you 2260
faythfully, I wyl ever take me to penaunce and praye whyle my
lyf lasteth, yf that I may fynde ony heremyte, other graye or
whyte, that wyl receyve me. Wherfore, madame, I praye you kysse
me, and never no more.'

'Nay,' sayd the quene, 'that shal I never do, but absteyne you 2265
from suche werkes.'

2233 *loke*, see [that]
2242-3 See C.
2249 *for* This must be taken in the (most unusual) sense of 'although': cf. l. 2103
2250 *deffende*, forbid
2255 *Sankgreall* (C)
2257-8 *of ryght*, in justice *take recorde of God*, take God to witness
2260 *royame*, realm (Fr. *royaume*)
2262-3 *other graye or whyte*, either grey or white (C)
2265 *absteyne you*, abstain (reflexive imperative)

And they departed; but there was never so harde an herted man but he wold have wepte to see the dolour that they made, for there was lamentacyon as they had be stungyn wyth sperys, and many tymes they swouned. And the ladyes bare the quene to hir 2270 chambre.

And Syr Launcelot awok, and went and took his hors, and rode al that day and al nyght in a forest, wepyng. And atte last he was ware of an ermytage and a chappel stode betwyxte two clyffes, and than he herde a lytel belle rynge to masse. And thyder he 2275 rode and alyght, and teyed his hors to the gate, and herd masse. And he that sange masse was the Bysshop of Caunterburye.

Bothe the bysshop and Sir Bedwer knewe Syr Launcelot, and they spake togyders after masse. But whan Syr Bedwere had tolde his tale al hole, Syr Launcelottes hert almost braste for sorowe, 2280 and Sir Launcelot threwe hys armes abrode, and sayd, 'Alas! Who may truste thys world?'

And than he knelyd doun on his knee and prayed the bysshop to shryve hym and assoyle hym; and than he besought the bysshop that he myght be hys brother. Than the bysshop sayd, 2285 'I wyll gladly,' and there he put an habyte upon Syr Launcelot. And there he servyd God day and nyght with prayers and fastynges.

Thus the grete hoost abode at Dover. And than Sir Lyonel toke fyftene lordes with hym and rode to London to seke Sir 2290 Launcelot; and there Syr Lyonel was slayn and many of his lordes. Thenne Syr Bors de Ganys made the grete hoost for to goo hoome ageyn, and Syr Boors, Syr Ector de Maris, Syr Blamour, Syr Bleoberys, with moo other of Syr Launcelottes kynne, toke on hem to ryde al Englond overthwart and endelonge to 2295 seek Syr Launcelot.

So Syr Bors by fortune rode so longe tyl he came to the same chapel where Syr Launcelot was. And so Syr Bors herde a lytel belle knylle that range to masse, and there he alyght and herde masse. And whan masse was doon, the bysshop, Syr Launcelot 2300 and Sir Bedwere came to Syr Bors, and whan Syr Bors saw Sir

---

2267 *departed*, separated
2269 *stungyn*, pierced (lit. 'stung')
2281-2 See C.
2284 *shryve hym*, hear his confession   *assoyle*, absolve
2286 *an habyte*, a habit
2295 *overthwart and endelonge*, from side to side and from end to end
2299 *knylle*, ring (cf. *knell*)

Launcelot in that maner clothyng, than he preyed the bysshop that he myght be in the same sewte. And so there was an habyte put upon hym, and there he lyved in prayers and fastyng.

And wythin halfe a yere there was come Syr Galyhud, Syr 2305 Galyhodyn, Sir Blamour, Syr Bleoberis, Syr Wyllyars, Syr Clarrus, and Sir Gahallantyne. So al these seven noble knyghtes there abode styll. And whan they sawe Syr Launcelot had taken hym to suche perfeccion they had no lust to departe but toke such an habyte as he had.   2310

Thus they endured in grete penaunce syx yere. And than Syr Launcelot took th'abyte of preesthode of the bysshop, and a twelve-monthe he sange masse. And there was none of these other knyghtes but they redde in bookes and holpe for to synge masse, and range bellys, and dyd lowly al maner of servyce. And 2315 soo their horses wente where they wolde, for they toke no regarde of no worldly rychesses; for whan they sawe Syr Launcelot endure suche penaunce in prayers and fastynges they toke no force what payne they endured, for to see the nobleste knyght of the world take such abstynaunce that he waxed ful lene.   2320

And thus upon a nyght there came a vysyon to Syr Launcelot and charged hym, in remyssyon of his synnes, to haste hym unto Almysbury: 'And by thenne thou come there, thou shalt fynde Quene Guenever dede. And therfore take thy felowes with the, and purvey them of an hors-bere, and fetche thou the cors of hir, 2325 and burye hir by her husbond, the noble Kyng Arthur.' So this avysyon came to Launcelot thryse in one nyght.

Than Syr Launcelot rose up or day and tolde the heremyte. 'It were wel done,' sayd the heremyte, 'that ye made you redy and that ye dyshobeye not the avysyon.' Than Syr Launcelot 2330 toke his eyght felowes with hym, and on fote they yede from Glastynburye to Almysburye, the whyche is lytel more than thirty myle, and thyder they came within two dayes, for they were wayke and feble to goo.

2303 *sewte*, suit, kind
2305-7 See C.
2314 *they*, he
2320 *waxed ful lene*, grew very thin
2322 *in remyssyon of his synnes*, for the remission of his sins (C)
2323 *by thenne*, by the time that
2325 *purvey them of*, arrange for them to have   *hors-bere*, horse-litter
2328 *or*, before
2331 *yede*, went
2332-3 See C.
2334 *wayke*, weak   *to goo*, for walking

And whan Syr Launcelot was come to Almysburye within the 2335
nunerye, Quene Guenever deyed but halfe an oure afore. And
the ladyes tolde Syr Launcelot that Quene Guenever tolde hem
al or she passyd, that Syr Launcelot had ben preest nere a twelve-
monthe: 'and hyder he cometh as faste as he may to fetche my
cors, and besyde my lord Kyng Arthur he shal berye me.' Where- 2340
fore the quene sayd in heryng of hem al, 'I beseche Almyghty God
that I may never have power to see Syr Launcelot wyth my
worldly eyen!'

'And thus,' said al the ladyes, 'was ever hir prayer these two
dayes tyl she was dede.'   2345

Than Syr Launcelot sawe hir vysage, but he wepte not
gretelye, but syghed. And so he dyd al the observaunce of the servyce hymself, bothe the Dyryge and on the morne he sange masse.
And there was ordeyned an hors-bere, and so wyth an hondred
torches ever brennyng aboute the cors of the quene, and ever Syr 2350
Launcelot with his eyght felowes wente aboute the hors-bere,
syngyng and redyng many an holy oryson, and frankensens upon
the corps encensed.

Thus Syr Launcelot and his eyght felowes wente on foot from
Almysburye unto Glastynburye; and whan they were come to 2355
the chapel and the hermytage, there she had a Dyryge wyth grete
devocyon. And on the morne the heremyte that somtyme was
Bysshop of Canterburye sange the Masse of Requyem wyth grete
devocyon, and Syr Launcelot was the fyrst that offeryd, and than
als his eyght felowes. And than she was wrapped in cered clothe 2360
of Raynes, from the toppe to the too, in thirtyfolde; and after she
was put in a webbe of leed, and than in a coffyn of marbyl.

And whan she was put in th' erth Syr Launcelot swouned, and
laye longe stylle, whyle the hermyte came and awaked hym, and
sayd, 'Ye be to blame, for ye dysplese God with suche maner of 2365
sorow-makyng.'

2336 *deyed*, had died
2347–8 *dyd al the observaunce of the servyce*, performed all the ceremonies
2348 *Dyryge*, Dirige (C)
2350 *and* is redundant
2352 *oryson*, prayer
2353 *encensed* is a verb; translate 'and incensed the body with frankincense'
2360 *als*, as well   *cered*, waxed
2360–1 *clothe of Raynes*, fine linen (C)
2361 *from the toppe to the too*, from head to foot
2362 *webbe of leed*, sheet of lead
2364 *whyle*, until

'Truly,' sayd Syr Launcelot, 'I trust I do not dysplese God, for He knoweth myn entente: for my sorow was not, nor is not, for ony rejoysyng of synne. But my sorow may never have ende, for whan I remembre of hir beaulté and of hir noblesse, that was 2370 bothe wyth hyr kyng and wyth hyr, so whan I sawe his corps and hir corps so lye togyders, truly myn herte wold not serve to susteyne my careful body. Also whan I remembre me how by my defaute and myn orgule and my pryde that they were bothe layed ful lowe, that were pereles that ever was lyvyng of Cristen people, 2375 wyt you wel,' sayd Syr Launcelot, 'this remembred, of their kyndenes and myn unkyndenes, sanke so to myn herte that I myght not susteyne myself.' So the Frensshe book maketh mencyon.

Thenne Syr Launcelot never after ete but lytel mete, nor 2380 dranke, tyl he was dede, for than he seekened more and more and dryed and dwyned awaye. For the bysshop nor none of his felowes myght not make hym to ete and lytel he dranke, that he was waxen by a kybbet shorter than he was, that the peple coude not knowe hym. For evermore, day and nyght, he prayed, but 2385 somtyme he slombred a broken slepe. Ever he was lyeng grovelyng on the tombe of Kyng Arthur and Quene Guenever, and there was no comforte that the bysshop, nor Syr Bors, nor none of his felowes coude make hym, it avaylled not.

Soo wythin syx wekys after, Syr Launcelot fyl seek and laye in 2390 his bedde. And thenne he sente for the bysshop that there was heremyte, and al his trewe felowes. Than Syr Launcelot sayd wyth drery steven, 'Syr bysshop, I praye you gyve to me al my ryghtes that longeth to a Crysten man.'

'It shal not nede you,' sayd the heremyte and al his felowes. 'It 2395 is but hevynesse of your blood. Ye shal be wel mended by the grace of God to-morne.'

2367–9 See C.
2373 *careful*, sorrowful
2374 *defaute*, deficiencies, inadequacy   *orgule*, arrogance (Fr. *orgueil*)   *that* is redundant
2378–9 See C.
2380 *mete*, food
2382 *dryed*, shrivelled up   *dwyned*, wasted away
2384 *kybbet*, cubit, eighteen inches
2385 *knowe*, recognise
2390 *fyl seek*, fell sick
2393 *drery steven*, sad voice
2394 *ryghtes*, rites   *longeth*, belong
2395 *nede*, be necessary

'My fayr lordes,' sayd Syr Launcelot, 'wyt you wel my careful body wyll into th' erthe, I have warnyng more than now I wyl say. Therfore gyve me my ryghtes.'   2400

So whan he was howselyd and enelyd and had al that a Crysten man ought to have, he prayed the bysshop that his felowes myght bere his body to Joyous Garde. (Somme men say it was Anwyk, and somme men say it was Bamborow.) 'Howbeit,' sayd Syr Launcelot, 'me repenteth sore, but I made myn avowe somtyme 2405 that in Joyous Garde I wold be buryed. And bycause of brekyng of myn avowe, I praye you al, lede me thyder.'

Than there was wepyng and wryngyng of handes among his felowes.

So at a seson of the nyght they al wente to theyr beddes, for 2410 they alle laye in one chambre. And so after mydnyght, ayenst day, the bysshop that was hermyte, as he laye in his bedde aslepe, he fyl upon a grete laughter. And therwyth al the felyshyp awoke and came to the bysshop and asked hym what he eyled.

'A, Jesu mercy!' sayd the bysshop, 'why dyd ye awake me? I 2415 was never in al my lyf so mery and so wel at ease.'

'Wherfore?' sayd Syr Bors.

'Truly,' sayd the bysshop, 'here was Syr Launcelot with me, with mo angellis than ever I sawe men in one day. And I sawe the angellys heve up Syr Launcelot unto heven, and the yates of 2420 heven opened ayenst hym.'

'It is but dretchyng of swevens,' sayd Syr Bors, 'for I doubte not Syr Launcelot ayleth nothynge but good.'

'It may wel be,' sayd the bysshop. 'Goo ye to his bedde, and than shall ye preve the soth.'   2425

So whan Syr Bors and his felowes came to his bedde they founde hym starke dede; and he laye as he had smyled, and the swettest savour aboute hym that ever they felte. Than was there wepynge

---

2401 *howselyd and enelyd*, given Holy Communion and the Last Sacrament (C)
2403–4 *Anwyk . . . Bamborow*, Alnwick . . . Bamburgh (C)
2404 *Howbeit*, Although
2406 *bycause of*, for fear of
2407 *lede*, carry (not 'lead')
2410 *a seson*, a [certain] time
2411 *ayenst*, towards
2414 *what he eyled*, what ailed him, what was the matter with him
2420 *heve*, carry (lit. 'heave')   *yates*, gates
2422 *dretchyng*, deceitfulness   *swevens*, dreams
2425 *preve the soth*, discover the truth
2427 *as he had*, as if he had
2428 *savour*, smell

and wryngyng of handes, and the grettest dole they made that
ever made men.   2430

And on the morne the bysshop dyd his Masse of Requyem, and
after the bysshop and al the nine knyghtes put Syr Launcelot in
the same hors-bere that Quene Guenevere was layed in tofore
that she was buryed. And soo the bysshop and they al togyders
wente wyth the body of Syr Launcelot dayly, tyl they came to 2435
Joyous Garde; and ever they had an hondred torches brennyng
aboute hym.

And so within fyftene dayes they came to Joyous Garde. And
there they layed his corps in the body of the quere, and sange and
redde many saulters and prayers over hym and aboute hym. And 2440
ever his vysage was layed open and naked, that al folkes myght
beholde hym; for suche was the custom in tho dayes that al men
of worshyp shold so lye wyth open vysage tyl that they were
buryed.

And ryght thus as they were at theyr servyce, there came Syr 2445
Ector de Maris, that had seven yere sought al Englond, Scotlond,
and Walys, sekyng his brother Syr Launcelot. And whan Syr
Ector herde suche noyse and lyghte in the quyre of Joyous Garde,
he alyght and put his hors from hym and came into the quyre.
And there he sawe men synge and wepe, and al they knewe Syr 2450
Ector, but he knewe not them.

Than wente Syr Bors unto Syr Ector and tolde hym how there
laye his brother, Syr Launcelot, dede. And than Syr Ector
threwe hys shelde, swerde and helme from hym, and whan he be-
helde Syr Launcelottes vysage he fyl doun in a swoun. And whan 2455
he waked it were harde ony tonge to telle the doleful complayntes
that he made for his brother.

'A, Launcelot!' he sayd, 'thou were hede of al Crysten
knyghtes! And now I dare say,' sayd Syr Ector, 'thou Sir Launcelot, there thou lyest, that thou were never matched of erthely 2460
knyghtes hande. And thou were the curtest knyght that ever bare
shelde! And thou were the truest frende to thy lovar that ever be-

---

2431 *dyd*, said
2438 See C.
2439 *quere*, choir [of the church]
2440 *saulters*, psalms (lit. 'psalters')
2441 *layed open*, exposed
2442-4 See C.
2458 See C.
2461 *curtest*, most courteous
2462 *frende*, see 'Lancelot', l. 2075*n*

strade hors, and thou were the trewest lover, of a synful man, that
ever loved woman, and thou were the kyndest man that ever
strake wyth swerde. And thou were the godelyest persone that 2465
ever cam emonge prees of knyghtes, and thou was the mekest man
and the jentyllest that ever ete in halle emonge ladyes, and thou
were the sternest knyght to thy mortal foo that ever put spere in
the reeste.'

Than there was wepyng and dolour out of mesure.   2470

Thus they kepte Syr Launcelots corps on-lofte fyftene dayes,
and than they buryed it with grete devocyon. And than at leyser
they wente al with the Bysshop of Canterburye to his ermytage,
and there they were togyder more than a monthe.

Than Syr Constantyn that was Syr Cadores sone of Cornwayl 2475
was chosen kyng of Englond, and he was a ful noble knyght, and
worshypfully he rulyd this royame. And than thys Kyng Constantyn sent for the Bysshop of Caunterburye, for he herde saye
where he was. And so he was restored unto his bysshopryche and
lefte that ermytage, and Syr Bedwere was there ever stylle here- 2480
myte to his lyves ende.

Than Syr Bors de Ganys, Syr Ector de Maris, Syr Gahalantyne,
Syr Galyhud, Sir Galyhodyn, Syr Blamour, Syr Bleoberys, Syr
Wyllyars le Valyaunt, Syr Clarrus of Cleremounte, al these
knyghtes drewe them to theyr contreyes. Howbeit Kyng Con- 2485
stantyn wold have had them wyth hym, but they wold not abyde
in this royame. And there they al lyved in their cuntreyes as holy
men.

And somme Englysshe bookes maken mencyon that they wente
never oute of Englond after the deth of Syr Launcelot—but that 2490
was but favour of makers. For the Frensshe book maketh mencyon, and is auctorysed, that Syr Bors, Syr Ector, Syr Blamour,
and Syr Bleoberis wente into the Holy Lande, thereas Jesu Cryst
was quycke and deed. And anone as they had stablysshed theyr
londes (for, the book saith, so Syr Launcelot commaunded them 2495

2465 *godelyest*, most excellent (from *goodly*, not *godly*)
2471 *kepte*, watched over   *on-lofte*, exposed (lit. 'on high')
2472 *at leyser*, taking their time (lit. 'at leisure')
2475-7 See C.
2485 *drewe them*, went   *Howbeit*, Although
2491 *favour of makers*, partiality of authors
2491-8 See C.
2493 *thereas*, where
2494 *quycke*, alive   *stablysshed*, settled

for to do or ever he passyd oute of thys world), there these foure
knyghtes dyd many batayles upon the myscreantes or Turkes.
And there they dyed upon a Good Fryday for Goddes sake.

Here is the ende of The Hoole Book of Kynge Arthur and of His
Noble Knyghtes of the Rounde Table, *that whan they were holé* 2500
*togyders there was ever an hondred and fifty. And here is the ende of 'Le
Morte Darthur'.*

*I praye you all jentylmen and jentylwymmen that redeth this book of
Arthur and his knyghtes from the begynnyng to the endynge, praye for me
whyle I am on lyve that God sende me good delyveraunce. And whan I am* 2505
deed, I praye you all praye for my soule.

*For this book was ended
the ninth yere of the reygne of Kyng Edward the Fourth,
by Syr Thomas Maleoré, Knyght,
as Jesu helpe hym for Hys grete myght,* 2510
as he is the servaunt of Jesu bothe day and nyght.

2497 *myscreantes*, infidels
2498 See C.
2508 See C.

Commentary

Lancelot and Guenivere

I

9. Malory's French source, the *Mort Artu*, reports Lancelot's return to Guenivere. Lancelot's incomplete success in the Grail-quest and the reason for it will be Malory's additions.

17. *prevy draughtis* The metaphor is from surreptitious drinking: not a laudatory comparison.

39. This is not a confession of hypocrisy. Lancelot is talking about things that he had concealed from himself as well as from others during the Grail-quest. Medieval men were well aware of many psychological processes they had no special names for. We would say, 'If I had not had an unconscious desire . . .'

55. The *that* that would be hateful is seeing Guenivere dishonoured.

71. This construction, *that* + subjunctive, has the force of a command.

79. Double comparatives and superlatives were acceptable even in literary English until the eighteenth century.

86. *Brother* is used with affectionate carelessness. Ector is Lancelot's brother; Bors is not. Lancelot's relationship to Bors is one of the loose ends of the *Morte Darthur*: Malory sometimes calls them cousins – thinking of their fathers as brothers – and sometimes uncle and nephew. But whatever the degree of kinship, Lancelot is always the leader of all his father King Ban's kindred, Bors among them.

104. *wyte you well* gives us the voice of the narrator himself for a moment in an emphatic phrase traditional in oral story-telling. Writers used these phrases partly because they were aware that most people would still have books read aloud to them rather than reading silently and alone. Cf. ll. 1277–8 and 'Morte', ll. 2088–9, 2126.

As the booke seythe Neither the *Mort Artu* nor Malory's English source, *Le Morte Arthur*, says this.

112–20. The guests at Guenivere's dinner form an important part of the aristocracy of Arthur's kingdom. They include the king's five nephews, his foster-brother Kay, seven of Lancelot's kinsmen, Palomides and Safyr from among Tristram's friends, and Pynell, one of Lamorak's cousins. In front of this assembly, not even the queen can commit murder and get away with it. Their feelings for one another are very varied, and have been set out in widely separated parts of the *Morte Darthur*. There is hatred between them as well as love: the (temporarily latent) hatred between King Lot's and King Ban's families that will cause the downfall of the Round Table, and the present cause of strife, the hatred between King Lot's and King Pellinore's families. Lot's sons Gawain, Gaheris and Aggravayne, and their half-brother Mordred ambushed Pellinore's son Lamorak, attacked him from all sides, stabbed him in the back, and mutilated his corpse.

142. These direct, immediate and total emotions are typical of Malory's characters.

146. This peculiar sense, not uncommon in Malory, is probably simply overwriting. It is probably only coincidence that the Fr. equivalent, *car*, was used or abused in the same way in the Middle Ages.

155. Mador is starting legal proceedings: *appeled* (lit. 'appealed') is the technical term for the kind of accusation leading to trial by battle. There were several kinds of trial by battle, and the one Malory has in mind was called the duel of chivalry. The *Mort Artu* was written before the duel of chivalry had reached its full development, and Malory has altered the story to bring it closer to the law as he knew it, although at the cost of one or two difficulties. Because he was writing for people who knew the process well, he takes much of it for granted.

The first stage was to formulate the challenge, agreeing precisely what to disagree about. This is more clearly seen in a later trial by battle than here, because here there is no one to dispute the challenge. (Compare the whole of this trial with the whole of the later one, ll. 2237–2478.) Guenivere cannot fight, her guests will not fight for her, and her husband is disqualified because he must, as King, preside over the Court of Chivalry that will try the case. When the terms of the challenge were agreed, the parties went before the court, where the trial formally began with the challenger repeating the challenge (orally or in writing, depending on the case), and the defendant denying it. As in other courts, the king's powers were normally exercised by a deputy, but the king could resume them if he wished. In the Court of Chivalry, his deputy would be the Constable of England, the country's highest-ranking military officer. But Mador demands justice directly from the king, and Arthur accepts the case.

When a case was presented, the court had first to decide if it had jurisdiction. Among other limitations, it was empowered principally to decide cases of treason, which did not include poisoning the king's subjects. Malory explains this anomaly by saying that in King Arthur's days *treson* had a broader meaning in law (ll. 164–5). When the court had established that the case was a proper one for it to try, it would make sure that both parties were resolute, set a time and place for battle, and direct the Constable, with the assistance of the Marshal of

England, to supervise the arrangements: the legal formalities, the fighting, and the degradation and execution – should he survive the combat – of the defeated party.

Arthur's conflicting feelings as judge and husband leave him in a state of shock, as the slight repetitiousness and confused connectives of his first speech show. Nevertheless, his decisions are quick and fair. Malory is no great lover of ceremonial and takes all the practical arrangements for granted, except one. The parties had to produce sureties that they could appear for the combat, or await trial in prison. From what Arthur has seen, it appears that none of the barons would stand surety for the queen, and it must be doubtful whether he, as judge, could properly do so. His last words to Mador are a discreet assurance that he will see to it that the queen appears, so that she can be spared the humiliation of imprisonment. Mador trusts Arthur, and accepts his word.

166–7. An impersonal construction, lit. '[It] causes regret to me about this trouble'.

178–9. *ye muste holde me excused* Understand 'for any seeming lack of respect'.

189–90. Cf. the English royal motto *Dieu et mon droit*, 'God and my right'.

217. Arthur knows that Bors was one of the twenty-four. He means that Bors will do for Lancelot what he would not do otherwise.

224–5. There is a sombre dramatic irony to Arthur's question. He has some grounds for suspecting that his wife is having an affair with his friend, but his love for them both, his fear of the consequences for his country, and his innate nobility of mind have made him banish suspicion from his conscious mind. Cf. ll. 1464, 2399, and 'Morte', l. 84.

233–45. Bors's speech extends itself almost involuntarily as his latent dislike of Guenivere is given its head. He has promised to make her love Lancelot again, which does not mean that he has to like her himself; and the strength of his dislike shows in the way he avoids saying a single word of comfort to her, and never mentions the possibility of her being innocent. He first refuses to help her lest he should be suspected of complicity in the murder; then, taking breath, he points out acidly that what she lacks is Lancelot, who had not been so scrupulous about right and wrong when she was in danger. Both this last idea and Bors's antithetical phrase about right and wrong recall the Grail-quest, and his motives here may include resentment that, after the sublime experiences of the quest, he should be dragged by his love for his cousin into furthering an immoral liaison. On a more mundane level, he feels and goes on to say that, by banishing Lancelot,

Guenivere has both brought her troubles upon herself and injured Lancelot's kinsmen to such an extent that it is a startling piece of effrontery for her to ask one of them for help. When he eventually agrees to fight, he makes it plain that it is for Lancelot's and Arthur's sakes, not for hers.

The gift of self-abnegation that Bors acquired on the Grail-quest was clearly not permanent, but his character is all the more human for his lapse.

271–2. The order of clauses is confusingly different from the order of happening. Understand 'the king and queen were very glad and thanked him warmly, and so departed'.

293–4. The repetition is for emphasis only. 'In the world' is to be taken literally, not in the sense of 'worldly' as opposed to 'spiritual', or 'lay' as opposed to 'clerical'.

300–15. With time and the absence of the irritant, Bors has achieved a less distorted view of Guenivere's situation.

301. In medieval English, as in a number of modern European languages, accumulated negatives do not cancel one another out, but add greater force to the negation.

303. The mutual support of lord and vassal gave feudal society its structure at every level, and set a pattern for relationships in the church, the family, and elsewhere. This pattern still survived when society became much less feudal than it had been. Generosity was one of the fundamental virtues of chivalry (see the *Introduction*), and the knights are here complaining that the queen does not live up to standards they would expect of her as well as of the king. Behind their complaint lies an unspoken assumption of the unity of good character: that the person who is generous with material possessions is likely also to be too generous-minded to poison even an enemy, and that avarice and murderousness are likely to go together.

The scale of gifts given to show goodwill on one side or evoke it on the other often far surpassed mere birthday presents. The quantity of money, land and offices changing hands in both directions could rival more conventional kinds of income: these are the *gyfftis* that Bors speaks of. As with their counterparts in modern business, their status varied greatly between the genuinely unsolicited gift, a duty, a bribe, a tax and an investment; but woe betide the man who dispensed with them. 'Maintenance' included these gifts but was expected to go far beyond them, to providing clothing and settling feuds, to helping in courtships and furthering law-suits: in fact to everything on which influence could be brought to bear. The recipient was expected to further his lord's interests proportionately, to the point of going to war for him if need be, perhaps even against his lord's own superior.

The lord needed his vassals as much as they needed him, and sometimes – particularly in fifteenth-century England – more. To be known as *a mayntayner of good knyghtes* was to be strong: to be thought otherwise was to be alone, helpless and desperate.

314–15. The metaphor was a commonplace.

331–2. Understand 'of (i.e. in) the world' at the end of Arthur's speech as well as earlier. When he speaks of Bors as the most perfect man in the world, Arthur is thinking of him as the only survivor of the three Knights of the Round Table who fully achieved the Grail.

338. This is the only reference to the officer who saw to whatever parts of the case the king did not take into his own hands.

345. Malory mentions only the essential points of these preliminaries. He ignores the careful inspection of combatants and matching of weapons, and condenses the three complicated oaths on each side into an asymmetrical oath by the challenger and a mere 'saying' by the defendant's champion.

366. The rest of the sentence changes without warning to the plural.

372. The lists were barriers marking out the edges of the fighting ground. They took their name from the material that was fastened on to the frame of the barriers proper. In tournaments, the barriers might be wide open at the ends to the countryside around, but in a duel of chivalry they always enclosed the ground entirely, except for gates east and west through which the combatants entered. The standard regulations demanded strong six-foot-high bars enclosing sixty by forty yards of hard level ground.

404. The impact of an armoured man and horse would make a lance slip backwards through the firmest grip, and increasingly elaborate ways were found of overcoming this difficulty. In the twelfth century, lances began to be made with a wide ring round them behind the hand grip, and this ring rested against the armpit and let the shoulder take the shock of the charge. Later, a bracket called 'the rest' was built out from the chest-armour so that the lance could be 'couched' in it, with the ring resting against it. This distributed the shock over the knight's whole torso.

408. Compare Chaucer's Squire, in the General Prologue to the *Canterbury Tales*, line A 84.

415. Because fighting in armour is a very specialised art and an obsolete one, the meanings of these words are not all known with certainty; *trasing* probably means 'moving back and forth in the same track', *traversyng*, 'moving from side to side to outflank an opponent', *racyng*, 'slashing', and *foynyng*, 'lunging'.

422. The upper layers of chain mail or plate armour always over-lapped the lower ones, so that heavy downward blows would glance off; but this made it possible for lucky or skilful upward blows to penetrate the layers at the join.

428. Malory deliberately makes Arthurian practice different from that of his own time. Mador is, so to speak, settling out of court. Under English law, the parties in a duel of chivalry could not withdraw. The law assumed that accuser or defendant had committed treason, or its equivalent, a false accusation of treason; and that God's providence would ensure that the traitor lost the battle. The loser, standing convicted of a capital crime, was executed at once. Once the process had been set in motion, the king, as the fount of justice and embodiment of the law, was the only person who could interfere with it. He could and often did stop the trial – even at the beginning, as in Shakespeare's *Richard II* – and deliver judgment (which need not be death) on the spot. Otherwise the trial must proceed and discover the traitor. Anyone except the king who tried to stop it was concealing treason; and in case their wounds should tempt them to do this, the combatants were forbidden to speak to one another. Mador and Lancelot make a settlement based on the assumption that there had been no treason, simply a mistake. This assumption undermines the whole basis of trial by battle; but Malory's interest is in practical justice, not in the consistency or implications of legal processes.

437. The Constable of England had three, and the Marshal two, of these officers, who were armed with headless spears for separating the combatants. All seven men, like boxing referees, would be in the lists all the time the battle was being fought. No smaller number could be sure of being able to enforce the rules of this deadly legal process.

444. A piece of bread dipped in wine: a common light refreshment in the Middle Ages.

447. *grauntemercy* This phrase often did not have the casual overtones that the modern English 'many thanks' almost always has.

457. Originally the essential part of knighting a man was girding him with the sword, not the blow on his shoulder. It was no longer quite that important in Malory's time, but even if it did not invalidate the ceremony, its absence would be a disgrace, like a wedding without a ring.

There was a special bond between a knight and the man who had knighted him. The impending tragedy is more poignant because Arthur knighted Lancelot, and Lancelot Gareth. Cf. ll. 1734, 1902, 'Morte' 60, and 866.

460. An ominous phrase. It is common enough to be spoken by Lancelot and understood by his hearers at much less than its full face

value, as an exaggerated way of saying 'whatever happens'. But there are a good many other indications that Lancelot's fine sense of honour becomes distorted when Guenivere is involved: cf. particularly ll. 238 and 'Morte', 176, and *nn*.

470. *leechcraft* meant 'medical treatment' because one of the commonest kinds of medical treatment was the use of leeches for bloodletting. When the treatment became obsolete, so did the word.

483. The subject is not Sir Pynell but an understood *hit*: 'and it was openly known . . .'

II

503. Fifteen days may be exactly a fortnight (fourteen nights), depending on how the ends of the period are calculated, but like the modern phrase it was often used approximately rather than exactly. *A fifteen* is an example of a construction used more widely in the Middle Ages, but surviving now in *a hundred, a thousand*.

504. *a justyse and a turnament* Malory's phrase is characteristic and misleading: it suggests that two separate activities have been arranged, jousting and a tournament. If fact, although Malory often describes tournaments in which there is individual jousting before the mêlée, he is here using the two words as synonyms (cf. ll. 652, 997, 1500, and *nn*). This use of 'doublets' is typical of him and his period, and he presumably chose the word *justyse* to reinforce *turnament* because jousting seemed to him the most important part of a tournament in bringing out the skill, strength, and courage of the participants.

Malory's word *justyse* (lit. 'jousts'), a new singular noun formed from the plural of 'joust', means a set of jousts. For other singulars formed from plurals for things distinguishable into parts, see ll. 1411, and 'Morte' 285).

504–5. Camelot was traditionally Arthur's chief residence, but the romances did not say where it was. A number of places in southwestern England have names beginning with *Camel-* (from Celtic word-elements meaning 'a winding stream'), but there is no reason to suppose that Malory or any other medieval English Arthurian writer knew of any of them. The importance of Winchester, on the other hand, went back beyond times that any medieval writer could have checked. It has been a Roman cantonal capital and King Alfred's seat of government, and in the Middle Ages was the site of a rich bishopric, a magnificent cathedral and a royal castle. In the fifteenth century, one of the most famous of Arthurian relics was displayed in the Great Hall of the castle: what purported to be the Round Table itself. It is still there, repainted on Henry VIII's orders to Tudor tastes and in Tudor colours, with the names of twenty-four of its knights abominably misspelt round the circumference. Malory could have known of it by common report, read of it in the revised version of Hardyng's *Chronicle*, or seen it for himself. Caxton mentions it in the preface to his edition of the *Morte Darthur*, and English historians and foreign travellers remarked on it throughout the following century.

By giving Camelot an identifiable location, Malory brings the whole Arthurian world a little closer to his own Britain. Rather oddly, Caxton's preface states flatly that Camelot is in Wales; but Shakespeare agrees by implication with Malory in *King Lear* (II. ii. 85).

508–12. These kings, and others who appear later, have become familiar in the earlier parts of the *Morte Darthur*. Arthur's realm contains various kingdoms subordinate to his, whence the *dyverse contreyes* (cf. ll. 1262–7 and *n*). Some of these are identifiable: *North Galis* is North Wales, a traditional Arthurian locality; but Malory never says where the King with the Hundred Knights is king of, or locates *Surluse*, Galahault's principality.

517–18. That occasion was the beginning of the Grail-quest.

522. *he seyde* We are to believe this, although Guenivere disregards it in her next exchange with Lancelot.

524. Arthur's depression and anger might be due to the situation rather than directed at his wife.

527. Guildford is half-way between London and Winchester, and in the fifteenth century it had a ruined royal castle, which might have seemed to Malory the most natural place for King Arthur to break his journey. Cf. ll. 504–5 and *n*.

529–34. The narrative leaves this speech very enigmatic. One explanation is that, while Guenivere is suffering from a slight illness and Lancelot from the after-effects of a serious wound, she thoughtlessly decides to send him on a long journey to save scandal, and then insults him by announcing this in a bland little speech that assumes that his only ailment is stupidity too great to notice compromising circumstances. Perhaps Malory is showing feminine guile at work: her speech is suspiciously blithe and innocent, and she may have decided on her own that Lancelot has recovered, and so have pretended illness to produce a situation where Lancelot's consideration for her will compel him to go to the tournament. Dialogue in the *Morte Darthur*, as in life, is often capable of more than one interpretation, and the relationship between Lancelot and Guenivere as Malory shows it is mature enough for them sometimes to be extremely blunt with one another without destroying it, and at other times to leave a great deal unsaid.

535–41. Lancelot's speech is sarcastic and elliptical with resentment. In his fourth sentence he intends to say ironically, 'I will take your advice because you are so wise', but in his anger he forgets the exact meaning of the previous sentence, and therefore says, 'I will take your advice because you have become so wise recently'. *I woll take my reste* informs the queen obliquely that Lancelot will be spending the night in his own bed, and even his choice of side at the tournament seems made mainly to displease her.

547–8. A semi-proverbial phrase.

581. *Wyght* included not only toughness but also other qualities desirable in a fighting man, particularly courage, energy and agility.

592. *As the book sayth* It is the English poem, not the French romance, that has Elayne's love begin at this point.

594. *le* should be *la*: Malory's grasp of French grammatical gender was uncertain. *Blanke* (Fr. *blanche*) may mean 'blonde' as well as 'beautiful'.

Tennyson, working from a very different source from Malory's, told a version of this story in his poem, 'The Lady of Shalott'. *Shalott* and Malory's *Astolat* derive from the same word.

595. *cam to and fro*, i.e. came and went while welcoming the visitor.

596. If his lady were prepared to give him one, it was common for a knight to wear a 'token' or 'favour' as a sign that he was fighting to please her and (if he could reveal who she was) to bring her honour if he won. Like most of the signs of the code of courtly love, a 'favour' could mean little or much. Lancelot accepts it as a courteous gesture to his host's daughter, and as a useful disguise (since he had previously been prudent enough to avoid wearing the queen's favour and adroit enough in courtesy to refuse any other woman's); but Elayne gives it as a sign of passionate and exclusive love.

598. The phrase is sometimes ambiguous in medieval English, since it had the modern meaning 'for your love' as well as the specifically medieval one 'for your sake'. But the context makes it clear that Lancelot intends the meaning that is now obsolete. Cf. l. 1233.

620. *whyght*, i.e. blank, without any heraldic device. They may also have been white in colour. Shields of a single plain colour were extremely rare in real life, but are quite common in the romances, particularly for unproved knights. The contrast with the complicated heraldry of the late Middle Ages was probably felt to be symbolic of a greater simplicity of life in the distant times in which the romances' stories are set. Cf. *Le Morte Arthur*, ll. 147–52.

633. *The Freynshe booke seyth* It actually says Arthur kept Gawain and Gareth with him on this occasion in case they and Lancelot wound one

another and ill-will arise from it; not that Arthur habitually did this, or that Lancelot always defeated Gawain.

652. Despite the phrase *justyse and turnement* (above, l. 504), Malory gives no hint that any individual jousting takes place before the general engagement.

674. Keeping together was the first essential for survival in battle.

695. *mercy* is a stock interjection of (admiring) surprise: cf. Wordsworth's poem 'Strange Fits of Passion I Have Known', stanza 7.

712–15. In Malory, *noble knyghtes* normally implies bodily, mental, and spiritual excellence. Its use here, where hatred has temporarily swept away chivalrous generosity, is effectively incongruous: a reminder of how dangerous are the strong sudden passions of Malory's characters, and how strength and courage can remain when knightly ideals have become distorted. These are two of the chief causes of the coming catastrophe.

Rebuke means primarily a reverse or setback. The shame that such a reverse brings can vary from a great deal, as Bors's company intends here, through very little to nothing (see ll. 1676–7).

725. Lancelot is Lavayne's 'master' because Lavayne has freely chosen to serve the greatness of mind, courtesy and warlike skill that compel his admiration.

The word implies neither compulsion on one side nor servility on the other.

746–50. *as the booke seyth* It does not. Malory has invented this incident showing, how Lancelot's wound, his instincts, and his trained reflexes nearly carry him into killing his three closest kinsmen. It takes the sight of their faces to bring him to his senses.

773. The impersonal construction, lit. 'that (i.e. the sore 'buying') causes regret to me'.

775–6. The impersonal construction, lit. '[it] pleases me'. Cf. previous note.

783. The construction is the subjunctive expressing a wish, as in ll. 799 and 805.

790–1. It is characteristic of Malory's frequent indifference to grammar that he omits any sign that the subject of *gaff* is not the subject of *drew*.

793–6. When the fragment of the spear is drawn out – which would be done with Lancelot kneeling and Lavayne supporting him as best he could – Lancelot first slumps back into a sitting position, and then faints and collapses completely, looking 'deadly', i.e. like death. Lavayne turns him to face the wind to help him breathe.

806. *cousyne jermayne*, 'first cousin'. According to this, Lancelot's

father, King Ban of Benwick, had been the brother of Bors's father, King Bors of Gaul. But see above, l. 86n.

832–6. The hermit's character comes out well from his speech. *Loved him the worse* is authentic knightly understatement, and *I am othirwyse disposed* has a clerical tone to it, as in the more modern phrase *dispositions at the hour of our death*. His experienced calmness contrasts markedly with Lavayne's near-panic: in particular, his first remarks sound very like a doctor's patter for soothing the relatives who might have to help with the patient.

Doctor, priest, and knight all in one, he sounds less like a typical hermit than like an epitome of the great military religious order, the Knights Hospitallers of St John of Jerusalem. In the 1430s, the Hospitallers had a Commandery, rather like a small hermitage, in Warwickshire, in the charge of a Sir Robert Malory who became Prior of the Order in England and later went to Rhodes to fight the Turks (cf. 'Morte', ll. 2491–8 and n).

844–6. *Worship* must be actively sought (see *Introduction*).

864–6. It could happen, though not often nor quite like this. The brilliant, generous, and aristocratic Bertrand de Born, whose reckless passions helped to turn Richard the Lionheart and his brothers against their father, King Henry II, ended his life as a monk in the strict Cistercian order.

897–9. Arthur presumably fears that some partisan feelings may linger after the tournament in which the unknown knight has worked such devastation on the Round Table, so he warns Gawain, who has shown a vindictive streak several times in previous tales, to behave himself if the stranger is in any state to notice.

920. This and the following speeches make this the first scene in which we can really understand Elayne. The first shock of meeting Lancelot has worn off, and she is left with a clear-eyed self-knowledge and an innocent immoveable pride that will destroy her.

941. The *case* might be any covering. It could be of cloth, and certainly need not have a frame or be rigid.

943–4. Sir Bernard's caution is a sign of how much medieval society needed its code of chivalry towards women. The author of a widely-read book of manners told his daughters not to cross the hall of their own castle at night, because once it was dark they might not be safe among their own household and guests.

959. Elayne is emphatic and so repetitive: even discounting the compound negative, modern English is not free enough to give a word-for-word equivalent. Understand 'for always before that time, [despite] all the knights I saw, I was in love with no one'.

250

960–8. Gawain misinterprets Lancelot's ambiguous acceptance of Elayne's token, and therefore encourages a love that would end the court gossip and whatever reality might lie behind it. Since his interpretation is wrong, he is making things worse for Elayne.

997. Arthur, and others later, refer loosely to the mêlée at Winchester as 'the great jousting' because jousting is the most important part of it, though not the whole. Cf. l. 504n.

1002. *none erthely woman*, 'any woman on earth', is for emphasis, and does not imply that Lancelot normally fought bearing (say) the image of the Virgin Mary on his helmet or shield, as some knights were said to do.

1014–44. While Guenivere is trying to pick a quarrel with Bors as a proxy for Lancelot, Bors stonewalls, patiently rational and showing no affection whatever for her. He says nothing to suggest that he is restrained by anything except fear of the impending catastrophe, a wish to please Lancelot, and his obligations to his own knighthood. When she descends to abuse, he warns her by implication that he will walk out if she continues (ll. 1020–1); and when he tells her that Lancelot loves no one lady more than any other, the fact that he makes no soothing exception for Guenivere herself is no doubt deliberate (cf. ll. 1149–50).

As usual in Malory, *langayge* means false, empty, or excessive words. Cf. ll. 1171 and 1543.

1031. *Fy*, said to be imitative of the sound people make on noticing a bad smell, implied stronger disgust in earlier English than does its modern use in children's stories. Translate by any exclamation of disgust. *Fy on*, 'shame upon'. Cf. Shakespeare's *Winter's Tale*, III. ii. 52.

1066. Kissing was a normal greeting between friends and acquaintances in the English upper classes at this time and later. Cf. Donne's poem, 'The Relique'. Some foreigners found this English freedom shocking.

1107. *unhappynesse* means 'misfortune', and is used of someone whose *hap* or luck has not gone well. It does not mean 'unhappiness', though a man who was unhappy in the medieval sense would no doubt usually be so in the modern sense as well. Cf. 'Morte', l. 1920n.

1125. One of the few proverbs in the *Morte Darthur* explicitly marked out as such. There is another, also spoken by Lancelot, at l. 2033.

1129. Also a proverb.

1145. *that* is a conjunction implying result, but the result of the whole previous situation and not the preceding main clause. Understand 'and'.

1158–9. In the Middle Ages, an agreement of any importance was usually confirmed with oaths, often rather to mark its importance than because it was thought that anyone intended to break it.

1169. *more mekar* Double comparative. 'Meek' here implies both usefulness and humility: what Malory calls *jantyl servyse*. Chaucer showed this ideal in the Squire on the Canterbury pilgrimage:

> Curteys he was, lowly and servisable,
> And carf biforn his fader at the table.
> *Canterbury Tales*, A 99

Classic courtly love expected this service only of the man, but Malory thought both lovers should give it to one another.

1176. Arming a knight was a skilled and laborious process, and at least two trained helpers were desirable. The knight could not do it alone. The pieces had to be put on in the right order or it might not be possible to put them on at all.

1183. The knight's lance was 'great' in contrast to lighter weapons such as throwing spears.

1198. *oute of mesure* is an ambiguous common phrase. It may mean 'beyond the virtue of "measure" or moderation', 'excessive', and then whatever it applies to is condemned as wrong. But it can also mean 'beyond measurement', which is the literal meaning here. As in most stock phrases, the full literal meaning is not always present, and in this passage 'very great' would be an adequate translation. Cf. ll. 1328–9, 1366–82, 1456, 1571–2 and *nn*.

The repetitions of this, as of other stock phrases of value, create at times a special kind of dramatic irony. Resonances from previous uses give the phrase a meaning beyond what the rather unsophisticated narrator seems to intend, so that, for instance, *out of measure* may be intended to mean 'extremely great' but provoke the reader to supply the meaning 'excessive'. Cf. ll. 712–15; and ll. 333 with 2497. Like the symmetries and ironies in the action that the narrator shows little sign of appreciating, this dramatic irony at his expense increases the sense of unseen and unknown forces at work behind the events, and increases the effect of verisimilitude, of the narrator following rather than controlling his story.

1213. The hermit is trying to make Lancelot breathe in this very small quantity of water, so that he will cough and choke and thus recover consciousness. It could be a very dangerous remedy in unskilled hands. The *thynge* may be a surgical instrument or the first object that came to hand for nose-blocking.

1266–7. *As the boke seyth* No source is known for this statement.

1269. Fighting in armour was extremely exhausting, and therefore stamina was highly valued among knightly qualities. Insofar as tournaments were training for war, they had to discover, encourage and reward it.

1272–3. *som maner adventures* This construction survived from an older stage of the language, and fifteenth-century users still probably felt obscurely that the genitive force lay in the first two words (here singular) and not in the last one (here plural).

1277–8. *lyke as ye have herde* Another survival from oral story-telling reminds us of the narrator's presence. Cf. l. 104*n*.

1282–3. The words have been carelessly ordered, since both *so*-phrases qualify both verbs. Understand 'bear down and smite down so many knights in so short a while'.

1312–21. Lancelot's speech is confused and tactless. His remark that he could have been married but had chosen not to be, though perhaps intended to commend the single life, is gratuitous; saying 'because you love me as *you say* you do' sounds as though he doubts her sincerity; replying to her offer of herself with a counter-offer of money is an insult; and offering to be 'her' knight as long as he lives is a travesty of her dearest hopes, all the crueller because courtly love had made that phrase one of the regular ambiguities of passion. All that can be said for Lancelot is that he has never met such realistic feminine directness before; he is taken off balance; and the sum he offers to settle on her and her husband is enormous. It was fifty times the income of Sir Thomas Malory of Newbold Revel and was only matched by the incomes of the dozen greatest magnates in Malory's England: the great majority of the peers in the House of Lords had much smaller ones.

1328–9. *overmuche sorowe* More than is good for her; the narrator implies nothing about whether Elayne should or could have restrained herself from grieving over Lancelot's rejection of her. Cf. l. 1198*n*.

1331–2. Lavayne's inability to leave Lancelot despite his sister's fate is only the latest of many instances showing Lancelot's dangerous power of evoking devotion from others. Malory as narrator never analyses this; he simply shows it in operation.

1335. Shakespeare remembered this incident as a pattern of heroic love, and summarised it and quoted this line in *The Merchant of Venice* (III. iv. 70–2).

1353. Malory gives another reminder of the envious troublemakers who are looking for a chance to trap Lancelot and Guenivere.

1354. *woode wrothe* One must judge from the context whether or not this popular phrase has its full literal meaning of 'mad with rage'. In this period it is often used as a term of praise when describing a man fighting: reckless fury can sometimes be an asset. Cf. l. 1611 and *n.*

1355. *by no meanys* means 'by no means', but also implies that a number of people have tried to act as 'mean' or intermediary, and all failed.

1366–82. Elayne's *erthely woman* is a statement of the naturalness of her plight. Only those who have vowed themselves completely to a supernatural heavenly love are bound to deny themselves this natural earthly love. She develops with characteristic clear-headedness the idea of love's naturalness: it is a quality that does not make her love pleasant or beneficial in any obvious way; her love is natural in the same sense as storms or earthquakes, and she speaks of it coming upon her by God's permission, implying a common theological distinction between things God wills directly as good, and evils he allows for purposes usually beyond men's knowledge. And so Elayne responds to her love as she might to such a disaster, asking that the suffering it causes her while she lives may be allowed, like any other suffering willingly accepted for God, to reduce the debt of suffering in Purgatory that she owes for past sins not completely expiated. Caxton seems to have found Elayne's theological ideas too daring: he cut the words from *unto God* to *Launcelot du Lake* inclusive.

oute of mesure may mean 'immeasureable' but it certainly means 'excessive': too much for her life and too much, as the preceding words show, for her virtue. The latter excess may be her request to be Lancelot's mistress, or her consenting to her own death, or both. Cf. l. 1198*n.*

1384. Though there were exceptions, it was normal amongst the gentry for the men to be able to write fairly easily and for the women to be able to write with difficulty if at all. So Elayne's request is not a sign that she is too weak to hold a pen.

1388–90. Elayne intends that her hand should stiffen in rigor mortis so that it will continue to hold the letter after she is dead.

1391. The medieval English word *clothys* meant both 'clothes' and 'cloths'. Elayne seems to be thinking mainly of using lengths of fabric on the bed as a rich setting for her dead body.

1392. The verb *to lead* here and in l. 1402 is used in an obsolete sense of carriage in a vehicle. It does not mean 'to lead' in the modern sense.

1393. The nearest point of the Thames to Guildford is Chertsey, 13 miles away.

1395. *thidir* is to Arthur's court at Westminster, though this is never said.

1405–6. *rubbed and rolled*, i.e. against the quayside outside Arthur's palace. Malory is thinking of a palace on the bank of the Thames, on the site of the present Houses of Parliament. There had been a royal palace on that site from before the Norman Conquest, and the present Parliament buildings, which are still called 'The Palace of West-minster', derive some of their legal privileges from their past status.

1425. Either Malory or one of his scribes has left out after *the fayryst woman* some such words as *that ever he saw*.

1440–2. The reasoning is compressed but clear. Elayne makes her 'complaint' (cf. l. 1360) to the ladies so that they will add their support to her request to Lancelot, so that he will do as she asks.

The *masse-peny* is an offering of money, in such contexts 'the offering' made at a Mass. The person who made it at a Requiem Mass accepted *ipso facto* the office of principal mourner, though others might, as they do here, also make offerings after the main one. Cf. 'Morte', l. 2184n.

1464–9. Lancelot's definition of love is important in itself (cf. Chaucer's Franklin's Tale, *Canterbury Tales*, F 765–67), but it is also a covert thrust at Guenivere, who has tried to constrain his love. Arthur replies only at the overt level, unconscious – perhaps by his own decision – of the abyss beneath. The similarities with the Franklin's Tale passage are striking, especially the use of personification. This is the only known passage in the *Morte Darthur* that may show the in-fluence of non-Arthurian English literature.

1471. *worshyp* here means 'honour' both in the most idealistic sense and in the sense of increase of reputation (see the *Introduction*). Trans-late 'It will be [greatly] to your credit that . . .'

III

1500. *turnement and justis* As previously (cf. l. 504n), the words are synonyms making up a 'doublet'.

This tournament begins with jousting between pairs of famous champions until there are enough of these on the field for a 'medlé' or general combat in which everyone could join.

1508–9. *Freshness* included liveliness, youthfulness and gaiety, and summed up all the qualities of springtime that medieval Englishmen valued as part of life at its best. Cf. Chaucer's Squire, who 'was as fresshe as is the moneth of May' (*Canterbury Tales* A 92).

1511. Since accumulated negatives increase the force of a negation, Guenivere's prohibition is very emphatic indeed.

1513. Because a 'favour' meant something, however little, it was indiscreet of Lancelot to wear one from a married woman, and especi-ally from the queen, even if he concealed the identity of its donor. He had not done so in the past, but Guenivere makes him do so now, to protect him by identifying him to his kinsmen, but also to put herself on a par with Elayne of Astolat.

1535. A passion for hunting was an English characteristic. The two most famous satires of the Renaissance, More's *Utopia* and Erasmus's *Praise of Folly*, both attacked it, and Erasmus especially ridiculed the enthusiasts' jargon.

The *treste* was part of the most elaborate kind of medieval hunt, the *chasse royale*, developed when the efficient killing of large quantities of game was an important source of food. *Treste* descends from an ancient form of *trust*, which in all the Germanic languages meant 'a man's obligations to his lord'. For a man living in a forest, those obligations included waiting with a dog at an appointed place during the *chasse royale*. *Treste* first meant this obligation, and then extended itself to the 'hides' where the men and dogs lay hidden, and from which, as the hunted beasts went past, the dogs were released to drive them towards nets or archers at a specially contrived funnel-like gap in a long hedge. This gap, as another 'appointed place', also came to be called a *treste*. The dogs in the hides had to be well trained, to keep silent until the quarry was past and then drive it in the right direction; and, no doubt for this reason, the lord – here the lady – came to breed and train hounds specially for this purpose (and for others), instead of using whatever the tenants could provide.

Treste survives in modern English only as *tryst*, 'rendezvous'.

1547. The hind takes refuge in the pool to cool herself and to kill the scent.

Go to soil translates Fr. *prendre souille*, 'to seek out a wallowing-place', as boar and deer do to cool themselves, in hot weather as well as after pursuit. This word *soil*, modelled on *souille* and meaning a watery or muddy place, has no etymological or semantic connection with *soil* meaning 'earth', 'humus'.

1552. The arrow is 'broad' because of its barbed head. This, as Lancelot finds, makes it almost impossible to extract even at the cost of a savage wound; and, in the case of a fleeing animal, the movement of its muscles would drive the head in even further.

1561. The lady's speech shows she fears no violence from Lancelot, so *mercy* does not have its full sense but is a stock interjection of (alarmed) surprise. Cf. l. 695*n*.

1571–2. The order of the sentences is not that of happening or motivation. Lavayne and Brastias are both downcast and angry because Lancelot has been hurt. The fact that Lancelot does not tell Lavayne (or, presumably, Brastias) who wounded him is an entirely separate matter. But careless ordering of the sentences misleadingly suggests that both are angry because Lancelot will not tell Lavayne who is responsible.

oute of mesure here means no more than 'very great'. Cf. l. 1198*n*.

1580–1. This is a clipped form of a proverb, not an assertion that God is a mere man.

1587–1602. When Lancelot and Lavayne arrive, they see one party in front of them on one side of the field; then Arthur's party comes in on the other side. *North Galys* is North Wales and *Bretayne* is Brittany; but *Goore* and *Claraunce* – though the former may derive from Gower in South Wales – are countries of the mind only.

1611. *wood wrothe* Like the colloquial modern English 'mad', the medieval phrase often has less than its full literal meaning. Cf. l. 1354*n*.

1614–15. Omission of subject and displaced clauses. Understand 'And he (i.e. Arthur) did very well, and then his spear broke'.

1629. Omission of subject. Understand 'and he (i.e. Bors) said to them all'.

1664–5. The Knights of the Round Table were supposed to support one another in battle, so Gareth has to exchange his distinctive shield for another if he is to support Lancelot without openly violating his obligation. Since a tournament is only a mock battle, the obligation does not bind him very seriously here.

1667–8. I.e., where the Welsh knight was sitting to rest himself. Malory may hint that Gawain, in gravely injuring someone, had been fighting too hard.

1672. *the booke seythe* No source is known for this episode.

1673. *semed* Malory is emphasising the excellence of the painting, which creates a convincing illusion of a maiden in the shield.

1703. *as the Freynshe booke seyth* No source is known for this episode.

1705–6. The sentence *And Sir Lavayne* ... would come more naturally after the one that follows it, in which *for all this* has nothing to do with Lavayne. Malory hesitated between dealing with one knight at a time, and putting all the actions first followed by all the reactions; and his solution is not the clearest possible.

1707–9. The explanation is characteristically elliptical. Malory leaves us to work out that Lancelot thought that only the two great knights named were capable of doing as well as the stranger; and because they were dead, Lancelot could not think who the strange knight could be.

1713. Cf. l. 86*n*.

1724. Kay rather slow-wittedly suggests that the reason Lancelot's cousins are not with Arthur is that they are somewhere else. Gawain's reply shows that he suspects that there is another reason as well.

1739–43. Gawain says that to beat Lancelot they would need still greater odds in their favour, and that such odds would disgrace them; Arthur replies that they would be disgraced even by continuing with their present advantage in numbers.

1773–8. *worshyp* means something between 'honour' and 'duty', with little of its sense of 'increase of reputation'. Understand 'I was bound in honour to . . .'

For the terms of praise in the next three paragraphs, see the *Introduction*.

1783. *the more bettir* Double comparative.

1789–91. The expression is wordy, but the thought has been proverbial in English since King Alfred's time.

IV

1796. In the Middle Ages, the rhythm of nature made human life, individual and social, slow down in winter. Winter reduced light, warmth, comfort, good food and travel; spring brought new life (*corrayge*) to everybody and *renewed* them. The most famous celebration of this in English is the opening of the General Prologue to Chaucer's *Canterbury Tales*. The lovers Malory writes of have been afflicted by dullness and the dead hand of winter, not by cowardice.

1804. The trees and plants stand by synecdoche for Nature, which does the renewing and of which they are the most conspicuous part.

1806. *servyse* was essential to the medieval view of love, whether of God, a feudal lord, or a mistress. The manner of service was *jantyl*, i.e. it had the qualities that a gentleman should have, among which was *gentleness* in the modern sense.

1815–23. The argument is based on the statement *for there was never* . . . Men and women of honour will by their very natures be lovers; when such a man loves such a woman, his 'worship' (i.e. both his character and his achievements) will draw her irresistibly to love; therefore he should not be afraid to love. Their love will have three characteristics: the *jantyl servyse* mentioned before, loyalty (vacillation is weak and dishonourable), and subordination to the love of God. (Cf. Chaucer's *Troilus and Criseyde*, I, 239–59.)

thy quarell muste com of thy lady The 'quarrel', literally the fighting the lover will do for his lady in quests and tournaments, stand for his whole behaviour.

1826. Proverbial.

1830. The narrator is comparing three eras: the time of writing, an unspecified 'old time', and King Arthur's days. In the old time, and 'likewise' in Arthur's days, love *was* troth ('loyalty') and faithfulness. This equivalence shows how strongly Malory felt the importance of loyalty in love. Nowhere else in the *Morte Darthur* does he comment directly on the morals of his age.

1833. Love now, says the narrator, is both hot and cold: i.e. it alternates from one to the other.

1837. To be 'true', love need only have two of the three qualities of 'virtuous' love: *jantyl servyse* and *wyse stabilité*. But if it does not *reserve the honoure to God*, it will not be virtuous and its very strength will be a danger. Guenivere's true love will destroy everything she values and cause the downfall of the Round Table; and yet, says the narrator, it earns her her *good ende*.

1866. *The booke seyth* It does not.

1876. *knowlecchynge* The precise modern equivalent is 'cognizance', a heraldic term taken from medieval French (cf. Fr. *connaissance*). The English ruling classes spoke French for centuries after the Norman Conquest, and this brought a very large number of French words into the English vocabulary. Some have remained in modern English, some have not; and those that have not were often displaced by native equivalents. Malory is using an Anglo-Saxon equivalent for the French word that heralds of his time used (cf. l. 2410); but in this case it was the French term that became part of modern English.

Even after the mid-fourteenth century, when French had ceased to be the first language of the English aristocracy, it retained great prestige: Chaucer's Prioress prided herself on her French. Some writers and speakers of English showed off their knowledge of French by using words that had not been thoroughly absorbed into English. Malory preferred established English, as his use of *knowlecchynge* shows. But cf. ll. 2780–3 and *n*.

1907–10. *Be as hit be may* and *I woll take you as I fynde you* are common expressions.

1916. The earlier *Howbeit* makes this *but* superfluous.

1941. *reuled*, lit. 'governed', usually implies 'sensible', because the government is that of one's self-control, reason itself, and the counsellor who is offering reasonable advice.

1946–7. *The Freynsh booke seyth* It does not. There is no large escort to make a proper stand in the queen's defence.

1960–1. *joy*, meaning both 'sexual enjoyment' and 'the pleasure he gets from my thinking well of him', is as conveniently ambiguous as much of the vocabulary of courtly love. This ambiguity lets the lovers communicate by innocent intermediaries (as here), and speak openly before third parties (see ll. 2074–5 and *n* below).

1962. A narrative commonplace.

1982-3. *the booke seyth* It does not.

2000-1. Lancelot is king of France (see 'Morte', ll. 1260-7), so he knows what he is saying.

2011-13. *The booke seyth* It does not. Lancelot's many adventures on his way to rescue Guenivere do not include swimming any rivers.

2036. Helmet and steel back and breast plates could weigh 90 pounds, and then there were weapons, shield, and armour for the legs and arms. A strong man could move about on foot in armour with agility, but not for long.

2045. Cf. l. 503 and *n*.

2053. *reremayne*, a technical term for this kind of blow. A fully-armed fifteenth-century knight wore gloves of velvet with gauntlets of boiled leather over them; the gauntlets were covered in turn with overlapping steel plates, and might have iron spikes ('gadlings') on the knuckles. His arm was in a steel sleeve, with steel joints at the shoulder and elbow, thick chain mail under the shoulder, and steel plates ('pauldrons') covering the shoulder-joint. A hand armoured in this way needed some strength even to raise it, but it could deliver a fearsome blow without any further weapon.

2074-5. After her first *Alas* at Lancelot's plight, Guenivere exults in his prowess. Her phrase is quasi-proverbial, but especially apt to her because one of the medieval English uses of *friend* was as synonym and translation of Fr. *ami* or *amie* (another conveniently ambiguous term – cf. ll. 1960-1*n* above), meaning both 'lover' and 'friend'. So, in Shakespeare's *Measure for Measure*, Lucio tells Isabella that her brother 'hath got his friend with child' (I. iv. 29). Cf. modern English *girlfriend*.

2108-9. Both sentiments are proverbial.

2114. This sequence of speeches shows Guenivere unable to stop herself concealing her real gratitude and admiration for Lancelot and using her power over him, in this case to tease him. Lancelot, who has been working himself up to fight to the death for her against huge odds, feels let down and understandably goes into something of a huff. He points out that he has only lost a horse and his temper (the latter because of the meanness of the attacks on him), whereas she may have lost her reputation. The queen agrees obscurely with him, but thanks him all the same and asks him to come in without making a fuss. This still leaves Lancelot 'amoved': Guenivere's words sound like agreement that his hurt is only *lytyll*, fighting fury take time to die down, and he may resent hearing Mellyagaunte's complicated treachery described as a *mysadventure* that simply 'befell' him – it is clear that Mellyagaunte's treachery rankles. One or more of these motives is still clouding his mind and preventing him from seeing that Guenivere is being the more far-sighted.

2117. *more wrotther* Double comparative.

2132–3. Guenivere puts her two questions mock-seriously in the language of moral theology before giving an explanation: her actions were intended 'wisely to make an end of all scandalous gossip'. But it still takes Lancelot two speeches before he can calm himself down again. This scene shows people who have loved one another for a long time: they know how to hurt and how to heal.

2155. *fayne* usually means 'glad', 'eager', but only in the prevailing circumstances. The circumstances that make Lancelot eager to ride in the cart are so peculiar that they change the meaning to 'compelled'.

2158–9. No 'French book' is known that says this, but it is not impossible. The story of Chrétien's *Lancelot*, in which Lancelot was called the 'Chevalier de la Charrette' was later incorporated into the prose *Lancelot*; so, in the expanded prose *Lancelot*, a certain number of the hero's *dedys and grete adventures* came after the incidents Chrétien had related. But cf. ll. 2768–75 and *n*.

2223. Because they had no efficient artificial light or heating, medieval Englishmen rose and went to bed much earlier than their descendants, to make best use of the sun. This explains *longe*, and may also partly account for the number of descriptions of dawn in early English literature.

2226. A common oath, not to be taken at full face value. *Good God!* is probably too strong, *Good lord!* about right as a modern equivalent.

2229. The *hede-sheete* was a special sheet that went on only at the head of the bed, covering the pillows. It often matched the ordinary upper and lower sheets.

2237. Defiling the king's wife by adultery had been made treason by an Act of Parliament of 1352.

Compare with this whole passage and its Commentary ll. 155–202, 333–436 and *nn*.

2277–8. *God woll have a stroke* . . . Proverbial, as is Lancelot's reply, *God ys to be drad*.

Strictly speaking, it is Mellyagaunte's part to challenge Guenivere, and Lancelot's to accept the challenge on her behalf, as her champion. But, by accusing Mellyagaunte of lying, Lancelot tricks him into wording the charge in such a way that Guenivere is innocent of it.

2284. Lancelot has denied before it was given, and then Mellyagaunte has given, a formal challenge to trial by battle: hence the clear careful phrasing on each side. Taking up the challenger's glove was the normal way of accepting his challenge; Malory then has them exchange the terms of the challenge in writing and under seal, according to the rules of the 'duel of chivalry'. The written documents would be presented to the Constable of England, the executive officer of the Court of Chivalry, and this would be the formal beginning of the trial.

2358–9. Even in this situation, Lancelot still uses the courteous pronoun for addressing a woman.

2365–6. The lady's argument, as she expresses it, is either not very logical or not very creditable; but it is difficult to be both graceful and consistent when one's bluff has just been called.

2370. Without the double sense of *worship*, Lancelot's speech would be unpleasantly egocentric.

2377. The war-saddle differed from an ordinary saddle in having its saddle-bow and cantle heavily built up to protect the rider and to help him keep his seat even under the full impact of another mounted knight's spear-thrust.

2410. The French phrase is the beginning of the formula always used to start the fighting; Arthur's *whoo!* is the formula a king used for stopping it. Cf. Theseus in Chaucer's *Knight's Tale* (A 1706).

2418. Great care was taken to emphasise the king's impartiality in duels of chivalry. It was expected that he would be present, but that he would leave the management of the trial to the Constable and Marshal of his country, unless he chose to exercise his right of stopping the trial and delivering judgment there and then. Arthur's behaviour is irregular because he is interfering in the trial while it is going on and anticipating the outcome of the combat. But his breach of the rules pales into insignificance beside Mellyagaunte's.

2444. *recreaunte* The technical term, from Fr. *recroire*, for a man who admitted himself beaten in a fight. The spectators' opinion of surrender gave *recreant* the meaning 'coward', and it became such an insult that people spoke of it as 'the loath word' to avoid allowing it to pass their lips. In Malory's fifth tale, one of Lancelot's cousins is prepared to be killed rather than admit himself vanquished by saying it. Mellyagaunte, of course, is not saying 'I am a coward', only 'I surrender'.

2458. See l. 437n.

2476. A man convicted of a false accusation of high treason was liable to the punishment for high treason, hanging, drawing and quartering, after which the quarters of his body would be sent to various towns where they would be left to rot as publicly as possible to discourage others. The 'drawing' might be one or both of two things: being drawn (i.e. dragged) on a hurdle through the streets to the place of execution; or being drawn (i.e. disembowelled like a chicken) when let down, still alive, from the hanging.

The effect of justice being seen to be done was so highly valued in medieval law that the sentence would be carried out even on a dead man (as late as 1660, the corpses of the leaders of those who had condemned King Charles I to death were disinterred and hung publicly in chains). Mellyagaunte is convicted by losing the battle, and his body has already been *drawyn* out of the lists – a passage would be broken through the rails for this, so that the disgrace would be more conspicuous – when his fellow Knights of the Round Table persuade the king to remit the rest of the sentence and allow the body to be buried.

V

2481. *The Freynshe boke makith mencion* The name Urry is not known in any other Arthurian story, but the prose *Lancelot* includes an incident in some ways similar to Malory's. An unnamed knight surprises two girls bathing, one of whom promptly shoots him in the thigh with an arrow. She is not said to be a *sorceras*, but a passer-by predicts that the wound will never be cured unless the best knight in the world removes the arrow. During the adventures that follow, nearly all the knights of the Round Table try to do this and fail: finally Lancelot tries, and succeeds.

2505. *the Freynshe booke saythe* The prose *Lancelot* does not mention the mother of the wounded knight.

2512. *that londe* rather than any other land. Her answer, interrupted by some lines in indirect speech, is that she has tried everywhere else.

2519. *hys modir*, i.e. the mother of Alpheus, the man who wounded Urry.

2547. Translate ambiguously: 'the most honourable man in Christendom'. The honour may be a matter of rank and reputation and heraldry, or of the spirit – in which case Malory is saying that, in some ways at least, Arthur is a better man than Lancelot – or it may be, as Malory likes it to be, a matter of both equally.

2585-9. Most of this group of knights are supporters of Gawain, either his friends or his kinsmen: at least Mellyot, Petipace, Galleron, Mellyon, Grummor, and Crosseleme. *Wynchelsé* is almost certainly Winchelsea in Kent, though Winksley near Fountains Abbey in Yorkshire has been suggested.

2591. *the booke seyth* No trace is known of either of the things attributed in this paragraph to Malory's source.

2611. *wordly* There is an implied contrast with Percival, the spiritual knight.

2612. *they* Percival and Galahad.

2615. *Sir Constantine* A slip: he has been included already (l. 2566).

2621. *Sir Trystram* A slip, confusing Gawain, who caused Priamus to be baptised, with Tristram, who did the same for Palomides.

2638. *the crosse* Presumably the one of his grave.

2654. The closest modern English can come to this is awkward: 'had not one . . . Nynyve been'. Translate, less clumsily, 'if one . . . Nynyve had not been'.

2667. The list contains 103 names, one of which appears twice. The lively parenthetical material may have defeated Malory's arithmetic, which was never his strong point.

2734–5. Quasi-proverbial. Cf. Absolom in Chaucer's *Miller's Tale* (A 3759).

2739. It is typical of Malory that the reader is left to imagine for himself the *ryche maner* of clothing provided by the king.

2762 The phrase *sought uppon their dedis* is odd, and the text may be corrupt.

2768–75. No known version of Chrétien's Knight of the Cart story includes the incidents Malory mentions. He may have known such a version, or invented it to give authority to the incidents. If he did know it, he may really have lost it, or he may have pretended to do so to explain his omission of material he did not want. Cf. ll. 2158–9*n*.

2772–4. In the trial by battle and perhaps for a *lytil aftir*, Lancelot, rode normally, on horseback; then he began his eccentric year of riding in a cart.

2779. In the only known manuscript, the next tale begins on the page on which this one ends. The phrase has been copied mechanically from a manuscript, almost certainly Malory's own, in which what it said was true.

2782–3. Malory uses French here, outside the story proper, perhaps for its literary and social cachet (cf. his use of English verse in the *explicit* of the last tale), perhaps as a kind of testimony to the 'French Book' he has so often cited as his authority.

Le Morte Darthur

I

The title At the end of his book, Malory calls the entire book *The Hoole Book of Kyng Arthur and of His Noble Knyghtes of the Rounde Table*, and the last of its eight tales 'Le Morte Darthur' (see the *explicit*, l. 2499). Unfortunately Caxton misread this, thought the title of the last tale was the title of the whole book, and said so so emphatically in his colophon that the book has been called *Le Morte Darthur* for years. So the two functions of the phrase must be distinguished, and this is best done by using inverted commas for the title of the tale and italics for the title of the book.

Le should have been *La* (cf. 'Lancelot', l. 594n), but this also is too firmly established to be altered now.

9. *unhappy*, 'wretched' in their situation (as bringers of *unhap*, 'bad luck') rather than in their feelings.

25–6. I.e., a sharer in your secret thoughts and one of the advisers who advise you to do as you now intend.

45–9. Gawain is recalling an incident related in the fifth tale of the *Morte Darthur*. The Dolorous Tower is probably Lancelot's own castle of Joyous Garde, which he renamed when he captured it from King Carados.

72. In early English society, a man's relationship with his sister's sons was much closer than with his brother's sons. He might have to fight for them because his sister could not.

Mordred's incestuous birth makes him both Arthur's son and Arthur's sister's son – and therefore makes Guenivere both his stepmother and his aunt.

79–80. If witnesses saw a man committing a crime, he was not entitled to defend himself in trial by battle.

84. On the contrary, in the French book Arthur encourages the plotters. Malory presumably altered this because he found such behaviour incredible in a man as honourable as Arthur (cf. 'Lancelot', ll. 224–5n). But once an accusation is made, he must hear it impartially; hence his next speech.

107–11. Two of these knights are Gawain's brothers and three his sons; Mador and Collgrevaunce had come in one group to the healing of Sir Urry, and the other five had all come in another. In *The Wedding of Sir Gawain and Dame Ragnell*, the only other story in which Gromore Somer Joure is known, he became Gawain's brother-in-law. Neither the origin nor the meaning of his extraordinary name is known.

Logris is the French romances' name for Britain, *Wynchylsé* is Winchelsea in Kent, and *Galoway* is Galloway in southern Scotland (not Galway in Ireland). *Gorre* is perhaps derived from the region of Gower in South Wales.

121. The relative pronoun *that* represents *goynge*, and is therefore the cognate object of *wente*; cf. *to go one's way*.

139–41. The French book says, as Malory refuses to, that the lovers were in bed together.

Compare, for the effect of pathos when a narrator has to treat matter obviously uncongenial to him, Chaucer's *Troilus and Criseyde*, V, 1050.

176–7. A common phrase like this can be used lightly to mean little more than 'whatever happens'. That Lancelot has no feeling that his cause at this moment is unjust is shown by his invoking Christ in it a moment later. But the context gives the phrase dramatic irony. In the past Lancelot has certainly sometimes been willing to act for Guenivere in a wrongful cause, and on the Grail-quest he confessed that at times he had in fact done so. It must be doubtful whether he has the right to resist, let alone kill, his lord's knights (however despicable their private motives) when they try to arrest him and the queen for a treasonable act that he and she have often committed. If the record of King Lot's family in broken promises and stabbings in the back justifies him in resisting arrest now, nothing in the future justifies his many attempts to defend the queen, inside and outside the law, from punishment for her real guilt. On the other hand, nothing could justify his not doing so: from now on, he is in a cleft stick.

186. Once again Guenivere has slipped into using the derogatory pronoun.

Guenivere's comparing herself to a martyr shows that she has no more thought than Lancelot that their cause might be unjust. Caxton seems to have felt her comparison in bad taste: he substituted *ony crysten Quene* for the *marter*.

254–7. Guenivere's cool judgment on Lancelot would be insulting were it not that her actions speak louder in implied compliment. She gambles her life on his ability to rescue her, and makes no more fuss about it than about her assessment of the damage he has done.

281–3. Both Bors's statements are proverbial.

306–8. The two knights follow Lancelot not because he won, but because the way in which he won revealed the kind of person he was, and the dangerous magnetism of that personality drew them to him.

a bridge Actually two bridges, one each, in quick succession.

318. Lamorak was from North Wales and Tristram from Cornwall; both were close friends of Lancelot. The 'fellowship' of a group of

great nobles is threatening society, because it takes precedence over the members' loyalty to their king. The situation was familiar in fifteenth-century England.

350. Both geographically 'to the four corners of the earth' and temporally 'until the Day of Judgment'.

366–73. Despite the symbolic unison of their voices, the reasoning is humanly laboured and uncertain. The threat to Lancelot's life is irrelevant to the syllogism his friends are trying to construct: you have fought to prevent her being killed in others' quarrels; your own quarrel concerns you more; therefore you must fight to prevent her being killed in your quarrel.

376. The blood is tangible in him, in his dead ancestors, and in his living kinsmen. Their honour is felt to be equally tangible, equally a common possession that one could corrupt for all. See the *Introduction*.

395. Bors hints that the reconciliation may reveal some trouble-makers at court, on whom the king's displeasure would fall.

400. For much of the *Morte Darthur*, Arthur's fitness to rule is highlighted by contrast with the envious, suspicious, perfidious, cowardly Mark, who always puts his own impulses before the good of his kingdom. Cf. 'Lancelot', ll. 2626–41.

402. The glaive, properly so called, was a stout one-edged blade on a staff with a handguard. It was popular with infantry, especially with royal bodyguards: unlike the sword and lance, it had no knightly associations.

412. The syntax is uncertain because the sentence is hovering between direct and indirect speech. *shortely* seems to modify *condiscended* (it certainly does not modify *rescow*), but in fact modifies an unreported verb from the speech being summarised, something like *we agree*.

438. *menour*, which is being used in a slightly inaccurate sense, is one of several legal terms in this passage. Malory is distinguishing two situations that would justify *hasty jougement* (a summary trial): being caught in the act, and being caught in overwhelmingly incriminating circumstances. In contrast, a man accused on circumstantial evidence had the right to the full process of law, which, if the charge were treason, included the right to challenge his accuser to trial by battle. Gawain argues in his next speech that the circumstances are not over-whelmingly incriminating, that there is enough doubt to allow trial by battle; but Arthur refuses to allow it.

457. This sentence is a new thought, not a development of the last one. So the *entente* is not that of rewarding Lancelot but that of getting him to visit her secretly.

459–60. The parallel cannot be kept without stiltedness in modern

English. Translate 'in order to avoid slander, which she feared'.

The generalisation that follows is a loose restatement of a proverb.

480. Actually three: Arthur has left out Gyngalyn.

529. *horse* This is an obsolete plural form surviving from earlier English, and still found today in 'horse, foot and guns'. Cf. ll. 989, 1463, 1566. Both known texts of the *Morte Darthur* passed through the hands of scribes each of whom seems to have modernised it where the other left it, perhaps without having noticed it.

543. *the Freynshe booke sayth* It only says so about Gareth.

545–6. The helmet of a suit of armour restricted the field of vision considerably.

550. The names of garments change almost as rapidly as fashions in garments themselves. Malory is probably being rather old-fashioned in both. For him, the undergarment is the *smock* and the ordinary dress is the *kirtle*, a long dress with a close-fitting bodice and sleeves, low waist and belt, and a full skirt. Over this, the *gown* or *houppelande* was worn as a coat, a long full dress with one of a range of elaborate neck-designs, a high waist and belt, and larger, sometimes enormous, sleeves. About 1400 this was the basic style, varied with individual taste. By the time Malory wrote, the kirtle was an undergarment, of which all that would normally be seen was a touch at the wrist, neck, and hem. A woman would only be seen in her kirtle if she were doing public penance. The gown had become the ordinary dress, upon which the ingenuity of fashion was lavished. Both kirtle and gown had changed a little since 1400, and were to change yet more rapidly in the decades after Malory died.

555–6. *as the Freynshe booke seyth* It does.

II

569–70. *kynge* is the subject and *felyship* the object of *hylde*, 'held'.

626. The continued reiteration of Gareth's name shows how much more Gawain loved his youngest brother than he did the other five members of his family who had been killed. Gawain also mentions that his brother had loved Lancelot more than him. Here a mere observation, this will eventually become a cause of great bitterness.

659–60. Gawain formally notifies Arthur of his intention to 'defy' him unless Arthur supports him in his cause. He has stripped the feudal relationship to its essential, mutual support in need. The *diffidatio* or renunciation of allegiance made each party independent, and ended their rights and duties to one another. It did not necessarily imply hostility, but – not surprisingly – hostility often followed. Cf. l. 1121.

685–7. Arthur's army is big enough to force Lancelot, if he remains in the open, to fight or die. If he fights, he will have to kill his friends or be killed by them, so he retires to a castle where he need do neither. His decision is a matter of conscience, not of courage: he is as afraid of winning as of losing.

694. *go* at this period very commonly applied to motion on foot, as opposed, for instance, to riding, swimming, or crawling.

702. Lancelot's argument seems to be that Arthur will lose the respect and support of his followers if he keeps them at an unpleasant and futile task. He is not talking of how his own party feel towards Arthur.

722–3. Malory has slipped between the two forms of address, *your person* and *the person of your highness*. Translate as the latter.

727. Lancelot's words imply both a speech on the queen's behalf, which would be *large* in that it would defend her against all the charges that might be brought against her; and an offer to fight for her, which would be *large* in that he would not refuse battle to anyone who asked for it.

735–7. Lancelot's love for Guenivere was challenged on his first quest in the *Morte Darthur*, told in the third tale; and he replied that no lady in the world was truer to her lord. There is no reason to believe that that was then untrue. He does not repeat his assertion now, but he says that he will fight anyone who denies it, so suggesting that it is true but avoiding a direct lie. This recalls his handling of Mellyagaunte.

Although after the death of Aggravayne Arthur is shown to be so angry that his impartiality might be doubted, this is entirely uncharacteristic of him. Contrast, for instance, his behaviour in the two trials in the seventh tale, where such slight lapses as a strict legalist might take exception to are entirely in favour of Guenivere. The rush of argument has carried the best knight in the world into equivocation and exaggeration.

740. A very significant phrase in the fifteenth century. It implied active and continued favour and protection. It does not here imply, as it often did, a disregard for the rights of other people and the claims of law and justice. Cf. 'Lancelot', l. 88.

751. The fundamental feudal virtues could be summed up as loyalty to all one's obligations to God and man, and courage to enable one to act as loyalty demanded, whatever the cost (but see the *Introduction*). So Gawain's insult, which denies Lancelot both, is as sweeping as it is succinct; and in a society where much depends on being seen to be capable, it is hard to ignore even though it is obviously said for effect.

269

773. Gawain also has been carried into exaggeration: this is absurdly and obviously untrue. Since, unlike his previous direct insult, it will not help to bring Lancelot to a fight, it must be ascribed to Gawain's own feelings. Under extreme grief, a previously unrevealed jealousy of Lancelot's power over his brother torments him, and he feeds it to urge himself on.

801. The French source portrays the king as hot-tempered, suspicious, ungrateful, and much less ready to be reconciled than he is here.

813–16. Lancelot, as leader, must do broadly what his followers as a whole are determined on, and they are giving him notice of what they want. Not only do they think a fight is inevitable, but they also want a demonstration of Lancelot's capacity to lead them in it, as a proof of his capacity to lead in other circumstances. Cf. ll. 659 and *n* and 1426–7.

824. *thus* is a mistake. It refers Arthur and Gawain to something Lancelot would know they knew nothing of.

841. Early medieval armies, all except the very largest, were normally divided into three 'battles'. which formed vanguard, centre and rear on the line of march, and right, centre and left on the battle-field. The 'battles' rarely had much internal organisation. A fight was a matter of choosing ground and time, charging with as much force and cohesion as possible, and slogging it out until one's own side or the other gave way. The system was like classic feudal land-tenure, to which it corresponded: simple, comprehensible, capable of a few important adaptations, and adequate when the men on both sides were in homogeneous, not very professional groups. Specialisation and training brought problems: even combining cavalry and infantry was difficult, and by the end of the Middle Ages complicated subdivided formations were in use. In Malory's lifetime, the English made a practice of dismounting every man, for use in these formations, and this won them Crécy, Poitiers, Agincourt, and other important battles. Malory is thinking of a very old-fashioned kind of army, consisting of cavalry only or in which only the cavalry mattered enough to be mentioned: the kind of army which lost Crécy so completely for France.

The *order and rule* Malory praises is keeping formation while forming up for the charge in sight of the enemy. It was the most complicated and therefore the most dangerous manoeuvre that could be expected of the kind of army he is thinking of.

866. Malory's subjunctive construction must be rendered by an imperative. How emphatic Lancelot's speech is can be measured by his using to Bors both the masterful pronoun and a threat of death.

927. *the Freynshe boke seyth* It does, but Malory has drawn even more on the English poem for this episode.

928. The seals were made of lead. The Latin name for such a seal, *bulla*, became the English name for the document, *bull*.

962. An impersonal construction with the dative, like *it repents me*.

971–2. *recommaunde me unto hys good grace* This phrase has three meanings, all of which Lancelot intends. It has the literal meaning 'recommend me to his favour', but since *your grace* was the normal fifteenth-century mode of address to the king and others with grace and favour to dispense, it also means 'commend me to His Majesty', and – on the level of protocol – 'present my compliments to His Majesty'. The modern *Your Majesty* was largely a sixteenth-century development.

975. Cf. l. 727n above.

993. Lancelot and Guenivere are dressed in the same style as their young attendants, but in a different fabric, a cloth of gold tissue instead of velvet.

994. The French book says only that the horses had silk foot-cloths. The English poem describes, but much more briefly than Malory does, a procession of Lancelot and the queen in white, and a hundred knights in green bearing olive branches. The rest will be Malory's invention.

997. A clause of result, not purpose.

1102–3. The suggestion is 'coatless', not 'trouserless': he would wear nothing equivalent to a modern jacket (doublet or jerkin) or overcoat (houppelande/gown and cloak). Lancelot is willing to accept a penance such as might have been imposed if he had killed his friends deliberately and without any mitigating circumstances. One of the terms of the reconciliation between the Lancastrians and the Yorkists in 1458 was that the Duke of York and the earls who supported him should found a chantry where the souls of those whom they had killed three years before while fighting against the king would be prayed for perpetually. Lancelot is offering to found about two dozen such chantries.

Sandwich was an important port, second of the Cinque Ports responsible for the defence of the Channel, and the port from which banished men had to leave the country; Carlisle was the northernmost place at which Arthur was said regularly to have held his court, and the centre of the West Marches defensive system against Scotland; they are about 225 miles apart.

1131. Gawain echoes the standard formula for a safeconduct such as Lancelot has been given (cf. ll. 939, 966–7).

1133. Gawain's use of the legal term shows that he sees his revenge as the execution of justice, to be carried out inexorably but in due form.

1135–6. According to Gawain, he and Arthur have come to an agreement that Lancelot should be allowed to come to see the king, but should be banished afterwards; otherwise Lancelot could only have seen Arthur unwillingly (*magré thyne hede*): by implication, as Gawain's prisoner.

1148–9. This was one of the most powerful images to the medieval imagination. The Wheel of Fortune was visualised as carrying men up and down between adversity and prosperity, and throwing them off suddenly, unpredictably and quite regardless of their merits. Arthur dreams of the Wheel before his last battle (l. 1812). It was a notion difficult to reconcile with that of God's providence, and most people just let the two co-exist in their minds.

In that 'old chronicle', the alliterative *Morte Arthure*, Arthur has at the moment of his greatest success an ominous dream of eight great kings lamenting their past or acting out their future subjection to the caprice of Fortune and her Wheel. They are the Nine Worthies, whose number he is destined to complete, and the first two of them are Alexander the Great and Hector of Troy, the men Lancelot names here. The idea that the nine greatest kings in the world were as subject to Fortune as the most ordinary man was so familiar that Malory did not need to have Lancelot explain it any further than he does.

1162. *treson* combines the legal sense of 'treason' and the moral sense of 'treachery'; *felony* likewise with 'felony' and 'villainy'.

1174–5. Arthur and Gawain have fallen short of the standard Lancelot expected of them.

1182–5. This speech, like many of Lancelot's is exhilarating because what would be empty boasts in other men are simple promises in him.

1197. Lancelot gives his castle its old name again (cf. l. 1060).

1210-12. Banishment is the last straw for Lancelot, and grief makes his speech repetitive and not very coherent. He is on the horns of a dilemma, and his last sentence tries to show how. If he goes, it will be recorded that he was banished for treasonable and treacherous adultery, and everyone will assume that he went because his friends would not fight for him, because they knew that he and Guenivere were guilty; and so he will be shamed. If he stays, people will assume that he could not bring himself to leave Guenivere, and therefore he and she must have been guilty; and so he will be shamed, too. There is, as he sees and struggles to say, no escape.

His friends respond with loyalty rather than logic – which is what he needs.

1218–19. The family is taken for granted here as the basis of loyalty and alliances.

1238. The weight of the meaning of *nobeles* is on the physical rather than the moral side, but both are intended. Cf. 'Lancelot', ll. 712–15*n*.

1253. Beaune is 500 miles from the sea. In Malory's time, a good deal of its wine would have been shipped from the Bayonne area to Cardiff, which was a major port for the wine and salt trade with the west coast of France.

1260. The people rush to see Lancelot, walking if they can and crawling if they cannot: a testimony of love and admiration for him.

1262–7. Lancelot divides his lands (the *Mort Artu* calls them 'Gaul') into three parts: 'France', Benwick-and-Guyenne and King Claudas's lands. 'France' seems to be northern France, the area least out of control of the medieval French kings in the Ile de France; Benwick-and-Guyenne is south-west France, an area the English long held and finally lost in 1453; and King Claudas's lands are presumably the rest, south-east France. The king of Benwick-and-Guyenne was to be suzerain of the other two kings (cf. 'Lancelot', ll. 508–12 and *n*). Earlier French writers made King Claudas's lands Berry, the province round Bourges, almost in the centre of modern France; but there is no reason to suppose that Malory knew of this.

1270–87. Each of the three kingdoms has its constituent duchies and counties, which are based on fifteenth-century political divisions. Most of those named are in the south-west, and the smaller the farther. *Lymosyn* is Limousin; *Payters*, Poitiers; *Overn*, Auvergne; and *Sentonge*, Saintonge. *Perygot* is Périgord; *Roerge*, Rouergue; *Bearne*, Béarn; *Comange*, Comminges; *Armynake*, Armagnac; *Estrake*, Astarac; *Pardyak* Pardiac; *Foyse*, Foix; *Marsank*, Marsan; *Tursank*, Tursan; and the *Lauwndis*, the Landes. *Provynce* is Provence; *Landok*, Languedoc; *Agente*, Agen; *Sarlat*, Sarlat; *Angeoy*, Anjou; and *Normandy*, Normandy.

III

1301. This is a deliberate campaign of devastation. Such compaigns grew increasingly common in late medieval warfare, their aim being to force the enemy to leave his castles and fight, or make peace. Because they did the maximum possible damage to non-combatants, they were thought unknightly and wrong; and a knight convicted of setting fire to a vineyard might be hanged by the other side or ostracised by his own. Arthur had previously shown himself a good king by fighting invaders who did this to his own people, and by minimising the damage to civilians when he invaded his enemies.

1313. Most of the alliteration, poetic diction, and tortuous word-order in the next three paragraphs come from imperfect assimilation of *Le Morte Arthur*.

1331. The towns would be walled and hence defensible.

1340–1. Proverbial.

1358. Malory does not bother to say the obvious, that a king would have his great barons with him when he listened to proposals of this kind, and that they would expect to give their opinions before he makes his decision, as in fact they do.

1383. The walk with long extended steps suggests precisely the impetuosity, vigour, and arrogance of Lancelot's knights.

1397. The besiegers, never previously mentioned, are the subject of *gan* and the object of the following sentence.

1421. *holys* was a normal word for 'windows', even in the fifteenth-century building trade; but it also meant 'holes', and Gawain may intend his *within holys and wallys* to call up an image of a creature lurking in the woodwork and masonry. The substance of his speech is a brute reassertion of his charge that Lancelot is entirely lacking in the primary feudal virtues. See l. 751n.

1435. Castle gates were their weakest points, and so always had at least one tower as an extra defence.

1471. *Than* is the narrator's time, not the time of the action of the story.

1485–6. *The Freynshe booke seyth* It does.

1497–8. Defence against an overwhelming onslaught meant staying in a near-crouched position, keeping as much behind one's shield as possible, and moving mostly with small steps. When Gawain's stamina is exhausted, both Lancelot's height and the length of his steps grow as he moves in to attack. Compare boxing.

1511–12. Lancelot is applying tournament rules with extreme punctiliousness when the rules of real warfare would have been more natural. He had killed three of King Lot's sons, and is looking for an excuse that will let him avoid killing the fourth and last. The strain shows in his single use of the pronoun *thou*.

1583. It is the English poem that says that Gawain's strength increased gradually. The French book says something very different: that his strength increased suddenly about noon; and that he deliberately fought harder just before noon, so that when it increased his enemy would be exhausted. Neither source says anything about *wynde* or *evyll wyll*.

1584. Malory seems to be distinguishing between *myght*, 'strength', and *wynde*, 'stamina', the ability to keep putting out one's strength. Lancelot was speaking of stamina when he praised Gareth as *well-brethed* 'Lancelot', l. 1288).

Cf. modern English *sound in wind and limb, broken-winded,* and *second wind*.

IV

1621. The calling of the Lords *is* the parliament. If there are any Commons, they are not important enough to be mentioned.

1640–2. This very modern siege is the only point at which Malory mentions guns. They are ascribed to Mordred here in a spirit like that in which they are ascribed to the rebel angels in *Paradise Lost*; the brutal weapons that destroy any possibility of chivalrous warfare match the nature of the characters who use them.

threw, 'committed', seems to be military jargon. The *engynnes* are siege-engines such as catapults and mangonels.

In 1460, an approaching Yorkist invasion forced the Lancastrian authorities in London to abandon the city and retire to the Tower, which the Yorkists besieged. Guns and infantry assaults were used by both sides, but the Tower was not captured and the garrison eventually negotiated its own terms for surrender. Sir Thomas Malory of Newbold Revel was apparently being kept in prison in London by the Lancastrians at the time, and it therefore seems likely that he was freed by the Yorkists and joined them in the siege.

1664–7. In 1461, the Archbishop of Canterbury was in hiding in Kent because of what *myschevous warre* might do.

1691–2. Translate 'Nothing can please us for any length of time'. This is Malory's only direct comment as narrator on fifteenth-century politics, and the repetitions underline his earnestness.

1695. Both in the literal sense 'joined his army', and the figurative one 'changed sides'. The same double sense is in *abyde*.

1702–3. These were the biggest fighting ships of the time. The galley was a long slim ship driven by sail and oars, and designed for ramming; the carrack, a tall broad sailing ship, designed for boarding an enemy. By Malory's time, both carried light guns.

1709. *currageous* means 'brave, eager, lively, forceful and fierce'. All these qualities together make it impossible to stop Arthur.

1722. Arthur is using the *thou* of affection, the usage common within the family, especially from older to younger members of it. It is in this spirit that Arthur mostly uses *thou* to his knights from here on (see *Introduction*). It shows his love for them, but at the same time it sets him a little apart – there is an analogue to the distance between parent and child in the mysterious fate that is enfolding him and separating him from the rest of humanity.

1746. In the French book, Gawain sends only a verbal message asking Lancelot to forgive him and to come and see his tomb. He also tells those around him that he had deserved the blow from Lancelot and that it had caused his death, but he does not say that Lancelot should be told of this or asked to come to Arthur's assistance.

In the letter, Gawain still addresses Lancelot as *thou*, but now it is the intimate use of the pronoun – as between brothers – not the hostile one. In the passage of public argument and persuasion in the middle of the letter, he wavers between it and the dignified *ye*; but he returns to *thou* for the close.

1755. This is drastically compressed. Gawain takes it for granted that it is a terrible thing to kill someone one likes and respects; so much so that it can be regarded less as a crime than as a punishment. It is to be considered, therefore, as something one deserves or does not deserve, and Lancelot does not deserve it, both because he is too good a man and because he has done everything his honour would allow to try to avoid it. Had Gawain been as objective about his brother Gareth's death as he is about his own, the final tragedy would have been averted.

1784–5. A Biblical usage, e.g. Matt. 27. 50.

1786–8. Gawain's skull in Dover Castle was another of Britain's famous Arthurian relics. Caxton says in his preface to the *Morte Darthur* that when he spoke of the doubts about Arthur's existence, Gawain's skull was among the evidence cited to sustain the counter-argument.

1790. Barham Down is six miles south-east of Canterbury. In the fifteenth century, it was used as a mustering ground for English forces going to France.

1807. Mordred raises his army in the south-eastern counties of England, where the Yorkists were strong. Unrestricted plunder in this area was promised to the Lancastrian army before the battle of Northampton in 1460. Fortunately for the inhabitants, the Yorkists won the battle.

1812–21. Arthur's dream of the Wheel of Fortune gives vivid imaginative form to fears produced by a time when everything he has is upon the hazard.

1854. Medieval science classified dreams on a physiological basis, contrasting *avisions*, which were prophetic and trustworthy, with *phantasms*, the deceptive products of waking preoccupations and digestive disorders. The bishop who speaks of a deceitful *sweven* (l. 2422n is thinking of a kind of phantasm.

The two difficulties were that, as Chaucer complains at the beginning of his *House of Fame*, there was no sure way of telling which was which; and that, as Chaunticleer in Chaucer's *Nun's Priest's Tale* and King Arthur here both discover, undesirable *avisions* have a way of fulfilling themselves whatever precautions are taken against them.

1871–2. This warning must have been given before occurrence of the events in the sentence that precedes it.

1907. Most French and Anglo-Norman surnames were derived from places and began with *de*, 'of'. In language, minorities tend to imitate majorities, and so surnames like *le Buttler*, 'the butler', became as here *de Buttler*, 'of Butler', even though there is no place called Butler for them to be 'of'. The same sometimes happened to *Malory*.

1920. Lucan means that Mordred is a Jonah, a manifestation of *unhap* itself, bringing mischance to himself and anyone near him. Arthur should stay away lest the destruction fall on him too. Mordred may also be *unhappy* in the modern sense, but Lucan is not suggesting that Arthur should leave Mordred alone out of pity for the state of his feelings.

1925–6. Lucan calls this a victory, but he is a dying man searching desperately for an argument to save his king's life. His monstrous logic emphasises the completeness of the tragedy.

1929. Semi-proverbial in style, but apparently Malory's invention. Shakespeare quotes it in a burlesque of the heroic in his *Midsummer Night's Dream* (V. i. 205).

1941. The broad ring on the spear, which was held behind the hand and against the rest during the charge.

1949. Malory's geography is in error: the sea nowhere comes to the edge of Salisbury Plain.

1983–4. Arthur's seemingly brutal words are not therapy to jolt Bedivere out of shock and grief. The mysterious realities that underlie the world of the *Morte Darthur* make the return of the sword more important than the king's life, and the king's life more important than Bedivere's grief.

1992 Malory has again been careless with verb-subjects.

2003–4. Like Gawain and Lancelot's kinsmen, Arthur *in extremis* invokes the feudal relationship in its most primitive form. He says next to nothing of honour or religion or the ideals of knighthood, but calls on the loyalty between the tribal chief, the bread-giver and ring-giver, and his house-carle, who repays the gifts with personal service, and if need be with his life. When Bedivere does not obey his commands, Arthur accuses him of a breach of this bond and this alone.

2011–12. This is to take *wap* and *wanne* as infinitives. *Wap* might be a noun and *wanne* an adjective, which would give a translation of 'the slapping of the waters and the gloomy waves'.

2052. Malory takes it for granted that Avalon is Glastonbury (see *Introduction*).

2056. The nearest part of Salisbury Plain is 25 miles from Glastonbury; the farthest, 40 miles away.

2059. *fayne* here means 'glad', but under the circumstances, not absolutely. Although Bedivere is not happy, he is relieved at being able to be unhappy in a weather-proof building. Cf. 'Lancelot', l. 2155 and *n.*

2071. Gold or silver coins, originally from Byzantium (now Istanbul), whence their name. The gold ones were worth about a pound, the silver ones about a shilling, in the English money of their time. Here the coins are a gift for the priest himself; the candles are an offering for the use of the church. Cf. 'Lancelot', ll. 1440–2*n.*

2088–9. Cf. 'Lancelot', l. 104*n.*

2090–5. Morgan le Fay is Arthur's sister and his most determined enemy (*le* should be *la* here too – cf. 'Lancelot', l. 594 and *n*), and the Queen of North Galis is an ally of hers. The Lady Nynyve, the chief lady of the lake, is Arthur's most consistent friend; and the Queen of the Waste Lands, who is Sir Percival's aunt and one of the visionaries of the Grail, seems to be on her side.

A small inconsistency has escaped Malory's notice: here he has three queens and one lady; earlier in this episode he spoke of one queen and three ladies.

2103. Malory as narrator leaves out two stages in his argument: but this tale [denies it, and has authority to do so, because] Sir Bedivere . . .

2109. The two most sacred relics of Christ's earthly life were the cross on which He was crucified and the sepulchre in Jerusalem in which His body was afterwards buried. How St Helena found the cross (AD 320) was one of the most famous stories in Christendom. She took the largest part of the relic to Constantinople (Byzantium under yet another name), and there almost everyone from her day to Malory's believed it to remain.

The Moslems captured the sepulchre when they took Jerusalem in 635, and the cross when they took Constantinople in 1453, seventeen years before Malory finished the *Morte Darthur*. It would have been the supreme act of a Christian king to lead a crusade that recaptured one or both of these sacred objects. The Christian kings of Malory's time never managed to stop fighting one another long enough to do this, but the crusading ideal exercised an attraction in England for at least another century.

The idea of King Arthur's return was traditional, but the idea that he would then lead a crusade to recover the True Cross may have been suggested to Malory either by the papal mission that was in England from 1459 to 1462 trying to encourage the king of England to join a crusade for that purpose, or by the alliterative *Morte Arthure* (ll. 3217,

3422–37). There it is said that Arthur was about to start a crusade, apparently to recover the Holy Sepulchre, when he was called back by Mordred's fatal rebellion. Malory takes Arthur's epitaph from the same poem (l. 4347).

2121. Many religious orders dressed in these colours, which were in themselves a penitential contrast to the vivid colours medieval people loved.

2123. Guenivere is not just entering a convent: she is taking on a life of penance to make what reparation she can for her previous sins. It is her knowledge of what she has to repent, brought home to her by the deaths of so many men, not the conventual life in itself, that deprives her of gaiety and liveliness.

V

2135. Treacherous both to the king and to the queen.

2169. To make sense of what happens next, it must be assumed that at this point the 'people' also tell Lancelot something of what happened to the king.

2176. Such *doles* as this were common on the death of a great noble.

2176–8. There is a clause missing here after *ale*, presumably *as they would*.

2182. Clerics in minor orders, junior to priests, and able to help at but not to say Mass.

2184. A Requiem Mass is the Mass offered for the repose of the soul of someone who has died. The first (Latin) word in the first of the special prayers that differentiate it from other Masses gave it its name. The senior priest would say the principal Requiem, and at this all the other clergy would sing and assist in the ceremonial, and the mourners would make their offerings in order of precedence. The other priests among the clergy would say their Requiem Masses privately as near as possible to the time of the principal one.

2194–5. Proverbial.

2205. Semi-proverbial.

2213. In this situation, loose-jointedness causes as much trouble as weight.

2225. Guenivere is calling upon the redemptive effect of the suffering that Christ endured on the cross for sinners.

2231–2. *On Goddis behalff* is a formula like *in the king's name* or *in the name of the law.*

2242–3. *of that* ('what') *I have promysed* The promise spoken of, by

279

implication that Lancelot would never give his love or the first place in his life to any other woman, has not been related in the earlier parts of the *Morte Darthur*.

2255. The manuscript breaks off with the word *Sankgreall*. One of the surviving copies of Caxton's edition breaks off three lines above, at *forsakyn*, so the rest of the text depends solely on the other copy of Caxton.

2262–3. The colours are those of the hermits' habits, and the whole phrase means therefore 'any hermit of whatever sort'. Religious orders were often distinguished by the colours of their habits rather than their official titles: Black Friars and Grey Friars for Dominicans and Franciscans, Black Monks and White Monks for Benedictines and Cistercians respectively; but in fifteenth-century England, where there was only one order of hermits, there was no strict need for such a distinction. The phrase must have survived from a time when hermitry was more varied.

2281–2. Lancelot's exclamation sums up a recurrent theme in the *Morte Darthur*. No proverbs were more quoted in the Middle Ages than those that spoke of the transience of earthly happiness.

2305–7. When St Bernard became a Cistercian in 1113, thirty other noblemen, including his own brothers, entered the Order with him.

2322. According to traditional Christian doctrine, even when a sin has been forgiven, the objective wrongness of the sinful act leaves a debt of justice to be made up. This is commonly illustrated by comparison with breaking some valuable object: even if the owner forgives the breakage wholeheartedly, perfect amends could only be made if what was broken was replaced. The debt of justice can be paid and the sins 'remitted' either by purgatory after death or by sufferings accepted and charitable acts performed in this life. Among the principal charitable acts are the Seven Corporal Works of Mercy, one of which is the burial of the dead.

2332–3. *lytel more than thirty mile* It is forty-eight by modern roads.

2348. The *Dirige*, so called from its first (Latin) word, was properly speaking the matins or morning service that would precede the Requiem Mass itself. But the name was extended to include the vespers or evening service on the previous night, and this is what Malory is speaking of. Modern English *dirge* comes from *dirige*.

2360–1. *Raynes* is Rennes in Brittany. The cloth was waxed to make it waterproof.

2367–9. In the first sentence, Lancelot denies that his sorrow is caused by *rejoysyng of synne* 'joy [I had] in sin'. He is so full of grief not, as the watchers might suspect, because he has lost the opportunity to make love to Arthur's wife, but for another reason, which the next two sentences explain.

Malory changes his mind halfway through the second sentence, and confusedly has Lancelot saying that Guenivere's beauty and nobility were in Arthur as well as in herself. The incoherence helps to make Lancelot's grief lifelike, but translate, to conform to Malory's final intention, 'the beauty and nobility that were . . .'

2378–9. There is no scene and no speech like this in either source.

2401. The dying man has a right to the rites of three sacraments: Confession (if he needs it), Communion and the Last Sacrament or Last Anointing. The ghost of Hamlet's father laments bitterly that he died deprived of them:

> Cut off even in the blossoms of my sin,
> Unhouseled, disappointed, unaneled.
>
> *Hamlet*, I. v. 77

enelyd, lit. 'anointed with oil'; because of the 'matter' of the sacrament.

2403–4. These two castles and Dunstanborough were captured by a Lancastrian raid in the struggle for the north of England in 1462. A large Yorkist army, including a Sir Thomas Malory, besieged and recaptured them.

John Hardyng's *Chronicle* said that Bamborough was built at a place called Mount Dolorous.

2438. From Glastonbury it is some 345 miles to Alnwick and some 360 to Bamborough. If the fifteen days is taken literally, it gives an average speed, quite credible for medieval English roads, of 23 or 24 miles a day.

2442–4. The custom was normal in the fifteenth century for the funerals of great nobles.

2458. The lament for Lancelot spoken by his brother has justly become famous. It seems, like much that is admirable about Malory's Lancelot, including large parts of his rôle in the second and fourth tales of the *Morte Darthur*, to be reworked from an earlier story about Sir Gawain. In this case, the probable inspiration is the alliterative *Morte Arthure*, in the lament for Gawain spoken by his brother (ll. 3875–85). The differences are a reminder of the different emphases possible within chivalry.

The alliterative poet repeatedly stresses vitality – the knight he praises is gay, active and proud – but the scope of his list of virtues is wide: goodness and God's grace figure at the beginning, fame somewhere in the middle, and even intelligence (*konynge*) finds a small place towards the end. However, neither love nor friendship is explicitly mentioned. Malory's Ector, in contrast, apart from such religious implications as may be in *Crysten knyghtes*, confines himself to the human relationships of chivalry: with enemy, lady and friend. This narrower scope gives his words a remarkable intensity, which is reinforced by skilful parallels and contrasts, all the more striking in a man who shows no sign of knowing of the meaning or existence of the word *rhetoric*. Each of the nine statements in the portrait is simple, superlative and exact. The repetition of the intimate family pronoun and the past tense of the most basic of all English verbs generates a strong elegiac mood, yet the emotion is kept from sentimental excess by the precision of the praise, in its qualifications (*of* erthely *knyghtes hand, of* [= 'for'] *a* synful *man*) and in the aptness of the concrete imagery.

The most paradoxical of these images (courteous with a shield, faithful on a horse, kind with sword-strokes) are central to the portrait and epitomise the *Morte Darthur*. In the world of common experience, courtesy can nowhere be more difficult, more praiseworthy, or more important than in battle. The images succinctly convey this, remind us that Lancelot's courtesy was most memorably shown in battle (e.g. l. 875), and qualify their own extravagance by allowing the possibility of other kinds of courtesy altogether, in (for instance) a spiritual knight, a sinless woman, or God Himself.

There is a pattern to these images, which grow in length, complexity, and concreteness from *hede*, too abstract and familiar to have any sensory component, through the physical to the social worlds. This pattern plays against two others: first that of the persons with whom Lancelot was concerned – all Christian knights in the introductory clause, then repetitions of enemy, friend and lady; and second, the pattern of the virtues that related him to them – Christian *chivalry* in the introductory clause, then a symmetry with *prowess* in battle first and last, *generous courtesy* within that, and *loyalty* in the centre. The complex patterns of sound and syntax and meaning suggest that the chivalry being described is indivisible, and the content makes clear that it is practical, personal and immediate, guiding strength to produce justice in a world much in need of it. This portrait recalls and transcends the original Round Table oath, which Lancelot has done more than any other single man to fulfil.

2475-7. Compare the end of Shakespeare's *King Lear*. Arthur's relationship to his son has similarities with that of Lear's to his ungrateful daughters, Constantine's situation resembles Albany's, and Lancelot's kinsmen's, Kent's. There are also similarities is the states of the two kingdoms: each purged and restored to health, but continuing without its former greatness.